REGIONAL PLANNING
FOR A SUSTAINABLE
AMERICA

REGIONAL PLANNING FOR A SUSTAINABLE AMERICA

How Creative Programs Are Promoting

Prosperity and Saving the Environment

CARLETON K. MONTGOMERY

RUTGERS UNIVERSITY PRESS
NEW BRUNSWICK, NEW JERSEY, AND LONDON

Library of Congress Cataloging-in-Publication Data

Regional planning for a sustainable America : how creative programs are promoting prosperity and saving the environment / edited by Carleton Montgomery.
    p. cm.
Includes bibliographical references and index.
ISBN 978-0-8135-5132-6 (hardcover : alk. paper)   1. Regional planning—North America. 2. Natural resources conservation areas—North America.   3. Sustainable living—North America.   4. North America—Environmental conditions.   I. Montgomery, Carleton.
HT395.N612R44   2011
307.1'20973—dc22

2011004703

A British Cataloging-in-Publication record for this book is available from the British Library.

Visit our Web site: http://rutgerspress.rutgers.edu

Manufactured in the United States of America

For my parents, Bob and Peggy

CONTENTS

PART V
Envisioning the Region

FIGURES

ACKNOWLEDGMENTS

I thank the many public servants, nonprofit activists, and academic researchers who contributed their unique experiences and knowledge to the chapters of this book. David Moore and the late Ray Corwin read the introduction and conclusion, making excellent suggestions and greatly improving the final product. Many conversations with Candace Ashmun, Dianne Brake, Michael Catania, George Hawkins, Peter Kasabach and his colleagues at New Jersey Future, Terry Moore, and John Stokes and his colleagues at the Pinelands Commission have taught me more than I can say about regional planning.

This book would not have been possible without the support of my employer, the Pinelands Preservation Alliance, the Alliance's trustees, and my colleagues on the Alliance staff. For their support in this and so many other endeavors, I am deeply grateful.

The Fund for New Jersey and the Stockton Alliance provided essential funding for the preparation and publication of this book. Three foundations—the Fund for New Jersey, the Geraldine R. Dodge Foundation, and the William Penn Foundation—provided funding to support the Regional Planning Comes of Age conference in 2006, which inspired this project and my subsequent work in creating this book. These foundations do enormous good in the communities they serve. I hope this book, too, will make a difference by helping people find better ways to manage our use of the landscapes in which we live.

REGIONAL PLANNING
FOR A SUSTAINABLE
AMERICA

INTRODUCTION

Carleton K. Montgomery

The dream of environmental, economic, and social sustainability through better land use drives the work described and debated in this book. "Land use" is an emotionally flat term, but it captures vastly important features of our society. It is the complex of policies and practices that shape the landscape; the pattern, design, and intensity of development; the infrastructure of sewer, water, roads, transit, and public institutions that serve that pattern of development; and the ways we exploit and conserve resources of land, water, plants, animals, and air. The programs discussed in this book are built on the recognition that our society can do land use better if we do it regionally.

The most fundamental obstacle to regional planning is also, surprisingly, its greatest virtue: the region is not built into our structure of government. Regional government—whether based on a metropolitan area, a watershed, or any other defining ecological, political, or cultural principle—is simply not part of America's established administrative matrix. But the fact that regionalist programs keep appearing shows they are needed. In the absence of established legal or constitutional structures, necessity has been the mother of invention. Indeed, for all the difficulties that come from being a late-born child in our constitutional system, regional initiatives have shown a degree of creativity, diversity, and inclusiveness that we might never have seen were regional government a part of our political inheritance.[1]

Good regional planning is planning for both conservation *and* growth. Managing growth to protect rural landscapes and natural resources has been the dominant motivation for most regional land use planning initiatives in America. But while conservation is a key motivation for regional planning, so too is the recognition that people are not going away—in most cases, more are coming. If it is people that

[1] Maps, documents and links relating to this book can be found at http://www.regionalplans.com. This book does not provide a historical account of the evolution of land use planning and the development of regional planning programs. Excellent historical accounts can be found in several sources, such as Bosselman and Callies (1971), DeGrove (2005), Mason (2008), and Weitz (1999).

threaten ecosystems and rural open spaces, it is also people who will save them by finding the formulas for truly sustainable growth.

Regional planners also believe regional governance can manage land use in ways that ensure prosperity in a rapidly changing, highly competitive world economy. Nothing in the modern economic world stands still for long. Much as many of yesterday's powerhouses became today's basket cases, so too can today's stars fall into decline as markets change, populations shift, and resources erode. Regions are the effective unit of economic productivity in North America today, not cities, suburbs, or states. Municipal and even state boundaries are becoming as irrelevant to the economic forces that shape their residents' lives as these boundaries have always been to the natural resources they rely upon. Regional policies can foster economies that are more efficient in their use of land and energy, better-equipped to compete, and diverse and resilient enough to prosper over time.

Regional planners seek to build communities that are successful for every member and segment of society. No society has yet been able to eliminate poverty or provide truly equal opportunities for all. But regional planning can provide tools needed to take on some of the basic drivers of the social problems regions face, such as the concentration of poverty in failing urban and suburban neighborhoods, the lack of quality affordable housing and transit near jobs, urban disinvestment, and aging infrastructure. Regional growth management programs aimed at limiting sprawl into rural and natural lands can encourage redevelopment in existing urban areas and distribute mixed-income housing development throughout a region.

THE REGIONALIST INSIGHT

Regional planning aims to match the scale of land use decision making with the scale of the resources and forces society seeks to manage. Only regions can encompass critical natural resources like freshwater aquifers, iconic landscapes, and entire watersheds. And only regions can begin to encompass the geographic reach of today's local economies, in terms of the labor, housing, job, land development, and retail markets that shape the day-to-day lives of communities and their inhabitants (Briffault 2000, 3–5). Of course, no "region" can be drawn to control all critical land use impacts affecting a region. At six million acres, the Adirondack Park encompasses nearly all the headwaters of the rivers and lakes within its boundaries, but the Adirondack Park Agency (APA) is powerless to influence the coal-fired power plants of the Ohio Valley, whose emissions have produced a deadly scourge of acid rain across the Adirondack Park, damaging many of those same rivers and lakes. Yet its vast jurisdictional breadth does enable the APA to manage the great majority of growth-related impacts in ways no municipal or county government could dream of—or likely even consider—doing. The case studies in this book show how regional planning programs can tackle environmental, economic, and social problems precisely because they are built to better match the regional scope of the challenges they are designed to meet.

The Folly of Local Government Land Use Control

Cities and towns working on their own cannot solve most of the major policy challenges arising from land use change, such as degradation of natural resources, maintenance of public water supplies, urban and suburban sprawl, transportation, affordable housing, fiscal health, and climate change. Municipal governments cannot protect great, emblematic landscapes like the Everglades, the Appalachian Mountains, the New Jersey Pinelands, Puget Sound, or Lake Tahoe. This point is especially obvious in the eastern United States, where even counties are geographically small. But it is equally true across America, where natural resources do not respect our arbitrary political boundaries, and very large, border-crashing metropolitan areas dominate our economic and cultural life.

Municipal zoning and infrastructure investments also cannot control the powerful forces shaping the movement and development of industry, transportation, and housing. Being fragmented and inherently parochial, the uncoordinated exercise of municipal powers is increasingly ineffective and collectively self-defeating.

Municipal governments have tremendous power that can be marshaled for the common good. But when they lack regional structures and visions, municipal governments tend to pursue their own parochial interests without regard to regional welfare, since their leaders are elected only by their own constituents. Even local officials who have a broader view face daunting odds if they try to shape their own town's zoning and other policies to serve broader goals. One town—even a central city—generally cannot achieve much on its own if its neighbors go their own way, and each town is under economic and political pressure to take advantage of any opportunity to be a "free rider." Regional resources, such as large intact forests and aquifers, are far beyond the power of most municipal governments to conserve, yet development decisions made by local governments represent the greatest threat to these resources.

Individual municipal governments have no power to control or manage regional sprawl. Indeed, the regime of atomized local zoning units is an engine, or at least a facilitator, of sprawl (e.g., Carruthers 2002a; Gillham 2002, 15–17; Richmond 2000). At most, local governments can address sprawl within their borders by limiting the density, price, and geographic extent of new development inside the town. But such uncoordinated controls are as likely to end up doing harm as good, since they may merely push growth faster and farther outward, promote poor and inefficient community design, and quickly use up land without accommodating the region's housing needs. They generally will not produce a pattern of development and conservation that protects regional environmental assets, promotes long-term economic health, or serves other regional needs.

If there is no regional structure or compact on which each town can rely, local officials cannot be sure other towns will not take advantage of opportunities when they arise, regardless of the impact on their neighbors. An unhealthy competition for public resources, commercial development, jobs, and wealthier residents naturally arises, leading to worsening disparities in the quality of local services, infrastructure, and amenities among different towns in the same region. While it may prove shortsighted, both wealthier and less-developed towns often believe it in their interest to compete for resources with their neighbors. In practice, wealthier suburbs do tend to win a disproportionate share of public infrastructure investment. Such towns benefit from the regional economy (for example, in having low-wage workers available), yet end up paying less than their fair share of public service costs. Through exclusionary policies like zoning and infrastructure investments shaped by the greater political power of wealthier towns, fragmented government encourages, and certainly has not alleviated, racial and economic segregation. Both central cities and many suburbs suffer from the effects of economic and racial segregation, the deterioration of once healthy communities, worsening traffic, and all the many ills of uncontrolled sprawl (e.g., Aoki 2005; Cashin 2000; Downs 1994, pts. 1–2; Orfield 2002, chaps. 2–3; Rusk 2003; Swanstrom 2001). In fact, the race for taxable development is often akin to a pyramid scheme in which ever more development is needed to feed the beast of expanding school and government budgets, since most new development ends up costing more in demands for services than it brings in through taxes. Nor can fragmented local governments deploy and manage the investments—in transportation, education, housing, and other infrastructure—that metropolitan regions need to prosper in the competitive global economy (Brookings Metropolitan Policy Program 2008; Hershberg 2001).

Regional Planning Is Better than State Planning

Regional agencies and structures are also better equipped than *state* government to address our land use challenges. Regional institutions are at once less arbitrary in their boundaries than states and better able to respond to the peculiar environmental, cultural, and economic forces at work in a particular region. State-level initiatives, therefore, succeed where they do not try to plan an entire state from the state capitol, but instead provide a strong mandate and sufficient powers for planning on a regional scale. The statewide growth management program that has seen the greatest practical success is Oregon's, but its success is clearly tied to that of Portland Metro—a powerful and truly regional planning agency. In contrast, the New Jersey State Development and Redevelopment Plan has not been successful, even though New Jersey is a small state and boasts three of the nation's strongest regional planning initiatives, as the State Planning Commission has failed to translate its overarching vision into effective, organic regional planning regimes. The state's highly successful regional planning initiatives in the Pinelands, Meadowlands, and Highlands were each created and operate independently of the state plan (cf. DeGrove 2005, 100–117; Ingram et al. 2009, 185). So regional approaches enjoy the virtues of flexibility and local knowledge we attribute to municipal government, while providing a means to overcome the limitations that render the established system of local, county, and state governments ineffective at managing landscape change and controlling sprawl.

A number of states have adopted statutes requiring local governments to adopt land use plans that incorporate good planning goals but omit procedures to ensure these plans satisfy specific, meaningful regional visions. It is telling that such reliance on municipal governments to interpret and implement regional policies, without any regional governance process, has not been successful at managing landscape change or at achieving desired outcomes for the environment. The critical evaluations of Florida's growth management initiatives and Chesapeake Bay Program in this book, as well as recent evaluations of North Carolina coastal communities and the Georgia, California, and Wisconsin smart growth planning laws, provide strong evidence that counties and municipalities operating outside a strong regional process are not well positioned to achieve sustainable land use management goals (Carruthers 2002a; Edwards and Haines 2007; Norton 2005).

Federal and State Environmental Regulations Cannot Save Ecosystems

Parcel-by-parcel enforcement of traditional zoning, wetlands protections, or antipollution laws also cannot protect functioning ecosystems and landscapes. Federal and state environmental regulations are based on the individual development parcel, the individual factory, and the individual permit application. To take the Clean Water Act as an example, experience shows that the goal of having states take control of nonpoint source pollution will only be met through regional planning of land use, stormwater, and septic systems. But, in both theory and practice, the Clean Water Act looks to municipal and site-specific design, not regional planning of development patterns and intensities. Even its wetlands standards apply to individual parcels or developments. While the first generation of environmental laws provides opportunities and good reasons for regional planning, they do not require, nor in practice have they brought about, regional solutions.

Regional planning of development patterns and transportation infrastructure is essential also to any effective strategy for reducing greenhouse gas emissions and mitigating the effects of climate change. Robert Yaro and David Kouris point out that, while scientists suggest the United States needs to reduce its carbon emissions by 60 to 80 percent below 1990 levels by 2050, we can also expect America's population to grow by 40 percent during that same period (chap. 23). How can America grow and prosper while also cutting its carbon emissions? The enormous amount of new development and redevelopment that will serve our growing population has to be designed for energy efficiency and mass transit use. Only regional land use planning and infrastructure investments can meet that demand. At the same time, these regional planning strategies will help society and natural systems adapt to the impacts of climate change that we cannot prevent. For example, regional growth management can protect the large forested landscapes that plants and wildlife will need as they try to shift their geographic ranges in response to new climate conditions.

AN ANALYTIC FRAMEWORK

Today's regional planning programs are as diverse as the landscapes and communities in which they work. To get a handle on their similarities and differences and highlight their innovations, I suggest the following seven features of regional initiatives provide a useful analytic framework:

- What are the goals of each program?
- How does each program define the "region" it covers?
- How does each regional program relate to local planning institutions and processes?
- What are the legal foundations and powers of each program, and what kind of autonomy do these provide for regional decision making?
- What land use strategies does each program use?
- What is each program's decision-making structure, and how does each answer the democratic imperative to incorporate state, regional, and local political elites, voters, and businesses into their decision making?

Regional Goals

Histories of regional planning in America describe the different eras, the evolving philosophies, and changing motivations and goals of regionalism over the past hundred or more years. Some commentators have given the name "New Regionalism" to recent efforts and suggest this era is focused on achieving economic goals through voluntary collaborations among state and local governments (e.g., DeGrove 2005; Frisken and Norris 2001; Swanstrom 2001; Wheeler 2002). Today's reality, however, is simply too eclectic, and the initiatives we find are simply too ambitious, to fit into such neat categories.

Most of the regional programs at work today place environmental resources at the center of the effort, but none are exclusively environmental. Many were sparked by recognition that their populations would continue to grow, but the sprawl that has dominated development in recent decades is bringing a host of negative, and worsening, effects—particularly traffic congestion, loss of open space, and degeneration of anchor cities and inner suburbs as wealth moves ever farther into newer suburbs. While all programs include economic health in some form among their stated goals, for some it would be more accurate to say they seek to accommodate rather than promote economic development. Most aspire to achieve some social equity goals, such as fostering decent and affordable housing, but only one or two could be said to place this goal at the heart of their programs.

In practice, the regional planning efforts discussed in this book seek to achieve concrete and quantifiable sustainability in terms of goals that may be framed as the following:

- Sustain native biological communities, biodiversity, and rare species populations despite habitat fragmentation, water quality degradation, and similar impacts of urbanization
- Preserve iconic landscapes—whether they are millions or thousands of acres in size—including their characteristic biodiversity, sense of place, beauty, and history

- Achieve sustainable levels and technologies in the exploitation of natural resources—especially water and land
- Create conditions in which cities, suburbs, villages, and rural communities will provide high levels of employment and fiscal health appropriate to their size and character, while having the resiliency to adjust to the long-term evolution and short-term vicissitudes of the global economy
- Foster communities where people will want to live for generations to come because these communities not only provide jobs but also meet residents' needs for security, education, good housing, efficient transportation, and vibrant culture—often in the face of contrary economic trends and forces
- Enable regions to compete in the global economy through cooperation in creating the infrastructure (roads, transit, water supplies, open spaces, and so on) needed to keep and attract people, business, and industry
- Cultivate a regional identity among the public and its government and business leaders—an identity that helps give special meaning to places and everyday activities, fosters active citizenship, and creates loyalty to the region
- And, increasingly, combat global warming through conservation and the efficient use of resources

Core goals both shape and reflect an agency's areas of focus and methods of work, but the language of a program's enabling statute or agreement does not necessarily capture the complex reality of how each one, in each era of its life, prioritizes—or perhaps juggles—competing claims on its powers. Programs in which environmental protection is the reason for their existence and dominant mission—such as the Adirondack Park, Pinelands, Highlands, Central Pine Barrens, and Tahoe Region—tend to focus their efforts on large-scale planning and the promotion of land acquisition to protect forest and water resources. These agencies look to permit and encourage development that is deemed compatible with environmental goals and is needed to "balance" conservation. Other programs—such as the Atlanta, Sacramento, and Envision Utah initiatives—place community prosperity as their guiding mission, recognizing that protection of open space and other natural resources is a key element of long-term success. These programs tend to focus more heavily on community design, infrastructure planning, and fostering public/private partnerships around development goals. In each case, then, the language of environmental protection or sustainable growth or, less often, social equity dominates but does not entirely control the discourse around policies and conflicts. The most successful programs find the narratives and real-life examples that give their public a coherent, compelling, and credible vision of how their work reconciles multiple values.

Defining the Region

Regional planning programs are necessarily built around a definition or delineation of the "region" they cover. All successful regionalist institutions began with a previously formed, though often weak, regional identity, which regional actors work hard to strengthen and embed as deeply as possible in the popular culture. In places like the Adirondack Park, Cape Cod, and the Salt Lake City area, there is a long-standing and very powerful sense of place and identity in which residents take pride regardless of regional planning institutions. In others, planners must work with a more fragmented public perception of the region in which they live. The multistate politics of the Chesapeake Bay Program illustrate a region defined by an iconic watershed containing multiple, fragmented geographic and political identities. And, in most cases, the rapid in-migration of suburban residents represents a constant challenge to sustaining a broad sense of regional identity. Yet planning initiatives can draw on a range of natural, political, and social features around which to build lasting regional institutions.

Natural versus Political Features. Regional planning programs define their geographic reach in three ways: natural features, artificial political or human-made boundaries, or a combination or compromise of the natural and artificial. The Tahoe Regional Planning Agency is the outstanding example of a planning agency whose region is defined solely by a natural feature, as its jurisdictional boundary matches the watershed of Lake Tahoe. Since the agency's overriding mission is to restore the natural qualities of Lake Tahoe, and the overriding threat the agency faces is contaminated runoff flowing into the lake from its watershed, the agency's "region" perfectly coincides with its mission. Similarly, the Cape Cod Commission covers all of Cape Cod, so it theoretically can influence all (or virtually all) land use affecting water quality in its streams and bays. Most regional planning programs do not enjoy jurisdictional boundaries that so well match the watersheds affecting their regions and missions, even where those missions are focused on environmental goals that are inextricably dependent on watershed-based processes and impacts.

The New Jersey Pinelands boundary, for example, was an essentially arbitrary compromise between the extent of the Pine Barrens ecosystem and a raft of political and economic pressures to reduce its boundaries. The resulting jurisdictional border bears little or no relation to the natural processes and flow of human impacts, which generally follow watershed boundaries. In the end, the Pinelands captured about 70 percent of the contiguous ecosystem but left out the cities that have been engines of sprawling growth, as well as much of the Kirkwood-Cohansey aquifer system on which the ecosystem relies for its survival. Perhaps most damaging, the Pinelands boundary excluded the greater part of Barnegat Bay's watershed, while including most of the Bay itself. Barnegat Bay, a large coastal lagoon that is an iconic natural resource for New Jersey, is now suffering from severe eutrophication due largely to the flow of nutrients that come with rapid, uncontrolled development of its watershed (Kennish et al. 2007). The Pinelands Commission has tremendous power over development patterns within its legally defined borders, yet its long-term ability to protect the ecosystem is compromised by arbitrary geographic limitations built into its enabling statutes.

Metropolitan planning programs like those of Atlanta, Sacramento, and Envision Utah have boundaries drawn on the basis of preexisting political subdivisions. This approach makes sense because, while all have environmental goals, their core missions are defined around the health of cities and suburbs rather than protecting a particular landscape or ecosystem. The Atlanta regional planning agency, for example, covers ten counties, while the Sacramento Area Council of Governments (SACOG) includes six counties and twenty-two cities. In both cases, the program's "region" is defined simply by the political jurisdictions surrounding a central city that dominates the region's politics, economy, and identity.

Metropolitan versus Rural/Suburban Plans. Cities are unique, powerful, and unpredictable creatures. Some of the most successful regional planning efforts are metropolitan plans shaped by and for a city—such as Portland and Sacramento. Others, such as the Adirondacks, the New Jersey Pinelands and Highlands, and the Columbia River Gorge, are essentially rural preservation plans that exclude any major city. These regions have pockets of urbanization within their boundaries but no dominant urban center of gravity. Standing between these extremes are programs for regions, such as Cape Cod, that contain a mix of suburban development and rural zones with no dominant big city. Ontario's Grow Plan for the Greater Golden Horseshoe is centered on a major city, with Toronto at its heart, but encompasses more than one hundred municipalities and over eight million residents. Regional planning, then, is not synonymous with metropolitan planning.

The exclusion of cities can bring significant benefits and weaknesses. Excluding cities can simplify the politics of a plan and present a clearer, more distinctive regional identity on which to build public support by skirting the potential conflicts between residents and politicians on either side of the rural/suburban versus urban divide. This was certainly true of the New Jersey Pinelands, where both federal and state Pinelands legislation of 1978–1979 excluded Atlantic City to the east (at the time gearing up for the casino industry) and Camden and its suburbs to the west (then, as now, housing a concentration of racial minorities and poverty). Yet the intensively developed cities on its borders are driving housing demand inside the Pinelands and taxing the aquifers on which the region's ecosystem and human populations rely. In excluding the cities, the Pinelands statutes deprived the Pinelands Commission of any power over forces that already compromise, and may one day undermine, its ability to fulfill its overriding conservation mission.

Big versus Small. Some planning efforts cover very big areas, such as the Adirondack Park and Puget Sound region, while others, such as the Sacramento and Atlanta programs, cover far smaller areas. The Cape Cod, New York Long Island Central Pine Barrens, and Lancaster County programs cover only the extent of a relatively small Eastern county. Yet size alone does not matter as much as one might think. The kinds of resources, activities, and political structures one uses to define the region are more important than the simple geographic extent of the region. None of the regions represented here is large enough to control all critical impacts, and the order of magnitude of the "region" (though not always the specific boundary) is less a free policy decision than an imperative driven by the geography, politics, and economics of the individual case.

There are evident advantages and disadvantages in drawing one's regional boundary large or small. The Chesapeake Bay Program is clearly challenged by the enormous size and complexity of its "region"—the 64,000 square mile Chesapeake Bay watershed. On the other hand, only a watershed-wide effort stands any chance of saving the Bay and meeting the program's mission, and the massive scale of the project has generated billions of dollars to fund its scientific and policy initiatives, far more than any other regional effort. At the other end of the scale, the jurisdiction of the Cape Cod Commission is dictated by the geography of the Cape Cod peninsula, and its ability to build on the preexisting identity of the Cape among a fairly homogenous population made it easier to win public support than might otherwise be the case. Its relatively small size creates major challenges, such as the difficulty of financing a large-scale conversion from septic to sewers needed to repair water quality, and the lack of large undeveloped tracts to serve as receiving areas for a transfer of development rights program. (See also Mason 2008, 82–87.)

A number of planners and academics are promoting the idea of "megaregions" as the best scale and regional definition for planning. Focusing on these very large megaregions makes sense when one considers both the need for powerful and diversified economic units to prosper in a highly competitive global economy and the fact that people are continuing to congregate in these very large urban/suburban agglomerations (chap. 24, this volume; America 2050 website; Dewar and Epstein 2007). In several of these megaregions, scholars, industry, activists, and government officials have begun discussing challenges like sprawl control, transportation infrastructure, economic development, and housing on a megaregional scale. It is too early to say how these discussions will ultimately influence investment and land use policies. At this scale, however, the regions usually cross multiple state boundaries and encompass a vastly complex array of land use, economic, and social issues, making a single, unified, mandatory planning regime very unlikely.

Relationship to Local Planning Institutions and Processes

The single most important feature of any regional planning program is whether it is mandatory or voluntary for municipal and county land use agencies. There is a spectrum in the use of carrots and sticks reflected in today's regional programs, but they all fall essentially into one of two categories: those where regional plans and standards are mandatory on lower levels of government and land use activity, and those in which regional plans and standards are essentially voluntary for local government.

Mandatory Plans. There are a number of well-established mandatory regional planning programs at work today, most of which are described in chapters of this book. They all feature a regional agency that has the power to impose its will, over some range of issues, on local governments within its jurisdictional boundary. The mandatory plans highlighted in this book are the following:

- Portland Metro (chap. 1)
- Columbia River Gorge National Scenic Area (chap. 2)
- Tahoe Regional Planning Agency (chap. 3)
- Ontario's Growth Plan for the Greater Golden Horseshoe (chap. 4)
- Adirondack Park (chap. 5)
- New Jersey Pinelands (chap. 6)
- New Jersey Highlands (chap. 7)
- New Jersey Meadowlands (chap. 8)
- Long Island's Central Pine Barrens (chap. 9)
- Cape Cod (chap. 10)

With the sole exception of the New Jersey Meadowlands program, these regional planning agencies do not replace local government's traditional land use role, but instead shape and supplement local rules and procedures to ensure that the regional pattern and standards of development and conservation are achieved.

Several initiatives, such as the Adirondack Park Agency, New Jersey's Pinelands and Highlands programs, and New York's Central Pine Barrens Commission are built around regional land use maps specifying permitted uses and densities in each zone, which local governments must incorporate into their traditional municipal zoning and land use ordinances. Portland Metro relies first and foremost on its Urban Growth Boundary, which I discuss further below. All of these programs also use a variety of environmental standards and innovative transfer of development rights (TDR) and cluster mechanisms to accommodate growth compatibly with their natural resource conservation missions. The New Jersey Meadowlands, in contrast, has assumed the zoning and development powers of its municipalities within the Meadowlands district.

Some programs, such as the Tahoe Regional Planning Agency and Pinelands Commission, review and must approve all development for consistency with regional environmental thresholds, plans, and ordinances. Others rely on preexisting county or municipal governments to implement regional plans. The Columbia River Gorge Commission's regional management plan is detailed and mandatory, but it relies first and foremost on the county governments to adopt its terms and ensure it is implemented within their jurisdictions. Similarly, Ontario's Growth Plan for the Greater Golden Horseshoe delegates much of its land use authority to municipal governments by statute, but the regional growth plans are mandatory. More deferential to municipal land use controls than other mandatory programs discussed here, the Cape Cod program relies on direct regulation only of the larger "developments of regional impact" and those in designated Districts of Critical Planning Concern. In addition to enforcing growth boundaries of various kinds, all mandatory programs also engage in a variety of assistance, financing, and training efforts to foster local buy-in, cooperation, and good practices.

Voluntary and Collaborative Plans. Today one finds a great many regionalist programs that are essentially voluntary or advisory for local governments, providing
several basic models for organizing such initiatives. Voluntary and collaborative
programs highlighted in this book are the following:

- Puget Sound Regional Council (chap. 11)
- Sacramento Area Council of Governments (chap. 12)
- Envision Utah (chap. 13)
- Florida's Growth Management Program (chap. 14)
- Atlanta Regional Commission (chap. 15)
- Maryland's Smart Growth Program (chap. 16)
- Chesapeake Bay Program (chaps. 17 and 18)
- Envision Lancaster County (chap. 19)
- Delaware Valley Regional Planning Commission (chap. 20)
- Delaware River Basin Commission (chap. 21)
- Maine's Beginning with Habitat (chap. 22)

Three of these voluntary programs are rooted in statewide growth management
legislation, but the state laws in each case are dramatically different from one
another. Puget Sound Regional Council (PSRC) arose from the Washington State
Growth Management Act of 1990, which directs the counties and cities of the Puget
Sound area to create a common growth management plan. PSRC is a voluntary
program because the state mandate it carries out is broad and aspirational, PSRC is
a forum of its member jurisdictions, and the regional plans it creates represent a
consensus of these members. The state of Florida has adopted a series of statutes
aimed at managing its phenomenal growth by setting standards for local and
regional land use planning while playing a direct role in planning for a small number of special areas, such as the Florida Keys. Though the state requires all local
governments to plan, it does not require their plans to conform to regionally con-
ceived land use visions, and the regional conservation programs for special areas
have not yet produced effective growth management plans. Maryland's Smart
Growth Priority Act of 1997 is famous as a groundbreaking statewide growth management strategy—and because its father, Governor Paris Glendenning, is credited
with coining the term "smart growth. " The act uses the power of the purse, rather
than direct regulation of development, to direct growth into designated zones by
withholding most state infrastructure funding from development projects outside
these growth areas. Yet Maryland's plan is fundamentally voluntary because
municipal and county governments need not conform their local master plans,
and builders need not conform their ambitions, to the state's designations.

The Chesapeake Bay Program is the largest of America's regional initiatives and
the most daunting to understand. A compact among the federal government, three
states, and the District of Columbia, the program so far lacks a common regional
vision of the pattern and design of land uses, but instead relies on setting measurable environmental criteria that the member states commit to try to achieve
through whatever land use efforts each state is prepared to institute within its own

borders. Of these states, only Maryland (and some of its counties) has adopted meaningful forms of regional land use management. Beginning in 2009, the Obama administration launched a new effort to reinvigorate the program (Chesapeake Bay Program 2009).

The Sacramento Area Council of Governments (SACOG) is one of many councils of government (COGs) in California. Authorized but not required by state law, COGs are really the creatures of counties and municipalities that voluntarily band together to carry out regional planning. SACOG is one of the most active, innovative, and successful experiments in such collaborative planning in the country. It has formal responsibilities under federal and state law for transportation planning (it is the region's Metropolitan Planning Organization) and for meeting state housing and greenhouse gas reduction goals.

Yet another model for voluntary regional initiatives can be found in the county-based planning program of Lancaster County, Pennsylvania. Lancaster County, like Cape Cod, has a strong regional identity and cultural heritage that are very important to many of its residents, but the county is suffering the effects of sprawl coming from a distant city and its own struggling urban areas. Its plans promote the use of tools like designated urban growth areas, incentives for redevelopment, and farmland preservation to safeguard the county's scenic character in the face of growing population. Because the county lacks land use power and does not provide infrastructure funding, it relies on local governments to participate in the planning process and then implement the resulting plans through their local ordinances.

Maine's Beginning with Habitat is an example of ecosystem-based land use management designed to use planning to protect biodiversity through intensive focus on specific landscapes or ecosystems—an approach embodied in a number of projects of widely varying structure and histories across the country (e.g., Layzer 2008). Maine's program is a state initiative aimed at persuading local governments to plan for key natural resources while retaining their control over land use regulation through traditional comprehensive plans and zoning ordinances. This partnership of state government, the U.S. Fish and Wildlife Service, and three nonprofit environmental organizations provides landscape-scale analysis of critical resources and works with local governments to protect these resources through traditional tools like riparian buffers, zoning, infrastructure planning, and land acquisition. The program is entirely voluntary, so its success depends on county and municipal leaders seeing the value of collective action—a task aided by broad recognition that Maine's natural scenery and resources are its greatest social and economic assets.

Envision Utah is unique among the initiatives highlighted in this book because it is a nongovernmental project. The Salt Lake City region is conservative in its views on private property and government regulation—making it at first glance one of the least likely candidates for successful, progressive land use planning. So the region's leaders found their way to an atypical structure for regional planning tailored to the region's culture. Envision Utah is administered by a private nonprofit and is led by a steering committee of forward-thinking citizens, business people, elected and appointed public officials, and nonprofit community leaders. Local governments can implement their parts of the regional plans through traditional land use powers, if they choose.

Legal Foundations, Powers, and Independence

With only a few exceptions, today's regional initiatives are government programs with a legal foundation in state, and sometimes both state and federal, statute. Regional agencies with regulatory powers are all, of necessity, created and authorized by state law (sometimes in combination with federal backing or ratification). In some cases, state agencies of general jurisdiction—such as departments of environmental protection—play a large role in planning and implementation. The provincial government of Ontario, for example, is carrying out collaborative, but mandatory, regional growth planning for its Greater Golden Horseshoe region. In most cases, however, mandatory regional planning is carried out through an independent agency with rule-making powers—such as Portland Metro, the Columbia River Gorge Commission, the Tahoe Regional Planning Agency, the Adirondack Park Agency, the Pinelands Commission, the Meadowlands Commission, Long Island's Central Pine Barrens Commission, and the Cape Cod Commission. The Highlands Council is unusual in that it holds the planning authority for the region, but the state's Department of Environmental Protection has the rulemaking authority to enforce the plan. The Adirondack Park, Meadowlands, Highlands, Cape Cod, Central Pine Barrens, and Portland Metro initiatives are all creatures of special state statutes (and in some cases constitutional provisions), while the Pinelands, Columbia River Gorge, and Tahoe programs are founded in state statutes underpinned by special federal authorizing legislation unique to each program.

There are even fewer generalizations to be made about voluntary programs. Maryland and Maine are examples of state governments undertaking regional planning but choosing not to compel local land use authorities to comply with state plans. Neither of these programs created separate regional agencies standing between the state/provincial and county/municipal governments. The state instead focuses on regions by working with the preexisting matrix of local governments.

Regional agencies without rule-making powers also include federal-state partnerships (the Chesapeake Bay Program and Delaware River Basin Commission), interstate compacts (the Delaware Valley Regional Planning Commission), state-authorized agencies (the Atlanta Regional Commission), and voluntary collaborations of local governments, sometimes having formal state sanction (the Puget Sound Regional Council, Sacramento Area Council of Governments, and Envision Lancaster County program). One, Envision Utah, is led by a purely private organization that convenes and staffs a committee of public and private-sector leaders for voluntary, collaborative action.

In all of these cases, regional agencies are run by a board that is, in some significant degree, independent of the state's governor or legislature and, indeed, of broader partisan politics. This real, though imperfect, autonomy is a critical part of the agencies' effectiveness and public credibility. In fact, the freedom to create such independent agencies is one of the ways the architects of regionalist structures benefit from the fact that regions are not part of the received constitutional hierarchy of government.

How is autonomy achieved? The principal mechanism is to spread out the appointment of members to the governing board among state, local, and, in many cases, nongovernmental representation. By this means, no one government—federal, state, or local—controls the agency. The Tahoe program, for example, gives local government representatives enough seats on their boards to veto agency actions if they act collectively. In the Pinelands, the state enabling legislation ensures that commission members are unpaid volunteers and cannot be employed by the state. Even in the case of Portland Metro, whose governing council is directly elected, the elections are nonpartisan, and members of the Metro Council may not hold multiple elected offices. While in many cases governors select some members of the regional agency's board (often with the advice and consent of the legislature) and may even have some form of veto power over decisions (such as the power to veto the minutes of the board), these agencies still retain substantial legal independence of the state executive.

It would be easy to exaggerate the separation of these agencies from politics, but their relative independence provides a degree of stability and protection from typical political gamesmanship that state executive agencies often lack. The dynamic plays out differently in each region and may evolve over time. Yet the public typically expects these agencies to operate independently of partisan politics and politicians.

Regional Strategies

In aiming to meet their lofty and difficult goals, regional planning initiatives are using a wide range of strategies, including the following:

- Growth management maps
- Urban growth boundaries (UGBs)
- Tax revenue sharing among political subdivisions
- Transfer of development rights (TDR)
- Controls on development of high-value natural or cultural resource areas
- Land and development rights acquisition programs
- Innovative regional infrastructure planning and strategic investments linked to regional land use policies
- Water resource planning, protection, and controls
- Smart-growth or sustainable community design policies
- Public engagement through inclusive planning processes

Growth Management Maps. Growth management maps are designed to permit (or encourage) new development in growth zones and forbid (or discourage) development in conservation zones. Versions of this strategy can be found among mandatory programs in the Adirondack Park, Cape Cod, New York's Central Pine Barrens, New Jersey Highlands and Pinelands, and Tahoe Region. In each of these cases, the regional map does not replace municipal plans and zoning laws. Instead, municipal plans and ordinances must conform to minimum standards of the regional plans, which aim to bring about a regional pattern of development and conservation while giving towns some discretion on detailed regulation of densities and uses.

Regional growth management maps enable regional agencies to create a large-scale pattern that allocates new development across a broad landscape in ways that protect natural resources and strengthen existing urbanized areas. When consistently applied over time, growth management maps also have the virtue of providing clear and predictable statements of what landowners and developers can and cannot do—thus minimizing parcel-by-parcel conflict and strengthening public expectations that at least some large parts of the landscape will be preserved if they support the plan.

Some voluntary programs use growth management maps as well, though they have no direct means of compelling consistency of local and county master plans with the regional plan. Maryland's statewide smart growth program, for example, designates growth zones, in part explicitly in the enabling statute and in part through local designations following criteria set in the statute. Maryland's Smart Growth Priority Act generally bars state funding of infrastructure in support of development outside designated growth areas, but does not require that local and county zoning match the smart growth map, nor does it forbid or regulate infrastructure or development outside the growth zones. The Atlanta Regional Commission has developed a Unified Growth Policy map that identifies the city center, suburban centers, corridors, and outlying rural areas in an effort to guide local government actions and investments.

No matter how wise the planners, no matter how good the data, no matter how creative the strategies adopted, events and the passage of time will eventually reveal defects in any regional plan. Like all laws, plans must be flexible, must leave some decisions for later action, and must be able to respond to changing economies and better scientific knowledge. Every plan, whether written in binding regulations or only in aspirational visioning documents, must include mechanisms for amendment. Yet this very ability to change and make exceptions also represents a fundamental threat to the success and survival of a regional plan built on creating stable patterns of growth and preservation.

Urban Growth Boundaries. The UGB is a version of the growth management map that limits the types and intensities of development outside designated growth areas around established cities and settlements. The boundary functions both to protect surrounding natural and agricultural lands from excessive development and to strengthen the city by satisfying growth pressures within the urban boundary. Oregon state law requires all cities to create UGBs and to use them to manage growth and discourage sprawl. Washington and Tennessee also require local governments to create UGBs. A number of cities and towns, particularly in California, have adopted their own versions of urban growth boundaries (Aytur et al. 2008;

Pendell et al. 2002). UGBs can be implemented through highly restrictive use and density rules outside the boundary, through limiting public services and investments in infrastructure such as roads, sewer, and water to new development inside the UGB, or through a combination of these approaches.

Portland Metro's implementation of Oregon's statewide UGB requirement is the preeminent example of the UGB approach. While the state statute does not specify the rules that apply inside and outside the boundaries, it does mandate many goals, procedures, target densities, and similar standards that local governments must build into their UGB regulations in order to combat sprawl and protect farmland and open spaces. In the case of Portland, the basic tool for making the UGB effective is severe limitation of nonagricultural development outside the UGB (chap. 1, this volume; Abbott 2002).

The use of UGBs raises at least four major challenges. First, one city's UGB may simply drive growth even farther from the urban center to nearby, unregulated green fields—thus weakening the city and worsening sprawl. In most contexts, therefore, it is essential that cities using UGBs coordinate their UGB and transportation planning with neighboring cities and counties to achieve a desirable regional outcome even where there is no common, overarching regional land use plan. There is not much data on how this phenomenon is affecting UGBs to date. Portland Metro addresses the issue by using a very large UGB (with more than 250,000 acres within the boundary as of 2008) and coordinating the setting of UGBs for all cities in a large region, as well as with neighboring governments across the state border in Washington.

Second, poorly planned, inefficient development within the growth boundary may, over time, defeat its purpose by absorbing too little of the demand for growth and pressuring planners to repeatedly expand the UGB. Growth boundaries, therefore, must be combined with zoning, design standards, and infrastructure investment that brings about sustainable, efficient development and redevelopment within the boundary. Portland Metro and the city of Portland have devoted a great deal of energy to urban and suburban design within the UGB.

Third, there will be constant pressure to make incremental extensions of the growth boundary; such incremental expansions will raise difficult political dynamics and concerns of favoritism in the choice of where to expand and where to hold the line. Since 2002 Portland Metro has expanded the UGB three times, for a total of 20,000 additional acres (just under a 10 percent increase). Each time the process has been difficult and controversial. Metro is working on a new, longer-term approach. Metro and the county governments are working to designate "urban reserves" beyond the current UGB that will be the priority for expansion, if needed, over the coming forty to fifty years. Metro is also focusing more energy on promoting efficient development within existing centers in order, among other things, to reduce the pressure to expand the UGB at its edge.

Finally, there is some evidence that growth boundaries (and other growth limits) can drive housing prices so high within a UGB that segments of the population are condemned to overcrowded conditions, spending too much of their income on housing, or migration to cheaper markets. The impact of the UGB on housing costs in Portland is hotly debated, but it is a legitimate concern any regional agency must address (e.g., Ozawa 2004; Staley et al. 1999). Land use policies within the boundary should work to ensure a diversity of housing types and specifically encourage construction of affordable housing.

Portland Metro looks to solve all three of these potential pitfalls through regional coordination, long-range planning, and very careful attention to what happens inside the UGB.

Regional Tax-Base Sharing. Sharing property and other local tax revenue among political subdivisions is a tool regionalism's advocates and theorists tend to love, but which only two places in the United States, the Twin Cities and the New Jersey Meadowlands, have adopted so far. Both in its promise and in the reasons that certain communities in any region will oppose it, tax-base sharing (TBS) encapsulates the challenges that regionalism faces in our society. Regionalist policies and institutions arise where enough people (leaders, the public, or both) decide regionalism will benefit everyone (or nearly everyone), while fragmented localism will ultimately harm everyone (or nearly everyone). With the sharing of local tax revenue, regionalists have to make that case in very objective, measurable terms of dollars and cents, and they must fight against an expectation of local control over money that is even more difficult to dislodge than that of local control over zoning.

Myron Orfield and Thomas Luce have set out the economic and social basis for tax-base sharing, described its success in the Twin Cities region, and provided additional examples of places where it can and should be adopted (chap. 27, this volume; see also Orfield 2002, Orfield and Wallace 2007). Where fragmented local governments raise their own funds through local taxes, they are driven to compete for taxable development, leading to irrational and often self-defeating encouragement of sprawling forms of growth. By removing or mitigating that fiscal motivation, TBS provides a basis for genuine cooperation and synergies through regional planning. TBS brings benefits to all communities participating in the system, both those that receive more of the shared tax revenue than they contribute and those that contribute more than they receive.

The New Jersey Meadowlands Commission's tax sharing program exemplifies this conclusion. The Meadowlands plan does not necessarily provide each municipality equal shares of revenue-producing development. Without tax sharing, the plan could create significant, corrosive disparities among the municipalities and neighborhoods. The tax sharing system requires each municipality to contribute 40 percent of property tax revenue on post-1970 development to the common fund. The commission distributes the common fund back to the cities based on the number of schoolchildren it is educating and the amount of land it has within the Meadowlands District. The program has won the allegiance of participating municipalities, and towns currently outside the district have raised the idea of joining (see chap. 8).

Transfer of Development Rights. TDR programs have become a key land conservation tool that many regional programs are using. Zoning alone cannot protect most natural and scenic resources, and TDR provides a mechanism for private industry to finance the permanent preservation of valued open spaces as one cost of the right to build—or to build in specified ways—on other lands. TDR programs can be constructed not just to direct development where government wants it to go, but also to get the kind of development government wants by, for example, reducing required rights purchases for favored designs, incorporation of affordable housing, or other planning objectives. A tool that holds great promise, TDR has been very successful in some places and a failure in others.

The New Jersey Pinelands TDR program and the farmland program of Montgomery County, Maryland, appear to be the most successful TDR systems in the United States, each having preserved tens of thousands of acres through deed restrictions (see also Fulton et al. 2004, Messer 2007, Walls et al. 2007). New Jersey has been an innovator in this field in two rather different contexts: the long-established Pinelands program and a statewide municipal TDR authority that is just beginning to prove its value. TDR is also incorporated, with varying degrees of success, into several other regional programs, including the Cape Cod, Tahoe Region, and Lancaster County initiatives discussed here. The Central Pine Barrens program includes a TDR system that is unusual in two respects: the transferable credits are, in effect, rights to discharge sanitary waste water, and rights can be used by developers working outside the Central Pine Barrens boundary (but within a Pine Barrens municipality). In fact, some credits are redeemable elsewhere in the county through the county health department.

The greatest challenge to building an effective TDR program lies in the need to create both a steady supply of rights, through strong incentives for holders to sell rights at a reasonable price, and a robust demand by developers for those rights, through requirements or powerful incentives to buy. Each program must be tailored to the economic, land tenure, and land use planning environment in which it will operate. Agencies overseeing these programs need to monitor and adjust the rules as conditions change through time. A healthy and resilient market requires lots of (willing) sellers and lots of (understandably reluctant) buyers.

TDR can be an important tool within a broader regional planning system. By the same token, TDR programs are most likely to succeed when set within an effective regional plan. A strong regional land use plan that allocates rights over large sending areas, and motivates developers working across large receiving areas to purchase and retire rights, is the most efficient way to create and calibrate supply and demand. TDR can fail on either or both of the supply and demand sides of the equation. In Cape Cod, the difficulty is the scarcity of undeveloped blocks large enough to serve as sending areas, while a recent study finds that the program in Montgomery County, Maryland, is one of many that have been bogged down by a lack of demand for rights on the part of developers (Walls and McConnell 2007, chap. 10; see also Messer 2007).

Controls on Development of High-Value Natural or Cultural Resources. Detailed regulation of natural or cultural resources is another tool to conserve high-value resources and concentrate growth where it makes sense regionally. Many regional planning initiatives incorporate a variety of controls on development of critical environmental areas, whether or not they use a regional growth management map. Critical areas might be rare species habitats, scenic vistas and recreation lands, ground water recharge areas, or historic sites. The Adirondack Park Agency classifies private lands based on factors including biological, scenic, and historical significance; these classifications are then built into the permitted types and intensities of development in the park's Land Use and Development Plan. The Central Pine Barrens program identifies and maps "critical resource areas" and authorizes municipalities and the commission to require that development projects identify, take account of, and protect these resources. The Tahoe Regional Planning Agency's regulations prohibit the demolition or alteration of designated historic sites without an agency-approved "resource protection plan." Maine's Beginning with Habitat program is based on identifying and prioritizing critical areas through science-based analysis, then persuading local governments to use traditional zoning and financial and land acquisition tools to shift development away from these sites. The power of this approach, even without mandatory regional protections on private development, helps explain why landowners and local officials in many places have fought hard to prevent even the mapping of critical resources.

The Pinelands Comprehensive Management Plan incorporates factors like threatened and endangered species habitat into the regional growth management area boundaries, but also bars development of critical habitats in all zones, both conservation and growth. The Tahoe regulations take a similar approach. This dual strategy can invite conflict, as owners or developers in designated growth areas are sometimes outraged to discover they still cannot build in a growth zone because someone found a local population of rare plants or wildlife on site. But the dual approach certainly makes ecological sense where boundaries were drawn with imperfect knowledge of the resources within each area and, in any case, are drawn at too large a scale to protect all high-value habitats and features spread throughout the region.

Land and Development Rights Acquisition. The purchase of land and development rights is our most common and most successful means of protecting natural and agricultural lands from development. It is also a vital tool for regional planning, and every regional program includes land acquisition planning among its strategies. Buying land or easements alone will not necessarily protect ecosystems, scenic vistas, or traditional working landscapes. Random purchases may not protect enough contiguous land in the right places to achieve ultimate conservation goals. Simply buying land as willing sellers come to one's door is bound to leave out certain habitats, rare species populations, headwaters, and geological formations needed to preserve a region's biodiversity. Acquisitions, then, should be guided by a coherent, regional plan that prioritizes purchases and focuses energy.

The Nature Conservancy's Ecoregional Conservation strategy and Maine's Beginning with Habitat initiative are outstanding examples of programs designed to ensure that conservation agencies have the data they need to protect the complete biodiversity of a region. Each applies a rigorous methodology to map habitats in light of ecological features such as habitat types, rare species, intact patch sizes, surrounding land uses, and viability (see chaps. 22 and 29). The work of the Eastern Shore Land Conservancy in Maryland illustrates how buying land can play a major role in a regional conservation project like saving the Chesapeake Bay, especially where there is no mandatory regional land use control in place. Public and private agencies have preserved over 280,000 acres, or about one-quarter of the remaining undeveloped land in the region. Importantly, the Eastern Shore Land Conservancy does not pursue land acquisition in isolation from planning, but places acquisition within a regional land use vision for which it has won the support of the six counties in its region. Its Eastern Shore 2010 regional vision, for example, sets specific goals for counties to direct 80 percent of new development into existing and designated growth areas through zoning and acquisition (chap. 30).

The conservation easement, as opposed to the outright purchase of land, is a key tool of land preservation for two reasons: it can be less expensive, and it safeguards the continued economic use of working landscapes, especially farms. A strong "hybrid" program will use zoning, funding for purchases of easements, transfer of development rights, and incentives like tax credits to encourage donations of land. This integrated approach can be found, in differing forms and degrees, in programs like those of the California Coastal Commission, New Jersey Pinelands, the Central Pine Barrens, and Baltimore County, Maryland (chap. 31).

Finally, land acquisition carried out on a regional scale has long been a prominent tool for protecting water resources. New York City's financing of massive and expensive land acquisitions in the Catskill Mountains is the most prominent example (chap. 26). This episode suggests that while it can be difficult to make an air-tight economic case for acquisition based on its costs and benefits for water supply protection, water users can understand themselves as part of a regional hydrologic system in which long-term success requires that they invest in the region's natural infrastructure. Land acquisition (unlike building physical infrastructure) is a strategy that can serve multiple popular goals of water supply protection, growth management, and open space preservation.

Innovative Regional Infrastructure Planning and Strategic Investments. Linking infrastructure planning and investment to regional land use policies, particularly for transportation, is a tool that should be integrated into all regional planning initiatives. It is fitting that many of the agencies discussed here are the designated Metropolitan Planning Organizations (MPOs) for their regions and play the leading role in transportation planning. This role enables the agency to plan for close linkages of housing and commercial development with transit and road networks. Portland Metro, the Tahoe Regional Planning Agency, Atlanta Regional Council, Delaware Valley Regional Planning Commission, Puget Sound Regional Council, and Sacramento Area Council of Governments are all MPOs for their regions. Hybrid models also exist: the Lancaster County Planning Commission serves as staff to its region's MPO, which is an independent body of citizens and officials. Regional planning agencies serving as MPOs are using their influence over transportation investments simultaneously to reduce commute times, fight sprawl, reduce greenhouse gas emissions, and meet state and federal clean air mandates. Today's integrated transportation/land use planning is a model of how regional planning serves economic, social, and environmental goals that many have seen as being at odds with one another, but in reality can only be reached together.

Given how intimately transportation and urban/suburban growth are tied, it is surprising that some otherwise powerful agencies, like the Adirondack Park Agency and Pinelands Commission, are not MPOs and tend to play only a secondary or permitting role in transportation spending. These disconnects are legacies of the particular history of each program. The Pinelands Commission, for example, was founded before the MPOs were created and only has the power to review transportation projects (like the widening of the two major freeways in the Pinelands or the construction of new freeways) as a permitting agency. This reactive role inevitably places the agency in a defensive posture in which it can, at best, try to mitigate the impacts of these projects, rather than shape a coherent long-term transportation network as an organic element of the regional land use plan. The lack of direct responsibility for transportation planning in such cases is an anachronism and can be a major weakness in the structure of regionalism.

The Atlanta Regional Commission and Sacramento Area Council of Governments exemplify agencies pursuing tightly integrated transportation and community design projects to foster transit-oriented, center-based development in locations that serve a regional vision. Ideally, these agencies have two key tools: planning and money. Placing transportation planning at the heart of their visioning and long-term plans enables regional agencies to influence the zoning regulations that set the pattern, density, and mix of land uses driving transportation demand. Envision Utah, as a private nonprofit, is not an MPO and does not have power over transportation investments, but it has nevertheless been able to influence transportation thinking and policy through its regional visioning processes and participation in specific demonstration projects.

Water Resource Planning, Protection, and Controls. Water management is an increasingly critical element of regional growth management. The subject of water resource planning is an enormous one, complicated by the great differences in climate, geology, laws, and cultural settings that shape competition for water across the continent. In some areas, the federal and state governments have created specialized regional water supply management agencies, such as the Delaware River Basin Commission highlighted in this book and Florida's regional water management districts. In other places, such as the Seattle region, local water purveyors, special districts, and governments are voluntarily cooperating on a regional basis to analyze water demand and supply.

The Delaware River Basin Commission (DRBC) is one of the specialized agencies that mediate the demands of competing water users across local, state, and even national boundaries. DRBC is a federally sponsored but state-controlled forum through which Pennsylvania, New York, and New Jersey hammer out the allocation of water and management of river flows through mutual agreement. The states have committed themselves through a compact to maintain minimum specified flow rates needed to sustain ecological functions and protect intakes. Although controlled by its member states, the commission serves them all as a neutral expert, in effect setting the bounds of negotiation by showing the states how much water, and from where in the system, they have to work with (chap. 21).

A long history of cooperative management in a context of relative water abundance has kept the Delaware River from becoming one of the notorious cases, such as the Colorado and Klamath Rivers, where there is intense and long-standing conflict among differing users—cities, farmers, fisheries, and native peoples. It is striking that the most contentious water battles in the West have typically not led to the creation of such neutral regional agencies, but are fought out in courts, federal and state executive branch offices, legislatures, and back-room negotiations.

Bruce Babbitt has trenchantly observed that "in the more than thirty years since the Clean Water Act was enacted, no state yet has produced a meaningful plan to clean up and restore its waters by managing land uses" (Babbitt 2005, 119). In this as in other fields, it seems that state government itself is ill-equipped to create and implement land use plans to protect natural resources from the diffuse impacts of development, such as nonpoint sources of nutrients flowing into ground and surface waters. Regional planning agencies, in contrast, offer the best hope of solving most of today's critical water quality problems because both the sources and impacts of nonpoint source contamination are so widespread. All programs highlighted here are concerned with water quality. At least two of them, the Chesapeake Bay and Tahoe initiatives, owe their very reason for being to the restoration of water quality to two of North America's great but damaged water bodies. The Chesapeake Bay was once an almost inconceivably productive source of seafood, while Lake Tahoe's intensely blue depths made it one of the most beautiful places in the world. Both of these water bodies have been damaged—but by no means destroyed—by excessive nutrients and sediment flowing from fertilized farms and suburban lawns, septic systems, construction sites, roads, and rooftops. Nutrient contamination plagues the shallow aquifers of Cape Cod and the Pinelands, as well as the Everglades and many of the continent's bays and estuaries. To succeed in these cases, government will need to protect and restore large forested areas, keep enough of each watershed free of development to preserve ecosystem functions, and limit new development to compact, resource-efficient forms—all land use policies that regional agencies are uniquely equipped to devise and carry out.

Smart Growth Community Design Policies. Smart growth or sustainable community design seeks to bring about (and where it exists, to preserve) compact, transit-oriented, mixed-use, energy-efficient development that creates public or civic as well as private and commercial spaces. In *The Regional City*, Peter Calthorpe and William Fulton make a powerful case that bad community design drives bad regional outcomes, while good community design is an integral part of good regional planning (Calthorpe and Fulton 2001, especially pt. 2). Community design can play three roles in a regional land use strategy: It can support an overarching regional pattern of growth and conservation zones; or, where no large-scale growth management map or UGB exists, it can be a principal tool for achieving regional goals through the cumulative effect of applying good design to all the new development in a region; and, finally, it can be combined with transportation spending to create transit-oriented centers.

The Tahoe, Portland, and Ontario programs are examples of regional land use plans that incorporate community design within a broader landscape plan. In the Ontario program, for example, the provincial government leads the regional planning initiative, producing a twenty-five-year growth plan to which municipal planning documents must conform. The plan institutes a framework of policies and targets to foster redevelopment and compact forms of new development, among other policies. Both Portland Metro and the Pinelands Commission mandate minimum densities for areas within the UGB to prevent local governments from defeating the plan through low-density zoning (see also Seltzer 2004). Envision Utah's Quality Growth Strategy does not use growth boundaries or a master plan that designates various growth and preservation zones on the landscape, but instead promotes compact, pedestrian-friendly, and mixed-use community design, infill rather than greenfields development, and transportation choices and water conservation measures that local governments are encouraged to implement by adopting model ordinances. The Atlanta and Sacramento initiatives are salient examples of programs that integrate transportation planning with plans for compact, transit-oriented centers.

A vital question is whether regional plans can succeed over time if they do not require or foster compact development, efficient land use, and transit within their designated zones for growth. If within a UGB or regional growth area development proceeds in the form of strip malls and familiar low-density, disconnected subdivisions, then land within the growth zones will be exhausted quickly. These areas will be prone to the same fiscal stresses and disinvestment that plagues many older suburbs, and pressure will grow to build out of the problem by expanding boundaries. The Pinelands and Portland plans address this concern in part through setting minimum zoning densities in certain growth areas. But putting limits on down-zoning is generally not going to be enough, since zoning allows, but does not require, developers to build at zoned densities. Some regional programs, like the Pinelands and Highlands, do not include formal rules or incentives to prevent sprawl within designated growth areas. Others, like Portland Metro and Tahoe Regional Planning Agency, recognize the dangers of poorly designed development as a central element of the regional program. The Central Pine Barrens statute, for example, mandates that the regional plan must "accommodate development, in a manner consistent with the long-term integrity of the Pine Barrens ecosystem and . . . ensure that the pattern of development is compact, efficient and orderly."

Public Engagement through Inclusive Planning Processes. Inclusive planning processes that involve the public in an intensive planning exercise have become a central feature of the newer regional planning programs. These public planning processes can be very effective in raising awareness of a region's identity and the shared future its residents can influence. They give the public a personal sense of responsibility for managing growth on a regional scale, overcoming parochialism or simplistic preconceptions. These forums are designed to provide participants with the following:

- Information about the challenges they face collectively, such as development trends, landscape patterns, and the impacts of growth
- A range of possible growth scenarios for the future
- Visualizations of current trends and future scenarios (particularly a current trends scenario contrasted with alternative possible scenarios)
- A means to deliberate among themselves toward reaching a consensus about the best vision of the future
- A means to express and share the results of their deliberations with the public at large

Out of the deliberation may arise a consensus vision of the most desirable future for the region—and an idea of the policies that could make that vision a reality. Through the media coverage it receives, the exercise should form the basis for a continuing public engagement into the future.

These visioning projects are not stakeholder negotiations. They aim to engage the public at large and generate public consensus around broad growth and conservation scenarios for the region. In contrast, stakeholder planning processes are typically structured by government to gather people formally representing a range of public and private interests—agencies, businesses, industries, and non-profits—to meet and negotiate specific proposals and report back to the convening agencies. (For an excellent discussion of the hazards of relying on stakeholder negotiations to create ecosystem-based regional conservation plans, see Layzer [2008].)

Envision Utah is particularly famous for its groundbreaking public visioning process, which began with workshops that developed four alternative growth scenarios, then invited the public to respond through a massive publicity initiative, before adopting a Quality Growth Strategy. Gerrit-Jan Knaap and his colleagues at the National Center for Smart Growth Research and Education of the University of Maryland have developed and applied a conceptually similar approach called Reality Check *Plus* (see chap. 32). Reality Check *Plus* focuses on the related questions of density and location for projected new growth through 2030, having participants place toy blocks on region-scale maps to represent their desired distribution of new jobs and housing in relation to existing development, infrastructure, and natural features. SACOG's visioning project for the Sacramento region provides another example. Using workshops at the neighborhood, county, and regional levels, on-the-ground case studies, and computer mapping, the Sacramento process has resulted in transportation and land use plans with broad public support (see chap. 33).

A striking feature of these visioning processes is that each succeeded in bringing diverse participants to a common recognition that they do indeed share a region with a distinctive identity and to a broad consensus on the most desirable path for their region. It appears that, at least in regions facing sprawl, most people really do, on reflection, want to see growth concentrated, open spaces protected, transit choices, and walkable, mixed-use commercial centers. When these ideas are made specific and concrete, dissent is bound to arise, but it is encouraging that the public in culturally very different regions (like Salt Lake City and Maryland) are seeing the advantages of contemporary "smart growth" landscape visions.

DECISION MAKING AND DEMOCRACY

Regional boundaries generally do not match existing democratic structures of municipality, county, and state. Regional plans, therefore, are often seen as undemocratic impositions from outsiders. The very structures that give regional agencies the benefit of at least partial independence from partisan political forces, moreover, also make them open to the charge of being antidemocratic. These are two reasons some regional planners believe only voluntary programs—in which multiple jurisdictions, each with its own democratically elected leaders, join together to pursue their common interests—are feasible or even appropriate for their regions. Some argue that regional agencies—whether common special purpose districts or the less common regional programs with broad growth management powers—threaten democracy by removing real power from local, participatory, community-building municipal governments (e.g., Briffault 2000, 16–17; Frisken and Norris 2001, 471–472; Frug 1999; Hills 2000; Reynolds 2007). My own experience is that this latter defense of municipal government is divorced from reality and fails to seriously engage the true dynamics and failings of fragmented local governance. Yet it surely reflects a genuine value in our popular culture to which any form of regional planning, whether compulsory or voluntary on local jurisdictions, must respond.

Regional governance agencies have succeeded in overcoming the challenge of satisfying democratic values in a variety of ways, each finding different structures and processes to provide responsiveness to the electorate. At the same time, these programs seek to build in safeguards to prevent the regional process from becoming captive to parochial local, economic, or partisan political interests. In sum, each aims to structure regional planning institutions whose culture and balance of powers will favor regional visions of the public good and regional policies to achieve those visions.

The regional planning programs discussed in this book do not replace municipal governments with regional governments, but instead, in a great variety of ways, seek to incorporate municipal governments and powers into a regional growth management and conservation plan. Virtually all the regional planning agencies

discussed here include representatives of relevant municipal or county governments in their regional decision-making body, but the extent of local control
or influence varies greatly. On the other hand, virtually all these programs
include within the regional decision-making body significant representation of
interests or agencies other than local governments, based on the recognition that
local governments, though democratically elected, do not necessarily represent all
the interests that need to be heard within the agency if it is to serve a truly regional
mission.

Only one regional agency, Portland Metro, is a free-standing unit of government whose leaders are directly elected by citizens of the region. Since 1979
Portland Metro has been governed by a six-person council whose members are
elected by district, with Metro's council president elected at large. Even Portland
Metro, with its exceptionally broad powers over land use, does not replace the
region's preexisting general purpose municipal governments.

All the other programs discussed here rely on having elected officials or their
nominees share power among themselves and, often, with others representing distinct interests within the state, region, or nation. Among programs with mandatory planning powers, some examples provide a flavor for the great diversity of
approaches. The Cape Cod Commission gives each of the Cape's fifteen municipalities one of the nineteen seats on the commission. The New Jersey Pinelands
Protection Act, in contrast, allocates seven of fifteen seats on the Pinelands
Commission to county representatives (who have always been residents, but not an
elected county politician) and no seats to municipal officials or their representatives. The Tahoe Compact between California and Nevada provides for the Tahoe
Regional Planning Agency to have fourteen voting members, of whom six are local
officials—but the compact also requires a super-majority vote on key regulatory
actions. The Adirondack Park Agency Act gives the least deference to local governments in assigning the power to select all of the agency's board members to the
governor, as the board consists of eight gubernatorial designees, plus the secretary
of state and commissioners of Environmental Conservation and Economic
Development.

Voluntary programs also must provide accountability to win public support.
Indeed, voluntary programs may have a greater need to prove their democratic
bona fides in order to keep local officials on board and pursuing the regional
vision. Several voluntary programs have gone to great lengths to win public credibility, not just through a responsive organizational structure but also by carrying
out extensive public engagement and visioning processes. As with mandatory
plans, voluntary programs have no common governing structure for providing
accountability and responsiveness to the public. Some planning bodies are simply
state administrative agencies, as in Maine and Maryland. Others, like Lancaster
County, are simply established county governments. Most, however, are specially
designed regional agencies that build local government representatives into their
governing boards. The Puget Sound Regional Council, created by agreement
among the region's counties and cities and designated as the region's MPO, is

governed by boards made up of elected officials from the constituent jurisdictions, plus state transportation officials. The Atlanta Regional Commission's board includes twenty-three local elected officials, as well as private citizens and a state representative. SACOG actually broadened its board in 2003 to include representatives of all twenty-eight member counties and cities (smaller cities had previously chosen a single representative to speak for them all). In contrast with all other programs highlighted in this book, the Utah initiative is led and staffed, but not really controlled, by an independent nonprofit NGO, Envision Utah. The project is guided by a steering committee that includes a wide array of state and local officials, business leaders, and nonprofit representatives. Independent of any state or local government agency, Envision Utah relies on intensive public visioning processes and education to build support for its ideas.

The governing boards of nearly all programs discussed here include positions representing interests other than locally elected governments. These programs reflect a recognition that relying solely on municipal (or county) representatives excludes two kinds of voices—elements of the region's population who are typically not well represented by municipal councils or elected officials, and residents of the state, and even the nation, who live outside the region's geographic boundaries but have a legitimate interest in the region. Portland Metro and SACOG are exceptions: no out-of-region and statewide representative, nor anyone not elected or representing an elected body, sits as a voting member on their governing boards. In contrast, the Cape Cod program adds a minority, a Native American and a county representative, as well as an appointee of the governor, to the fifteen municipal representatives on its nineteen-member commission. The Pinelands program allocates seven seats on the commission to state residents nominated by the governor as representative of statewide interests and one to a representative of the U.S. secretary of the interior. The Tahoe Compact specifies that at least six members of the Tahoe Regional Planning Agency must be persons who are *not* residents of the Tahoe region, in order to ensure statewide interests are represented.

The chapters that follow provide real-world examples of regional planning at work. The regional projects discussed in this book do take different forms. Their working definitions of sustainability, their measures of success, the strategies and tools they use, the resources on which they are focused, and the geographic scales on which they operate vary widely. They are trying different ways of integrating public accountability and responsiveness into political structures that have no established place in our constitutional system. But they all share three qualities in common: the recognition that our use of land shapes all other features of our society; the goal of achieving genuine sustainability in human use of and impacts on valued landscapes and resources; and the insight that achieving that goal requires taking a regional perspective and fashioning land use management strategies on a regional scale.

Program	Chapter	Year established	Mandatory (M) or voluntary (V) on local government	Defined by natural (N), metro (M), or state (S) borders	Acreage	Authorizing legislation: state (S) both federal and state (B)	Board members: elected (E), appointed (A), or state executive agency (SE)[a]
Adirondack Park Agency (NY)	5	1971	M	N	6.0 million	S	A
Atlanta Regional Commission (GA)	15	1947	V	M	1.9 million	S	A
Cape Cod Commission (MA)	10	1990	M	N	250,000	S	A
Chesapeake Bay Program (DC, MD, PA, VA)	17, 18	1983	V	N	38.0 million	B	A
Columbia River Gorge National Scenic Area (OR, WA)	2	1986	M	N	292,500	B	A
Delaware Valley Regional Planning Commission (NJ, PA)	20	1965	V	M	1.4 million	B	A
Delaware River Basin Commission (DE, NJ, NY, PA)	21	1961	M	M	8.6 million	B	A
Florida Regional Planning Programs	14	1972	V	S	Statewide	S	Not applicable
Highlands Council (NJ)	7	2004	M	N	860,000	S	A
Lancaster County Regional Planning (PA)	19	2005	V	County	570,000	S	A, E
Long Island Central Pine Barrens (NY)	9	1993	M	N	102,500	S	SE
Maine Beginning with Habitat	22	2000	V	S	Statewide	S	SE
Maryland Smart Growth Programs	16	1992	V	S	Statewide	S	SE
Meadowlands Commission (NJ)	8	1969	M	N	25,000	S	A
Twin Cities Metropolitan Council (MN)	25, 27	1967	M	M	1.9 million	S	A
Ontario Places to Grow	4	2005	M	M	8.3 million	Provincial	Provincial government
Pinelands National Reserve (NJ)	6	1978	M	N	1.1 million	B	A
Portland Metro (OR)	1	1992	M	M	296,514	S	E
Puget Sound Regional Council (WA)	11	1991	V	M	4.0 million	B	A
Sacramento Area Council of Governments (CA)	12, 33	1980	V	M	670,000	S	A
Tahoe Regional Planning Agency (CA, NV)	3	1969	M	N	300,000	B	A
Envision Utah	13	1997	V	S	Statewide	None	A

Figure I.1. Regional Planning Programs in this Book

Program	Chapter	Growth management maps	Urban growth boundaries	Transfer of development rights	Controlling development of high value natural areas	Conservation land acquisition	Regional infrastructure planning
Adirondack Park Agency	5	✓			✓	✓	
Atlanta Regional Commission	15	✓					✓
Cape Cod Commission	10	✓			✓		✓
Chesapeake Bay Program	17, 18	✓			✓	✓	✓
Columbia River Gorge National Scenic Area	2		✓				✓
Delaware Valley Regional Planning Commission	20						
Delaware River Basin Commission	21						
Florida Regional Planning Programs	14						
Highlands Council	7	✓		✓	✓	✓	✓
Lancaster County Regional Planning	19	✓			✓	✓	✓
Long Island Central Pine Barrens	9	✓		✓	✓	By member governments	✓
Maine Beginning with Habitat	22	✓			✓	✓	✓
Maryland Smart Growth Programs	16	✓		County programs			✓
Meadowlands Commission	8	✓			✓	✓	✓
Twin Cities Metropolitan Council	25, 27	✓			✓	✓	✓
Ontario Places to Grow	4	✓	✓		✓	✓	✓
Pinelands National Reserve	6	✓	✓	✓	✓	✓	✓
Portland Metro	1	✓	✓		✓		✓
Puget Sound Regional Council	11	✓		✓	✓	✓	✓
Sacramento Area Council of Governments	12, 33	✓					✓
Tahoe Regional Planning Agency	3	✓		✓	✓	✓	✓
Envision Utah	13	✓		✓			✓

Program	Chapter	Metropolitan planning organization (MPO)	Water resource planning	Tax revenue sharing	Smart growth community design	Focus on affordable housing	Public visioning and planning processes
Adirondack Park Agency	5						
Atlanta Regional Commission	15	✓	✓		✓	✓	
Cape Cod Commission	10		✓			✓	
Chesapeake Bay Program	17, 18		✓				
Columbia River Gorge National Scenic Area	2						
Delaware Valley Regional Planning Comm.	20						
Delaware River Basin Commission	21		✓				
Florida Regional Planning Programs	14						
Highlands Council	7		✓		✓	✓	
Lancaster County Regional Planning	19					✓	
Long Island Central Pine Barrens	9		✓				
Maine Beginning with Habitat	22		✓				
Maryland Smart Growth Programs	16						
Meadowlands Commission	8		✓		✓	✓	✓
Twin Cities Metropolitan Council	25, 27	✓	✓	✓	✓	✓	
Ontario Places to Grow	4	✓	✓	✓	✓	✓	
Pinelands National Reserve	6		✓			✓	
Portland Metro	1	✓	✓		✓	✓	✓
Puget Sound Regional Council	11	✓				✓	✓
Sacramento Area Council of Governments	12, 33	✓			✓	✓	
Tahoe Regional Planning Agency	3		✓		✓	✓	
Envision Utah	13		✓			✓	✓

Note: Because each program is uniquely structured, it is difficult to fit them all into simple categories, but this table provides a quick summary of key features of the programs discussed in the book. It is important to remember that, for example, the use of growth management mapping will mean very different things in different programs.

[a] In many cases, some members of appointed boards are elected officials to other posts and are thus ex officio members of the regional agency board.

Figure I.1. Continued

PART I

MANDATORY PLANS

CHAPTER 1

REGIONAL GROWTH MANAGEMENT IN THE PORTLAND METROPOLITAN AREA

Andrew Cotugno and Richard Benner

The 1.4 million people of the Portland metropolitan region reside at the confluence of two great rivers of the West, the Columbia and the Willamette. The valley of the Willamette is a highly productive agricultural area generating over $2 billion in farm-gate receipts in 2007. Of the three counties that surround the metropolitan area, Clackamas ranks second and Washington third in the state for the value of their farm products. Mount Hood rises to the east of the region, with the Columbia River Gorge National Scenic Area on the mountain's north slope. The Tualatin Mountains on the northwest side constitute a significant wildlife corridor between the region and the Coast Range. Across the Columbia is the city of Vancouver, the second fastest-growing city in Washington State.

The region's natural beauty and bounty have led its residents to develop a fierce devotion to the landscape and the lifestyle it affords them . Metro, the nation's only popularly elected regional government, is chartered by voters of the region to protect its high quality of life. This quality of life and the region's reputation for its efforts to protect and enhance it are among the reasons it is one of the fastest growing in the United States. This irony is not lost on residents of the region, who devote much time to contemplating the future.

THE STATE CONTEXT FOR METRO

Metro operates within a state context that has been critical to the achievement of the region's vision. In 1973 the Oregon legislature enacted Senate Bill 100, the legislation that set the state on its unique planning course. The law requires every city and county to adopt a comprehensive plan that meets nineteen statewide planning goals (which have the force of law). These goals address issues ranging from citizen involvement to housing, the economy, and protection of farm and forest land.

Upon its founding in 1979, Metro, too, became subject to the statewide planning goals. For Metro, the most important goal is the one that requires every city or urban region to establish an urban growth boundary (UGB) to limit the extent of urbanization and protect farm and forest land outside UGBs. Metro assumed responsibility for the UGB surrounding twenty-five cities and the urbanized portions of three counties that comprise the urbanized region. As discussed later, Metro's growth concept calls for a compact development form. The statewide planning program plays a key role in the successes the Metro region has achieved by prohibiting urban development and requiring every county to protect farm and forest land outside UGBs. This ensures that cities near Metro (with their own UGBs) do not sprawl onto rural land between the cities and Metro, and by preventing nonfarm, exurban development on these rural lands.

FORMATION OF A REGIONAL GOVERNMENT

Concern about regional issues in the Portland area extends back to 1925 with the formation of a legislative committee to study the problems of local governments in the Portland metropolitan area. Over the next five decades, regional governance evolved into two agencies, the Metropolitan Service District (MSD) and the Columbia Region Association of Governments (CRAG). Both were created under a typical model for associations of governments. MSD was created to deliver regional services efficiently and assumed responsibility for operation of the metropolitan zoo and the solid waste disposal system. CRAG was created to coordinate planning for land use, transportation, water quality, and criminal justice. Each had a governing body of predominantly local elected officials, with significant crossover between them.

By the mid-1970s Oregon and the Portland area were going through a significant shift in policy direction. The state had established the statewide planning program described earlier. The city of Portland was aggressively working to reverse the decline of its downtown and retain strong, family-oriented neighborhoods. The region was embroiled in controversy over proposed urban freeway construction that would have had dire impacts on neighborhoods. And the nation was beginning to tackle significant environmental issues, particularly air and water pollution and energy conservation.

Amid this mix of issues, a "good government" coalition of representatives from government, business, and civic organizations called for the creation of a new regional governance structure equipped with authority to tackle these issues and accountability to the public. The experience with MSD and CRAG had demonstrated that a voluntary association produced an approach to decision making aimed at the lowest common denominator, hidden from the public eye. Assisted by a grant from the National Academy of Public Administration, the Tri-County Local Government Commission drafted a legislative proposal that was adopted in large part by the 1977 Oregon legislature.

The legislation authorized an elected regional government, subject to approval by the voters of the three-county region. The bill called for elimination of CRAG and reorganization of MSD into a freestanding unit of government rather than an association of local governments. It provided for a twelve-member council elected by districts and an executive officer elected at large to manage the organization. It assigned the duties of CRAG and MSD to the new entity and gave it the power to tax and to ensure local plans were consistent with regional plans. In addition, it shrank the boundaries from the larger boundaries of CRAG and MSD to the area of contiguous urbanization. In May 1978, the voters of the three-county region voted 55 to 45 percent to create Metro. That November voters elected the initial Metro Council and executive officer. The change in government went into effect in January 1979.

The late 1980s produced a major evolution for Metro. After a decade of operation, it became apparent that the region needed authority to make governance decisions on its own, without having to seek state legislation for every change in Metro's authority. The legislature authorized and voters statewide approved a change to the Oregon Constitution allowing Metro a home-rule charter. As the charter commission was drafting the charter for consideration by Metro's voters, Metro was going through its first state review of the UGB. Enlightened local elected officials used the charter to broaden Metro's land use planning functions beyond responsibility for the UGB. As a result, the charter declared the livability of the region for future generations to be Metro's primary planning responsibility. It required Metro to adopt a fifty-year Future Vision and a long-range Regional Framework Plan with which city and county comprehensive plans would have to comply. It also called for establishment of a Metro Policy Advisory Committee (MPAC), composed predominantly of local elected officials, to advise the Metro Council on any land use action that would apply to local governments. The charter was approved by the region's voters in 1992.

REGIONAL TRANSPORTATION PLANNING

The mid-70s also brought a shift in transportation policy for the region. The initial segments of a regional freeway system had been built, but there were dueling visions for expansion of the region's transportation system. The metropolitan planning organization, CRAG, had adopted a major freeway expansion plan developed by the state highway department. Meanwhile, TriMet, the newly created public transit agency, called for significant transit expansion. Three new segments of the interstate system were embroiled in controversy.

To overcome this stalemate, the Governor's Task Force on Transportation was formed to sort out the region's policy direction. The result was cancellation of two of the three interstate segments that were bogged down in controversy, as well as the overall freeway expansion plan. Instead, policies were redirected toward a multimodal transportation system. To strengthen the regional approach to transportation planning and decision making, the role of the regional agency was strengthened at both the staff and elected levels.

Since this shift, regional collaboration on multimodal transportation issues has been focused at Metro. At the policy level, there is a dual decision-making structure consisting of the Joint Policy Advisory Committee on Transportation (JPACT), composed of local and Metro elected officials and key transportation agency representatives, and the elected Metro Council. This structure was established to meet the federal requirements for a "metropolitan planning organization" calling for a decision-making structure that includes elected officials of general-purpose governments and agencies that provide transportation services. To support this structure, a professional staff carries out regional transportation planning, light-rail project development, travel-demand forecasting, land use, economic and demographic forecasting, and, more recently, transit-oriented development and demand management.

A key ingredient of this regional function has been the responsibility to manage allocation of flexible transportation funds. Throughout the late 1970s and 1980s, these funds came from the transfer of interstate funds from the two canceled freeways. After 1991 they flowed from new flexible funds provided by federal transportation legislation.

For a sustained thirty-year period, Metro and its regional partners have aggressively developed a regional light-rail and streetcar system, numerous smaller projects to support a more compact urban development pattern, and an expanding system of bus, bike, pedestrian, and trail projects.

2040 GROWTH CONCEPT: THE REGION CHARTS A COURSE

Metro established the UGB for the region in 1979, with a supply of land intended to accommodate twenty years of growth. A recession that ran into the early eighties slowed development inside the UGB. But the region's economy came roaring back later in the decade, and its population grew faster than the rest of the nation. Leaders in the region understood that the UGB would not, by itself, stop sprawling development patterns *within* the UGB. Metro developed a base case scenario in 1992 to show what the region would look like in 2040 under existing zoning within the UGB. Development at low densities would exhaust the remaining supply of land inside the UGB and force UGB expansion onto 120,000 acres, much of it productive farmland. Dependence on the auto and the length and number of trips would rise. Air quality would decline, and infrastructure costs, especially for new roads, would be daunting.

Leaders in the region rejected the base case and called for new policies to build up, not out. Polling done for Metro showed a majority would accept slightly higher densities in their neighborhoods if necessary to avoid UGB expansion onto farmland. Metro developed three growth scenarios—growing out (large expansion of

UGB); growing up (no UGB expansion); growing up, out, and in neighbor cities (small expansion, higher densities, and growth in cities just outside the UGB)— and publicized them throughout the region. After unprecedented public involvement, Metro selected elements from the scenarios and composed the 2040 Growth Concept, a long-range regional plan adopted in 1995. The plan called for modest UGB expansion (18,600 acres through 2040), relying on a tight UGB to encourage more efficient use of land, and for new policies in local comprehensive plans to facilitate higher densities in focus areas. During public review there was some opposition from development interests, mostly from those whose principal market was close to the edge of the UGB, with a business model reliant on larger tracts of vacant land. Nonetheless, the cities and counties of the region embraced the 2040 Growth Concept and immediately began to implement it by changing zoning in the focus areas.

The 2040 Growth Concept merges land use planning and transportation planning to reinforce the objectives of both. It concentrates mixed-use and higher-density development in thirty-nine centers, thirty-three light rail station communities, and along 400 miles of corridors that connect many of the centers. The concept then plans for high-capacity transit (principally light rail) to connect the central city (Portland) and eight regional centers. Bus service, often ten-minute headways, connects thirty town centers with the central city and regional centers.

The 2040 Growth Concept builds on this fundamental land use and transportation superstructure. The central city serves as the hub of business and cultural activity in the region. The regional centers are centers of commerce and civic services in a market of hundreds of thousands of people. Town centers provide localized services for tens of thousands within a three- to five-mile radius. At a finer grain, the concept recognizes the importance of main streets as traditional neighborhood commercial hubs within walking distance of surrounding residential districts. The growth concept will bring infill and a mix of uses to some residential areas, mostly in centers and along main streets and corridors. But an estimated 80 percent of traditional residential areas are not affected by these changes.

The 2040 Growth Concept also calls for protection of the region's most important industrial areas, especially growing industry clusters and port, airport, rail, and other transshipment facilities. Finally, it weaves green infrastructure among the centers and neighborhoods and calls for new open spaces throughout the region.

To bring the 2040 Growth Concept to life, the Metro Council relies on traditional land use and transportation strategies and new tools developed with cities and counties in the region. These strategies and tools are collected in Metro's overarching Regional Framework Plan (RFP), adopted in 1997. The council adopted an Urban Growth Management Functional Plan to implement land use strategies in the RFP through city and county comprehensive plans and zoning ordinances. The council adopted a Regional Transportation Plan to implement transportation strategies and build the multimodal transportation system called for in the 2040 Growth Concept. The council also adopted a Metropolitan Greenspaces Master Plan to guide investments in parks and greenspaces. Each of these implementation plans is part of, and must be consistent with, the RFP. Recognizing that plans and regulations alone do not, themselves, build better communities, the council aligned its transportation and other investments to encourage development in centers, corridors, and main streets.

BUILDING A COMPACT URBAN FORM

The fundamental growth management strategy in the 2040 Growth Concept is to develop in a compact urban form, using lands inside the UGB as efficiently as possible. Maintaining a tight UGB is the first element that has succeeded in channeling market forces from a sprawling edge to a series of vibrant centers. State law requires Metro to review the capacity of the UGB every five years to ensure it provides a twenty-year land supply. But the law directs Metro to seek needed capacity from more efficient use of existing urbanized land before adding land to the UGB. This requirement reinforces the 2040 Growth Concept, which is supported by an analytical and decision-making process that stresses redevelopment and infill (dubbed "refill" locally). Metro has developed a detailed and sophisticated land-monitoring process to inventory vacant land and track the rate of refill. This analysis exceeds the requirements of state law and helps defend Metro decisions in court.

Metro's most recent process provided a twenty-year development capacity (2002–2022) by relying on refill at the rate of 29 percent for residential, 45 percent for industrial, and 52 percent for commercial, plus a modest expansion of the UGB (20,000 acres). This means Metro expects 29 percent of new dwellings over the twenty-year period will be built through redevelopment or development of existing parcels of less than one-half acre, and 45 percent and 52 percent of new industrial and commercial jobs, respectively, will locate on already developed sites and through redevelopment. This approach has a self-reinforcing feature: as the region takes actions to increase the refill rate, a higher rate can be accounted for in subsequent reviews, further reducing the need for UGB expansion.

The UGB is only one tool available to Metro and its partner local governments. The region employs a wide array of regulatory, incentive, and investment tools and constantly works to expand and extend the tool kit. The first Metro action after adoption of the 2040 Growth Concept, with the urging of MPAC, was to call for removal of zoning barriers to higher densities in centers. MPAC negotiated a series of household and employment growth targets, with regional equity in mind. The targets became Metro mandates; every city and county went through a local rezoning process to provide the targeted capacity. Now, under Metro rules, cities and counties can distribute and redistribute residential capacity as they choose, but they cannot reduce capacity below the targets. Because the growth concept calls for focusing development in centers and corridors, Metro also set housing unit and employment targets for these areas as a subset of each overall city and county target. Metro also adopted parking ratios to encourage development in centers and corridors. The ratios allow no parking minimums larger than an established regional minimum, and no parking maximums larger than an established regional maximum.

This widespread rezoning generated opposition in some parts of the region. The voters of Milwaukee, a first-ring suburb southeast of Portland, recalled its mayor and two city councilors over their support for the extension of light rail from Portland and planned upzoning. Several years later (2002), an antiplanning group gathered sufficient signatures to place a measure on the regional ballot that would have repealed Metro's authority to mandate upzoning in communities in the region. The measure was voted down by the region's voters, but only after the Metro Council placed an alternative measure on the ballot—which passed— limiting its own authority to require cities and counties to increase density in certain single-family neighborhoods. Because the growth concept focuses high density in nodal centers rather than single-family neighborhoods, passage of the measure has not interfered with progress toward the growth concept.

Nonregulatory tools to encourage development in centers and corridors include aggressive prioritization of transportation improvements toward those that leverage development in those areas. Foremost has been the steady expansion of the regional rail system. The goal is to connect light rail to every regional center and make every intervening station an opportunity to establish high-density station communities. More recently, the expansion of the region's light rail system has been supplemented by a central city streetcar system, providing convenient local circulation and leveraging a significant level of high-density residential development.

The region also places a priority on allocating certain categories of federal highway funds to projects that leverage development in centers and corridors. The result has been a decade of projects to improve the amenity value of targeted downtown main streets, sidewalk improvements, bike paths and trails, bus stops, and access improvements for the centers and corridors. Of particular note is the allocation of flexible federal highway funds that are converted to federal transit dollars to help fund transit-oriented development through the use of the Federal Transit Administration's Joint Development regulations. The most common use of this tool has been land value write-downs for developments that include higher density and mixed use beyond what the market would support on its own.

Although the region's long-range vision places significant emphasis on centers and corridors, several important actions have been taken to affect the broader low-density landscape. When the 2040 Growth Concept was adopted in 1995, the smallest single-family lot zoning outside Portland called for a minimum lot size of 7,500 square feet. Due to widespread upzoning, there is now a significant supply of 4,000–5,000 square foot lots, and the market has responded dramatically. In addition, Metro requires all local governments to allow accessory dwelling units in their single-family zones. These provide an affordable housing opportunity, with minimal intrusion on single-family neighborhoods. To ensure efficient use of industrial land and protect freight transport facilities, Metro requires cities and counties to prohibit large-scale retail in the region's most important industrial areas.

None of this planning comes free. Programs have been developed to fund local, city, and county actions to implement the 2040 Growth Concept. For more than a decade, the Oregon Department of Land Conservation and Development has operated a planning assistance grant program, and the Oregon Department of Transportation has provided funds through a Transportation/Growth Management grant program. In 2006 Metro adopted a construction excise tax on building permits regionwide to fund planning for the lands newly added to the UGB.

Green in the City

When Metro and the cities and counties of the region committed to more efficient use of land in centers and corridors, they recognized that more intensive development must be matched with better access to parks and open space. Driven by federal and state water quality and fish and wildlife habitat requirements, and the call from conservation organizations to think of the region's floodplains, wetlands, streams, and riparian areas as "greenfrastructure," the region developed complementary greenspaces strategies: acquisition, regulation, and a broad program of public engagement and incentives.

Metro began its effort with a master plan for parks and greenspaces, developed in conjunction with cities, counties, and other public open space providers. The Metropolitan Greenspaces Master Plan was the blueprint for a regional system. In 1995 voters of the region passed a measure sponsored by Metro and a coalition of local governments, businesses, and conservation organizations to authorize $136.6 million in general obligation bonds to purchase land for parks, trails, greenways, and open spaces. The measure enabled Metro to acquire over 8,000 acres across the region and local government park providers to invest $25 million in park and open space improvements.

The success of the 1995 measure led to passage of a second in 2006, this one for $227.4 million. Metro expects to add 3,500 to 4,500 acres to the region's parks, trails, greenspaces, and natural areas. The 2006 measure set aside $44 million for cities, counties, and park districts for projects to protect water quality and habitat and to improve access and facilities. To educate and engage residents in the effort to protect the region's green infrastructure, Metro earmarked another $15 million for grants to schools, neighborhood associations, community groups, and nonprofits for projects of a neighborhood scale. These measures succeeded because the campaigns for public support and the plans for improvements were developed collaboratively by Metro and the other local governments in the region.

Metro has turned to regulation where it is the most appropriate way to protect water quality and guard against flooding. For floodplains, streams, wetlands, and riparian areas, Metro established criteria for development, emphasizing avoidance and mitigation. Metro offered cities and counties the choice between adoption of a model ordinance that guaranteed Metro approval or their own techniques, reviewed by Metro for conformance with regional criteria. Each city and county has now adopted conforming ordinances.

Protection of upland habitat posed a greater challenge. Upland habitat is more expensive than water bodies and their riparian areas and affects the developable portions of many more properties. State voters passed a property rights measure (Ballot Measure 37) in 2004 while Metro was developing its habitat protections, making a full regulatory program unachievable. Instead, in its 2005 Nature in Neighborhoods program, Metro combined regulation of the most important habitat with voluntary efforts to protect other habitat. Both approaches are reinforced with model ordinances, technical assistance, and grant funds to accomplish the objectives of the program. Cities, counties, and special districts are currently implementing Nature in Neighborhoods.

A Work in Progress

Metro added more than 20,000 acres to its then 235,000 acre UGB in three related expansions in 2002, 2004, and 2005. In the wake of the arduous process that led to the expansion, Metro and the cities and counties of the region are rethinking the region's approach to growth management. Among concerns expressed are the following: (1) the cyclical nature of the UGB process forces local governments to devote precious time and resources to the edge of the region rather than to its centers, corridors, and main streets; (2) state planning laws that emphasize protection of farmland can have the effect of directing expansion to areas not well suited for compact, mixed-use development; (3) the region needs to look further into the future than twenty years in order to offer longer-term certainty for infrastructure planning inside the UGB and for agricultural operations outside the UGB; and (4) for a variety of reasons—ranging from reduced federal funding and property tax limitations adopted by Oregon voters—the region is finding it difficult to extend urban services to the areas Metro added to the UGB. To address these concerns, Metro and the other local governments in the region agreed to pursue new approaches. A series of studies and forums yielded an agenda for change.

Most significant was the successful effort in 2007 to change state planning law to authorize long-term planning for the region. Metro will designate urban reserves to signal the direction of UGB expansion for the next forty to fifty years. The three counties will designate rural reserves of farmland, forestland, and important natural landscape features that will be off limits to UGB expansion for the same forty to fifty years, to provide longer-term security to farm and forest operators, and to define the shape of the urban region. A unique feature of the new legislation is that all four local governments must agree on the designation of both kinds of reserves. The four governments began an three-year designation process in January 2008. If successful, designation of reserves will also make expansion of the UGB less contentious and litigious.

Equally important, Metro is leading an effort to develop new tools to encourage development in the region's centers, corridors, and main streets and minimize expansion of the UGB. Metro is helping local governments to reexamine traditional tools, such as urban renewal, and rediscover underutilized tools, such as discounted system development charges and various state income tax credits for higher-density development. Using these tools, the region will encourage the private sector to "build 2040."

Third on the agenda is to alter the way Metro makes critical growth management decisions, such as expansions of the UGB. Today's method of UGB expansion is determined largely by state statute and administrative rules. These laws require Metro to examine the capacity of its UGB every five years, and to add capacity if needed, based on a twenty-year population and employment forecast, to ensure a twenty-year supply. Metro and the cities and counties are designing a performance-based system to determine whether new development capacity is needed and when to add it. This "metering" of capacity would be continuous rather than cyclical, as under the current system.

Finally, the region is conducting an inventory of its infrastructure needs in hopes of persuading the 2009 legislature to authorize new methods of paying for sewer, water, stormwater, and transportation services. This work will influence the addition of capacity to the UGB by putting new capacity where services are available or financially feasible.

A Property Rights Detour

After many defeats of statewide ballot measures (1970, 1976, 1978, 1982) aiming to repeal the statewide planning program, opponents finally found a formula that would subvert it without calling for repeal. Ballot Measure 7 amending the Oregon Constitution passed in 2000, providing that if any unit of government enacted or enforced a regulation that reduced the value of a property after the date that the property was acquired by the current owner, the government had to compensate the owner for the reduction or waive the regulation. The Oregon Supreme Court struck down the measure as a violation of procedural provisions in the Oregon Constitution. The proponents of Measure 7 answered with Ballot Measure 37 to amend Oregon statues (rather than the constitution), which passed with over 60 percent of the vote in 2004.

A nightmare ensued in which the state, cities, counties, and Metro were flooded with thousands of claims based on existing regulations, ranging from farmland protections to billboard limitations. Governments were overwhelmed by the volume of claims. They were unable to review them to determine whether the regulations had actually caused reductions in value. Because none had money to compensate, governments at every level simply chose not to enforce the regulations and granted waivers to the claimants. More than 2,000 claims were filed with governments in the Metro region, most involving proposed developments of farm and forest land outside the UGB. The state and the three counties of the region approved hundreds of waivers that, had they resulted in development, would have undermined the region's effort to contain sprawl. But development under the waivers encountered a variety of obstacles that slowed land use applications following waivers. In the meantime, aided by a steady stream of media on the large subdivisions, billboards, shopping centers, and other big projects authorized across the state by the waivers, the legislature sent a replacement—Ballot Measure 49—to voters in November 2007. The measure limited claims to those seeking new residential dwellings only, dramatically reduced the magnitude of the development allowed under waivers, and raised the bar for proof of reduction in value. Metro compared likely results for the region under Measure 49 with feared results under Measure 37 and estimated that Measure 49 would reduce the amount of new residential development outside the UGB by 85 percent. Prospectively, Measure 49 applies to new regulations that reduce property value and will discourage adoption of them. But implementation of the 2040 Growth Concept Planning relies very little on new regulations. Instead, regional efforts now focus on removal of regulatory obstacles and investments to facilitate refill in centers, corridors, main streets, and light rail station communities.

Things Look Different Here

The results of the Portland metro area land use and transportation policy direction are among the most studied topics in urban planning. Frequent independent studies find the Portland area remarkably different from other metropolitan areas, and the region's efforts are beginning to pay off. Here are a few indications:

- A Smart Growth America study of eighty-three metropolitan areas rating sprawl based on centeredness, street connectivity, mix of uses, and density found Portland metro to be the eighth least sprawling in the country (Ewing et al., n.d.).
- The Brookings Institution in 2007 rated metropolitan areas for walkability and found Portland metro area to be the fifth most walkable region in the country (Leinberger n.d.).
- The League of American Bicyclists awarded the city of Portland its gold status for bike-friendly cities. Summer daytrips across the four principal Willamette River bridges to downtown Portland rose from 2,855 in 1991 to 14,563 in 2007, a 410 percent increase and 11 percent of all trips across the bridges. Some 4.4 percent of Portland commuters biked to work in 2006 (U.S. Census Bureau 2007).
- The latest annual congestion study by the Texas Transportation Institute reveals an interesting story for the Portland metro region. While the region ranks twenty-fifth in population, it ranks twenty-first for "travel time index," a ratio of peak hour auto speeds to free-flow auto speeds. It appears that there is more congestion due to the higher density concentrating vehicle trips. But a closer look yields a more complete picture. The Portland metro area ranks twenty-eighth in excess fuel consumed per peak traveler, thirty-third in delay per peak traveler, and thirty-third in congestion cost per peak traveler. In other words, the road network carries more congestion than one would

expect, but the traveler is not as burdened by this congestion: the compactness of the region brings destinations closer and shortens trip lengths. Finally, the Portland region ranks thirteenth in the contribution that public transit plays toward congestion relief, substantially higher than the size of the region would suggest (Texas Transportation Institute 2007).

- According to the Federal Transit Administration, the Portland metropolitan area ranks twenty-third in population, while TriMet, the region's principal transit provider, ranks tenth in overall annual ridership and eighth highest in annual ridership per capita. Transit ridership and mode share continue to increase (Federal Transit Administration 2005).

- The Federal Highway Administration's Highway Performance Monitoring System (HPMS) shows the Portland metropolitan area's average daily vehicle miles traveled per capita is lower than the national average and declining, while the national trend continues upward. This saves 1.4 million tons of greenhouse gases each year (at 19.4 pounds of carbon/gallon burned). According to economist Joe Cortright (2007), driving less than the national average also puts $2.6 billion per year in local spending power back into the local economy (Federal Highway Administration, n.d.).

- Despite growth pressures in the region (which is home to over 40 percent of the state's population), farm sales in Washington, Clackamas, and Multnomah counties have increased each year for the past five years (Oregon Department of Agriculture 2008).

- A common criticism of a tight urban growth boundary is the impact on housing affordability. It is a simple matter of supply and demand, say the critics: constrict supply for a growing demand and prices go up. The region's overall growth strategy, however, is to manage growth, not to restrict it, by adding land to the UGB when needed to ensure a long-term supply. Furthermore, the real availability of supply, taking into account actions to support redevelopment and multifamily housing, keeps the region's housing relatively affordable.

- According to the Surface Transportation Policy Project's report *Driven To Spend*, households in the Portland region do spend a higher share of their household income on housing than the national average (34.5 percent vs. 32.9 percent). However, according to the historical housing price index maintained by S&P/Case-Schiller, housing price escalation in the Portland region has been nearly the lowest of the major West Coast metropolitan areas. Furthermore, also reflected in the report is a comparison of the share of household income spent on transportation, which shows the Portland region with nearly the lowest of all regions studied. Finally, the combination of household income for housing and transportation (the two highest costs typically faced by a household) shows the Portland region to be, again, nearly the lowest of all regions studied. The region's strategy is successfully contributing to lower transportation cost with minimal impact on housing cost.

- Over the past fifteen years, Metro has protected open space through stream and wetland setback regulations and public acquisition. Regulations have protected over 38,000 acres of wetland and riparian areas, and acquisition has protected nearly 2,000 acres of open space inside the UGB and nearly another 7,000 acres in large blocks outside the UGB. Another 4,000 acres are now being acquired.

CHAPTER 2

REGIONAL PLANNING FOR THE COLUMBIA RIVER GORGE NATIONAL SCENIC AREA

Sy Adler, Carl Abbott, and Margery Post Abbott

Three stories high, square, and solid as a tan boulder, the Skamania County Courthouse was the most imposing building in the small town of Stevenson, Washington. Set above a sloping park and the town's main drag of State Route 14, the courthouse looks south across the Columbia River to towering bluffs on the Oregon side. On October 16, 1986, county workers had their eyes glued to cable television coverage of the U.S. House of Representatives as it considered creating a Columbia River Gorge National Scenic Area. There was no doubt about sympathies in the courthouse—89 percent of Skamania County voters had agreed with a 1984 ballot measure demanding that the state and federal governments keep their hands off local land management. Nevertheless, the House passed the National Scenic Area Act on October 16, and the Senate, a day later. President Ronald Reagan signed the legislation on November 17.

The Skamania County Commission, outgunned in state and national politics, responded with symbolic politics. For the next week, the American flag fluttered at half-mast in front of the courthouse. No president had died, no national hero was gone, but many residents in the rural communities and small towns of the gorge believed that the new federal law marked the end of a way of life.

Skamania County's official dismay demonstrated a deep division about the proper management and preferred future of the Columbia River Gorge. To scenic area supporters in Portland, Seattle, Washington, D.C., and the gorge itself, the legislation represented the success of fifty years of struggle for environmental values; it was a rational way to manage inexorable economic change. To the Stevenson residents who wandered into the offices of the *Skamania County Pioneer* to get the news and shake their heads, the scenic area looked like a death blow to the old resource economy and those who had shaped their lives around timber and farming.

Fast forward nearly a quarter century and attitudes have changed. Stevenson has developed several tourist-oriented businesses on its main street, while on the outskirts rises the 245-room Skamania Lodge, built with funds made available by the National Scenic Area legislation. The county has attracted enough urban commuters that it was recently included as part of the Portland metropolitan area. Twenty miles upriver, the small city of Hood River has become a windsurfing and recreation mecca. Another twenty miles farther east, the city of The Dalles is now home to a substantial branch operation of Google, attracted both by abundant electricity from Columbia River dams and by the environmental amenities secured by the scenic area legislation. Most telling are opinion surveys for the Friends of the Columbia Gorge, the advocacy group that pushed the original legislation and has monitored its implementation. In 1998, 60 percent of gorge residents had a favorable opinion of the scenic area and 37 percent a negative opinion. In 2007 the figures were 68 percent favorable and 21 percent unfavorable. Responding to a related question, 43 percent of residents thought that the legislation has helped the gorge, compared to 32 percent who think that it has been harmful.

THE COLUMBIA RIVER GORGE AND THE NATIONAL SCENIC AREA

The Columbia River Gorge itself is a deep cut through the volcanic rocks of the Cascade mountain chain, carved by the flow of the Columbia River and by towering floods of glacial melt water roughly 15,000 years ago. It was a trade route for Native Americans, a pathway for Meriwether Lewis and William Clark, and a link on the Oregon Trail. It is now one of the nation's major transportation corridors, with barge traffic, Interstate-84, the Burlington Northern–Santa Fe Railroad along the north bank of the river, and the Union Pacific Railroad along the south bank. The river itself is punctuated by two huge hydroelectric and navigation dams (Bonneville Dam and the Dalles Dam), while the landscape ranges from dense conifer forests climbing up 3,000-foot bluffs in the western half to sunny rimrock cliffs and grasslands toward the eastern edge.

The gorge and its scenic area are also politically and socially complex. The Columbia River forms a state boundary, meaning that the gorge is shared by the states of Oregon and Washington. The scenic area abuts the fast-growing Portland-Vancouver metropolitan area at its western end (population 2,137,000 in 2006, ranking twenty-third in the United States), but it also includes a dozen long-established towns that developed around agriculture and logging. The current population of approximately 55,000 within scenic area boundaries includes old families and new arrivals, entrepreneurs and environmentalists. Latinos, Asian Americans, and members of several Indian tribes add to the demographic mix.

The federal scenic area legislation embodies multiple goals. It is a balancing act that tries to preserve and enhance natural and scenic values while protecting the livelihoods of gorge residents. The motivation of the Friends of the Columbia

Gorge, the organization that did the most to mobilize political support for the legislation, was to protect scenery and natural systems from Portland-Vancouver suburban sprawl and from scattershot proliferation of second homes. To gain passage, however, the legislation acknowledged the importance of preserving a vital gorge economy. Its two goals therefore read as follows:

1. Protect and provide for the enhancement of the scenic, cultural, recreational, and natural resources of the Columbia River Gorge.
2. Protect and support the economy of the gorge by encouraging growth to occur in existing urban areas and by allowing future economic development that is consistent with paragraph 1.

The federal legislation divided an eighty-five-mile stretch of the gorge into three categories. Special Management Areas are 115,000 acres of largely federal land where little development is allowed. General Management Areas are 149,000 acres of largely private land where carefully controlled development within the parameters of a comprehensive management plan is expected. Thirteen Urban Areas, totaling 28,500 acres, are exempt from the legislation, with land use decisions remaining under local control.

The legislation also allocated management of the scenic area among multiple partners. The U.S. Forest Service has responsibility for the Special Management Areas. Four Native American tribes—the Nez Perce, Yakama, Umatilla, and Confederated Tribes of Warm Springs—have an explicit role in identifying historic and cultural resources. A Columbia River Gorge Commission oversees overall implementation and has responsibility for the General Management Areas.

The Columbia River Gorge Commission was created by the federal legislation but is a bistate agency funded in equal amounts by Oregon and Washington. Three members are appointed by the governor of Oregon, three by the governor of Washington, and one by each of the three Oregon and three Washington counties that share the gorge. These counties are very diverse: Clark County, Washington, and Multnomah County, Oregon, are largely metropolitan, with undeveloped eastern edges within the National Scenic Area. Hood River and Wasco counties in Oregon have strong agricultural economies and the small cities of Hood River and The Dalles. Skamania and Klickitat counties in Washington have the smallest populations.

The U.S. Forest Service and Gorge Commission worked together to create the management plan that was adopted in 1991 and revised in 2004. The plan covers the following:

1. Land use designations, using the broad categories of agricultural land, forest land, open space, commercial land, and residential land spelled out in the legislation
2. Policies for protection and enhancement of scenic, cultural, natural, and recreation resources
3. Action programs for recreation development, economic development, enhancement of gorge resources, and public education
4. Administrative roles for the various partners in scenic area management

The management plan, administered originally by the Forest Service and now by the Gorge Commission, was developed with the expectation that counties would assume implementation within the General Management Area after adopting suitable ordinances. Counties and municipalities are not required by federal or state law to adopt the management plan, so counties must be persuaded to adhere to the plan because of the environmental and economic benefits the regional plan brings. If a county declines to adopt an implementing ordinance, the Gorge Commission retains control over land use changes within the National Scenic Area. Five of the six counties adopted ordinances implementing the regional plan by the mid-1990s. One, Klickitat County, Washington, the county most removed from urbanization pressures, has declined to do so.

The 1986 federal legislation also provided for specific funds to reduce the levels of economic activity in some parts of the gorge and increase economic activity in other parts, in effect trying to move employment toward the urban centers. There have been funds to encourage tourism and recreation, used for the Skamania Lodge conference center, the Gorge Discovery Center museum in The Dalles, restoration of segments of a historic highway from the 1910s for hiking and biking, and other recreation development. In contrast, the U.S. Forest Service has acquired 31,000 acres of Special Management Area land from willing sellers, reducing the likelihood of recreational development or clear cutting.

Planning and Management Changes over Twenty Years

The Columbia River Gorge Commission and its staff were inserted into a very complex ecology of public and private organizations and interests. Much of its time since 1987 has been taken up with defining and redefining its role in relation to these other entities. The level of funding from the Oregon and Washington legislatures is an indication of its changing status. In nominal terms the Gorge Commission budget did not fluctuate much between 1987 and 1997, although it declined in inflation-adjusted terms. State allocations for the commission decreased during 1997–1999, rebounded in 1999–2003, and again fell for 2003–2005; in real terms, the 2003–2005 budget was the smallest one since the commission was established. Oregon and Washington granted significant increases during 2005–2007 and 2007–2009 that enabled the commission to enlarge the professional staff, but both states cut their general fund allocations for 2009–2011 by 20 percent. The Oregon legislature did set aside a special $25,000 appropriation, instructing the commission to request it after submitting a report documenting its efforts to persuade Klickitat County to adopt ordinances to implement the gorge management plan, and a scheme to charge Klickitat County for implementation expenses if it failed to do so. Some of the ups and downs have reflected general changes in state revenue collections. The earlier reductions also occurred because legislators representing gorge constituencies who were critical of Gorge Commission actions persuaded their colleagues to decrease support for the agency. The increases in 2005–2007 and 2007–2009, which produced the largest ever commission budgets in real terms, were associated with improvements in state economies, changes in the political party composition of the state governments, and efforts by the commission to increase support for its programs both locally and at the state capitols.

The rollercoaster budget ride has limited staff capacity to monitor, enforce, and evaluate the incremental and cumulative consequences of the decisions made by investors and regulators inside and outside the scenic area. In catch-22 fashion, it has also impeded efforts to resolve the conflicts perceived by state and local stakeholders, some of which led to the budget cuts. The severe 2009–2011 reductions necessitated staff cuts that will make it very difficult for the commission to address several of the issues identified below.

The strategic plan adopted by the commission in April 2006 responded to these tensions. In addition to the two major goals outlined in the National Scenic Area Act cited earlier, the commission also saw it as critically important to do the following:

1. Increase citizen participation in decision-making processes
2. Coordinate effective and consistent implementation of its management plan by county governments
3. Provide a gorge-wide approach to issues, make efficient use of public resources throughout the gorge, and support interagency projects and problem solving

As previously noted, many gorge property owners bitterly contested the creation of the scenic area and the bistate commission, and believed that the commissioners and staff who adopted the original management plan in 1991 were too closely aligned with the resource protection interests of Friends of the Columbia Gorge (FOCG). Those beliefs lingered throughout the 1990s and were manifest in strained relationships between some of the counties and the commission during plan implementation.

As part of its continuing effort to address those critical attitudes and to increase its acceptance by gorge residents and officials, the commission in 2006 hired as its executive director someone who grew up in the gorge and who has family still resident in the gorge. This executive director has tried to transform formerly adversarial relationships into collaborative, win-win partnerships with gorge property owners, developers, and county governments, all within the context of the commission's responsibility to balance resource protection and development.

Since its inception, the commission has been aware that counties varied widely with regard to their technical capacity to implement the management plan, as well as their political commitment to enforce it. The commission's own limited staff capacity to monitor and enforce highlighted its concerns about the effectiveness of plan implementation efforts and the cumulative impacts of what was happening on the ground. A major battle involving the Gorge Commission, Skamania County, and longtime gorge residents who wanted to build their dream house erupted in mid-1998, when the commission discovered that the half-completed house appeared to violate the act and county ordinances, especially the requirement that new construction be visually subordinate to its setting when seen from key viewing areas. The Bea house saga, which attracted national attention, illustrated the monitoring and enforcement problems the commission confronted. After the commission belatedly moved to intervene, the Washington Supreme Court ruled in 2001 that while the commission was authorized to appeal the county's approval of the proposed house during the period allotted for an appeal, "which it had declined to do," it was not empowered to invalidate a county's final decision on an application to develop.

Disciplined by the court in this way, the commission's need both to increase its own capacity to monitor and enforce and to enhance the technical capacity of county planning commissions and their staff to implement the plan consistently became even more pressing. Adding to the concern was a set of monitoring reports prepared by commission staff that were funded by a special project grant from the federal government. In fiscal year 2000, around the time those monitoring reports were being done, Gorge Commission staff reviewed just 37 percent of county development decisions. The Bea case put the counties on notice, though, that their practices were likely to be scrutinized more closely in the years ahead. In addition, passage of growth management legislation in Washington in the early 1990s produced more attention to plan making and implementation, and the gap in technical capacity between the counties on the Oregon and Washington sides of the river began to narrow. However, court decisions found that, in the absence of a federal zoning law, when interpretation is necessary to make a zoning decision at the county level the commission must apply the relevant state law when dealing with an appeal. These decisions highlighted the commission's concern with the consistency of implementation throughout the gorge, a concern shared by Friends of the Columbia Gorge. To increase consistency, commission staff in fiscal year 2005 reviewed 75 percent of the county decisions and began meeting more frequently with county planners and elected and appointed officials to discuss plan implementation. County planners during the process of revising the management plan gave important input about vague and ambiguous goals and regulations, and generally about what was and was not working well in the field. Commission staff used their own hands-on experience regulating development in Klickitat County to inform the revision process as well.

The relationship between the commission and Friends of the Columbia Gorge has been at times contentious. Friends supports commission budget requests at the state capitols and sometimes intervenes on its behalf during litigation. Friends of the Columbia Gorge also challenges the commission in court when it thinks that commission action may threaten resource protection. It has continued to play the watchdog role in relation to both commission decisions and decisions made by the counties. Indeed, FOCG reviews every county-level decision. It has also undertaken planning-related projects such as a buildable lands inventory and a buildout analysis, and has urged for years that the commission explicitly address cumulative impacts. In order to provide some technical capacity, FOCG asked the regional chapter of the American Society of Landscape Architects to analyze the cumulative impacts of development on gorge scenic resources. It also brought landscape architects in to help successfully resolve a dispute with a property developer, an example of FOCG engaging in negotiation as a complement to its watchdog role.

Friends has itself attempted to win greater acceptance among gorge residents and to change the long-standing perception that it represents primarily a metropolitan area point of view. In 2000 the organization opened a gorge field office and has boosted its local membership. It helped to start trail conservancies, composed primarily of local people, to work on recreation projects in partnership with the Forest Service. A Skamania County commissioner has worked with Friends on a trail-related land acquisition project and has led one of the popular gorge hikes that Friends sponsors. There is a similar relationship with a Klickitat County trail group. Friends have helped to organize local groups that share its interest in preventing the construction of a proposed Indian casino in a gorge urban area. Moreover, a major gift in 2005 launched it on a new path of operating a land trust. Modeled on the Piedmont Environmental Council in Virginia, the only other organization Friends has identified that combines advocacy, litigation, and land trust activities, the trust is staffed by a fourth-generation gorge resident who is also a Realtor.

Friends and the commission recently clashed over the 2004 revisions to the scenic area management plan. Friends charged in state court that the revisions weaken protection for the resources the commission was mandated to protect and permit too much commercial and industrial development. Friends similarly used the federal courts to challenge the secretary of agriculture's concurrence with the revisions. Friends believes that the Gorge Commission is increasingly aligning itself with those interested in local development, and it sees itself as having to uphold the national interest that created the scenic area. The Oregon Court of Appeals upheld the commission-approved amendments in all but one case; it agreed with Friends that allowing the expansion of existing industrial uses violated the National Scenic Area Act. On appeal the Oregon Supreme Court sustained much of what the lower court decided; however, it reversed the court of appeals on two issues, finding that the management plan revisions did not comply with scenic act requirements to protect cultural and natural resources from adverse cumulative impacts.

The federal district court agreed with Friends that the secretary of agriculture had erred in concurring with two of the commission-approved plan amendments permitting more residential and commercial development in Special Management Areas; however, the court concluded that most of Friends' claims, especially those regarding failure to address cumulative impacts, were not ripe for review. Friends is appealing those aspects of the district court decision to the Federal Ninth Circuit Court of Appeals. Settlement discussions were under way in autumn 2009.

The Forest Service now has a less prominent role than in earlier decades. In 2001 Congress adopted an amendment to the National Scenic Area Act that prospectively set 2004 as the ending date for private landowners to offer their land for sale to the Forest Service, or to have the zoning on their land changed to the less restrictive General Management Area designations if the Forest Service failed to accept a bona fide offer within a three-year period. In response to the congressional action, nearly 200 offers to sell, representing about 6,700 acres, were submitted. The Forest Services did not have access to nearly enough money to respond positively to many important offers. Friends retained a lobbyist, former U.S. senator Slade Gorton (Washington), a critic of aspects of the original management plan, to help secure additional funding for the Forest Service.

The Gorge Commission is also expanding its role as a regional planner, functioning as a catalyst that brings together various public and private stakeholders to shape the evolution of the National Scenic Area. The commission worked closely and effectively with the state transportation agencies, the counties, and the Forest Service about integrating resource protection objectives into corridor plans that prioritized safety issues. It helped to create forums for discussing workforce housing issues. There are several other critically important regional-scale issues that it is currently confronting and will confront in the years ahead.

Issues and Challenges

Seventeen years ago, Gorge Commission members Joyce Reinig (Hood River County representative), Nancy Sourek (Skamania County), and Pat Bleakney (Klickitat County) wrote a minority report on the management plan. Representing largely rural counties, they disagreed with several features and identified two unresolved issues that remain problems today. In an interview in February 2008, Reinig, now the longest-serving member of the commission, reiterated these concerns. One is the lack of criteria and procedures for dealing with urban area expansions. The other is the use of open space zoning within the General Management Area without funds available to purchase such lands. In the following section, we discuss these long-standing issues along with several other ongoing concerns and emerging problems.

Urban Area Expansion

In 2008 The Dalles, near the eastern edge of the National Scenic Area, benefited from the arrival of a Google data center. Since then, real estate prices have risen quickly, and the firm's arrival has brought about 200 new jobs—a big deal to a community of approximately 25,000 people—and raised expectations for further high tech development. In response to this new energy, the city of The Dalles is planning to request expansion of the urban area boundary set by the National Scenic Area to include another 620 acres of urbanizable land, an area equivalent to about 15 percent of the current urbanized area. The expansion proposed would allow housing, industry, a regional shopping center, and other commercial uses on what are now cherry orchards or undeveloped land.

The response from environmental groups has been intense, with Friends of the Columbia Gorge leading efforts to lobby against this expansion, calling it inconsistent with the National Scenic Area Act. In addition, the cities of Hood River and Lyle (Washington) are also considering expansion requests. The act specifies that the commission can make "minor" revisions to the urban area boundaries. Major revisions require an act of Congress, thus making the definition of "minor" a matter of considerable debate. Once land is designated as within an urban area, land use decisions are exempt from provisions of the management plan. The commission in the past has made two small adjustments to correct what were clearly mapping errors. The entire process is complicated by the Oregon land use system, which predates the National Scenic Area. It also prescribes creation of urban growth boundaries (UGBs) and requires that each UGB encompass sufficient land for twenty years of development—an explicit criterion not found in the National Scenic Area legislation. After intense study and hearing, the commission indefinitely tabled proposed changes in July 2009 because of strong opposition from both environmental groups and from cities and counties, leading to basic disagreement within the commission. However, revival of development pressures with recovery from the recession may again push the issue forward.

General Management Area Open Spaces

Driving I-84 down the gorge and looking at the Washington side, one sometimes notices the incongruous reality of fresh clear-cuts on land well within the scenic area. Congress was clear about the establishment of open spaces within the portion of the scenic area identified as the Special Management Area and appropriated funds for purchase of land in those areas. However, roughly 5,500 acres in the General Management Area have also been designated as open space. No money is available for purchase of these lands, creating a significant imbalance. While it seemed a politically necessary compromise at the time to secure passage of the National Scenic Area Act, the decision to restrict funding for land acquisition to the Special Management Areas has since been widely regarded as a serious weakness in the original legislation. Absent funds to purchase land outright, or to purchase scenic easements, the largely regulatory approach taken to protect resources in the General Management Areas has always generated a great deal of conflict, especially on the Washington side of the river, where there is more privately owned land.

Environmentalists and local activists alike agree that change is needed, and the Friends have been active in purchasing key lands in the Special Management Area to retain them in their natural state. Also, there is some indication that even the timber companies involved would not be opposed to stopping all logging as long as they are compensated for their land. The Gorge Commission took the lead following adoption of the original management plan to foster the creation of a land trust to provide an alternative means of resource protection in the General Management Areas. In addition to that land trust, other trusts have been active in the gorge, including the one recently created by FOCG.

Major Recreational Use Development

Changing demographics in the gorge caught most everyone by surprise in its speed and the dislocations involved. The decline of the timber industry in the gorge was not simply a result of the act, however, as it was part of widespread changes across the Pacific Northwest. A visually prominent result of these economic changes is the closure and abandonment of the Broughton Mill, located on the river bank on the Washington side near Bingen and across from Hood River. Some communities, such as parts of Skamania County and Hood River experienced an influx of professionals, and of people willing to commute to Portland for work. Demand for recreational uses grew by leaps and bounds.

This confluence of events led to the current proposal to convert the abandoned Broughton lumber mill site into a major recreational housing development. The site is zoned for commercial recreation, allowing some camping and recreational vehicle sites, but the developer has been seeking a much larger development that would require the Gorge Commission to amend the management plan. Amid strong reactions from the Friends and others, commission staff released a report in January 2008 recommending no full-time homes but increasing allowable average unit size and lifting the lid on the number of units, relying on a master plan and detailed site-specific review to ensure compatibility and visual subordination. The commission was challenged to balance two interests. Some see the decision as a major precedent that will lead to more such projects. Others see it as a one-time action that will make reasonable use of a derelict site to generate jobs to make up in at least small part for those lost with the closure of the mill. After intense discussion, the commission in spring 2008 sided with the latter argument by a 10–2 vote and approved a modified development proposal. A challenge to this action by Friends was pending at the Oregon Court of Appeals in autumn 2009.

The Broughton Mill debate is an example of what Friends of the Columbia Gorge sees as a "scale and scope" problem. They worry that the gorge is now attracting outside investors who hope to do large-scale developments and build houses out of scale with the preexisting built environment. The commission staff a few years ago appealed county decisions to allow 4,000–6,000 square foot houses as incompatible with their neighbors. Since each county has its own land-use ordinances and thus its own standards about what "compatibility" means, there has been considerable variation in what was allowed. When opponents such as 1,000 Friends of Oregon and Friends of the Columbia Gorge describe the Broughton proposal as "urban scale" and the commission staff state that their recommendations will "prevent creation of a new town that could become a de facto urban area," they are continuing the same discussion.

Protection of the Air and Water

In contrast to the acreage that the commission, Forest Service, and counties manage through land use controls, the scenic and economic qualities of the gorge are also affected by the fluid resources of air and water. Stretching for hundreds of miles through Canada and the United States, the Columbia River's quality and character are only marginally influenced by actions within the gorge. The same is true of air quality, as weather systems funnel stiff winds through the gorge and prevailing winds bring Portland pollutants. In order to deal with air and water issues, the commission needs to work with state and federal agencies whose activities both inside and outside the gorge have substantial impacts on the scenic area.

One such critically important issue is air quality impacts on visibility and cultural resources such as Indian petroglyphs. A 2000 report by the U.S. Forest Service documented a very serious acid fog and rain problem in the gorge that was degrading those key resources. The problem largely originates outside the gorge and raises the question of whether the Gorge Commission is authorized to require the state environmental quality agencies to act so as to address the problem. The commission decided to partner with those agencies and the federal government to sponsor a multiyear investigation. While the commission and its partners sort out the technical, legal, financial, and political feasibility issues, Friends of the Columbia Gorge and several allies have initiated court action against Portland General Electric, which owns an older, coal-fired power plant east of the National Scenic Area that is an acknowledged major source of the air quality problem. Another issue that remains to be clarified is whether the state agencies that regulate forest practices are required to implement the National Scenic Area Act and the management plan.

The National Scenic Area Act left it to the commission to decide whether or not to directly seek protections for the Columbia River itself, and the management plan does not address the river. Recent years have brought increasing pressure on the waters of the Columbia and increasing awareness that both water quality and the temperatures essential to salmon and other fish are under stress. Even the volume of flow is at risk of significant human adjustment. Oregon in 2008 funded a feasibility study of withdrawing Columbia River water during high flow to recharge eastern Oregon aquifers. The pending U.S.-Canada negotiations on the renewal of the treaty governing water use between these two nations have raised additional concerns. It is not clear yet if or when the commission might take up this focus, but the current director is actively monitoring such issues and seeking to be a player wherever appropriate.

The Indicators Project

What are the long-term effects of the management plan? No one really can say in concrete terms. Some statistics gathered early on in the planning process now seem to be irrevocably lost in the stress created by minimal budgets and cuts in staff. But as the first decade of the twenty-first century approached its end, the commission undertook a major project to identify and implement a procedure to measure the impacts of the National Scenic Area—both its successes and where it has fallen short. Task forces were established to draw on expertise of groups like the American Society of Landscape Architects, as well as on the knowledge and perspectives of local residents.

Within this process, FOCG has hoped to define ways of measuring cumulative impacts of development and as a result to shape future commission decisions about development proposals. The Friends worked with the American Society of Landscape Architects to study the visual impacts of construction in the gorge and obtained a grant to study the cumulative effects of buildout. They found that 1,790 developable lots (32 percent of all nonpublic tax lots) remain within the National Scenic Area, with the most in Wasco County on the east end and Skamania County toward the west end. They cite this as evidence of the "clear need for cumulative effects standards and effective monitoring."

The Vital Signs Indicators Project, a top priority for the commission and its executive director, began in 2007 and released a report in May 2009. The project aimed to develop measures to assess the condition of the scenic, natural, cultural, and recreation resources in the gorge, as well as the condition of the gorge economy. Those assessments were intended to guide the commission's adaptive management efforts and to create new and strengthen existing partnerships with gorge communities and public agencies. A community advisory team and a technical advisory team composed of academic members and representatives from state and federal agencies worked with commission staff to generate a list of fifty-one indicators, twenty-four of which are covered in the report. The condition of many key gorge attributes was evaluated for the first time, enabling the commission and its partners to establish useful baselines. The challenging next steps involve assessing the planning and management implications of the indicator data and institutionalizing a process for ongoing monitoring in the context of the commission's reduced staff capacity.

The Tribes

The Yakama and the Confederated Tribes of Warm Springs both hold substantial claim to the Columbia River basin and still rely on this area for traditional fishing, hunting, and gathering, as well as a place which has long been their home. The act specifically mentions the importance of archeological and cultural resources, but no position on the commission was designated for a tribal representative and no funds were allocated to be used for the benefit of the tribes. Oregon for years did name someone from the Warm Springs tribe as one of its representatives, but the tribes have not always been full partners in the preservation of this area. Interest within the tribes is increasing for engagement with management issues, and Jill Arens, executive director for the commission, has actively sought to build on this interest as she works to create partnerships at the state, local, and federal level with all parties whose actions affect the gorge.

CONCLUSION

One of the most controversial projects proposed for the gorge is not under the purview of the commission. The Warm Springs Tribe is actively seeking to build a casino in Cascade Locks, an urban area specifically excluded from the provisions of the management plan. Opposition does not necessarily parallel support for the National Scenic Area, but the Friends and other strong environmentalists have always been uneasy about the exclusion of the thirteen cities from provisions of the act. Issues such as air pollution and the construction of 400-foot-high wind towers just beyond the eastern edge of the scenic area are also gaining attention, just as protection of the river itself is becoming of more concern.

These tensions, which are part of the act itself and the compromises necessary for its passage—definition of Urban Areas and the particulars of drawing their boundaries, open space designations, the absence of tribal representatives on the commission—reflect the complexities of attempting to protect the gorge. The National Scenic Area encompasses a region eighty-five miles long, extending from the Columbia River roughly to the crests of the surrounding mountains and ridges. It is a gloriously beautiful landscape with cliffs, waterfalls, broad expanses of forest, and wildflower meadows. It is also a region of successful agriculture and increasing housing demand.

The initial hope of some advocates for the establishment of a national park on these lands was not realistic, given its large population base and role as a major national transportation corridor. The balancing act between the needs of the communities in the gorge and the desire to protect the landscape has rightly been described as a dance. At times, however, the partners are pulling hard in different directions, and resolution is only possible in the courts.

Attitudes toward the National Scenic Area are slowly—some might say inexorably—changing. Increasing numbers of gorge residents, especially in Hood River and Skamania counties, are Portland-Vancouver area commuters. Environmental or land use conservation values are increasingly strong as the character of the electorate shifts, as evidenced in November 2007 by favorable votes in Hood River and Wasco counties on Measure 49, a ballot measure that preserved the core of the Oregon planning system in the face of a strong property rights movement. After more than twenty years, the National Scenic Area regulations seem like part of the landscape to residents who have grown up with them or arrived from elsewhere, a tool which gorge residents can use to help control their own future.

CHAPTER 3

RESTORING THE TAHOE REGION WITH COMPREHENSIVE REGIONAL PLANNING

Gordon Barrett

The Tahoe Regional Planning Agency (TRPA) exercises an exceptionally broad range of powers to plan land use change, economic development, transportation, community design, infrastructure, and habitat restoration and management for the Lake Tahoe Region, which is generally the watershed of Lake Tahoe. The TRPA was formed in 1969 through a bistate compact between California and Nevada. The compact, which was ratified by the U.S. Congress and signed into law by President Nixon, was amended in 1980 to strengthen and clarify the TRPA's regional mission. The agency is charged with protecting the environment of the Lake Tahoe region through planning and regulation. It is one of only a few watershed-based regulatory agencies in the United States. By working at the regional level, TRPA's plans, regulations, and permitting authority apply across political boundaries and encompass the entire 501-square-mile Lake Tahoe region.

The TRPA was established to protect the Lake Tahoe Basin's extraordinary mountain beauty, which is considered a national treasure. The lake itself is one of the largest and deepest in the world. The startling clarity of the lake's water has drawn people to its shores for centuries. Soon after John C. Fremont recorded sighting Lake Tahoe in 1849, its forests were targeted by loggers supplying timber for the Comstock silver mines in Virginia City, Nevada. After the logging era ended in 1890, the area turned to seasonal tourism at a modest scale while the basin recovered from the effects of rampant deforestation. With the opening of year-round highways in the 1950s, legalized gaming in Nevada, and the 1960 Winter Olympics, the area became the target of large-scale development.

The need to protect Lake Tahoe has been a concern for more than a century as conservationists and others have voiced concern about the impacts of logging, ranching, and tourism on the Lake Tahoe environment. Efforts to designate Lake Tahoe a national forest or national park did not gain wide support in Washington, D.C., primarily because much of the land in the basin was already privately owned and had been developed or logged. But concerned citizens continued lobbying for environmental protection as the ski resorts expanded, meadows were filled for development, and stateline casinos went high-rise. Fortunately, Lake Tahoe was becoming known throughout the world as a national treasure for its pristine environment and crystal clear waters.

The debate came to a climax in the late 1960s after two decades of rapid growth. Review of development permitted by local zoning predicted a future population of 800,000 people—a population that would have rivaled that of San Francisco. Local plans called for more growth and even a freeway encircling the lake. The impacts to the lake's famed clarity were significant, yet unregulated growth continued. That is why governors and lawmakers in California and Nevada approved a bistate compact that created a regional planning agency to oversee development at Lake Tahoe. The agency's jurisdiction was unique in that it is watershed/airshed–based and spans territory in two states and multiple local jurisdictions. Because of the compact's bistate role, the agreement was sent to the U.S. Congress in 1969, which ratified the compact. The TRPA was a creation of the compact (it is neither a state agency nor a federal agency) and had planning and permitting powers throughout the region. It should be noted that local governments were not supportive of this effort and lost lawsuits in both states contesting the validity of the compact. Even today there are those who still feel that the agency should have all elected representatives.

Although development potential was reduced to 350,000 people under the 1972 TRPA Regional Plan, significant development was still occurring. The TRPA Governing Board was dominated by local officials, and they had a voting structure that favored approval of projects. In response to limited progress on environmental protection and approvals of additional subdivisions and casinos, the two states and federal government revised the compact in 1980 to make it more effective in protecting the Tahoe environment. The revised compact changed the Governing Board's membership and voting procedures, strengthened environmental protections, and froze gaming industry construction.

The TRPA Governing Board adopted the regional plan in place in 1987, after years of controversy and community unrest. This consensus-based plan stopped new lot and block subdivisions, resolved the issue of the buildout of sensitive lots, and set forth a community planning process to resolve commercial development issues. The plan further established urban boundaries at less than 15 percent of the area and lowered the holding capacity to approximately 125,000 people. The TRPA has made strides toward achieving environmental standards over the past twenty years and is collaborating with partner agencies and the community on the update of the next long-range regional plan.

The 1980 Compact Requirements

The 1980 compact emphasizes the TRPA's overarching mission of protecting and restoring the environmental quality of Lake Tahoe, but it also states that the agency's plans and regulations shall "provid[e] opportunities for orderly growth and development consistent with" the region's environmental carrying capacity. The compact suggests that environmental and economic imperatives are fundamentally consistent here because a healthy Lake Tahoe is not only a value in itself, but also the prerequisite for the economic success of a region whose economy is built on tourism and recreation. With this philosophical underpinning, the 1980 compact brought four basic changes to the TRPA and the way it carries out its mission.

The compact changed TRPA's governance structure to achieve a better balance of statewide, regional, and local perspectives to shape the agency's policies. Today, the agency is led by a fifteen-member Governing Board made up of six local government officials and eight officials and appointees from the two states. The representation is split evenly between the two states, with one nonvoting presidential appointee. The voting structure requires super majorities for project approvals and ordinance approvals. Staff and a nineteen-member Advisory Planning Commission provide support and recommendations to the Governing Board. The compact specifically requires that at least six members of the board not be residents of the Tahoe region, ensuring that statewide concerns are well represented.

In addition, the TRPA is required by the amended compact to adopt environmental threshold carrying capacity standards, called thresholds, to drive the TRPA's policies and measure their success. The thresholds are environmental standards necessary to maintain a significant scenic, recreation, educational, scientific, health, or natural value of the region. There are nine threshold categories: air quality, water quality, noise, vegetation, fisheries, wildlife, scenic, soil conservation, and recreation. Within these categories there are adopted numeric, management, and policy standards that must be maintained. From these standards, the TRPA has established thirty-six threshold indicators to be monitored. An example of such a standard is the 33.4 meter winter annual average clarity standard for the lake. (California and Nevada water quality agencies are developing a total maximum daily load [TMDL] program to determine the sediment and nutrient loadings that can be permitted consistent with achieving this standard.) These threshold indicators are monitored and reviewed every five years to determine progress toward attainment. Further allocations of development are linked to the results of these five-year threshold evaluation reports.

The TRPA is further required by the compact to adopt an integrated regional plan that has a land use element, transportation element, conservation element, recreation element, and public service element. The TRPA is then required to adopt and enforce ordinances designed to achieve the thresholds and the goals and policies of the plan. All plans and ordinances are required to be consistent with the attainment of the thresholds. A key strategy of the regional plan is the designation of land use districts (such as conservation, residential, and commercial) with permitted uses, intensities, and infrastructure standards for each district.

Since the compact establishes TRPA planning, regulatory, and environmental authorities, TRPA is not subject to any local or state planning requirements. The regional plan and TRPA ordinances do not replace, but overlie and supplement, traditional local zoning and master plans. When conflicts arise with local government or other agency standards, the compact states the most restrictive standards apply. Generally those are the TRPA standards. The TRPA promotes joint adoption of plans such as community plans to eliminate conflicts.

The 1987 regional plan is made up of several documents. In addition to the adopted environmental threshold carrying capacities, the plan includes the goals and policies plan that provides the overall conditions that the agency aims to achieve, the code of ordinances that provides regulations to achieve the goals and policies, and the plan area statements that provide the specific zoning for the region. The Environmental Improvement Program (EIP) provides the list of capital improvements and programs needed to achieve the goals, since regulation alone cannot achieve the thresholds. (These documents and the compact can be found on the TRPA website at http://www.trpa.org.)

Finally, the compact requires the TRPA to review and approve all development projects before they can be built or carried out. A project is any activity that may have an impact on the natural resources of the region. In general, anything from housing additions on up requires a TRPA permit. All projects must be found consistent with attainment of thresholds and consistent with TRPA plans and ordinances. The TRPA has delegated some project review to local governments and agencies through memorandums of understanding.

In addition to its mission under the compact, the TRPA is also responsible for certain planning activities under the Federal Clean Air Act, the Federal Clean Water Act, the California Transportation Development Act, the Intermodal Surface Efficiency Act, and the California Clean Air Act. Most significantly, the TRPA is the designated 208 Planning Agency. The TRPA Board, with the addition of a U.S. Forest Service representative, acts as the designated Transportation Metropolitan Planning Organization (MPO) for Tahoe. The TRPA's planning and regulatory authorities go a long way in establishing these other plans and regulations; but the TRPA still requires collaboration for implementation due to the fact that the TRPA does not have taxing authorities or the ability to construct projects. It should be noted that the 1980 compact also created a Tahoe Transportation District (TTD) with taxing authority and project management authorities to assist the TRPA. Unfortunately, however, TTD has been hamstrung by its inability to establish local revenue sources.

COMPREHENSIVE PLANNING AND ACTION PROGRAMS

The TRPA and its mission represent a uniquely broad range of responsibilities to address environmental, economic, and cultural values at both regional and local levels. The TRPA uses a five-year strategic plan to help focus its short-term efforts and yearly reviews to determine progress. The TRPA has adopted a three-pronged strategy to meet these responsibilities and restore the environment of Lake Tahoe:

- Implement a regulatory program minimizing the negative impacts of new development
- Improve the environment through a $1.5 billion capital improvement program repairing damage caused by past development
- Scientifically research the effectiveness of the regulatory and capital improvement programs via adaptive management

The regulatory program has been in place for more than thirty-five years and, since 1987, is reevaluated every five years along with all other programs. As noted above, TRPA approval is required for all proposed projects within the region. To move forward, these projects must be found to be compatible with the overall goal of threshold attainment, state and federal air and water quality standards, and the standards of the agency.

TRPA regulatory standards include typical development standards found in a planning agency. These include subdivision, grading, height, density, design, and use standards. In addition, the TRPA has resource protection standards for vegetation, fisheries, wildlife, air and water quality, shorezone, and cultural resources. The TRPA enforces its standards through a compliance program and ultimately through civil court actions. TRPA ordinances also include programs for the following:

1. Allocation of Development Systems. TRPA establishes rates of growth by limiting commercial, tourist, residential, and recreational development through growth allocations. As an example, the TRPA limits the number of residential units that can be built each year. Based on a local jurisdiction's performance on meeting environmental targets, the TRPA distributes 210, plus or minus, yearly "allocations" to the jurisdictions to allow processing of permits for these units.

2. Transfer of Development Systems. Because TRPA has established finite limits on amounts of development and seeks to relocate potential and existing development to the most appropriate areas, it has established transfer of development systems for commercial floor area, tourist units, residential units, and land coverage. As an example, there may be a single family house located on a lot in a streamzone. This existing residential unit may be transferred to a lot with better land capability and supporting infrastructure. The TRPA would also allow the transfer of the impervious land coverage associated with the single family house. If the lot has no development on it, the TRPA gives it a development right for a residential unit and allows the right to be transferred along with the potential land coverage. Actual construction of the unit on the receiving lot would require an allocation, which in itself may be acquired to transfer. The latter example is driven more by legal reasons of reasonable use, since TRPA prohibits or limits development of certain sensitive lots.

3. Land Banks and Buyout Systems. Although the TRPA does not have the
   authority to own other property, TRPA ordinances do enable land banks and
   buyout programs. The TRPA has assisted in establishing such programs for the
   State of Nevada (Nevada State Lands) and for the State of California (Tahoe
   Conservancy). These agencies, along with the U.S. Forest Service, acquired
   8,560 sensitive lots for $219 million between 1982 and 2003.
4. Mitigation Fee Systems. The TRPA established mitigation fees to offset project
   impacts for air quality, water quality, excess land coverage, and shorezone
   development. These fees are based on offsite impacts or impacts that cannot be
   mitigated on site. The fees are distributed generally to the local governments
   in which the project is located to implement the EIP projects determined to
   mitigate and achieve threshold targets.

While regulation is one of the pillars of the regional plan, the TRPA has discovered that this is not enough to achieve thresholds. Thus the agency also emphasizes
the capital investment and scientific research components of its strategy, which are
embodied in the Environmental Improvement Program. Since the TRPA does not
have taxing authorities, nor does it construct projects, it is heavily dependent on its
partners to implement and fund these improvements.

The following are examples of accomplishments resulting from this partnership
under the 1987 regional plan:

- Approximately 266 environmental improvement capital projects completed,
  with more being planned
- $48 million in research/monitoring funded
- Tahoe Science Consortium established
- 3,064 acres of sensitive land acquired
- 13,000 acres of wildlife habitat improved
- 739 acres of wetlands restored
- Stormwater treatment installed on 26 miles of state highways
- 55 miles of dirt forest roads revegetated and 374 acres revegetated
- 25 restoration projects planned or completed to restore Upper Truckee River
  watershed
- 21,293 acres treated for ecosystem recreation and/or fuel reduction
- 2,388 linear feet of lake shore acquired for public use
- Construction and/or planning for 127 miles of new multipurpose trails
- 20 transit facilities constructed or improved, with transit ridership up to
  1.5 million annually
- 82 public facilities constructed or improved for recreation and access
- More than 4 miles of overhead utility lines moved underground

MEASURING SUCCESS

To assure that the regulations and accomplishments are meeting the TRPA's goals,
the TRPA has established environmental threshold carrying capacities and tracks

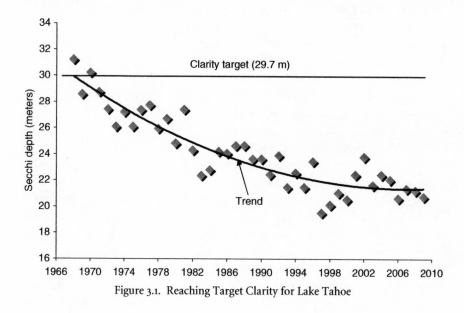

Figure 3.1. Reaching Target Clarity for Lake Tahoe

thirty-six indicators to determine threshold attainment status. The TRPA tracks both overall attainment targets and interim five-year targets for nonattainment indicators. Of the thirty-six threshold indicators that the TRPA tracks for overall attainment, approximately ten are in attainment for 2006. This means that monitoring indicates that the threshold meets the adopted standard. Monitoring results find that twenty-two of the indicators are in nonattainment in 2006, which means they do not meet the standard. The status is unknown for the remaining four indicators, meaning the TRPA did not have the data to make the determination.

Some of the nonattainment indicators are close to attainment. If a near-attainment category is considered for indicators that are very close to the standard, then eight of these are in near attainment and fourteen are in significant nonattainment. Significant nonattainment includes indicators that will not be attained in the near future, have negative trends, or are not making interim targets. Approximately twenty out of twenty-six of the indicators did not meet their interim targets. Figure 3.1 represents an example of tracking an indicator (water clarity) against a clarity target. The graph demonstrates that the TRPA is starting to turn the corner on achieving the ultimate target.

THE TRPA's FUTURE

For the agency to be successful, it must be a symbol of environmental responsibility and stewardship and provide a legal means to govern the region. The agency's hope is to be recognized throughout the world for what it contributes to planning and the science of resource protection.

The TRPA and its mission are one-of-a-kind and represent an unprecedented attempt to address environmental, economic, and cultural values at both regional and local levels. The solution is not solely in regulatory authority, but also in being the lead organization responsible for creating and implementing collaborative, regionwide solutions to environmental protection.

Much of the effort put forth is groundbreaking, as the problems the TRPA is addressing, such as dealing with ever-growing demands on strictly limited resources from growing populations in and surrounding Tahoe, have no textbook remedies. The great challenges the agency faces make it a lightning rod attracting a wide range of opinions and emotions. The TRPA is charged with achieving ambitious environmental thresholds while also promoting important social and economic values. For example, the shortage of affordable housing, while not a compact mandate, is a key social and economic issue in the Tahoe Basin, as it is elsewhere in the nation. While recognizing that this problem is far beyond the TRPA's authority to resolve, the TRPA is attempting to foster the development of moderate and affordable housing through planning and regulatory incentives that are consistent with the environmental goals of the regional plan. Recent wildfires have brought fuels management and safety to the TRPA's attention. The TRPA has developed regional wildland-urban interface treatment plans and is attempting to resolve conflicts with current water quality, vegetation protection, and scenic regulations to help prevent future catastrophic fires. Again TRPA can assist and facilitate but cannot resolve these challenges by its authority alone.

The TRPA is primarily an environmental land use planning agency, but it recognizes the need to resolve the interdependency of environmental, economic, and social well-being in the Tahoe Region. Environmental groups, property rights advocates, business interests, and numerous government agencies agree that tourism and successful, locally owned businesses are the key to economic vitality at Lake Tahoe and are dependent on the attractiveness of the region's environment. The TRPA's future regional plan will allow for a measured rate of residential, commercial, and recreational growth, balanced with the implementation of mitigation measures to achieve the desired restoration. This collaboration to resolve our challenges will be reflected in the TRPA's next twenty-year plan.

CHAPTER 4

ONTARIO'S GROWTH PLAN FOR THE GREATER GOLDEN HORSESHOE

Brad Graham

Canada is an increasingly urban country. Eighty percent of the country's population lives in urban areas, and by 2020 this number is expected to rise to 85–90 percent (Prime Minister's Caucus Task Force 2002, 1). This is not a uniquely Canadian phenomenon. Around the world economies are changing, labor markets are shifting, and urban regions, not countries, are emerging as competitive forces, vying with one another for investment. Success is increasingly dependent on urban regions being able to attract and retain knowledge workers by offering a high quality of life and providing places that are attractive, exciting, and diverse. In the United States, twenty of these urban regions now account for 70 percent of America's gross domestic product (Lang and Nelson 2007).

The Province of Ontario's Greater Golden Horseshoe, an area centered around the City of Toronto, is Canada's largest urban region. It encompasses 110 municipalities covering 12,355 square miles (32,000 square kilometers) and is home to 8.4 million people, roughly a quarter of Canada's population (Statistics Canada 2006). This economically and culturally diverse region is Canada's financial and economic center, as well as the destination of nearly half of all immigrants to the country (Statistics Canada 2006). By 2031 the Greater Golden Horseshoe is forecast to grow by an additional 3.7 million people and 1.8 million jobs, almost double the combined growth of other Canadian regions, such as British Columbia's Metro Vancouver Region and Alberta's Edmonton/Calgary region.

The challenge for Canada's urban regions is to plan for growth in a way that maximizes its benefits while minimizing its costs. Modeling has shown that if business-as-usual development were allowed to continue in the Greater Golden Horseshoe, by 2031 it would consume 386 square miles (1,000 square kilometers) of rural and agricultural land, and commute times would increase by 45 percent

(Neptis Foundation 2002). Research has also begun to link sprawl to climate change, and there is growing evidence that low density, dispersed development patterns are a major contributor to the rising obesity epidemic and other poor health outcomes (Abelsohn et al. 2005).

Addressing these problems is particularly difficult in urban regions, where decision making can be fragmented across several jurisdictions. In Canada, land use planning is the constitutional responsibility of provincial governments. In Ontario, planning is governed by the Province's Planning Act, which is administered by the Ministry of Municipal Affairs and Housing. The Planning Act delegates various planning functions and authorities to local municipalities. In a few circumstances, municipal planning decisions need to be approved by the province, but in most cases approval authority has been delegated by the province to the municipalities. Municipal planning decisions can be appealed by any private citizen or landowner, or by municipalities or the province, to the Ontario Municipal Board (OMB), a quasi-judicial independent administrative tribunal that hears applications and appeals on land use planning and other municipal matters. Planning is viewed as a partnership, with the province establishing the policy framework and municipalities making decisions within that framework. Each municipality is responsible for developing an official plan, a statutory document that sets out the municipality's land use policy directions for long-term growth and development.

The province of Ontario's *Growth Plan for the Greater Golden Horseshoe, 2006,* is a response to these challenges. Working with stakeholders, municipal decision makers, and the public, the province passed the Places to Grow Act, 2005. (The full legal name of the legislation is Places to Grow Act, 2005, Statutes of Ontario 2005, chapter 13.) The act enables the provincial government to put in place regional growth plans for any part of the province. These plans enable decisions that sustain a robust economy, build strong communities, promote a healthy environment, and make efficient use of infrastructure.

In June 2006 the province released the first growth plan developed under the Places to Grow Act, the Growth Plan for the Greater Golden Horseshoe, which is an integrated plan that contains clear, measurable targets and sets a framework for growth and development over a twenty-five-year period.

THE DEVELOPMENT OF THE GROWTH PLAN

The Growth Plan for the Greater Golden Horseshoe was over five years in the making and is the product of careful consensus building. For years, many local leaders, developers, and environmentalists had called for a coordinated plan and strategy for growth in the region: one that recognized the unique challenges of an urban region as diverse as the Greater Golden Horseshoe. While there was consensus around the nature of the problem and the need for action, what exactly such a plan should contain was not as clear.

In 2001 the province formed five regional smart growth panels comprising leaders from municipalities, environmental groups, the development sector, business, and academia to advise the province on issues related to growth management. The smart growth panel responsible for the Greater Golden Horseshoe—the Central Ontario Smart Growth Panel—was chaired by the Mayor of Mississauga (a major city adjacent to Toronto), Hazel McCallion. Panel members traveled across the region, meeting with local residents, elected officials, and stakeholders. In April 2003 the panel released a report outlining forty-four recommendations for tackling urban sprawl and achieving a more coordinated approach to planning.

The Growth Plan for the Greater Golden Horseshoe, launched in the summer of 2004 with a discussion paper, built on the work and recommendations of the Central Ontario Smart Growth Panel. The discussion paper marked the beginning of over two years of extensive public and stakeholder consultation and engagement, which included public town hall meetings, speaking engagements, facilitated multi-stakeholder workshops, meetings of key sectoral groups, dialogue with elected officials, and one-on-one meetings with stakeholders. This process culminated in June 2006 with the release of the growth plan.

The Growth Plan for the Greater Golden Horseshoe

The Growth Plan for the Greater Golden Horseshoe sets a clear framework for managing growth over a twenty-five-year timeframe. It is a plan that carefully considers the way development occurs in existing urbanized areas and also changes the way that new development occurs in greenfield areas.

The growth plan's guiding principles include the following:

- Create complete communities that offer more options for living, working, shopping, and playing
- Revitalize downtowns to become vibrant and convenient centers
- Reduce traffic gridlock by improving access to a greater range of transportation choices
- Provide greater choice in housing types to meet the needs of people at all stages of life
- Curb sprawl and protect farmlands and greenspaces

The plan contains a number of planning innovations:

- It is a plan that covers the entire urban region, which includes 110 municipal jurisdictions.
- It provides coordinated forecasts to 2031 for both population and employment growth that regional municipalities must use as the basis for their local planning.
- The plan supports urban redevelopment and intensification by requiring that by 2015 a minimum of 40 percent of all new residential development occurs within the existing built-up areas of municipalities, through infill, redevelopment, and intensification. The plan applies the target to each individual county or regional municipality to ensure that lower intensification

rates in suburban municipalities cannot be offset by those of the major cities. For example, outside of the City of Toronto, the average rate of intensification in these municipalities is approximately 15 percent (Urban Strategies Inc. 2005). The intensification target will be monitored through an innovative methodology based on GIS-coded building permit and assessment data that allows for consistent tracking across all municipalities.

- To further encourage reurbanization and downtown revitalization, the growth plan identifies twenty-five urban growth centers in the Greater Golden Horseshoe, typically the downtown areas in the region's large and midsized cities, and sets minimum density targets for them.
- The growth plan establishes strict policies to ensure that new greenfield development is more compact and complete—that is, development that easily and efficiently meets people's needs for daily living throughout their entire lifetime. It sets a minimum density target of fifty people and jobs combined per hectare (2.47 acres) and contains design standards that require a mix of land uses, high-quality public open spaces, and street configurations that support transit, walking, and cycling.
- There are rigorous criteria for settlement area boundary expansions that must be met as part of a municipally initiated comprehensive review.

The plan also recognizes the strategic importance of protecting employment lands and contains policies to help municipalities plan for and protect these areas from conversion to nonemployment uses.

IMPLEMENTATION

A plan remains just that unless it can be implemented; and implementing a plan across a diverse urban region, with multiple municipal jurisdictions, presents a challenge. One important method of implementing the plan is through decisions under the Ontario Planning Act, as amended, and local official plan conformity exercises. (The full legal name of the legislation is the Ontario Planning Act, Revised Statutes of Ontario 1990, c.P. 13.) The Places to Grow Act requires all planning decisions under the Province's Planning Act, including those by municipalities and by the Ontario Municipal Board, to conform to the growth plan's policies. In addition, all local official plans (the equivalent of town, comprehensive, or general plans in the United States) must be brought into conformity with the growth plan. This will ensure that municipal planning is coordinated with and contributes to the implementation of the growth plan.

However, the growth plan will not be implemented through legislation alone. Provincial infrastructure investment is another important mechanism. Responsibility for the growth plan is placed within the Ontario Ministry of Energy and Infrastructure, a ministry that brings together capital investment planning and growth planning. This ensures that provincial infrastructure investments are matched with growth plan priorities, such as increasing transit use and downtown revitalization. Through ReNew Ontario, the province's first-ever five-year infrastructure investment strategy, more than C$7.5 billion will be invested in the Greater Golden Horseshoe. The province's MoveOntario 2020 initiative will invest more than C$17.5 billion in a rapid transit action plan for the Greater Toronto and Hamilton Area by 2020. Other investments will support downtown revitalization in several urban growth centers, such as a new courthouse facility in downtown Oshawa, waterfront redevelopment in downtown Toronto, and a center for the arts in downtown St. Catharines.

Implementation of the growth plan is also supported by a wide range of other new provincial tools and initiatives, including the following:

- The award-winning Greenbelt Plan, 2005, which protects 1.8 million acres (728,000 hectares) of farmland and greenspaces from urbanization at the heart of the region
- The regional transportation agency, Metrolinx, established in 2006, which is responsible for developing a regional transportation plan released in 2008 in coordination with the Growth Plan for the Greater Golden Horseshoe to tackle congestion and create an integrated, user-friendly transit system in the Greater Toronto and Hamilton Area (the most densely populated area inside the Greater Golden Horseshoe)
- Planning Act reforms that provide new tools for municipalities, such as powers to control elements of urban design as part of the site plan control process, expanded ability to use the development permit system to fast-track development approvals that fit with a municipality's vision, and the ability to use community improvement plans to support brownfield redevelopment
- Legislative reforms to reduce risks and address liability and regulatory barriers to brownfield redevelopment
- Legislation that will allow the use of tax increment financing

Recognizing that the success of the growth plan depends greatly on the actions and acceptance of individual municipalities, developers, residents, and businesses, the province is also implementing an extensive training and public engagement program. This includes the development of user-friendly public information materials and visualization tools; an improved website; a youth engagement project for high school students to learn about planning, urban design, and smart growth; "Places to Grow" summits to bring together local and community leaders to discuss best practices; and delivering training sessions on the plan to local elected officials, municipal staff, and practitioners.

Finally, the province is producing key pieces of research and analysis to support the implementation of the growth plan. This work includes the mapping of a built boundary in each municipality in the Greater Golden Horseshoe to measure intensification; determining the size and location of urban growth centers; an assessment of the economic outlook and demand for employment land in the region; as well as work on transportation, water and wastewater, natural systems, prime agricultural lands, and mineral aggregate resources. These materials will assist municipalities in implementing the growth plan in their communities.

Conclusion

The importance of urban regions to national economies and the global trend toward a greater concentration of people in these regions is well documented. With the growth plan for the Greater Golden Horseshoe, Ontario has put in place a model for how a provincial government can plan strategically for growth at the scale of an urban region. It is a model that is garnering significant attention. In 2007 the growth plan became the first winner from outside the United States to receive the American Planning Association's prestigious Daniel Burnham Award. That same year, the plan was also recognized with an Award for Planning Excellence in the category of reurbanization from the Canadian Institute of Planners and an Ontario Professional Planners Institute Award of Distinction. While these awards are a strong endorsement of what Ontario is doing to plan for growth, the province recognizes the importance of continuing its work with municipalities, developers, environmentalists, and the public to help change the way that communities are developed in Canada's largest urban region.

CHAPTER 5

ADIRONDACK PARK

THE GREAT CONSERVATION EXPERIMENT

Ross Whaley and Brian Houseal

The Adirondack Park was born in controversy. Unregulated clear-cutting of forest lands led to widespread fire, significant erosion, and devastating flooding. Population centers to the south, meanwhile, were concerned that unchecked logging would degrade the water quality of their reservoirs, which provided their drinking water, as well as abundant water flows for the Erie Canal, the principal avenue of commerce for western expansion. In 1885 the New York state legislature set aside lands as a forest preserve amid concerns for the water and timber resources of the region.

In 1892 a line was drawn around the forest preserve lands, establishing the Adirondack Park's boundary. It was assumed at the time that the private lands within the so-called blue line would be bought back by the state. The forest preserve was later protected by the New York Constitution's Article XIV, called the "Forever Wild" clause, unique worldwide as the only time a state or national constitution has embedded the concept of wilderness into its fundamental social charter. New York residents have fiercely defended this article and their wilderness for over 110 years.

Today, the Adirondack Park covers six million acres, covering one-fifth of New York State's entire land area. It is the largest publicly protected area in the contiguous United States. The park is larger than Yellowstone, Yosemite, Great Smokey, Glacier, and Grand Canyon National Parks combined. It is a unique mixture of public and private land, with the state owning 48 percent and 52 percent privately owned. Its 131,807 residents live in 103 towns and villages scattered throughout the park. There are another 200,000 seasonal residents, and several million tourists visit the park each year. It is a place where protected wilderness, open space, and people coexist.

ECOLOGICAL IMPORTANCE

The park has a vital ecological role. Forests contain more than 90 percent of the living matter on land on the planet, yet forests are not nearly as widespread around the world as many might think. The eastern United States contains the bulk of the remaining temperate deciduous forests in the world. The Adirondack Park does not have the highest level of forest area in the eastern United States, largely because of its high concentration of lakes and wetlands. But vast stretches of intact forest land in the park contain the largest remaining temperate deciduous forests in the world and the largest old-growth forest east of the Mississippi.

The park has more than 30,000 miles of rivers and streams and more than 11,111 ponds and lakes large enough—5,000 are at least an acre—to be mapped on a USGS quad sheet. Approximately 14 percent of the park is composed of wetlands, ranging from boreal peat lands to examples of flood plain forests, and lake emergent and deep water systems. At the park's highest elevations, some alpine plant communities still exist. These are remnant plant communities of tundra, left from the postglacial retreat that began 12,000 years ago. In New York State this community is restricted to twenty acres on nineteen summits; eighteen in the High Peaks, and all in the Adirondack Park.

Conservation and habitat protection have worked in the Adirondacks, and many species that were extirpated due to overhunting and habitat loss have reintroduced themselves to the region. The moose that was extirpated in the nineteenth century began returning in the 1960s. The black bear, bobcat, beaver, and otter, whose populations were greatly decreased in the nineteenth century, recovered in the twentieth century.

A RESOURCE FOR RECREATION

With over 60 million people located within a day's drive, the Adirondack Park is a valuable natural landscape surrounded by extensive urban and suburban development and will certainly increase in importance in the future as a globally unique ecological resource. As a recreational resource, the park offers some of the best opportunities in North America. Whiteface Mountain and the Village of Lake Placid have been rated the number one ski destination in eastern New York for the past three years by readers of *Ski* magazine. Anglers frequently land the catch of a lifetime. Paddlers have a multitude of scenic rivers and streams to navigate. Miles of hiking trails weave through the woods, some leading to a summit of an Adirondack peak, while others meander quietly to a secret spot. Outdoor recreation is a significant contributor to the park's economy and one of the main reasons people choose to live here.

GOVERNANCE AND REGULATION

New York State's constitutional declaration in 1894 that the public lands of the Adirondacks would be kept "Forever Wild" was the first major controversy over the park. The second was the creation of the Adirondack Park Agency (APA) in 1971. The Adirondack Park Agency Act endowed the APA with zoning responsibility over the private lands and oversight for planning on public lands across the entire six-million-acre park. The act directed the APA to develop long-range land use plans for public and private lands within the boundary of the park. All members of the APA's board are chosen, directly or indirectly, by the governor. This includes eight public members appointed by the governor and approved by the Senate, plus the secretary of state and commissioners of the Department of Environmental Conservation and Department of Economic Development (or their designees). At least five of the agency's eleven members must be residents of the park. The agency prepared the State Land Master Plan, which was signed into law in 1972, followed by the Adirondack Park Land Use and Development Plan (APLUDP) in 1973.

The agency strives to conserve the park's natural resources and assure that development is well planned through administration of the Adirondack Park Agency Act, the APLUDP, the New York State Freshwater Wetlands Act, and the New York State Scenic and Recreational Rivers System Act. Application of the agency's regulations begins with the official Land Use and Development Plan map, which covers both state land and private land. Building densities and recommended uses are defined through the APLUDP, which designates a series of land use areas based on resource characteristics, intrinsic land development capability, and the availability of supporting public services.

There are seven state land use classifications, ranging from the most restrictive wilderness to intensive use for areas of heavy use. There are five private land use classifications. The least restrictive is hamlet; the most restrictive is resource management. The classification of a particular area depends on the following:

- Existing land use and population growth patterns
- Physical limitations related to soils, slopes, and elevations
- Unique features such as gorges and waterfalls
- Biological considerations such as wildlife habitat, rare or endangered plants or animals, wetlands and fragile ecosystems
- Public considerations such as historic sites, proximity to state lands, and the need to preserve the open space character of the park

The purpose of the classification system is to channel growth into the areas where it can best be supported and to minimize the spread of development in areas less suited to sustain such growth. The agency's development of private land is based on controlling density or intensity of development. The APLUDP does not generally restrict *uses* on developable private land. All private land is designated as one of the following classifications, and each land use classification has specific "overall intensity guidelines" that are implemented through municipal zoning ordinances:

Hamlet: To encourage development in these areas, the regulations provide no limits on density or intensity.

Moderate intensity use: Average number of principal buildings is limited to 500 per square mile, with a 1.3 acre average lot size.

Low intensity use: Encourages low density residential development at a 3.2 acre average lot size.

Rural use: Aiming to retain a rural character, this area permits residential development at an 8.5 acre average lot size.

Resource management: In order to protect the natural open space character of these areas, development is permitted at fifteen buildings per square mile and average lot sizes of 42.7 acres.

Industrial use: Industrial and commercial uses are permitted with no intensity limits.

Forest Preserve Lands and Waters

One the most compelling issues facing the APA and its sister agency, the New York Department of Environmental Conservation (DEC), is ensuring the forest preserve lands will survive their popularity. A vast number of people crave the solitude, peacefulness, and rugged challenges provided by the Adirondacks' wildlands. Through hard work and collaboration, the APA and DEC have completed or initiated work on management plans for all thirty-eight units of forest preserve. As of September 2006, ten plans had been adopted by the DEC commissioner, and the rest were in various stages of review or drafting.

The purpose of these management plans is to document the condition and ecological values of each unit and to set out specific management practices that will protect or restore its natural and historic resources and provide for compatible public recreational uses. The unit management planning process can become passionate at times. The agency staff works in accordance with the rules and regulations as defined in the State Land Master Plan, which can conflict with a popular form of outdoor recreation or may determine a beloved manmade structure such as an abandoned fire tower is nonconforming. Avoiding a difficult decision is not an option, and the agency works diligently to ensure unit management plans comply with the master plan. It is not always easy, and decisions are never embraced by all user groups. But the agency is committed to upholding its legislative responsibilities. Protection of the natural resources is paramount.

Other State Agencies and Local Government

Other layers of government and regulation come from state agencies such as the Department of Transportation and the Economic Development Agency, which overlap their regions in ways that do not correspond to the boundaries of the park and often treat it like any other area in the state. There are also the governments elected on the county, town, and village levels.

The current patchwork of government agencies and units is confusing to the general public due to state and local bureaucracies reluctant or unable to change due to legislative mandates, agencies without clear priorities, multiple layers of state and local regulations, little actual enforcement, and a frustrated citizenry worried about their economic future. Local communities are watching their property taxes climb, houses become less affordable, their population age, and young people seek opportunities elsewhere. Many communities know they need to plan for their futures and to secure the resources to get there. But they lack the expertise and funds to carry out comprehensive planning. After thirty years of the Adirondack Park Agency Act mandate to enable local planning, only 19 of the park's 103 towns have approved local land use plans.

KILLER THREATS

Those are the problems on the ground. There are several so-called killer threats to the ecological integrity and wild character of the Adirondack Park that the current governance and policy framework must also address. The big threats to the park include the following.

Air pollution. Global climate change, acid precipitation, and mercury contamination are caused by emissions coming principally from midwestern coal-burning power plants. As a result of climate change and warming waters in streams and ponds, native brook trout are dying. It also snows later and melts earlier than it used to, and agriculture suffers from too much spring rain and flooding. Due to the effects of acid rain, a quarter of the park's lakes are biologically dead; sugar maples are failing to reproduce in the western, windward side of the park; and high-elevation spruce forests are being lost. Mercury in the waters has reached a level at which the DEC advises pregnant women and small children not to eat several species of fish from Adirondack lakes.

Water pollution. In addition to atmospheric deposition, some of the park's waters suffer from elevated phosphorous and bacteria levels from failing septic and municipal treatment systems and nonpoint runoff. In some rural communities, excessive use of road salt has penetrated ground water, damaged municipal supplies, and degraded aquatic ecosystems.

Invasive species. The Adirondack Park still has extensive areas of forests and waters that are not infested by invasive species, but the invaders are spreading along roadways and waterways. As climate change progresses, the spread of pests and pathogens in the forests will severely impact ecology and economies.

Inappropriate development. The park's villages and hamlets are often located around major lakes with high development densities, little setback from waterfronts, and significant vegetative clearing to open views. As the lakeshores become built out, the second wave of development moves upland on steep slopes and along ridgelines, marring previously scenic and wild landscapes. The park's backcountry is being fragmented by fifty-acre mini-estate subdivisions, which meet APA zoning requirements but diminish prospects for working farms and productive forestlands. Proposed telecommunication towers and 400-foot-high wind turbines will mar views from adjacent wilderness areas. Increased motorized uses will disturb the solitude of wild forests.

An assessment of past performance would probably demonstrate that the current governance and policy framework may not be equipped to confront these threats. An effort must be made to rethink how our natural resources and ecosystems are used, and how to design a built landscape that is both environmentally and economically sustainable. This effort will require tremendous political will and leadership to restructure governmental mandates and institutional arrangements at the local, regional, and state levels.

The Future of the Adirondack Park in a Rapidly Changing World

Given what is known about the killer threats, what will the park look like thirty to fifty years from now, and what can be done today to mitigate those threats on the physical landscape, especially from global climate change?

Based on the 2001 Northeastern Regional Overview report for the U.S. Global Change Research Program, the Adirondacks could face a five- to ten-degree Fahrenheit increase over the next fifty to one hundred years and possibly a 20 percent increase in annual precipitation. Similar conclusions were reached by the Northeast Climate Impacts Assessment Team in their 2007 report, *Confronting Climate Change in the Northeast.* The effects of such sudden changes in climate are unknown, but scientists predict that the composition of forests may shift to species currently extant in the southern Appalachians. Native communities of plants and animals will undergo significant alterations, with the probable loss of niche-sensitive species and expansion of more opportunistic pest species. The increase in precipitation will require the redesign of much of the built infrastructure as flooding overwhelms highway culverts and bridges and damages other infrastructure in low-lying areas. The probable impacts of climate change challenge us to rethink how our natural systems and built landscape are designed and used, and to innovate now for capital expenditures to guide those developments over the next fifty years.

What is needed to address global climate change—essentially an air pollution problem—is national legislation that requires deep cuts in carbon dioxide and other greenhouse gases. The Clean Air Act and subsequent amendments that put into effect a cap-and-trade approach to address acid rain offer a successful market-based approach. New York State, as a major energy consumer, has an opportunity to follow California's recent example by placing caps on carbon dioxide emissions and to move the Regional Greenhouse Gas Initiative to a cap-and-trade approach.

At the Adirondack Park level, innovation and smart growth approaches are needed to address the future of the region in this rapidly changing world. Here are some ideas:

1. Comprehensive regional planning. Environmental strategies to address the killer threats should be the primary consideration for the future of the park, but with local communities and their economic development integrated into

those strategies. Comprehensive planning from the local community level must be strengthened and extended across the entire park to brand its unique natural, cultural, and historic assets. Development activities that would lead to irreversible and irreparable degradation of the ecological integrity and biological diversity of the park should be prohibited.

2. Land use management. Ecosystem management principals, policies, and practices should be implemented by all agencies with mandates to act within the park. Contiguous forest preserve units should be combined and managed holistically along with adjacent private lands, rather than the current piecemeal unit management planning process.

3. Core wilderness areas. To mitigate the effects of climate change, increased protection and expansion of large core areas with sufficient habitat are needed to assure long-term survival of viable populations of all native species, as well as options to restore extirpated species.

4. Regional habitat connectivity. The extension of the blue line borders of the park should begin now to establish buffer zones and wildlife migration corridors between remaining natural areas to permit native species to adjust to the coming impacts of climate change. Initially, focus should be placed on restoring river corridors and floodplains and on enhancing known migration routes. Stronger efforts will be needed to reconnect previously natural corridors from the Adirondacks to Tug Hill in the east, to Algonquin Provincial Park in Canada, along the Lake Champlain–Richelieu River to the north, east to Vermont's Green Mountains, and south along the Hudson River valley.

5. Permeable transportation corridors. It is time to rethink and redesign major transportation corridors, such as interstates 87 and 81 and other major state routes, to prevent the spread of invasive species and to permit sufficient and realistic wildlife migratory routes along flyways, wetlands, water courses, and other terrestrial pathways. The same linear natural open spaces can be used to sequester carbon, control flooding, remove contaminants from water bodies, and provide nonmotorized recreation opportunities.

6. Sustainable economic development. Economic incentives need to be created for carbon sequestration, energy conservation, and renewable energy sources, as well as increased capital investments in the forest products industries to create carbon neutral biomass energy generation, ethanol, and related products. Incentives could also be provided to restore Champlain Valley organic agriculture and local distribution networks, reducing dependence on food supplies transported from long distances. By restoring an Adirondack style of architecture with local designs, materials, and labor, there will be a reduction in transportation costs and an increase in employment. Smart growth approaches can be used to concentrate housing and utilities infrastructure within local villages and hamlets, provide affordable broadband access, and enable people to live and work in the same place while competing globally.

7. Improve governance and policy framework. To accomplish these actions, there should be renewed consideration of the proposal made more than a

decade ago to create an Adirondack Park Authority, with both public and private lands under its management, and to establish an Adirondack Park Service to manage the public lands of the forest preserve. At a minimum, the park should be consolidated under one DEC administrative unit for all lands within the boundary. Consolidation of duplicative county, town, and village public services should be undertaken through meaningful local participation to get the future institutional arrangements right.

In conclusion, the Adirondack Park has been a marvelous hundred-plus-year experiment, an experiment that has succeeded on many levels. And just as it served as a model for the twentieth century, we must move ahead to continue the experiment as a model for the twenty-first.

CHAPTER 6

PINELANDS NATIONAL RESERVE

SAVING A UNIQUE ECOSYSTEM IN THE NATION'S MOST DENSELY DEVELOPED STATE

John C. Stokes and Susan R. Grogan

In 1978, after many years of study and debate, Congress passed §502 of the National Parks and Recreation Act, creating the Pinelands National Reserve, 1.1 million acres of private and public lands, and calling for the adoption of a comprehensive management plan to manage growth and protect natural resources on a regional basis. The following year, the state of New Jersey adopted the Pinelands Protection Act, answering the call of the federal legislation by creating the Pinelands Commission and tasking it to write and implement the Pinelands Comprehensive Management Plan (CMP). The Pinelands Commission adopted the CMP in 1981. The Pinelands plan is, therefore, a true amalgam or partnership of federal and state authority. In one recent case a federal district judge ruled that even railroads (which are generally exempted from state and local oversight) were bound by Pinelands regulations.

The federal legislation provided a sound basis for regional growth management in the Pinelands, recognizing the national importance of protecting the unique natural resources of the New Jersey Pinelands. It outlined the goals for regional land use management in the Pinelands, outlined the approach to be taken in achieving those goals, ensured federal cooperation, and authorized federal financial assistance to New Jersey for planning and land acquisition.

THE PINELANDS COMMISSION

The Pinelands Protection Act created an independent fifteen-member commission, specified goals for the plan, granted broad planning authority to the commission, and mandated state and local governments to comply with the CMP. The

Pinelands Commission is made up of seven members nominated by the governor and confirmed by the state Senate, one member from each of the seven counties that are partially within the Pinelands, and one designee of the U.S. secretary of the interior. The commission appoints an executive director, who serves as its chief administrative officer and oversees the commission's other staff, now numbering about forty-five.

The members of the commission represent a diverse group of interests. Members have included farmers, conservationists, professional planners, professors, pastors, realtors, and numerous former mayors or members of township councils, planning boards, school boards, and environmental commissions. Commissioners are not paid and must devote a significant amount of personal time to their Pinelands duties.

There are three peculiar jurisdictional limits that can cause confusion. First, the Pinelands area has always been excluded from New Jersey's State Development and Redevelopment Plan, or "state plan," so the CMP and the state plan do not directly interact. Second, the state Pinelands Protection Act created a Pinelands area that is not coterminous with the 1.1 million acre federal Pinelands National Reserve boundary. Although the Pinelands CMP includes land use and environmental recommendations for the entirety of the Pinelands region, the Pinelands Commission exercises direct regulatory jurisdiction only within the 927,000 acre Pinelands area. Much of the Pinelands National Reserve that is outside the state-designated Pinelands area is located within New Jersey's preexisting coastal zone management zone. In this so-called overlap area, the New Jersey Department of Environmental Protection implements land use and development controls that are designed to implement the state's coastal policies *and* achieve consistency with the CMP. Finally, the Pinelands Commission and CMP do not have a direct role in meeting New Jersey's famous constitutional mandate to provide for affordable housing in zoning and land use ordinances. When the state legislature adopted the Fair Housing Act to provide a regulatory structure to satisfy this mandate, it also amended the Pinelands Protection Act to bar the Pinelands Commission from considering affordable housing either in its permitting or its regional planning functions.

The Pinelands Commission prepares, amends, and implements the development regulations embodied in the CMP as they relate to the Pinelands area. But the commission also has important nonregulatory programs, including land acquisition, scientific research, infrastructure investments, community planning and education, and interpretation. The commission's science program, for example, monitors the ecological health of the Pinelands and studies specific issues relating to human impacts on Pine Barrens ecology. The program's scientists have published numerous articles in peer-reviewed journals, informing the commission's policy deliberations with data and analyses of exceptional scientific integrity.

The commission also monitors the region's economic health. Twenty-three economic indicators representing four primary areas of inquiry—population and demographics, land and housing values, commerce, and municipal finance—are analyzed on an annual basis to compare the Pinelands' economy with that of the surrounding region. The results consistently show that the Pinelands outperforms the surrounding area in many economic areas, including higher housing values, lower unemployment rates, and lower taxes.

The Comprehensive Management Plan

The heart of the Pinelands CMP is its regulatory features, which cover land use policies, environmental standards, municipal and county conformance, permitting oversight, and state consistency. The plan's land use policies are embodied in nine land use management areas into which the Pinelands is divided. The CMP identifies specific land uses and intensities of development that are permitted in each management area. About 60 percent of the Pinelands area is highly regulated to conserve the essential natural character of the landscape and its various native habitats; about 10 percent is reserved for upland and wetlands agriculture; and about 13 percent is set aside for typical residential and business development in designated regional growth areas and traditional towns and villages. The balance of the region comprises transitional areas that generally separate conservation and development areas, and federal enclaves (military bases and a large Federal Aviation Administration facility), which have their own management area designation. As the CMP map shows, the conservation areas—the preservation and forest areas— are generally in the middle of the Pinelands, and the growth zones are generally around the Pinelands' perimeter. Pinelands towns and villages, which preexisted the Pinelands program and were naturally scattered throughout the region, are given definite growth boundaries.

The Preservation Area District encompasses 288,000 acres of the central Pine Barrens ecosystem and includes the full range of Pine Barrens habitats and natural communities. Among globally important resources included in the Preservation Area District are the exceptionally fire-prone pygmy pine forests, or pine plains, where pitch pines and shrub oaks grow only to about six feet in height. Land use in the Preservation Area District is restricted to resource-based uses of forestry, berry agriculture, and low-intensity recreation. Blueberry and cranberry farming is permitted here because these native berries are adapted to the region's acidic, droughty, and low-nutrient soils. New residential and business development is not generally permitted in this area. The central Pine Barrens area also includes the Special Agricultural Production Area, a 40,000 acre zone where the highest concentration of cranberry farms exists. The rules for the Special Agricultural Production Area, like those for the surrounding Preservation Area District, are very restrictive but they also accommodate farm housing and other small-scale development options needed to ensure that these farms are able to operate successfully.

In the 246,000 acre forest area, resource-based uses of forestry, agriculture, and low-intensity recreation are permitted, but so is low-density residential development. Municipalities can use zoning, density transfer, and/or clustering techniques to concentrate residential development on smaller lots in portions of their forest areas, so long as the overall density of the forest area is no greater than one unit per 15.8 acres of developable upland (that is, not wetlands). This equates to an average residential density throughout the entire forest area of one dwelling unit per 28.0 acres.

In recent years, the commission became concerned that some of the forest area was being fragmented by sprawling, large lot developments, a situation that reduces the health of large forested habitats. Therefore, in 2009, the commission adopted a set of new rules that *require* municipalities to institute clustering in both the forest and rural development areas. These rules require new residential lots to be one acre in size, much smaller than has been the case in the past, with the balance of the property permanently deed restricted to reduce forest fragmentation.

The regional growth area is set aside for traditional residential and business development. The Pinelands CMP mandates that municipalities adopt zoning ordinances that authorize a certain amount of residential development within these regional growth areas. This authorized level of development, which also provides developers the opportunity to use transferable development rights, varies by municipality due to different market, infrastructure, and land tenure conditions. Municipalities cannot "down-zone" these areas below the authorized density levels. Although hundreds of different zoning districts with varying densities exist within regional growth areas, on average, they permit a density of three homes per acre of land.

Of course, traditional zoning does not guarantee that developers will actually build at the maximum permitted densities. Experience to date has been that actual construction averages about 64 percent of the maximum densities authorized in regional growth area zoning districts. This pattern seems to reflect the broader market trend of recent times toward construction of larger houses on larger lots. This fairly low realization rate illustrates that the use of traditional local zoning policies to implement a regional plan may not fully achieve regional goals—in this case, the goal of satisfying regional demand for new housing in a limited portion of the region's land mass.

PINELANDS DEVELOPMENT CREDIT PROGRAM

A transfer of development rights program, called the Pinelands Development Credit (PDC) program, is also a key part of the Pinelands land use program. The PDC program, which allows development to be transferred across municipal borders, is one of the most successful TDR programs in the country, having protected more than 58,500 acres of land to date. The goals of the Pinelands Development Credit program are to protect the environmentally critical preservation area and the largest concentrations of farmland, to accommodate development in suitable parts of the protection area, and to mitigate windfalls and wipeouts for landowners.

The PDC sending area is made up of the three most restrictive Pinelands management areas: the Preservation Area District, Agricultural Production Area, and Special Agricultural Production Area. As of 2004, these sending areas together contained 106,000 acres of privately owned, undeveloped land that had not already been restricted by any easement or deed restriction. The CMP allocates PDCs to properties in these sending areas based on specific formulas that take into account property type and existing development. For example, farmed land receives one right per 4.9 acres; undeveloped nonfarm uplands, one right per 9.8 acres; and undeveloped wetlands, one right per 49.0 acres.

The PDC receiving areas comprise regional growth areas. The CMP sets overall residential density requirements and minimum PDC obligations for each regional growth area. Municipalities then designate specific zoning districts and densities but have to make the net zoned densities at least equal the minimum requirements of the CMP. In order to provide an incentive for developers to buy PDCs, the program requires municipal zoning to give a density bonus for residential developments that use PDCs. In most cases, neither the CMP nor the municipal zoning ordinance *require* builders to buy PDCs. Instead, they only need to buy PDCs if they want to take advantage of the density bonus. In 2004 the regional growth areas contained approximately 40,000 acres of privately owned, developable land in twenty-four municipalities, providing opportunities to use approximately 3,400 PDCs (which equates to 13,600 development rights). More recent estimates, based on current development trends, indicate that only 1,275 PDCs (5,100 development rights) are likely to be used.

The value of a Pinelands development credit is determined by the private market. Owners of land in the PDC sending areas are not required to sell their PDCs. The price increased from about $18,400 per credit in 1985 to a high of about $120,000 per credit in 2005. Prices have since declined, with a median sales price of $64,000 per credit in 2009. The price varies with supply and demand, and individual buyers and sellers can negotiate whatever terms they like to transfer PDCs. To date, the PDC program has returned more than $88 million to property owners in the development-restricted sending areas. A separate agency, the PDC Bank, facilitates the severance and sale of Pinelands development credits.

The PDC program has also been adapted for use in association with certain municipal variances and for other unusual projects in the Pinelands area. In each of these cases, the party proposing development (whether a public agency or private business) was required to purchase and redeem PDCs as part of the Pinelands Commission's approval. Examples include the following:

- A developer was permitted to reactivate an expired variance for a preexisting sewered retirement community site, resulting in a bonus of 196 homes, while the PDC requirement resulted in the protection of 585 forested acres in two other Pinelands municipalities. In total, 3,576 acres regionwide were protected.
- As part of the approval for a regional school district to build a new high school serving 2,000 students on a turf farm between village and growth areas, the district was required to purchase PDCs resulting in preservation of 2,166 acres in forested and agricultural areas.

By many measures, the PDC program has been very successful. From 1980 to 2009, 7,047 rights were severed from sending properties; 58,537 acres of land were permanently protected; 4,987 rights were sold or transferred; 1,110 resales were made; and 4,446 rights had been used or were proposed for use in pending projects. The remaining PDC supply was estimated to be approximately 6,600 rights in 2007. Each PDC equates to four development rights.

The Pinelands CMP also includes a density transfer program as a means to help landowners meet minimum lot requirements by using density from other contiguous or noncontiguous parcels. All Pinelands municipalities are required to include the density transfer program in their land use ordinances for all Pinelands forest and rural development areas. The density transfer program and PDCs operate on the same concept: an applicant can build on a smaller lot by utilizing density from another noncontiguous parcel. The "sending parcel" must be deed-restricted for no future development except low-intensity recreation, ecological management, and forestry, with certain provisions made for the continuation and expansion of existing agricultural activities. While PDCs, which were created in 1981, allow increased density in regional growth areas, the density transfer program, launched in 1992, facilitates development of small existing lots, and deed restriction of other parcels, in forest and rural development areas. The density transfer program was originally intended to facilitate development of existing undersized lots. However, municipalities may also designate receiving areas where creation of new undersized lots may occur, and they may designate sending areas from which noncontiguous lands must be acquired in order to build in the receiving areas. So far, the program has operated on a relatively small scale, enabling the development of about 120 homes on undersized lots and the permanent protection of 1,300 acres in the Pinelands forest and rural development areas.

Environmental Development Standards

In addition to the permitted land uses in each management area, the CMP imposes universal development standards in all Pinelands zones in order to protect wetlands, vegetation and wildlife, air quality, water, and scenic and historic resources, as well as to promote safety in a very fire-prone region and control waste management. These standards include rules that apply to all development, as well as specific rules for resource-based uses such as forestry, sand and gravel mining, agriculture, and recreational development. Examples of universal standards that play a large role in the commission's work are water quality standards that are five times more protective than federal drinking water standards, protections of critical habitats of threatened and endangered plant and animal populations, rules requiring generous wetland buffers (usually ranging between 200 to 300 feet from wetlands), and standards requiring that storm water generated by new development be infiltrated on site.

New Jersey is a home rule state, so development is reviewed by municipal planning and zoning boards and construction officials according to their own local zoning and land use regulations. The Pinelands Commission ensures that the regional CMP is implemented at the local level through extensive municipal conformance measures.

First, the Pinelands Commission must approve, or certify, all municipal master plans and land use ordinances, and any amendments to these plans and ordinances, for them to have any legal effect. Municipal ordinances must conform to the regional land use policies and must incorporate all the Pinelands development standards of the CMP. In theory, therefore, no development should be approved through the municipal process unless it meets Pinelands CMP requirements.

Second, the commission double checks all local development approvals to ensure conformance with the CMP. These local approvals, which include subdivisions, site plans, building permits, and septic permits, are not effective until the commission has signed off on them. The commission also directly approves public development proposals sponsored by municipal, county, state, and federal government agencies. About 1,500 public and private development applications are received each year.

In many places outside the Pinelands, planners and residents worry about excessive variances that cumulatively undermine well-constructed master plans and zoning ordinances. In the Pinelands, the commission can set aside a variance given by a municipal zoning board of adjustment if it concerns a requirement of the CMP and fails to meet the CMP's own waiver standards. The tests are much more difficult for a Pinelands "waiver of strict compliance" than for a variance granted pursuant to New Jersey's Municipal Land Use Law. As a result, the commission sees relatively few applications for waivers.

During the first thirty years of the Pinelands program, less than 1 percent of all approved residential development (about 135 homes) has been located in the Pinelands preservation area and less than 4 percent in the forest area. About 66 percent of new development is located in the 8 percent of the Pinelands area within the regional growth area. Some regional growth areas have seen a great deal of development, and residents often ask how the Pinelands Commission, charged with protecting the Pinelands, can allow this kind of intensive growth to take place in the region. The answer lies in the underlying premise of the Pinelands regional plan: that growth will not be stopped but will be channeled into preexisting towns and villages and other appropriate areas so that the most sensitive parts of the Pinelands can be conserved.

Nonetheless, the Pinelands Commission recognizes that regional land use and development policies do not automatically translate into progressive community development practices. Rather, regionwide policies need to be refined and adapted to local conditions to advance sustainable development practices. Utilizing generous grants from the Geraldine R. Dodge Foundation, the commission has engaged top-notch consulting teams to help several growing municipalities prepare innovative plans that promote sustainable community design. These plans are prepared by the consulting teams under the direction of visioning teams whose members consist of local government and community leaders.

Adopting a similar approach to fine tune regional conservation policies at a more localized level, the commission has also launched a subregional conservation planning initiative. The first such plan covered the Toms River Corridor, a

17,000 acre portion of the Toms River watershed that supports one of New Jersey's extensive coastal estuaries. As a result of this plan—which was prepared by the Pinelands Commission and municipal, county, and state officials, with help from NGOs and scientists—the two participating municipalities have enacted local ordinances to reduce the size of development areas, thereby increasing to almost three-quarters the amount of land in conservation zoning designations; instituted mandatory clustering provisions that will permanently protect 11,000 acres of land; and reduced impervious coverage, nonpoint pollution, wastewater, and water supply demands. In addition, a 600-foot-wide wildlife conservation corridor was established on each side of the river and one of its tributaries—the first of its kind in New Jersey. These innovative local measures complement a regionwide program to permanently protect important natural resources through the PDC program and through coordinated purchases of land by all levels of government and several NGOs. As a result of those efforts, more than 53 percent of the Pinelands is now afforded permanent protection.

CONCLUSION

Despite the strength and success of the CMP, the Pinelands Commission continually monitors the Pinelands program to identify and address weaknesses, new opportunities, and emerging issues. In addition to the initiatives described earlier, some of the other notable projects now under way include reexamining future growth demands in and around the region to assess whether Pinelands growth area policies need to be revised to better address those demands; strengthening the PDC program's ability to protect important conservation and agricultural lands; reexamining the boundaries of Pinelands management areas in light of more current ecological data collected as part of the commission's ongoing environmental monitoring efforts; researching state-of-the-art wastewater treatment technologies that can be used in rural areas to significantly reduce septic system pollution; and leading a $5.5 million research project to determine how best the 17-trillion-gallon Kirkwood-Cohansey aquifer can meet future water supply demands without adversely impacting the Pinelands' ecology.

The Pinelands plan has been very successful in achieving its goals since its adoption in 1981. But it is broad public support that will have the greatest influence on the long-term prospects for protecting the Pinelands. Public concern about the future of the region was the impetus behind the initial Pinelands protection program, and continuing public support will remain critical as the program evolves. An informed and educated public who appreciates this very special place is the best guarantee that the governmental and nongovernmental stewards of the region continue to take responsible actions to conserve the Pinelands for generations to come.

CHAPTER 7

PLANNING FOR TOMORROW IN THE HIGHLANDS OF NEW JERSEY

Eileen Swan

Carved out after the Wisconsin glacier retreated around the year 10,000 BC, the New Jersey Highlands region primarily consisted of tundralike vegetation that eventually yielded to grasslands and finally the forests that still cover much of this region today. Many years after the geology and geography of this region were changed by natural and man-made forces, the federal government and the State of New Jersey decided that the natural significance of this area must be protected to preserve a clean and reliable source of drinking water for more than half of New Jersey's residents and to provide precious open space in the most densely populated state in the country.

On March 7, 1906, New Jersey governor Edward C. Stokes approved a joint resolution establishing a five-member commission "to investigate the practicability and probable cost of the acquisition by the State of the title to the potable waters of the State." The commission's task was to examine the extent, character, ownership, and value of the state's potable water supplies. The 1907 report noted the importance of the Highlands watersheds, explaining:

> The Highlands watersheds are the best in the State in respect to ease of collection, in scantiness of population, with consequent absence of contamination; in elevation, giving opportunity for gravity delivery and in softness as shown by chemical analysis. These watersheds should be preserved from pollution at all hazards, for upon them the most populous portions of the State must depend for water supplies. There has been too much laxness in the past regarding this important matter.

Federal involvement with the Highlands region began in 1990, when the secretary of agriculture authorized the U.S. Forest Service, to prepare a report of the region. The New Jersey Highlands region is part of the four-state Highlands system consisting of over 3.5 million acres of land, including portions of Connecticut, New York, New Jersey, and Pennsylvania. U.S. Forest Service studies in 1992 and 2002 served as a significant impetus to reigniting the effort to protect the critical natural resources of New Jersey's Highlands region.

The State of New Jersey took a significant step in protecting these natural resources by first designating the Highlands region as New Jersey's first special resource area in the 2001 State Development and Redevelopment Plan and second by passing the Highlands Water Protection and Planning Act on August 10, 2004. The Highlands Act comes twenty-five and fifteen years after the respective state initiatives to address regional planning under the Hackensack Meadowlands Development Act and the Pinelands Protection Act. The Highlands Act designates a Highlands region of 859,358 acres—an area that provides water for well over half of New Jersey's populations through a combination of surface water reservoirs and ground water aquifers. The streams and rivers of the Highlands also support sensitive ecosystems, public recreation, and scenic values.

The Highlands region includes land in eighty-eight municipalities in seven counties in northern New Jersey and is divided into two areas: the preservation area and the planning area. The preservation area consists of nearly 415,000 acres located in fifty-two municipalities. Upon passage of the Highlands Act, these lands were immediately subject to its stringent environmental standards and are presently governed by rules and regulations subsequently adopted by the New Jersey Department of Environmental Protection. Nearly 445,000 acres are in the planning area located in eighty-three municipalities within the seven Highlands counties. There are five municipalities that lie entirely within the preservation area, forty-seven that have land in both areas, and thirty-six that have land only in the planning area. In November 2007 the Highlands Council, the state planning body created by the Highlands Act, issued a Final Draft Regional Master Plan (RMP) for the Highlands region. In July 2008 the council adopted the final RMP, which is guided by the goals and mandates of the Highlands Act to protect and enhance the significant values of the abundant and critical resources in this area.

HISTORY OF THE HIGHLANDS

The Highlands region is known for both its beauty and its natural resources. Rolling hills, pastoral valleys, steep ridges, forests, and critical wildlife habitats give way to lakes and streams. It stretches from Phillipsburg in Warren County at the southwest part of its border to Mahwah in Bergen County, the most northeastern part of the region. The Highlands Act sets forth boundaries for the preservation area and planning area, where conformance with the RMP is required in the preservation area and voluntary in the planning area.

Farming has always been a part of the Highlands. Farmers in the low fertile valleys consumed much of their own food or fed it to livestock. Dairy products, grain, fruits, and vegetables were grown or produced on farms and fields that were enclosed by natural, wooden, or stone fence lines, giving each tract a sense of independence and distinction that still exists in portions of the Highlands today.

The first key industry of the region was ironworks. The Highlands was found to contain one of the richest iron oxide deposits in the world. Iron oxide, also known as magnetite, is an iron ore with the highest iron content. The area also had an abundance of water and lumber, which were needed to process the raw ore into metallic products. The Mount Hope Mine in Rockaway Township, Morris County, is believed to be one of the oldest and largest iron mines in the United States, dating back to 1710.

Industrialization changed the face of the Highlands, as it did in so many regions of New Jersey. People started to settle permanently in the area because the ironworks operations needed full-time employees. Subsequently, communities sprouted up around these areas, which included housing, churches, schools, and stores. Industrialization also changed the natural environment of the Highlands. Many subsurface mines were established in the Highlands to extract ore. The water supply was used in many of the iron mines. The vast forests of the northern Highlands provided an abundant source of timber for producing charcoal, leading to nearly total clear-cutting of the forests over time.

Industrialization demanded a better way to move raw materials and goods throughout the region. The Morris Canal was completed in 1830 to connect Newark and the Hudson River to the Delaware River. This canal prevented an early demise of the iron industry in New Jersey by providing coal from Pennsylvania as a source of fuel for the forges.

While industrialization was occurring, agricultural uses also increased. Crops were adapted to provide dairy products for daily consumption and seasonal produce for the growing New York and New Jersey metropolitan area. The late nineteenth and early twentieth centuries also witnessed a gradual transformation of parts of the agricultural landscape from commercial farming into country estates of the upper middle class.

The Highlands Water Protection and Planning Act

Over the last hundred years, federal and state agencies have recognized and studied the significance of the Highlands region. These include the creation of reservoirs in the Highlands for northern New Jersey cities; the findings of the New Jersey Potable Water Commission report issued in 1907; the establishment of the North Jersey District Water Supply Commission; the U.S. Department of Agriculture Forest Service study conducted in 1992 and updated in 2002; and the recommendations of the 2003 New Jersey Highlands Task Force.

The Highlands Water Protection and Planning Act states that the Highlands is an essential source of drinking water for more than one-half of New Jersey's population and contains other exceptional natural resources, such as clean air, contiguous forestlands, wetlands, pristine watersheds, habitat for fauna and flora, historical sites, and recreational opportunities for the state's residents. It also recognizes that these resources are a vital part of the public trust.

The Highlands Act seeks to protect these public trust resources through a "comprehensive approach," including the immediate imposition of stringent water and natural resource standards in the preservation area, a reorganization of land use powers to emphasize regional planning for the entire Highlands region, and a "strong and significant commitment of the State to fund the acquisition of exceptional natural resource value lands."

The act created the Highlands Council, an independent agency of the State of New Jersey that consists of fifteen members whose powers, duties, and responsibilities are set forth in the Highlands Act. Five of the fifteen council members must be municipal officials from the Highlands region, and three must be county officials from the Highlands region.

A REGIONAL MASTER PLAN FOR THE HIGHLANDS

The RMP seeks to evaluate how best to protect the natural and cultural resources of the Highlands region while striving to accommodate a sustainable economy. It establishes the capacity limitations for future growth within the Highlands region related to both natural systems, such as protection of our drinking water supplies, and the built environment, such as wastewater and transportation infrastructure. The RMP evaluates the costs, and often unintentional consequences, of local land use planning decisions; assesses the environmental and economic benefits of natural resource and open space protection, particularly as they relate to water supply; and further develops the tools and methods necessary to institute growth control measures, where necessary, to safeguard critical natural resources.

The RMP embodies a regional vision for the Highlands region and will be implemented at all levels of government. Through plan conformance by municipalities and counties, financial and technical assistance by the Highlands Council, and state and federal coordination, the RMP will provide for the protection and preservation of significant values of the Highlands region for the benefit of the residents.

The Highlands Act required that the RMP include specific components that address the following issues:

- Resource assessment
- Smart growth
- Transfer of development rights program
- Transportation
- Finances
- Local participation
- Coordination and consistency
- Preservation area requirements

The RMP establishes a regional planning framework for resource protection as a complement to local land use planning efforts. The plan provides strategic opportunities for communities to consider and act upon based on an understanding of the cumulative and regional impacts of local land use decisions. The RMP also provides a framework to coordinate the policy and planning decisions made by federal and state entities to ensure that these decisions and public investments are guided by the goals of this plan.

After the first draft of the RMP was released in November 2006, the Highlands Council received more than 3,600 comments from 1,000 individuals during a 160-day public comment period. Many of the changes made to the final RMP were in direct response to these comments. For example, the Land Use Capability Map (LUCM) was expanded from one to five maps that identify overlay zones, water availability, water supply and wastewater utility capacity, and septic system yields. The Land Use Capability Map Series was developed by using the Highlands Council's Land Use Analysis Decision Support (LANDS) model, which has the ability to represent indicators, capacities, and constraints at a scale of one-twentieth of an acre (or 2,500 square feet, in 50-square-feet cells). The LANDS model includes more than fifty data layers that have been refined as a direct response to suggestions raised during the public comment period for the first draft of the Highlands Council's RMP.

The map series allows for a better portrait of areas for potential development and redevelopment. The map series identifies areas within the Highlands region that may be able to support additional development but may have water supply or sewerage constraints that could be addressed through local planning. These efforts will continue to guide future development away from environmentally sensitive and agricultural areas while utilizing existing infrastructure and making it more efficient.

The LUCM defined overlay zones that will be a guide to land use and conservation efforts in the Highlands region. The three primary zones identified by the council are:

- Protection Zone. This zone consists of land critical to maintaining the water quality, quantity and sensitive ecological resources and processes. Land acquisition in this zone is a priority, and development will be extremely limited.
- Conservation Zone. This zone features agricultural lands interspersed with associated woodlands and environmental features that should be preserved when possible. Nonagricultural development will be limited in area and intensity.
- Existing Community Zone. This zone contains regionally significant concentrated development signifying existing communities. Infrastructure is likely to already exist in this zone that may support compatible development and redevelopment.

In addition to the three primary zones, three subzones within the Conservation Zone and Existing Community Zone were identified. These additional landscapes recognize regionally significant sensitive environmental features where development is subject to standards concerning resource protection, water use, and degradation of water quality. These subzones are the following:

- Conservation Zone—Environmentally Constrained Subzone—consists of significant environmental features within the Conservation Zone that should be preserved and protected from nonagricultural development.
- Existing Community Zone—Environmentally Constrained Subzone—consists of significant contiguous critical habitat, steep slopes, and forested lands within the Existing Community Zone that should be protected from further fragmentation.
- Lake Community Zone—consists of patterns of community development around lakes to prevent water degradation and promote natural aesthetic values within the Existing Community Zone.

The RMP includes goals, policies, and objectives for protecting the Highlands region and designates 75 percent of the land in the region as environmentally sensitive. The RMP classifies 643,037 acres as environmentally constrained, an increase from the 557,507 acres that were identified as environmentally constrained in 2006. While the council confirmed the extensive amount of sensitive lands in the preservation area, the council also identified significant portions of the planning area as environmentally sensitive (over 60 percent or 270,000 acres of the nearly 445,000 acres).

The RMP also includes mapping of the areas with the highest potential to serve as a transfer of development rights (TDR) receiving zone. In New Jersey, TDR programs have been established for a number of purposes, including preserving farmland to maintain agricultural viability and protecting ecologically important lands to maintain ecosystem health and high water quality. TDR is a land use tool that permits the transfer of development potential from areas identified for preservation, called sending zones, to areas that are more appropriate to accommodate increased growth, called receiving zones. Landowners in the sending zones receive compensation for the transferable development potential of their property that has been restricted in support of preservation. Payment for this lost development potential comes from purchasers who buy credits representing the lost development potential of parcels in the sending zone. The credits then entitle the purchaser to build in a receiving zone at a density greater than that permitted in existing zoning. The Highlands Act created a voluntary TDR program where financial incentives are used to encourage municipalities to create receiving zones. The incentives include enhanced planning grants up to $250,000 and reimbursement for costs of amending local ordinances. In addition, the municipality has the authority to charge impact fees up to $15,000 per unit to defray the costs of that development, and they receive priority status for state infrastructure spending. While the RMP includes mapping of the areas with some potential to serve as TDR receiving zones, all growth is voluntary under the plan and thus the decision rests with the municipality. Areas mapped as having some potential must go through a resource analysis and an infrastructure capacity analysis before any designation can be made. After the adoption of the RMP, Executive Order 114 was issued and includes $10 million in initial capital funding to launch the Highlands Development Credit Bank. To address the fact that the receiving areas are voluntary and the timeline to create such areas has had an impact on preservation area landowners, the bank has initiated a program to offer to buy development credits from landowners who demonstrate a financial hardship.

One of the major emphases of the Highlands Act is protection of water resources. The RMP does so through many critical methods. First, stringent controls are placed on the use of ground and surface waters that flow through the Highlands to ensure that streams and the reservoirs they feed are not dried up during droughts. For many of the region's natural resources, the Highlands Council utilized a watershed-based assessment to evaluate resource integrity and protection needs. The watershed boundaries used for the analysis in the RMP were fourteen-digit hydrologic units (i.e., subwatersheds or HUC14s). There are 183 HUC14 subwatersheds located partially or entirely within the Highlands region. The Highlands Council analyzed the natural water sustainability of the Highlands region to determine the amount of water required to protect aquatic ecological integrity and the amount "available" for water supply, and commercial, industrial, or agricultural uses. The analysis entailed using stream base flows as a surrogate for water sustainability because the protection of base flow is critical to maintaining healthy aquatic ecosystems and protecting potable surface water supplies, particularly during periods of drought.

Second, water contamination is controlled by strictly regulating the density of new septic systems, with average densities ranging from ten acres to twenty-six acres per septic system, within the planning area, and incorporation of existing preservation area controls that require from twenty-five to eighty-eight acres per septic system. The plan also requires special development controls to limit water quality impacts in areas with sewers. Additional programs focus on reducing ground and surface water contamination sources that already exist, to improve existing conditions. Third, the quantity of ground water is protected through stringent controls on the development of prime ground water recharge areas. Finally, the sensitive ecosystems of the region's streams and lakes are protected by imposing stringent buffer requirements on new development.

In addition, the RMP reflects the results of cooperative efforts with the New Jersey Department of Agriculture to refine agricultural preservation priorities. It also includes more detailed language regarding cluster development and strict criteria governing its use. New evaluations on transportation infrastructure were conducted, and the data was used in the LUCM, TDR potential receiving areas, and the redevelopment and infill analysis work.

The RMP provides a more detailed approach to plan conformance by municipalities and counties, with provision for initial grants to help local governments determine how the RMP relates to their current plans and ordinances. The plan also includes a specific set of goals, policies, and objectives, as well as specific programs to carry them out.

Once the council adopted the RMP in July 2008, the plan conformance process began. This agency is in its infancy, but as Plato said, "The beginning is the most important part of the work." The RMP consists of six chapters:

1. An introduction to the Highlands region providing a history of the origins of both the region and the Highlands Act.
2. An analysis of the Highlands region, including an assessment of the region's resources and existing communities.
3. An analysis of the character of the Highlands region at a regional and local community scale and a framework envisioning the future of the Highlands.
4. A statement of policy guidance setting forth the goals, policies, and objectives necessary to implement the Highlands Act.
5. A series of programs designed to ensure that the goals, policies, and objectives for the Highlands region are met.
6. An implementation framework describing the necessary roles of the entities that will guide the successful implementation of the plan.

The major policy areas covered in the RMP are organized in the following manner:

- Natural resources—addresses the significant natural resources of the Highlands region and the protection strategies necessary to maintain and enhance their value. Includes the critical resources subject to protection under the RMP, including forest resources, highlands open waters and riparian areas, steep slopes, critical habitat, carbonate rock, open space, and lakes, rivers, and ponds.
- Water resources and utilities—addresses policies associated with establishing the existing capacity limitations of water and wastewater infrastructure necessary to provide for drinking water supply and wastewater treatment. Also includes policies and programs that support cost-effective, innovative, and efficient provision and use of utility capacity.
- Agricultural resources—outlines land management and land use policies necessary to support and maintain a viable agricultural industry. It seeks to balance the need to protect important natural resources that enhance both the resources and the people's livelihoods.
- Historic, cultural, archaeological, and scenic resource protection—includes strategies to address the existing status and threats to the Highland's historic, cultural, and scenic assets. Also recognizes the importance of these resources to the towns, villages, and cities of the Highlands regarding their history, local character, and culture.
- Transportation—includes policies and programs to address transportation system capacity and transportation system preservation and enhancement measures within the context of natural and cultural resource protection goals and smart growth principles of the RMP.
- Future land use—addresses land use, smart growth, community design, and housing. Provides policy guidance on community planning activities that

utilize regional development, redevelopment, enhanced growth opportunities, smart growth principles, and design standards.

- Landowner fairness—provides several mechanisms to mitigate impacts on landowners, including the transfer of development rights (TDR) program, land acquisition, exemptions, and waivers.
- Sustainable regional economy—evaluates regional employment and income conditions, as well as a series of baseline economic indicators, to help explain regional conditions in order to establish a means for evaluating economic segments over time, so Highlands-related trends can be distinguished from general trends regarding factors such as jobs, housing, business mix, performance of local economic support programs, and community facilities.
- Air quality—addresses the connection between land development patterns, automobile transportation, and the creation of air pollutants affecting the Highlands region.
- Local participation—promotes local, county, regional, state, and federal program coordination and provides the programs and tools to implement the RMP at municipal and county levels.

Land use planning decisions are generally made on the basis of local considerations, with limited opportunity to consider the broader context of these decisions. Sensitive and regionally significant environmental resources are not limited to political boundaries, nor are the impacts from bad land use decisions.

With respect to affordable housing, the RMP requires that conforming municipalities implement both the resource protection requirements of the RMP and the New Jersey Supreme Court's Mount Laurel doctrine to provide—through its land use regulations, sound land use, and long-range planning—a realistic opportunity for a fair share of its region's present and prospective needs for housing for low and moderate income families. The legislature, in the Highlands Act, specifically anticipated the need for New Jersey's Council on Affordable Housing (COAH) and the Highlands Council to coordinate their planning efforts. The act requires that COAH consider the RMP prior to making any determination regarding the allocation of the prospective fair share of housing need in the Highlands region. In addition, the Fair Housing Act has been amended to authorize regional planning entities, including the Highlands Council, to identify and coordinate opportunities for affordable housing on a regionwide basis in consideration of infrastructure, employment opportunities, and transportation, and to allow under certain conditions a transfer of up to 50 percent of the affordable housing obligations from one municipality to another.

The Highlands Act provides municipalities, counties, state entities, and federal agencies with a unique opportunity to address land use planning and resource protection in a regional context. The RMP serves as a foundation to guide future land planning decisions related to resource protection, conservation of agricultural landscapes, and economic growth and development.

CHAPTER 8

RESTORATION, CONSERVATION, AND ECONOMY IN THE NEW JERSEY MEADOWLANDS

Robert Ceberio

The regional planning tools deployed by the New Jersey Meadowlands Commission demonstrate the power of taking a regional approach to policies that, in states like New Jersey, have long been the prerogative of local councils and planning boards. The Meadowlands example also illustrates the benefits that can be gained through regional planning tools even in an area like the Meadowlands, which has been intensively developed and settled for hundreds of years and has suffered devastating environmental damage and industrial blight while remaining a hotbed of economic activity.

HISTORICAL BACKGROUND

The Meadowlands once comprised at least 25,000 acres of tidal wetlands and waterways. Most of the wetlands have been heavily exploited, drained, and "reclaimed" since European settlement. With the industrialization of the region during the nineteenth and twentieth centuries, the Meadowlands received heavy doses of sewage and industrial wastes from cities and factories upstream along the Hackensack River. The damming and dredging of the Hackensack River and the diversion of river water into municipal water systems altered the ecology of the surviving wetlands and greatly increased the salinity of these marshes. The Meadowlands has also served as one of the region's garbage dumps; there are at least thirty-four historic dumps in the Meadowlands District.

The greatest single impact on the Meadowlands, however, must be the filling and development of the wetlands themselves. The economic development and land use history of the area has been driven by its proximity to New York City across the Hudson River and by the cultural perception that the Meadowlands was a wasteland whose only value came through being transformed into buildable land that could be "put to good use." The southern portion of the Meadowlands, which reaches to Newark Bay, is now Port Newark, Elizabeth, and Newark Liberty International Airport. While these facilities may be a familiar site to the millions of travelers who drive the New Jersey Turnpike, few probably realize the freeway, airport, and everything they see around them were once swamps. In fact, most of the Meadowlands has been filled and developed for a wide range of industrial, urban, and commercial purposes, except for a swath of open space along the Hackensack River, which drains into Newark Bay and, ultimately, New York Harbor. This surviving open space is surrounded by some of the most intensively developed and exploited land in the world, with the Manhattan skyline just a few miles to the east.

Despite this history, several thousand acres of wetlands have survived and are being nurtured back to health by the cooperative efforts of the Meadowlands Commission, state and federal agencies, local industry, NGOs, and citizens. At the same time, the region's cities and industrial zones are seeing a resurgence through substantial redevelopment of brownfields and the fiscal cooperation among the municipalities of the Meadowlands District.

The Meadowlands District and Meadowlands Commission were created by state legislation titled the Meadowlands Reclamation and Development Act in 1969—long before the existence of New Jersey's Department of Environmental Protection, the Pinelands Commission, the Highlands Council, and most of the landmark federal environmental laws that apply today. The Meadowlands District is 19,485 acres, or 30.4 square miles, and includes parts of fourteen municipalities in two counties. Today, 8,400 acres of the district is open space, mostly wetlands; the rest is a mix of heavy industrial, commercial, and transportation uses. About 80,000 employees work within the district, one-quarter in manufacturing. There is little residential land use within the district (about 10,000 people live in the district), but more than 400,000 people live in the portions of Meadowlands municipalities outside the district boundary. Only 2 percent of the district is vacant upland. There are several Superfund and brownfield sites, and some abandoned or underutilized properties, in the district.

The mandate of the Meadowlands Commission is to plan for environmental protection, economic development, and solid waste management. The early focus of the commission, however, prioritized development over environmental protection. Originally titled the Hackensack Meadowlands Development Commission, the agency's initial focus was reclaiming additional wetlands for industrial and urban uses. Early proposals included plans to convert significant wetland acreage to upland or landfill to accept garbage from New York City. The Army Corps of Engineers offered to provide $350 million to drain the surviving wetlands for flood control and development purposes. Up to 1986, the master plan for the Meadowlands proposed what today is considered an excessive amount of commercial, residential, warehouse/distribution, and office space for the region.

New Directions

In 1986 the commission began revising the master plan to reflect changes in both environmental laws and cultural attitudes toward wetlands and their value. (For example, New Jersey's coastal zone management rules recognized the Meadowlands as a special area.) But it was not an easy process. The commission was often ambivalent about balancing economic development and environmental protection goals, and there was a lack of support from local communities and the state.

By the late 1990s, however, the commission changed its approach, with a new focus on strategic planning and working with constituencies. These reforms prompted the commission to submit its ideas for the new master plan to a rigorous and extensive public process, gathering input from environmentalists, developers, and other stakeholders to establish criteria for the new land uses. The commission also underwent a formal name change from the Hackensack Meadowlands Development Commission to the New Jersey Meadowlands Commission—reflecting the changing philosophies of how to achieve both economic and environmental goals.

The changes in the commission's organizational culture reflected changes in the economic development mind-set. A fiscal impact statement became a key component for master planning. A more careful consideration of costs and benefits encouraged the commission to move away from filling in wetlands and building large amounts of brand new infrastructure. Planning started to rely more on existing infrastructure through redevelopment and infill development.

When the new master plan was finally adopted in 2004, it aimed to achieve four basic goals:

- Protect and enhance the 8,400 acres of surviving wetlands
- Balance redevelopment and new development of uplands, with a strong emphasis on redevelopment of brownfield sites
- Foster an integrated multimodal transportation network
- Retain and grow commercial, industrial, and financial businesses and jobs

Given the rarity of undeveloped uplands in the district, the plan focuses on redevelopment of underutilized and abandoned brownfield sites to fuel the growth element of this vision.

The response to the 2004 master plan was mixed at first. Developers were unsure about the changes and municipalities were worried about land value and tax ratables, as 100 million square feet of zoned commercial space was reduced to 25 million square feet in the final plan. The 2004 plan also added thousands of residential units to support a more balanced mix of land uses. But through discussions with the commission, stakeholders became more comfortable with the 2004 plan. Communications and outreach were important in overcoming skepticism. Negotiations provided benefits to all the stakeholders involved. For example, a condition for a convention and visitors bureau in the Meadowlands was the promotion of ecotourism, which would generate weekend business for nearby hotels.

This experience convinced the commission that a regular review of this master plan was essential, and in 2009 the agency began a five-year review of the plan through meetings with members of the business community, municipal leaders, and environmentalists.

So far, the plan appears to be successful in guiding development and preservation, and the region's economy appears to be growing stronger each year as millions in new ratables have been added to the Meadowlands District. By trying to make the Meadowlands District a vibrant and successful regional center for business, industry, and community—one that includes efficient land uses that are compatible with its natural resources—the 2004 plan aims to be a model of smart and sustainable growth and an antidote to sprawl. Ten strategies are embodied in the plan to meet this vision:

- Mix land uses
- Take advantage of compact building design
- Create a range of housing opportunities and choices
- Create walkable neighborhoods
- Foster distinctive, attractive communities with a strong sense of place
- Preserve open space, farmland (yes, we still have farmland here), natural beauty, and critical environmental areas
- Strengthen and direct development toward existing communities
- Provide a variety of transportation choices
- Make development decisions predictable, fair, and cost effective
- Encourage community and stakeholder collaboration in development decisions

These strategies are, of course, every progressive planner's wish list of good outcomes. But the Meadowlands Master Plan, when coupled with the commission's mandates and programs, is a genuine and sophisticated effort to make these strategies real and effective.

The Meadowlands Master Plan and implementing regulations are geared to incentivizing the development of brownfields over greenfields, and to prevent further damage to surviving wetlands. This makes both environmental and economic sense. In the Meadowlands, brownfields are less expensive, and the commission coordinates with the New Jersey Department of Environmental Protection to help developers obtain permits for projects the commission supports. Wetlands, in contrast, are heavily regulated to restrict development, creating additional risk for developers whose projects would affect wetlands.

How It Works

The Meadowlands Commission implements this master plan through both regulatory and incentive programs. Under its enabling legislation, the commission serves as both the planning board and the zoning board of adjustment for all development in the district—replacing New Jersey's usual municipal system for the portions of each town that are in the Meadowlands District. The commission, therefore, sets zoning and other land use standards for the district through the master plan and enforces these standards through its review procedures for all new development. This approach ensures that the master plan is applied in a consistent fashion across municipal boundaries, so that the benefits of the plan are enjoyed by the region as a whole.

The commission's staff acts as a typical municipal planning and zoning board. Although the commission does not require a public hearing unless the developer is seeking a variance or special exception from the land use requirements, public hearings are held when the commission considers land use changes within its special redevelopment districts. (Within the district, the commission staff also implements the state's Uniform Construction Code, reviews occupancy certification applications, and conducts routine site inspections. Staff also monitors the district for violations regarding fill operations, construction, dumping, property maintenance, and/or housing.) The commission processes about eight hundred development applications per year.

The Meadowlands Commission also deploys a variety of other tools to bring about the vision embodied in the 2004 master plan. The commission does not rely on state appropriations or local tax money, but rather on revenue from development fees, methane gas mining, and solid waste operations. This funding supports a range of programs.

Tax Sharing

During the creation of the 1972 master plan, the Meadowlands Commission recognized that a local tax sharing system was essential to making the regional planning principles work for all municipalities within the district. In New Jersey, local governments and school districts are supported almost entirely by real estate taxes collected by local governments. Since the Meadowlands master plans allocate zoning for industrial, commercial, residential, and open space uses based on a *regional* vision of benefits to the district, such decisions could provide tax benefits to some municipalities far more than others. The tax sharing system is designed to balance the fiscal inequities that would inevitably arise and encourage municipal support for a regional plan that benefits the district as a whole. Under the plan, each community receives a proportionate share of the property taxes from "new" (post-1970) development, regardless of which municipality the development lies within. In this way, everyone shares in the growth and the associated costs.

The Intermunicipal Tax Sharing Account was authorized by amendment to the New Jersey Meadowlands Commission and Redevelopment Act in 1972, and the New Jersey Supreme Court has upheld the constitutionality of the tax sharing system. The tax sharing system has been working for nearly forty years. Real estate taxes are still set and collected by the municipalities, and each municipality keeps all the taxes it collects from pre-1970 development. Post-1970 property is taxed at the same rates as all other property in the municipality. Under the sharing plan, each municipality retains 60 percent of the revenues it collects, after payment of county taxes and deduction of pre-1970 ratables; receives a payment from the pooled funds for school pupils equal to the cost of educating these children; and receives a payment reflecting the percentage of property the community has in the Meadowlands District (regardless of its land use type or assessment).

MAGNET

In December 2004 the Meadowlands Commission created a five-year funding plan called Meadowlands Area Grants for Natural and Economic Transformation (MAGNET), financed by the commission's development fees. The MAGNET program has distributed $27.3 million in grants to foster economic and environmental revitalization through four funds:

- Municipal Fund ($15.1 million)
- Environmental Fund ($7.1 million)
- Economic Development Fund ($1.2 million)
- Commission Capital Improvement Fund ($3.2 million)

The Municipal Fund provides direct property tax relief through the Municipal Assistance Program (MAP). The Environmental Fund provides resources to protect and restore wetlands and open space, develop new trails and parks, and finance important research. The Economic Development Fund finances the Meadowlands Employment Opportunity Initiative to generate new jobs, the Meadowlands Liberty Convention and Visitors Bureau, and a Transportation Planning District to disentangle the transportation chokepoints in the district. And the Commission Capital Improvement Fund finances Meadowlands Commission program development and public resources. This fund allowed for the commission to expand its role as a hub for science education through the creation of the Center for Environmental and Scientific Education and the William D. McDowell Observatory. This fully "green" building, which provides classroom space for more than 10,000 students a year, was the first public building in New Jersey to obtain LEED Platinum certification—the highest level possible—from the U.S. Green Building Council. The building serves as a teaching tool for educators and also as an example for professionals looking to build sustainably.

Municipal Assistance Program

MAP incentivizes regionalization and shared services among the Meadowlands municipalities by providing them with direct funding for projects that would otherwise be funded by local property taxpayers. The fund has also paid for costly equipment—like special equipment to inspect and clean sewer lines—that is maintained by the commission for free by district municipalities. Since its inception in 2002, MAP has distributed $6.7 million in grants for municipal vehicle purchases, such as police cars and fire trucks, as well as local parks and other infrastructure projects. This program builds on and supplements the district's tax sharing program.

Transportation Improvements

In 2005 the commission created a Transportation Planning District, and two years later it adopted a plan that identified transportation needs within the district, recommended specific improvements, estimated the cost for these upgrades, and provided a mechanism to support these efforts through development fees. The plan, which extends through 2030, plays an important role in the commission's goal of improving the mobility of passengers and freight within the district. The commission is currently looking to implement an automated traffic signal system that would vastly improve vehicle flow in some of the district's worst choke points. This project is slated to begin in Secaucus and North Bergen and extend to other district municipalities in the near future.

Alternative Energy

A logical extension of the commission's focus on green and sustainable design and construction has been its support for alternative energy projects within the Meadowlands District. In 2008 the commission adopted an energy master plan similar to the state's plan that called for decreases in fossil fuel use and an increase in the district's reliance on solar, wind, and other alternative energies. Specifically, the plan calls for the district to reduce power consumption by 20 percent by 2020 and install twenty megawatts of renewable power by the same date.

To put the plan into action, the commission plans to contract with a company that will cover a portion of a former landfill in Kearny with solar panels. The project received support from the state's Board of Public Utilities, which provided $8.5 million in federal stimulus money to the commission to jump-start the project in August 2009. The commission is also looking to cover other former landfills with a "solar carpet" technology that reduces erosion while generating power, and it has plans to construct a solar "roof" on its parking lot to provide electricity to the agency itself. In addition, the commission is working with several local municipalities and school districts to help them determine the solar power potential of their buildings' rooftops.

Affordable Housing

The commission works with district municipalities and developers to address affordable housing requirements imposed by statute, case law, and the New Jersey Council on Affordable Housing. In 2010 it appears the state may abolish the Council on Affordable Housing, and it is unclear whether constitutional or legislative affordable housing mandates in New Jersey will change yet again. In recent years, the commission has updated its housing policies multiple times to keep pace with evolving requirements

The 2004 master plan called for mixed land uses—with the inclusion of potential residential areas in what traditionally had been largely industrial zoning—and encouraged the creation of walkable neighborhoods with a range of stores, homes, and open space close to mass transit options. But affordable housing obligations often created tension within communities as leaders struggled to balance legal requirements with the fear that the community would not have the resources needed to provide necessary services to new residents. These tensions often play out in court challenges that can result in decisions that further impact local zoning and housing policy. In one case, for example, a court-ordered special master is still overseeing zoning in Carlstadt—including the portion within the Meadowlands District boundary—as a result of a builder's remedy lawsuit the municipality lost nearly five years ago.

Another significant impact on the commission's housing policy arises out of the former Xanadu entertainment venue, which currently appears to be attempting to open under new ownership. In May 2007 the state appeals court found that this massive project would create a significant need for low-income housing nearby, and the court additionally determined that the commission has a "constitutional responsibility to plan and zone for affordable housing." The commission responded with guidelines that require staff to review almost all projects to ensure that the development site in question is actually appropriate for housing.

In July 2008 Governor Corzine signed a law that further revised state affordable housing requirements and appeared to give regional planning entities, like the Meadowlands Commission, more responsibility to plan for low-income housing. The commission established a task force consisting of commissioners, mayors, housing advocates, and the public, which has met several times to guide further changes to the commission's regulations. This panel will continue to be of great assistance as the commission prepares to respond to changes now anticipated under Governor Christie's administration.

New Jersey State Plan

New Jersey's 1985 State Planning Act includes a number of aims and strategies that are similar to the Meadowlands District Master Plan, the first of which was created in 1970. The act involves eight distinct goals: conserving natural resources, protecting the environment, protecting historic and cultural resources, revitalizing urban centers, providing housing for working people, creating appropriate public facilities, promoting growth, and coordinating these goals with the mission of other planning agencies.

The most recent state plan, updated in 2001, also shares many similarities with the Meadowlands District Master Plan of 2004. The 2001 state plan focused on watersheds, an acknowledgment that environmental boundaries, not just man-made dividers, must be considered when planning for growth. The state plan emphasizes the need to protect open space while encouraging development in existing urban and suburban areas—something that is critical in the Meadowlands and was embraced in the redrafting of the district master plan in the early 2000s. The state plan also stresses the need to embrace sustainable development, a concept that is a cornerstone of planning in the Meadowlands District, and further

underscored the need to coordinate planning goals and strategies with state
and local agencies.

———

For over forty years, the record of regionalism has grown and flourished through
a partnership of government, environmentalists, developers, and municipalities.
It is a prime example of how economic and environmental goals can meet and
grow together rather than conflict. To paraphrase a *New York Times* editorial
about the 2004 master plan: If it can happen in the Meadowlands, it can happen
anywhere.

CHAPTER 9

CHANGING THE LAND USE PARADIGM TO SAVE NEW YORK'S CENTRAL PINE BARRENS

Raymond P. Corwin

One of the last remaining tracts of native pine barrens along the eastern United States Atlantic coast, the Central Pine Barrens of New York is an invaluable natural area in the middle of a population of more than three million in the Nassau-Suffolk region, immediately east of New York City. Suffolk County is New York state's southeasternmost county, encompassing over 900 square miles of terrestrial and marine environments at the eastern end of Long Island.

Three of Suffolk County's ten towns jointly host the 102,500 acre, state-designated region known as the Central Pine Barrens. This region is the largest remnant of a forest thought to have once encompassed over a quarter million acres in the bicounty area. The Central Pine Barrens' 160 square miles (approximately 18 percent of Suffolk County's land area) overlies a significant portion of the region's sole source aquifer, as designated by the U.S. Environmental Protection Agency. The predominantly undeveloped and undisturbed core of this region overlies high quality groundwater suitable for use as drinking water for a portion of the population.

Reflecting its geologic origins and hydrology, the Central Pine Barrens contains terminal moraines, kettlehole ponds, groundwater fed rivers, and a rich suite of species and ecological communities. Vegetation includes pitch pine woodlands, pine-oak forests, coastal plain ponds, swamps, marshes, bogs, and streams. The dominant tree species in the barrens is the pitch pine (*Pinus rigida*) which is highly fire adapted and resistant. Dense growth of scrub oak (*Quercus ilicifolia*) and smaller heath species such as black huckleberry (*Gaylussacia baccata*), blueberry

(*Vaccinium pallidum* and *V. angustifolium*), sheep laurel (*Kalmia latifolia*), and wintergreen (*Gaultheria procumbens*) are common. Freshwater wetlands often feature red maple (*Acer rubrum*), tupelo (*Nyssa sylvatica*), and Atlantic white cedar (*Chamaecyparis thyoides*). Mourning dove (*Zenaida macroura*), American crow (*Corvus brachyrhynchos*), white-tailed deer (*Odocoileus virginianus*), raccoon (*Procyon lotor*), red fox (*Vulpes fulva*), masked shrew (*Sorex cinerea*), eastern mole (*Scalopus aquaticus*), and Fowler's toads (*Bufo woodhousei*) are found as well. The moth and butterfly fauna is especially rich; twelve species of rare Lepidopterans are known from the Central Pine Barrens (Central Pine Barrens Policy and Planning Commission 1995, vol. 2).

In addition to its value for ecological habitat and water quality protection, the Central Pine Barrens provides an accessible and irreplaceable refuge for walkers, hikers, hunters, fishing enthusiasts, bicyclists, photographers, runners, joggers, naturalists, scientists, canoeists, kayakers, families, visitors, and residents. The barrens provides separation among, and preserves the distinct identities of, the numerous communities that lie along the region's borders. A tour of the barrens also reveals the historic and cultural aspects of life on Long Island, stretching back to colonial and pre-European contact days. Indeed, it reveals the glacial origins of the island itself, a geological heritage shared with other Atlantic coastal areas such as Cape Cod, southern New England, and portions of the New Jersey coastal barrens.

In 1993, after more than a quarter century of controversy, confrontation, litigation, and untold debates, the New York State Legislature passed, and then Governor Mario Cuomo signed, the Long Island Pine Barrens Protection Act (codified under New York Environmental Conservation Law Article 57).

BORN OF CONTROVERSY: THE BATTLE OF THE WOODS LEADS TO A COMPROMISE

As with so many natural areas across the United States, the future of the barrens was not the focus of public debate or government action until much of the region had succumbed to steady development. From the original estimate of 250,000 acres from Nassau County eastward to the twin forks of eastern Long Island, the post–World War II development boom consumed much of the western fringes, leaving virtually all of the remaining barrens in Suffolk County proper.

The east-west commutation patterns of the 1950s and beyond pushed the road network, housing patterns, and the suburban frontier steadily eastward. In 1960 Suffolk County made its first modern era land purchase for the sake of ecological preservation, persuaded by the internationally renowned ornithologist and local resident Dr. Robert Cushman Murphy (in whose honor a roughly 3,000 acre county owned tract of wetlands and uplands is now named). Although already the steward of several active-use parkland tracts prior to that date, the county from that point forward became—and remains—the regional leader among government agencies in purchasing land areas for the primary purpose of environmental protection. Today, Suffolk County protects over 20,000 acres in the preservation area of the Central Pine Barrens. It is also a reasonable assertion that from that same date forward, the seeds of a future conflict-to-crisis-to-compromise situation were putting down firm roots in central Suffolk County. These seeds would fully mature in a painful but productive process over the next three decades.

Not far behind, New York State became a significant preservation landowner in the late 1970s, with the receipt from the Radio Corporation of America (RCA) of over 7,000 acres in two separate tracts at Rocky Point and Southampton, lands that had served as a worldwide radio communications and research facility since the early 1900s. These acquisitions are now known as the Rocky Point Natural Resource Management Area and the David A. Sarnoff Preserve (after the former RCA founder and chair), respectively. Complementing these holdings was the prior receipt by the state of approximately 1,000 acres of the former U.S. Atomic Energy Commission lands (the bulk of which now form the Brookhaven National Laboratory site).

Following this jump-start, the state also began an aggressive acquisition program, and today it holds title to over 13,000 acres within the Central Pine Barrens preservation area, either through the State Department of Environmental Conservation or the State Office of Parks, Recreation and Historic Preservation. Adding to these holdings are public acquisitions of land by several additional state, county, town, and other governmental entities; currently, twelve separate government entities own approximately 40,000 acres—approximately three-quarters—of the 55,000 acre Core Preservation Area within the larger Central Pine Barrens.

In parallel with the unfolding of these land preservation programs, site by site, project by project, battles erupted all across the barrens, as virtually every new residential, commercial, or industrial development proposal became a new focus of publicity, controversy, contention, and, ever more increasingly, litigation. The cascade of confrontations came to a focal point with the 1989 filing of a sweeping environmental lawsuit by the private nonprofit Long Island Pine Barrens Society against the Planning and Zoning Boards of the Towns of Brookhaven, Riverhead, and Southampton, as well as the Suffolk County Department of Health Services, challenging in a single action approvals by these bodies for over two hundred pending land use projects. These projects ranged from single site plans to massive residential developments and large scale shopping and retail centers.

The action sought to compel these agencies to examine the cumulative environmental impact of these pending projects as a whole on the sole source aquifer and the pine barrens ecosystem. Development interests sought and obtained intervenor status during the course of the litigation. This action worked its way through the state courts until late 1992, with victories claimed by both sides along the way. In the closing weeks of 1992, the New York State Court of Appeals, the state's highest court, ruled in favor of the defendants, stating that while a cumulative environmental impact analysis was clearly needed and justifiable given the severity of the threat to water quality and ecological habitat, the court was powerless to order one since the existing State Environmental Quality Review Act did not provide a basis upon which the court could proceed. Instead, in a rare example of dictum from the court, the justices clearly placed the burden for addressing this dilemma in the hands of the legislative branch. In so doing, the court settled a point of law but simultaneously guaranteed that a new act in the saga of pine barrens preservation would unfold in a new venue—the state legislature—with the start of the new year.

THE LEGISLATIVE SOLUTION: AN INTERGOVERNMENTAL STATE COMMISSION, A PLAN, AND A CONSEQUENTIAL DEADLINE

Responding to the growing calls in early 1993 for a final plan for the Central Pine Barrens, the New York State Legislature sought a legislative approach with state backing for the entire region. Long Island environmental, building, economic, ecological, and water quality interests came together that year to craft what might be an acceptable form of legislation, resulting in the passage in July 1993 of the act. Among the major provisions of the act were the following:

- Definition *within the act itself* of the geographic area to which the law would apply. This delineation consisted of two geographic regions: the core preservation area and the compatible growth area (colloquially referred to as "the core" and "the CGA," respectively). Taken together, these adjacent areas constitute the Central Pine Barrens of the act.
- Creation of a new, intergovernmental, five-member state commission with the mandate to produce and implement a mandatory land use plan for the entire area. This newly formed Central Pine Barrens Joint Planning and Policy Commission is defined to consist of an appointee of the governor, the Suffolk County executive, and the supervisors of the towns of Brookhaven, Riverhead, and Southampton.
- Mandating the production, review, and unanimous approval of the comprehensive land use plan *within two years of the passage of the act*, or suffer the penalty that failing to do so would automatically activate a built-in sunset provision that would erase the act and all of its provisions, thus returning the situation to its pre-act status. The unanimous approval required to avoid sunsetting includes a formal ratification by the town board of each of the three towns *before* the commission can give its final (and *unanimous*) approval.

SETTING THE GROUND RULES: CREATE A UNANIMOUS PLAN, THEN ENFORCE IT

The act provided separate provisions for reviewing and deciding land use approvals within the core versus the CGA. Within the core, the act itself (and not the separate plan) contains the criteria that must be met by a development applicant in order for the commission to grant approval (which is in addition to, not in lieu of, the normal requirements and approvals from all other agencies and levels of government). Within the CGA, the act provided that the commission promulgate interim goals and standards for development immediately, and place final standards and guidelines for regulating CGA development into the plan to be produced within two years.

The next twenty-four months were indeed packed, with reviews of development applications in both the core and the CGA conducted simultaneously with the creation, direction, and consolidation of numerous topical plan development committee reports into a coherent draft plan document. The act did not simply require the production of a plan within a two-year period; rather, and quite uncharacteristic of many land use planning statutes at the state level, its provisions were highly specific and calendar driven. These requirements provided—and mandated—a clear, discrete sequence of milestones and work products, each marking a progress point along the two-year time line leading toward completion of the final and legally binding (once adopted) plan. The commission enlisted the aid of numerous cooperators: government agencies from the federal to the village level, plus special districts; elected and appointed officials; private organizations and individuals; contractors; citizens; business groups; environmental organizations; historic resource specialists; recreational groups; academic interests and researchers; and many others.

As each milestone was approached and met, the final step drew nearer: discretionary approval by each of the three town boards for the involved towns, and final approval by the commission through a unanimous vote. A disapproval of the final plan by any of the three towns, or a nonunanimous vote by the commission, would effectively end the process, allowing the sunset provision to come to life and effectively vetoing the entire effort. The Central Pine Barrens Comprehensive Land Use Plan received all required approvals by late June 1995, however, and the final, unanimous approval of the plan by the commission, and its signing by Governor George Pataki, occurred on June 28, 1995. The plan has been in effect since that day.

COMPACT, EFFICIENT, AND ORDERLY: TRADITIONAL DEVELOPMENT PATTERNS AND SHAPING THE FUTURE LANDSCAPE

Anticipating the continued growth of central Suffolk County, the act identified separate goals for the core and the CGA and overarching goals for the overall Central Pine Barrens zone. Specifically, the act mandated that the plan, with respect to future land use, "discourage piecemeal and scattered development" and "accommodate development, in a manner consistent with the long term integrity of the Pine Barrens ecosystem and . . . ensure that the pattern of development is compact, efficient and orderly" (NY ECL 57–0121(2)).

Historically, much of the now designated CGA has been host to an often incongruous mixture of typical suburban development patterns. These include linear strip commercial development along roadways, rectilinear grid residential housing, more recent vintage clustered residential development with pockets of open space and curvilinear road networks, and interspersed commercial and industrial development (portions of which predate the post–World War II eastward development flow). The resulting mix of land uses, traffic generation, and daily activity periods has challenged engineers, planners, open space advocates, and infrastructure developers. This mix has also endangered continuance of the individual communities' characters and landscapes that initially created the distinct sense of place of each of the area's hamlets.

Based upon this statutory charge, and given the history and present land uses of the Central Pine Barrens today, what does the plan seeks to achieve? In addition to protection and maintenance of the core area's natural resources, the CGA contains several significant development centers or concentrations with intervening areas of light or scattered development that the plan must address. The CGA also harbors several subareas of extant pine barrens natural resources not adjacent to the statutorily designated core area, essentially islands of native habitat. A long-established road network crisscrosses the region, portions of which date from the colonial era, while other portions reflect more modern development patterns. The plan seeks to protect those remaining natural areas, identify areas suitable for additional development redirected from the core through the development rights transfer program, and ensure that new development proposals—wherever they arise within the CGA—meet certain strict standards.

Under the act, these provisions were incorporated within the individual towns' codes, and the towns serve as the first point of review—as well as compliance and enforcement—for CGA land use projects. CGA projects not conforming to those standards are referred by the towns to the commission for review through hardship permit applications.

To encourage compact, efficient, and orderly development, the plan provides standards and guidelines for development in the CGA. These standards address, for example, nitrate and nitrogen groundwater discharge; sewage treatment discharge placement; compliance with Suffolk County health codes for development and chemical storage; wetlands buffers, delineations, and conservation easements; stormwater recharge; vegetation clearance; unfragmented open space; fertilizer dependent vegetation; native plantings; special species and ecological communities; and receiving entities for open space dedications. In addition, the plan provides special provisions for the following:

- Identifying and reviewing developments of regional significance. These are large projects as measured by various quantitative criteria, such as number of residential units or square feet of commercial or industrial space.
- Development projects, regardless of scale, that lie physically within geographic subsets of the CGA identified in the plan as critical resource areas. These are areas within the CGA that harbor natural resources of statewide or regional significance, as identified during the plan development process. These CRAs are identified in the plan by both maps and parcel numbers.
- Identification of specific land areas both within the CGA and outside the Central Pine Barrens (but within the three involved towns) to which development rights may be transferred (i.e., receiving areas) from the plan's

sending areas (i.e., the core preservation area and select sending sites within the CGA itself). Notably, these receiving areas were identified initially by the individual towns during the original plan development and approved by the commission by virtue of their inclusion in the final plan. Cumulatively, the plan seeks to achieve minimum ratios of receiving capacity to sending potential for each town, as part of an effort to assure the economic value of every credit generated.

Land use review and permitting is a major and direct responsibility of the commission. No development can proceed within the region unless it is either exempt from the commission's jurisdiction (as identified in the statute proper) or meets the land use standards in the plan. ("Development" is a defined legal term within the statute; "nondevelopment" is a colloquial term used to refer to land use projects exempt from the pine barrens law and the commission's jurisdiction.)

Projects subject to commission jurisdiction are reviewed by staff, heard through the public hearings of the commission, and decided by the commission within 120 days of the application being deemed complete (unless extended by mutual agreement). Staff requirements include dedicated and part-time environmental planners, staff counsel, director's time, and, of course, commissioners' and related staff time.

Under 2004 amendments to the pine barrens law, the commission, along with the state attorney general and the three towns, have law enforcement authority for the plan, permits and conditions, stipulations, and so on. Toward this end, the commission has recently hired a part-time compliance and enforcement coordinator to provide pre- and post-permitting site visits, investigate land use complaints, and perform conservation easement monitoring duties related to the development rights program.

Pine Barrens Credits: Moving Development Rights across the Landscape

The 1993 act authorizes the commission "to establish regulations, values, and standards which may include a system of bonuses and incentives in order to purchase, sell, hold and trade development rights.... such transfers may cross municipal and special district boundaries" (NY ECL 57–0119(6)(j)).

Further, Section 57–0121(6) of the law specifically requires that the Plan . . . shall provide for, address and include but not be limited to the following: . . .

(f) Identification of sending districts in core preservation and compatible growth areas and receiving districts in compatible growth areas and outside the Central Pine Barrens area for the purpose of providing for the transfer of development rights and values to further the preservation and development goals of the land use plan and methodologies and standards for procedural equity and appropriate values in establishing rights and values consistent with the provisions of section two hundred sixty-one-a of the town law.

. . . .

(m) Land protection mechanisms, including, but not limited to, acquisition, conservation easements, rights and values transfers, purchase of development rights, donations and clustering, planned unit development, land trusts, exchanges between privately and publicly owned lands, or other zoning activities consistent with the provisions of this article.

With this unusually broad and inclusive mandate, the statutory foundations of the Pine Barrens Credit (PBC) program were in place. During the 1993–1995 plan development and approval period, the commission worked with business, environmental, civic, and governmental organizations to craft the mechanics of the program. As defined in the plan, the primary purpose of the PBC program is

to maintain value in lands designated for preservation or protection under the Plan by providing for the allocation and use of Pine Barrens Credits (PBCs). The Pine Barrens Credit Program will also promote development which is compact, efficient and orderly, and which is designed to protect the quality and quantity of surface water and groundwater and the long term integrity of the pine barrens ecosystem. (Central Pine Barrens Joint Planning and Policy Commission 1995, vol. 1, chap. 6)

Under the PBC program, eligible private lands within designated sending areas—the core preservation area plus selected sending sites within the compatible growth area—are provided with a letter of interpretation, similar to the same instrument used in the New Jersey Pinelands Development Credit program. The letter states the number of credits to which a defined real property parcel is entitled, along with the factual basis for that estimate. Property owners can administratively appeal the proposed allocation, and each appeal is explored by the commission in a formal public hearing. Once a final decision is made, the property owner receives a new letter of intention with the allocation adjusted or left intact from the original.

Willing property owners can then proceed to the second and final stage, wherein a conservation easement is placed upon the property, with the commission as the grantee, simultaneous with the granting of a Pine Barrens certificate in the name of the owner for the final credit amount. Easements can be customized or standard. Customized easements must be approved individually by the commission.

The Pine Barrens credit program is voluntary and one of several options open to property owners. Historically, it has attracted owners of relatively small pine barrens parcels, compared with parcels traditionally purchased outright by other levels of government. Through 2007, approximately 1,345 acres have been protected through permanent easements held by the commission, representing 657 parcels, with an average parcel size of slightly over two acres.

Interestingly, the average size of an enrolled parcel during the first several years of the credit program was approximately 0.80 acres, and this size increased to slightly over 2.0 acres by 2008, as the value of the credits increased steeply, thus attracting larger parcel owners to apply for credits. Credit values across the three pine barrens towns started at values ranging from $7,500 to $10,000 per credit in 1996 (the first year in which transactions were recorded), and as of 2008 were uniformly within the $98,000 to $100,000 per credit range.

While the commission, as a regional entity, controls the issuance of credits (including tracking, numbering, exchanging, sales monitoring, etc.), it is the Suffolk County Health Department and the three towns of Brookhaven, Riverhead, and Southampton that actually redeem the credits for various land uses above and beyond normal sanitary discharge or zoning regulations (but subject to certain maximum incentives). Credits, which are based on sanitary wastewater ground discharge limits, are essentially "rights to discharge," and all redemption uses are currently based on the quantitative discharge values (e.g., gallons per acre per day of discharge rights) established as safe by the Suffolk County Health Department for the sole source aquifer over which the Central Pine Barrens land lies. Credits are currently used for additional homes in a residential subdivision, additional square footage or floor area in various commercial or industrial uses, or intensity increases such as greater capacity for theaters, restaurants, and other places of public assembly.

Interestingly, one consequence of the intrinsically broader geographic jurisdiction of the Suffolk County Health Department and its role in redeeming credits has been the transfer and redemption of credits across municipal boundaries, whereas an individual town will only accept credits from the portion of the core preservation area located within that town. These intermunicipal transfers—which may be "town to town" or "town to village"—comprised approximately 9 percent of all credit redemptions as of the end of 2007, and approximately half of these redemptions involve transfers to "non pine barrens" towns within Suffolk County.

As part of the commission's statutory mandate and ongoing review of the larger plan, the possibility of alternative, non-bricks-and-mortar uses for credits are being explored. The statute terms this idea of allowing redemption of credits to encourage other economically attractive use or applications "transfer of development values." These might include, for example, prorated tax breaks on previously developed properties in downtown or hamlet center receiving sites, where the statute encourages compact, efficient, and orderly development. This will possibly extend the appeal of credits to a larger class of individuals, such as property holders and managers, than simply development firms.

With the maturation of the program, the commission has recently begun an active easement compliance and monitoring program, assuring that the easement conditions are being observed; this becomes increasingly important over time, as the original property owners—the original grantors of the easement—sell their properties to other parties. It is significant to note that successful operation of the Pine Barrens credit program requires three staff skills: clerical, analytical, and legal. The operational aspects of the credit program are supervised by a specialized clearinghouse board of advisers appointed by the commission, while the commission itself sets overarching policy for the board and the program. The clearinghouse makes financial decisions, invests and uses the approximately $3 million in funds available for purchase of credits (although rarely used now), and makes operational policy.

While other agencies in the region operate land acquisition (i.e., fee simple) programs, the commission instead focuses on the Pine Barrens credit program. The commission holds the resulting conservation easement but is not the owner of any actual real estate. As of 2008 approximately 1,345 acres, representing 657 parcels, have been voluntarily enrolled in the credit program. This represents approximately 2.5 percent of the overall 55,000 acre core area. Although this acreage is dwarfed by the approximately 40,000 acres of publicly owned land within the core area, it nonetheless represented a significant option for those enrolled landowners.

FROM PLANNING TO STEWARDSHIP: SPANNING THE SPECTRUM OF LAND MANAGEMENT RESPONSIBILITIES

In addition to its land use regulation and development rights transfer responsibilities, the commission is charged with promoting interagency and interorganizational stewardship. Currently, there are twelve separate public agencies owning protected lands within the Central Pine Barrens (not including the various other public agencies owning land for other purposes, such as roads, office buildings, etc.). These agencies vary widely in the size and total extent of their holdings, and there are a small number of private conservation holdings within the Central Pine Barrens as well.

In addition to this span of public landowners, there are twenty-five separate agencies with law enforcement duties in or including the Central Pine Barrens, more than forty fire departments or fire-related agencies, and over eighty schools within the area. To address this broad spectrum of stewardship, coordination, outreach, and education needs, the commission has a set of topical councils or committees established by the plan or resolution, along with appropriately specialized staff and finely focused work plans to support these efforts. These topical entities include a Protected Lands Council (made up principally of public landowners), a Law Enforcement Council (active with interagency field patrols and enforcement), a Wildfire Task Force (focusing upon specific regional needs such as a fire weather program, a wildfire training academy, and interagency wildfire field training), a Research Committee (sponsoring an annual scientific and technical conference), and an Education Committee (promoting pine barrens related environmental education in middle and secondary schools, working toward a regional visitors center, etc.).

MONITORING AND METRICS: WHAT DEFINES PROGRESS?

With the maturation of the Central Pine Barrens as a regional planning area—and of the commission as a regional planning body—there inevitably and necessarily arises a desire to track changes. Society seeks to answer the colloquial question

"How are we doing?" with specific, often quantitative, answers. In regional planning generally, we often turn to numeric measures: population growth experienced or projected, natural acres of land protected, acres developed, units of housing built or replaced, miles of roadways or lanes added or expanded, dollars spent on land protection or park management, types of land use applications filed, building permits issued, and many more. This is necessary in order to determine whether regional planning in a given area is effective.

Within specific disciplines, the measures become more focused. Planners look at the mix of housing units built or projected. Natural resource managers look at acres of protected lands requiring physical restoration or other hands-on management. Given the breadth of the commission's responsibilities and the sheer diversity of the region, there are potentially dozens of candidate metrics for the Central Pine Barrens. We select our measures, however, with an eye toward complementing the metrics and monitoring our independent sister agencies across the governmental spectrum. One agency may focus upon groundwater quality testing, while another tracks land acquisition programs, and yet another undertakes ecological health measurements. The commission recognizes that every agency has a role to play in monitoring our common—and singular—landscape and contributes its chosen specialized metrics to the interagency jigsaw puzzle that defines the status of the Central Pine Barrens. Specifically, we have focused upon land use analysis, the Pine Barrens credit statistics, interagency land preservation achievements, and regional stewardship project results.

Perhaps the most closely watched area of commission operations, and one area in which the metric question is visible, is its direct responsibility for land use review. Since its inception in 1993 through the close of 2007, the commission issued decisions on 129 development projects (with many more having been handled at the town level), of which 106 were approved and 23 disapproved. The projects were divided approximately evenly between the core area and the CGA; there were 69 CGA project decisions (53 approvals, 16 disapprovals) and 60 CGA project decisions (53 approvals, 7 disapprovals). From a slightly broader land use project review perspective, these 129 "decided" projects are part of a larger set of 183 projects that have been actually before the commission for hearings, policy determinations, or other action, with the difference (54 projects) having some "other" disposition (e.g., withdrawal, determination of nonjurisdiction, etc.). Finally, the larger perspective of projects reviewed by staff and handled without direct attention by the commission itself would yield measures in the hundreds. Which of these levels of metrics, if any, accurately reflects land use trends within the Central Pine Barrens since 1993?

THE CENTRAL PINE BARRENS IN THE TWENTY-FIRST CENTURY: WHAT CAN WE EXPECT?

The greatest lesson from the commission's experience to date has been the need for setting goals and being flexible. This theme echoes in all areas of the commission's endeavors: land use planning, project review, development rights transfers, stewardship, enforcement, fire management, recreational access, research, and so on. With finite resources—as with any organization—the commission and its numerous partners have learned to set and keep firmly in sight a set of reasonable and attainable future goals while simultaneously dealing with the unfolding and occasional surprises of daily operations.

Evolving organizationally, the commission has increased its staff specialization, introduced yearly work plans for its newest fields of work, and assured that its efforts are firmly rooted in its statute and the overall plan, both of which provide filters for determining what to do and what is beyond the scope of its work. Yet the commission is but one agent of change in the Central Pine Barrens. There are, as one should expect in a suburban county such as Suffolk and in the New York metro region, millions of citizens, literally hundreds of private organizations (both for profit and not for profit and covering dozens of topical interests), and dozens of governmental agencies and branches from the federal to the village level. All play a role; all influence the barrens. The Central Pine Barrens is not an island within the New York metro area; rather, it is—by its very geographic definition—physically subject to the planning, land use, recreational, and other trends occurring throughout the region.

Since the 1995 adoption of the plan, the spectrum of opportunities—a Central Pine Barrens synonym for challenges—within the Central Pine Barrens has steadily broadened. While preservation of the barrens and its twin natural resources of water and ecology have remained the focal point of community effort, the nuances of daily management and policy have become richer and deeper. New topics and terminology have become part of the process, and new paths to consensus have become essential. Fire management, invasive species, light pollution and management, hamlet centers, historic resources, mixed use developments, innovative development right redemptions, wildland urban interface, regional stewardship projects, interagency compliance and enforcement, open space fragmentation, community identity, and many other topics now commingle with traditional zoning, project review, and municipal government discussions.

The world is more populous, and natural resources around the globe are more valuable than ever before. The Central Pine Barrens of New York is no exception to this. The resources of the barrens comprise a variant of the age-old challenge of the commons. Paradoxically, however, it is within the very problem of a more populous world—and a more populous barrens—that we find perhaps the most essential resource of all to meet this evolving challenge: people themselves. Only through a concerned but committed citizenry—we are all, after all, citizens at our core—can we reach a civilized agreement on how to proceed. Whether the question is a protected lands management plan, a land use decision, a financial decision, or a compliance strategy, there can be no substitute for ongoing community communication and decision making.

Return, then, to the "measure of success" question regarding the 1993 act. Is such a single measure possible? If forced to pick one, I would say that perhaps it is simply the ability to assure that we can pass the Central Pine Barrens on to the next generation of citizens so that it continues to be treasured and valuable. Toward that end, we must pass on a community management approach that is the following:

- Founded in law
- Oriented toward progressive and measurable goals defined through consensus
- Flexible, with ongoing monitoring of the plan's effectiveness and formal plan amendments as experience and changing conditions warrant
- Realistic and practical from day to day
- Energized daily by citizen participation and interest from planning to implementation
- Worthy to pass on to the next generation

Perhaps anticlimactically, we must admit that there simply is no concept of "we are done" for long-term planning of a region such as the Central Pine Barrens. Perhaps the better question is, "Are we doing our best at all times for the future?"

CHAPTER 10

CAPE COD

PROTECTING A LAND OF
SAND AND WATER

John Lipman and Maggie Geist

Cape Cod is a long, narrow spit of sand extending into the Atlantic Ocean. It is a place of great beauty, exceptional but highly vulnerable natural resources, and ever-growing popularity for both seasonal and year-round living. One county, Barnstable, covers all of Cape Cod. County governments in Massachusetts are especially weak and largely irrelevant to issues of land use, community design, and environmental protection. The exception is Barnstable and Dukes (Martha's Vineyard) counties, which established through state legislation special land use agencies at the county level to deal with growth-related pressures. Since 1990, when the Cape Cod Commission Act was passed, the Cape has enjoyed regional government structures and land use planning for the entire Cape—a state of affairs that is essentially unique in Massachusetts, home to the storied New England town meeting and a very strong tradition of home rule in land use matters.

The regional governance and planning processes, however, have not replaced but have been added onto the received home rule structures. Land use planning in Cape Cod, moreover, is an endgame. Because there are no large undeveloped parcels left, any land use plan for the Cape has to plan for the state of complete build-out. Forty-four percent of the Cape's land is developed, 39 percent is protected, and only 17 percent remains developable and unprotected. The land use issues include not only how that remaining open land is developed, but also how redevelopment should progress in developed areas and how the quality of growth can be ensured. These three factors—the Cape's natural history and values, the creative tension between regionalism and local self-determination, and the limited remaining space for growth—set the challenges the Cape Cod commission is charged to solve.

Cape Cod covers 413 square miles and has 560 miles of coastline and 350 lakes and ponds. Is Cape Cod really a "region"? In the Massachusetts context, it certainly must be considered a region, simply because it encompasses fifteen independent municipalities and constitutes a distinctive geography with its own history and self-image.

Beyond the confines of being a peninsula, Cape Cod's geology plays a central role in its environmental health. Being made essentially of sand, the Cape's soils are extremely porous and do not treat nutrient contamination well. Nutrients, such as the nitrogen contained in septic system effluent, leach rapidly through the soil, and there is little organic material to bind these nutrients within the soil. Cape Cod has dozens of coastal bays, which historically were carpeted with thick beds of eelgrass that provide necessary habitat to many economically important fish and shellfish. This light-loving flowering plant–which is not to be confused with algae (phytoplankton and seaweed)—forms the foundation of the coastal water ecosystem. But due to an excess supply of nutrients to these waters in recent years, eelgrass has declined precipitously and has been replaced by fast growing algae. Many of the Cape's ponds also have suffered from eutrophication due to excessive nutrients.

The main source of the nutrients is effluent from the Cape's many thousands of septic systems. Almost 85 percent of the Cape's homes and other buildings use on-site septic systems. Such on-site septic systems do not remove or treat nitrogen, which enters the groundwater and makes its way into streams, ponds, and the coastal bays and estuaries where it causes eutrophication. The few centralized treatment facilities on the Cape, moreover, are old and are not equipped to remove nitrogen as well as more modern plants can do. The very high cost of centralized wastewater treatment and concerns that the provision of sewers and treatment plants would spur unwanted growth have contributed to the fact that Cape towns have relied primarily on on-site septic systems.

Since nutrients travel through groundwater, which does not respect municipal boundaries, and multiple towns are typically affected when surface waters are polluted, wastewater management is indisputably a regional issue for Cape Cod. The high cost of fixing the problem also argues for a regional plan and regional cooperation. At the same time, these sands hold vast quantities of fresh water supplied by precipitation and contained in a single, shallow aquifer that lies beneath the Cape. This aquifer provides the Cape's drinking water but is vulnerable both to excessive exploitation and to contamination by septic effluent and other pollutants.

As with so many places along the Eastern seaboard, Cape Cod saw rapid development and population growth from the 1950s on. The Cape's population rose 19.1 percent from 1990 to 2000; now about 230,000 people live in 160,000 homes, including both year-round and seasonal residents. With seasonal residents and tourists, the summer population is estimated to reach about 500,000. During the 1980s and 1990s some towns more than doubled in population. Trades and services make up 39 percent of the Cape's economy, and retail accounts for 30 percent. The critical impacts of the Cape's sprawling residential development include loss and degradation of threatened plant and animal habitats; nitrogen contamination from septic systems that pollutes lakes, ponds, and bays, as indicated by algae blooms and reduced eel grass beds; too many docks, piers, and man-made erosion protections on the shoreline; and traffic and its resulting pollution.

PARTNERSHIPS FOR SMART GROWTH

Two organizations in particular work to help protect Cape Cod from poorly planned and excessive development and its associated impacts. They are the Association to Preserve Cape Cod (APCC), a private nonprofit advocacy group, and the Cape Cod Commission, a regional governmental agency started in part at the urging of APCC. These organizations represent an important balance—an advocacy group that educates and motivates public policy and a government agency that formally establishes and implements that policy.

The Association to Preserve Cape Cod was founded in 1968—a time when the Cape had fewer than 100,000 inhabitants—in response to a proposal to dredge Nauset Marsh on the outer Cape. The founders understood that despite the fifteen towns comprising it, Cape Cod was a single geographic entity and that an organization with a regional perspective was necessary to safeguard the natural resources and quality of life of this narrow peninsula. The founders also recognized that the two ingredients that define Cape Cod—sand and water—were the source of its allure, but also the reason why the Cape is so vulnerable to pollution and other human impacts. For four decades, APCC has been the voice for Cape Cod's environment, steadfastly working for the adoption of policies and programs that protect and enhance Cape Cod's natural resources and quality of life.

APCC's legislative accomplishments are many and include passage of the Cape Cod Commission and the Land Bank Acts; designation of Cape Cod's coastal waters as ocean sanctuaries, of Cape Cod as a sole source aquifer, and of Stellwagen Bank as a national marine sanctuary; and creation of the Upper Cape Water Supply Reserve, the Cape Cod Business Roundtable, and the Cape Cod Water Protection Collaborative.

APCC is currently focused on managing growth by working to direct growth to existing town centers and away from natural resource areas. Key challenges are outmoded state and local land use laws that encourage commercial and residential sprawl and do not provide for protection of critical natural resource lands; lack of workforce housing due to the attractiveness of Cape Cod to second-home owners and retirees; and woefully inadequate wastewater infrastructure, as Cape Cod has relied on on-site septic systems that deliver excessive amounts of nutrients to surface waters, leading to eutrophication.

CAPE COD COMMISSION

In the late 1980s, concerns about the rapid pace of development and the potential impacts on the Cape's resources, particularly its water and its transportation network, led to a call to create a better way to manage development and plan for the region's future. This call led in 1988 to the passage of two referenda: one seeking a one-year moratorium on development and the other asking the state legislature to empower the county government to exercise home rule powers. Both passed by a large margin, apparently reflecting the public's desire for some means of reigning in development, preserving the Capes' scenery and other values, and planning for economic health on a Cape-wide basis.

With the support of Governor Michael Dukakis and Senator Paul Tsongas, the state enacted the County Home Rule Charter and Cape Cod Commission Act in 1990. Governor Dukakis signed state legislation creating the Cape Cod Commission in January 1990, and the commission was approved by Cape voters in March 1990. Ten years later, the voters of Barnstable County voted to rename their county government the Cape Cod Regional Government—a change widely considered an important symbolic recognition of the Cape's unified identity.

The Cape Cod Commission Act greatly expanded Barnstable County's influence and power over land use decisions. The purposes of the act include the following:

- Preserving natural resources, including wildlife, plants, and habitats for endangered species
- Preserving coastal resources
- Protecting groundwater, surface water, and ocean water quality
- Balancing economic growth
- Providing adequate capital facilities, including transportation, water supply, and solid sanitary and hazardous waste disposal facilities
- Increasing affordable housing
- Preserving historical, cultural, archaeological, architectural, and recreational values

The act established a nineteen-member Cape Cod Commission as the regional regulatory and planning agency of the county government. The act charged the commission with preparing and implementing the regional policy plan; reviewing and regulating projects of regional significance as developments of regional impact; and recommending specific areas of the Cape as districts of critical planning concern (DCPCs). The commission includes fifteen members who represent each of the fifteen municipalities, plus a minority representative, a Native American representative, a county commissioner, and a governor's appointee. The commission has a professional staff of about thirty-five.

The Cape Cod Commission Act also created a committee of state cabinet agencies to coordinate the plans and actions of the various state agencies that affect Cape Cod. The committee includes representatives of environment, transportation, economic affairs, labor, and other state functions.

Implementing Policies

The commission provides regional planning, technical assistance, and regulation of larger developments. The commission created a Cape Cod Regional Policy Plan, first adopted in 1991 and updated twice since then. The plan provides a vision to protect resources; a blueprint for municipal comprehensive plans; and regional standards for developments of regional impact. Municipal conformance with the regional policy plan is voluntary.

Technical Assistance and Guidance

Besides adopting the regional policy plan, the commission provides guidance for local comprehensive plans. Towns are not obligated to adopt comprehensive zoning and land use plans, but fourteen out of fifteen Cape Cod towns either have adopted plans or are in the process of completing plans. The commission's help in this process not only provides expertise and resources the towns generally do not have on their own small staffs, but also helps ensure that local plans further the goals of the regional policy plan. The commission has written fourteen model bylaws addressing a host of topics for municipal regulation, including issues like development impact fees, wetlands and wildlife habitat protection, inclusionary zoning, clustering, and transfer of development rights (TDR). While some towns are using some of these approaches, others, including development impact fees and TDR, have yet to be adopted in any substantial way by any Cape Cod town.

The commission also partners with municipalities on the whole range of planning issues, such as wastewater, transportation, affordable housing, natural resource and open space protection, economic development, and historic preservation. The commission provides significant technical assistance to local governments on water resource assessments, planning and zoning, affordable housing, open space protection and trails planning, traffic data collection and studies, and geographic information system (GIS) support. For example, commission staff are working with the towns to create comprehensive wastewater management plans. These detailed plans address questions such as how the town will meet wastewater disposal needs at build-out, where current septic systems are not working to protect water quality, and where new development can safely use on-site septic systems as opposed to requiring off-site treatment. Reflecting the continuing role of local control, it is up to each town whether its wastewater plan will be growth-neutral, growth-restricting, or growth-promoting.

Districts of Critical Planning Concern

The commission is empowered to establish districts of critical planning concern (DCPCs) for areas having exceptional natural, scenic, historic, or recreational values. Areas can be nominated for designation as DCPCs by towns or the commission itself, but in practice all DCPCs have been proposed by towns. Because it is so difficult to change zoning in Massachusetts—requiring approval by two-thirds of residents—DCPCs offer an essential mechanism for towns to control development in important areas. Once a place is designated as a DCPC, a temporary development moratorium is imposed while the town puts protective regulations in place applicable to all new development in the DCPC.

As of 2007 the commission had designated seven DCPCs. An example is the Six Ponds DCPC in Harwich. The area encompasses nearly 1,300 acres of land and water, including Aunt Edies, Black, Cornelius, Hawksnest, Olivers, and Walkers ponds, in the northeastern part of Harwich. The town nominated the district to protect water resources, wildlife habitat, and open space/recreational opportunities, as well as to develop growth management strategies. The town approved implementing regulations to increase minimum lot sizes, reduce lot coverage, protect buffer areas along scenic road corridors, increase pond buffer areas, and promote flexible cluster developments.

Another example is the Bournedale DCPC, an area of nearly 2,000 acres in the town of Bourne, along the Cape Cod Canal. The town nominated the district to protect drinking water quality and rare species habitat, to preserve the water supply and the area's unique historic character, and to assure an adequate and safe transportation network. The town implemented regulations that reduce development density, mandate cluster development, and reduce the amount of commercially zoned land.

Review of Developments of Regional Impact

The commission's principal regulatory role is to review developments of regional impact (DRIs). Developments qualify as DRIs if they have 10,000 square feet or more of commercial space or thirty acres of residential use, or if they are referred by the town as a DRI because of the likelihood of regional impacts. There are other thresholds that trigger commission review as well. The commission has the power to deny DRIs that do not meet the standards of the plan. After commission review and approval, a DRI must still meet all applicable local regulations and zoning (local review and permitting is suspended during the commission's review). Commission approval of a DRI does not bind the town to approve the development.

The commission reviews DRIs for conformance with minimum performance standards that include the following:

- A land use pattern that directs growth to centers or developed areas
- Protection of water resources, limiting nitrogen to five parts per million (ppm) of groundwater sitewide in order to protect drinking water and coastal embayments
- Protection of coastal resources and marine industries
- Protection of sensitive areas and critical wildlife habitat
- Transportation standards that mitigate trips and encourage alternate modes of travel
- Provision of 10 percent of residential units as affordable housing
- Architectural and design standards that preserve historic buildings and landscapes
- Economic development standards that promote well-paying jobs and encourage redevelopment and reuse.

DRIs are also required to provide open space proportional to the land area of the development and depend, in part, on the kind of planning district in which the development is to occur. For example, development in growth incentive zones requires protection of one acre for every two acres being developed, while development in significant natural resource areas requires two acres of preservation for each one acre developed. The commission can require that the land be protected to include high natural resource values and be contiguous with existing open space or wildlife corridors, among other standards. To qualify, open space must be permanently deed restricted or donated to a public or private conservation agency. Often a state conservation restriction is also required.

While the DRI process has been successful in addressing the impacts of the largest developments on Cape Cod, the amount of commercial development that gets reviewed is relatively small compared to the development that falls below commission thresholds. Perhaps less than 20 percent of commercial development proposals, and far fewer residential developments, get reviewed.

Relationships with Towns and Business

The commission's relationships with Cape towns vary. The state has a strong home rule ethic, but municipalities actually have little power to control their destinies. Some towns want the commission to be tough on DRIs, or on certain DRIs, while others chafe when the commission raises obstacles to a proposed DRI the town's leaders want. The towns all take advantage, to some degree, of the many services the commission offers them, such as assistance in planning and zoning, transportation planning, environmental studies, open space planning, economic development planning, assistance with grants and funding, and referral of DRIs.

The business community generally supports the commission as beneficial to the Cape but has a natural concern about regulation. The commission is talking with the business community about ways to change regulations to make smart growth easier and to make the regulatory process simpler and user-friendly. APCC helps foster relationships between the commission, environmental interests in general, and the business community. For the past several years APCC has collaborated on a number of growth management initiatives with the Cape Cod Business Roundtable (BRT). The BRT is a group of civic leaders from the business, housing, environmental, and planning communities that APCC founded to address and resolve regional issues. Early on, the BRT determined that its work would go beyond studies and the release of position statements. The BRT resolved to actively implement its recommendations through policy development, technical assistance, education, and advocacy.

Based on analyses of Cape towns' existing land use and zoning regulations by APCC and the BRT, several actions were taken. Workshops and conferences were convened to promote the desirability of mixed use and greater density in town centers, and the need for housing options in town centers. At the same time, the BRT began to analyze and comment on proposed zoning bylaw changes in Cape towns that were related to growth management.

The workshops revealed a broad concern about added density and height in villages and town centers. Despite the fact that multistoried buildings were not uncommon on Cape Cod in the past and that the villages most admired for their quaint New England character are the most densely developed ones, workshop participants expressed concern about changing bylaws to allow greater density. One workshop attendee asked to be shown what these proposed changes might look like. From this simple request has come the development of a very successful method to help communities visualize the results of zoning decisions.

A key component of the method is the use of realistic photovisualizations in a community-driven town center visioning process. Illustrations are of great assistance in helping a community to translate the complex language of zoning. But realistic photovisualizations accomplish more. Unlike sketches or architectural drawings, photovisualizations are realistic, and community members can recognize their town center. The visualizations allow the community to see what their town center could look like at build-out under current zoning or under different development scenarios.

Lack of adequate wastewater infrastructure has been a major reason Cape towns have resisted changing zoning bylaws to allow greater density. Directing growth to existing town centers, therefore, has to be coupled to providing adequate wastewater treatment to protect water quality. Overall, water quality remains a preeminent issue on Cape Cod. In 2003, recognizing the important connection between business and environmental protection, the BRT released a call to action for water quality recommending the creation of a regional entity to resolve the problem of inadequate wastewater infrastructure. In response, the county commissioners appointed a task force to explore the recommendation. After several months of deliberation, the task force unanimously recommended that the county create a regional entity, and late in 2005 the Cape Cod Water Protection Collaborative was formed. Consisting of representatives of the towns and region, the collaborative is working on finding funding sources for wastewater infrastructure as well as exploring management solutions, especially as they relate to watersheds shared among towns.

In 2006 the BRT released another call to action. This statement focused on growth management, and one of its recommendations was a review of the Cape Cod Commission to foster better land use planning. In response, the Barnstable County commissioners appointed a twenty-first-century task force to examine how the commission can be more effective, help implement local comprehensive plans, and better reconcile regional and local needs. The task force recommended a number of changes. Among these were proposals to increase use of growth incentive zones and development agreements to promote development in some areas and to limit and streamline DRI reviews in places where growth should be accommodated. The commission is developing a regional land use vision map to designate these areas. Many in the public have seen the task force as representing the voice of the business community, which generally favors easier development approvals, although the task force actually represents a broad cross-section of civic interests.

MEASURING SUCCESS

The commission and APCC have been most successful through the regulation
of DRIs, though these involve only 15–20 percent of the Cape's development.
Through DRI requirements, 2,200 acres of open space have been permanently protected; 108 affordable housing units were built, seventeen as ownership units and
ninety-one as rental units; and $6.7 million has been spent on traffic mitigation
and projects designed to protect resources. Other areas of success include natural
resource protection and planning, education and citizen involvement, technical
assistance, and wildlife habitat management. The commission has been moderately successful at the following:

- Downtown revitalization. In growth incentive zones, where towns conduct
  advance planning, the commission can waive most of its development review,
  thereby streamlining the process.
- Affordable housing. There is more, but not enough. As elsewhere in the
  country, it is very difficult for government to bring about affordable housing
  where market forces are working in the opposite direction. Barnstable County
  has not found the formula for success in this area, but it remains a priority.
- Transit services, which include a summer shuttle. More ambitious ideas for
  transit have run up against the generally low density and decentralized nature
  of development on the Cape, making it difficult to generate the volume of
  ridership necessary to justify the costs of new transit infrastructure.
- Wastewater planning. Despite progress in planning with towns, wastewater
  remains one of the greatest challenges for Cape Cod. The extensive reliance on
  septic systems, and the enormous cost of converting these systems to
  centralized sewer systems, has meant that nutrients from septic effluent
  continue to degrade many wetlands, ponds, marshes, and bays.

It is important that the commission and APCC recognize where they have not
been successful or where successes have fallen short of expectation. These areas
include the following:

- Influencing local comprehensive plans and zoning. Ten of fifteen
  municipalities have been certified as consistent with the regional plan, but
  serious changes to zoning to implement those plans remain a challenge. Much
  zoning on the Cape has not been changed since before the plan went into
  effect. Rapid growth in the last three decades coupled to the difficulty of
  changing zoning (a two-thirds vote is required at town meeting) has meant
  that smart growth tools, such as cluster development and transfer of
  development rights (TDR), either were not enacted by towns or were enacted
  too late to have an impact on redirecting growth to appropriate areas. Existing
  cluster bylaws have often been ineffective because most new residential
  subdivisions are smaller than the minimum acreage thresholds under these
  by-laws and because developers increasingly choose to build under traditional
  standards.

- Adopting transfer of development rights programs. Only two towns have TDR by-laws, but the structure of the bylaws coupled to the lack of receiving areas with sufficient infrastructure to accept denser growth, and the lack of enough open space to serve as sending areas of development rights, have frustrated these programs. The major challenges are to establish sending and receiving areas, a means of valuing credits, and a mechanism (such as a credit bank) for administering transactions.
- Wastewater management. More than 85 percent of the Cape relies on on-site septic systems. As noted, huge investments are needed to convert these to centralized treatment.
- Impact fees. So far, no towns have adopted impact fees, largely because the state has no experience with impact fees (they are not allowed except under the Cape Cod Commission Act or home-rule petition) and because of restrictive case law.
- Residential development. With relatively weak zoning enabling laws, powerful property entitlements for landowners, lack of centralized wastewater infrastructure, and fragmented municipal government structure, it is very difficult to make meaningful changes to zoning necessary to control the amount, nature, and pattern of residential sprawl.

The commission is acutely aware of these issues. There is a broad consensus that the commission should protect natural resources, scenic values, and quality of life on the Cape while also promoting a strong and sustainable economy. But there is substantial pressure on the commission both from the public, many of whom believe the commission has not done enough to prevent overdevelopment of the Cape, and from the business community, which argues the commission's reviews often discourage healthy economic activity.

Recognizing the admittedly daunting challenges Cape Cod faces today, the commission is focused on the following:

- Promoting changes in local zoning to bring about center-based development, using smart growth zoning in downtown areas and downzoning in outlying areas
- Changing regional policies of the plan to encourage center-based development and other smart growth policies
- Expanding transit facilities
- Bringing about affordable and workforce housing
- Building regional wastewater systems, especially in polluted areas, to replace antiquated septic system approaches to health and land use controls
- Improving relationships with towns and the business community to make the commission more effective in achieving its mission

APCC and the BRT will continue advocating for managed growth by finding ways to encourage housing in town centers and deter growth from critical resource lands. At the end of the day, compact development provides housing options, creates vibrant town centers, protects natural resources, limits traffic congestion, and reduces the costs of provision of infrastructure.

PART II

COLLABORATIVE
AND VOLUNTARY
PLANNING INITIATIVES

CHAPTER 11

INTEGRATED PLANNING FOR A SUSTAINABLE FUTURE IN PUGET SOUND

Robert Drewel

I have lived in the central Puget Sound region nearly all my life. I graduated from the University of Washington in 1970 around the time of the "Boeing Bust," when a billboard famously asked, "Would the last person who leaves Seattle please turn out the lights?" But most people stayed, and more came, in large part because of the region's spectacular setting, quality of life, and growing economic opportunities. Tall evergreens, amazing views of the Cascade and Olympic mountains, abundant lakes, rivers and streams, and Puget Sound itself are part of daily life here. Parks, trails, and other green spaces within the metropolitan area are close by, and the region is a jumping-off point for exploring the wilderness.

The shared values of enjoying and sustaining the natural environment and the livability of our communities are central to the planning mission of the Puget Sound Regional Council. As our region has grown and changed, people have looked for ways to preserve what makes this region special. Regional planning has provided local communities with a flexible framework for working toward a common vision for the future.

A central theme in our regional growth planning efforts is the integration of environmental, economic, transportation, and land use planning, and the important nexus among these issues. The regional vision centers on sustainability, linking planning for growth management, economic development, environmental health, efficient transportation systems, and education, arts, and culture. We recognize that to address climate change, remain globally competitive, and preserve what makes central Puget Sound such a great place to live, we need to work together as a region and develop holistic solutions. The old fights—"roads versus transit" or "suburbs versus central city" or "economy versus environment"—are increasingly irrelevant as our region's public and private leaders collaborate on the best ways to move into the future.

Growth—past, present, and future—is the primary force driving our efforts to plan regionally. Lots of people have moved to central Puget Sound in the past four decades, attracted by job opportunities and quality of life. Between 1970 and 2000, the region grew by more than 1.3 million people. The region grew at a particularly rapid pace during the 1980s, adding more than 500,000 people—about 2.1 percent a year. The region's jobs base more than doubled during that same period, rising from about 760,000 to 1.9 million. Over the last decade, our population grew by another 430,000, at a rate 30 percent faster than the national average. By 2040 the region is expected to gain an additional 1.3 million people and 1.1 million more jobs.

The most obvious effect of this growth has been traffic congestion and a growing urban footprint. For decades, land use policies and unplanned development spread housing and jobs farther apart. The number of vehicle miles traveled increased nearly three times faster than population between 1980 and 1992. Vehicle miles are now growing at about the same rate as population and job growth. However, with significant growth of people and employment anticipated through 2040, travel demand is forecast to increase another 40 percent by 2040.

The region's environment has been affected by growth. While vast new wilderness areas have been created in our federal forests and the management of working forests has improved, many other forests and farms have been lost to development. Water quality and the health of the Puget Sound ecosystem have been degraded. While most point-source pollution has been capped, stormwater runoff remains a significant concern. The region's abundant rainfall runs off roofs, roads, parking lots, and farms, collecting pollution along the way, which ends up in the rivers and streams that flow into Puget Sound. As we plan for the additional growth that is coming, the region is working to address these environmental impacts through a comprehensive strategy that incorporates planning for the economy, housing, transportation, land use, and air and water quality.

Regional Planning Responds to Growth

Building on a solid tradition of regional planning dating from the late 1950s, the region's jurisdictions created the Puget Sound Regional Council (PSRC) through an interlocal agreement in 1991. Also at that time, local leadership adopted VISION 2020: Growth and Transportation Strategy for the Central Puget Sound Region. VISION 2020 represented one of the first national examples of a coordinated regional strategy to address land use and transportation.

PSRC's members include seventy-one of the region's cities and towns, the four counties, tribes, the ports, and state agencies such as the Washington State Department of Transportation and Transportation Commission. The agency is the designated metropolitan planning organization (MPO) for the region. From its origins, PSRC has been charged with specific responsibilities under federal and state law for transportation planning, economic development, and growth management, serving as a forum for local governments and transportation agencies to plan for the future of the region. PSRC's primary decision-making body is its general assembly, composed of the elected officials from the member jurisdictions. PSRC also relies on an executive board of local elected leadership to oversee routine functions and policy boards that focus on growth management and transportation. PSRC, therefore, is very much an agency of and by its member municipalities and counties—not an independent body operating over our counties, towns, and cities.

The theme of better managing growth emerged in new state legislation, the Growth Management Act, enacted in 1990, that responded to public concerns about the effects of rapid growth and development. The growth management law requires local governments in fast-growing and densely populated areas to develop and adopt comprehensive plans. It also requires multicounty planning policies for the region's four counties and their cities. Local governments have agreed to use the Puget Sound Regional Council to develop and adopt these planning policies.

VISION 2020 was updated in 1995. The new regional growth, transportation, and economic strategy responded to requirements of the Growth Management Act and called for focusing new population and employment into urban areas, creating vibrant centers, and connecting centers with an efficient transportation network. The Puget Sound Regional Council also adopted a regional transportation plan, Destination 2030, which called for a coordinated, multimodal transportation system to support the growth vision.

Together, these efforts have set the stage in recent years for PSRC to work with local governments, business, labor, civic, and environmental interests and individuals to develop a common vision for the region's future, expressed through three integrated planning efforts: VISION 2040, the region's growth vision; Transportation 2040, the region's long-range transportation plan; and the Prosperity Partnership, which develops and advances the regional economic strategy.

VISION 2040

In April 2008, the region's leadership overwhelmingly adopted VISION 2040 as the new long-range growth management, economic, environmental, and transportation strategy for central Puget Sound. It provides specific guidance on how the region can accommodate an additional 1.3 million people and 1.1 million new jobs by the year 2040 while enhancing the region's environment and overall quality of life.

Through VISION 2040, the region has established new, stronger policies to direct future housing growth to designated urban growth areas (93 percent of total growth) and decrease the amount of growth in the region's rural areas (7 percent of total growth). Additionally, VISION 2040 encourages more growth to be directed to cities that contain one or more regionally designated growth centers and other strategic locations that are well served by existing and planned transportation infrastructure. Approximately 16 percent of the region is within the urban growth area, 1,000 square miles out of 6,300 square miles. The land outside the urban growth area is designated as rural or natural resource (including agricultural, mining resource, forest, and publicly owned forest and natural areas).

VISION 2040 is expressly based on the premise that the region's economic, environmental, and quality of life goals can—indeed, can only—be achieved in concert:

> The central Puget Sound region's surroundings create stunning backdrops for our cities and towns, contribute to our economic prosperity and quality of life and lend themselves to many recreation activities. . . . The way land is developed affects air and water quality, the climate, the natural environment, and human health. Development patterns and the siting of infrastructure have an impact on the character of communities as well as the natural environment.

VISION 2040 takes a bold and innovative approach by weaving the concept of environmental sustainability into land use, economic, and transportation policies. It has four parts: the environmental framework, the regional growth strategy, multicounty planning policies, and implementation actions.

The environmental framework provides the context for planning, development and environmental management in the region. The organizing goal of VISION 2040 is to meet the needs of the present without compromising the ability of future generations to meet their needs.

The regional growth strategy promotes sustainable development, providing specific guidance to achieve a development pattern with fewer environmental impacts and a more compact urban form. The growth strategy provides numeric guidance for distributing population and job growth to seven types of regional geographies that play distinct roles in the region's future:

- Metropolitan cities (five cities—3 percent of the region's land area) and core cities (fourteen cities—3 percent of the region) include cities that together contain more than two dozen designated regional growth centers. The regional centers are intended to attract residents and businesses because they include services and jobs, a variety of housing types, access to regional amenities, high quality transit service, and other quality of life features.
- Larger cities (thirteen cities—2 percent of the region) are larger suburban cities that have a significant amount of population and employment. Centers within these cities will be locations of redevelopment and increased activity as they become more secondary job centers.
- Small cities (fifty-one cities—2.5 percent of the region) are subdivided into three types to reflect the wide variety of smaller cities and towns throughout the region. City and town centers within these cities will support development and services at intensities appropriate to smaller municipalities.
- Unincorporated urban growth areas (4.5 percent of the region) capture a wide variety of urban lands, both lightly and heavily developed. Future growth in

these areas would be prioritized in areas that are affiliated for annexation into nearby cities.

- Rural areas and natural resource lands (84 percent of the region) describe the different types of unincorporated areas outside the urban growth area and include very low-density housing, working landscapes, and open space. Minimal growth is planned for these areas.

The regional growth strategy calls for directing the majority of growth to the metropolitan and core cities to help relieve development pressure on rural and natural resource lands. The regional growth strategy does not anticipate significant expansion of currently designated urban areas. The great majority of growth will be accommodated through infill and redevelopment of already urban areas.

Multicounty planning policies, adopted under the state's growth management act, address six major topics: environment, development patterns, housing, economy, transportation, and public services. The multicounty planning policies help cities achieve consistency on regional planning matters and guide a number of PSRC's processes related to certifying plans and approving federal funding for transportation projects. In general, central Puget Sound has a local, bottoms-up approach to achieving regional goals, through which cities can tailor their local comprehensive plans to meet their own unique goals and desires while also meeting the requirements of state growth management law and regional policies.

Finally, VISION 2040 includes a section on implementation, which describes actions to achieve the multicounty planning policies, as well as a monitoring program to track progress. Most of the actions to achieve VISION 2040 will occur at the local level. Zoning, development regulations, and other tools to shape how our communities function are managed by cities and counties, which make decisions informed by their local comprehensive plans. As noted previously, these local plans must be consistent with VISION 2040; one of PSRC's responsibilities is to review and certify city, county, and transit agency plans for consistency. This certification is required for jurisdictions to receive federal transportation funding managed by PSRC.

Transportation 2040

An essential component of realizing VISION 2040 is developing an effective and environmentally sound transportation system. In our recent update of the regional transportation plan, called Transportation 2040, we asked the question: How can the region best provide the mobility required to support a growing population to the year 2040, sustain the region's environment and economic vitality, improve system safety and efficiency, and enhance the region's overall quality of life?

Based on extensive public outreach and input, PSRC developed a set of future scenarios or alternatives representing different mixes of transportation projects, all of which were run through computer models to see how they performed in terms of congestion relief, air quality, travel time, and other measures. Concerns about climate change and energy use are influencing thinking about transportation.

In 2007 the Washington state legislature enacted policies to reduce greenhouse gas emissions and vehicle miles traveled. The Transportation 2040 alternatives considered how those policies might best be addressed. We also looked at ways to better manage the system using technology and active traffic management techniques successful in other parts of the world, and researched how tolling could affect traffic congestion and the region's ability to fund needed transportation infrastructure. A profound challenge as we developed the plan was to propose an innovative, sustainable financing plan given the uncertainty about traditional transportation revenue sources such as the gas tax.

The final Transportation 2040 plan, adopted in May 2010, directly supports the land use, environmental and economic policies in VISION 2040, and serves as the basis for prioritizing the federal funding available through the Puget Sound Regional Council, about $160 million a year on average. All projects receiving federal funding must be reviewed and found consistent with the regional transportation plan to proceed.

PROSPERITY PARTNERSHIP AND THE REGIONAL ECONOMIC STRATEGY

Central Puget Sound is home to internationally known business innovators such as Boeing, Microsoft, Starbucks, Amazon, Costco, and Nordstrom. Growing numbers of technology companies such as Google and Adobe have moved in. Biotech and clean technology companies are thriving. Realizing that our economic health is not assured, however, the Puget Sound Regional Council helped launch the Prosperity Partnership in 2004. The partnership is a growing coalition of over 300 government, business, labor, and community organizations advancing a regional economic strategy.

The Prosperity Partnership is working on two fronts. A series of foundation initiatives support the fundamentals of the regional knowledge-based economy, including education, technology commercialization, new and small business support, reforming the tax structure, transportation, social capital, and quality of life. For example, the Prosperity Partnership has worked to increase the production of bachelor's degrees in high-demand fields such as computer science, engineering, and health care. The partnership also helped lead a regional coalition that successfully secured $12.9 billion in new state funding to meet priority transportation needs.

Secondly, the Prosperity Partnership is focusing on growing seven important industry clusters: aerospace, clean technology, information technology, life sciences, logistics and international trade, military, and tourism. For each cluster, the Prosperity Partnership brings together a diverse group of key stakeholders to develop tangible actions that will improve the business climate for these clusters. This process includes collecting and analyzing economic data, convening working groups, and developing recommendations from the groups that indicate specific steps, timelines, and implementation responsibility.

Progress So Far

There are many indicators that we are moving in the right direction.

Land Use and Development

Large and small cities are developing or enhancing their downtown and commercial areas with an emphasis on mixing housing, employment, shopping, and transit in centers to create walkable, active communities. An increasing share of new housing is being built in designated urban growth areas, up from 77 percent in 1995 to 88 percent in 2006. Of the new residential growth that occurred within the urban growth area since 1995, roughly half of it was absorbed by communities in the urban core well served by existing public facilities and services.

The region's five metropolitan cities—Seattle, Bellevue, Tacoma, Everett, and Bremerton—are strong and vibrant. These five cities are continuing to grow, adding more than 80,000 people between 2000 and 2010. Since 2000, the share of the permitted new housing units in the region's twenty-seven designated regional growth centers has continued to increase: 14 percent of total regional permitted housing units have been in centers, which represent only 3 percent of the land in the urban growth area. While these trends show substantial progress, the continued growth we face will require a redoubling of efforts to ensure we achieve the VISION 2040 growth strategy.

Transportation

Sound Transit, the regional transit authority for the urban portions of King, Pierce, and Snohomish counties created in 1996, is building and operating an extensive network of regional express bus routes and light rail and commuter rail systems in the most congested parts of the region. Rail and transit stations are providing the catalyst for many communities to promote economic development and housing around stations. A major new 15.6-mile light rail corridor links Sea-Tac International Airport with downtown Seattle while also providing service to several major urban centers in between. A second phase of the Sound Transit system approved by voters in 2007 will invest an estimated $17.2 billion in expanded regional express bus, light rail, and commuter rail services. In recent years, voters have also approved other measures in Seattle (Bridging the Gap), King County (Transit Now), and Snohomish County (Swift) to fund transportation improvements. State funding will provide a total of $7.6 billion (year of expenditure dollars) in new revenues for investment in the region's highway system., making travel safer and faster for people and freight.

Economic Development

The Prosperity Partnership has helped the region support sustainable economic development through a variety of cluster-based and foundational initiatives. For example, the partnership successfully led a statewide coalition that codified state policy goals for access to an additional 10,000 high-demand bachelor's degrees per year by 2020 and secured $90 million for 2,000 additional degrees starting in 2008. The Prosperity Partnership also helped form two statewide trade associations—the Aerospace Futures Alliance and the Washington Clean Technology Alliance—and has been one of the key drivers in creating Global Health Nexus Seattle, a new nonprofit organization focused on branding the central Puget Sound region as the epicenter of global health discovery, delivery, and development.

Environment

In the last two decades, the central Puget Sound region's commitment to environmental health and conservation has been expressed through a number of successful public and private efforts:

- In Tacoma twelve miles of Commencement Bay were declared a Superfund site in the early 1980s. After many years of cleanup, the city's waterfront along the Thea Foss Waterway has become the center of the downtown revival.
- The Cascade Land Conservancy has worked with public and private landowners to conserve over 120,000 acres of forests, farms, and open space in the region.
- Since 1990 the Mountains to Sound Greenway has successfully conserved a greenway along 100 miles of Interstate 90 reaching from Seattle to Central Washington—encompassing over 750,000 acres of open space, historic towns, and working farms.
- In 2007 the governor and state senate leaders established state goals for greenhouse gas reductions.
- Washington is also the first state to phase out the use of toxic chemicals known as PBDEs, which can harm human neurodevelopment and are responsible for depleting marine wildlife populations in Puget Sound.

Those are just a few examples of the work being done to achieve regional environmental goals. Many other activities by cities, counties, and community groups, including stream restoration, new walking trails, farmers' markets, and many others, are improving the region's environmental health and quality of life for people who live here.

CONCLUSION

More of us are living in urban places. It is estimated that half the world's population is now living in cities, and that trend is expected to continue. The Brookings Institution's Blueprint for American Prosperity has called attention to the economic importance of metropolitan regions, noting that the central Puget Sound region is one of 100 metropolitan areas that together are responsible for 75 percent of the nation's gross domestic product. These same regions hold the bulk of the primary assets of the nation's economy: human capital, innovation, quality places, and infrastructure. It is important that federal policy should support and nurture the essential role metropolitan areas play in the U.S. economy.

The challenge facing central Puget Sound and other metropolitan regions is to plan appropriately for our future, so in ten, twenty, or one hundred years, people will be living in places with clean air and water, open spaces, quality schools, and good jobs to go to. Streets will be safe, arts and culture will abound, and we will have options for how to get around. In central Puget Sound, we recognize that the only way to accomplish our regional vision for our people, our prosperity, and our planet is to work together, harnessing the incredible talents, energy, and resources from our smallest towns and biggest cities. We believe that to be a successful region for the long term, land use, economic, and transportation decisions must be integrated in a manner that supports a healthy environment, addresses global climate change, achieves social equity, and is attentive to the needs of future generations.

CHAPTER 12

INTEGRATED LAND USE, TRANSPORTATION, AND AIR QUALITY PLANNING IN SACRAMENTO

Mike McKeever

The Sacramento Area Council of Governments (SACOG) is the body through which the region's twenty-two cities and six counties work collaboratively to plan the future transportation and land use patterns for the region. Under federal law, SACOG is the designated metropolitan planning organization (MPO) for the region. Every four years it prepares a long-range metropolitan transportation plan that, among other things, must comply with the Federal Clean Air Act. SACOG is responsible under state law for planning to meet the region's housing needs. In addition to its federal and state statutory responsibilities, SACOG is a voluntary association of cities and counties whose activities may be expanded as its members' needs dictate. SACOG's thirty-one member governing board includes at least one elected representative from each of its twenty-eight local government members. While SACOG carries out integrated land use, transportation, and housing planning for the entire region, it does not mandate compliance with its regional land use vision, titled the Blueprint. Instead, the Blueprint represents a consensus among its members based on their recognition that they share common challenges and will succeed through common strategies. This chapter describes SACOG's Blueprint growth strategy, the land use planning principles that underpin the Blueprint, and several land use, transportation, and air quality metrics that measure the plan's performance.

The Blueprint is a strategy to guide growth through the year 2050 adopted by the SACOG board in December 2004. Immediately after adopting a metropolitan transportation plan in 2002, the board initiated the Blueprint project to determine whether traffic congestion, air quality, and overall quality of life could be improved in the Sacramento region through changing the current pattern of development. The process was designed to combine the best technical information with a comprehensive, bottom-up citizen and stakeholder engagement process to determine the region's preferred future growth pattern. SACOG designed the process to produce a vision for the region that had sufficient technical grounding and political support to serve as the basis for SACOG's next metropolitan transportation plan and, more broadly, to shape the region's future.

The Sacramento region is comprised of six counties (Sacramento, Placer, El Dorado, Yolo, Yuba, and Sutter) and twenty-two cities. Over the past fifteen years the region has grown very fast. Until the last few years much of the growth had been in a pattern typical of most metropolitan areas in the country: lower density and spread out, creating an imbalance of jobs and houses within the major subareas of the region. Larger lot subdivisions, farther and farther away from the region's employment centers, dominated the housing market, with retail centers and professional service jobs eventually following. Growth in primary, or base sector jobs, has been dominated by government and other service sector employment.

The adopted Blueprint is comprised of a map that shows where different types of growth should occur (e.g., housing, employment centers, retail, etc.) through 2050 and seven growth principles:

- Housing choice and diversity
- Use of existing assets
- Compact development
- Natural resources conservation
- Quality design
- Mixed use development
- Transportation choices

The map and growth principles set out a strategy for managing a projected increase of nearly 2 million people, 1 million jobs, and 840,000 housing units. The long-term 2050 time frame was selected purposely to stretch beyond the typical twenty- to twenty-five-year planning horizons of existing land use and transportation plans.

MAJOR FEATURES OF BLUEPRINT GROWTH STRATEGY
Housing Choice and Diversity

The Blueprint changes the mix of future housing products significantly compared to trend (base case) conditions in the region. In 2004 detached single lots from 5,500 square feet to several acres in size represented 68 percent of the existing housing stock and 80 percent of the new housing being constructed. The Blueprint calls for only 31 percent of the new residential units to be built in this larger lot, format with nearly seven out ten in an attached format (townhouses, row houses, condominiums, or apartments) or small lot (e.g., 3,000 to 4,000 square foot lots with detached units) format.

The project conducted market research on homebuyer and renter preferences that showed a strong interest in the higher density products, particularly when placed in a setting that reduced driving distances to jobs and services. The market interest was particularly strong among households fifty-five and older, with two-thirds of people in this category stating a preference for small lot or attached products for their next residential move. This is important because the project's demographic research projected that two-thirds of the growth in households in the region through 2050 would be people in this fifty-five and older category, with only 21 percent of the growth in households with children. By 2007, the third year of Blueprint implementation, 68 percent of new housing starts were small lot single family or attached, a dramatic change from the trend line in 2004. A full 96 percent of new for sale residential lots in developments five lots or greater were small lot single family or attached.

The Blueprint will create much greater housing product choice for consumers. Many will still want a traditional product. Although these will constitute a much smaller share of new construction, such homes will be added to the very substantial existing inventory of larger lot single family homes. The density of the new housing will be on average approximately three times higher than the base case densities. Since housing is the land use that consumes the most land, the density of new development is critical in shaping the landscape. Low density residential subdivisions stretch the urban footprint farther and farther, creating challenges for the region's transportation system and other infrastructure.

Use of Existing Assets

The SACOG region is blessed with an abundant supply of flat land. In 2004 virtually no growth was occurring through redevelopment (i.e., more intense development on parcels with existing buildings that are either in disrepair or have a market value below the value of the land). SACOG used the simplified economic pro forma feature of the I-PLACE³S (Planning for Community Economic, Environmental and Energy Sustainability) software to estimate the redevelopment potential for downtowns and transportation corridors throughout the region. The analysis showed there is a great deal of land ripe and appropriate for redevelopment. The Blueprint scenario relies on redevelopment of existing built parcels for 13 percent of the housing growth (109,000 units) and 10 percent of the employment growth (100,000) jobs. The Blueprint also relies on infill (i.e., new buildings on existing, vacant lots) for a substantial portion of future growth. Approximately four out of ten new jobs (400,000) and housing units (320,000) occur within walking distance of fifteen-minute or shorter transit service during the peak afternoon and evening commute hours.

Compact Development

The result of the higher density housing products and aggressive utilization of redevelopment and infill opportunities is a growth pattern that uses land much more efficiently. The base case scenario requires 661 square miles of land for new urban development through 2050, while the Blueprint requires only 304 square miles for the same amount of growth in population, housing, and jobs—a reduction of 357 square miles needed for future urbanization.

Natural Resources Conservation

The Blueprint's more compact future urban footprint creates the potential to preserve significant amounts of agricultural and natural resource lands in the future. While the Blueprint does not constitute a detailed open space, farmland, or natural resources management plan for the region, the 2050 maps for Blueprint and base case show that the Blueprint could reduce impacts as follows: 64 fewer square miles of agricultural land converted to urbanization, 31,300 fewer acres of significant resource lands (e.g., wetlands/vernal pool complexes, hardwood stands), and 36,000 fewer acres of development in floodplains.

Quality Design

The detailed design features of development determine its overall quality as well as some aspects of travel behavior. Variables such as the building's relationship to the street, setbacks, placement of garages, sidewalks, parking, landscaping, the aesthetics of building design, and the design of the public right-of-way (e.g., short block lengths, grid street pattern, connectivity) increase walking, biking, and transit use and reduce the length of auto trips. In 2050 only 34 percent of the people in the base case scenario would live in neighborhoods with good or excellent pedestrian features. Twice that many, 69 percent, would live in neighborhoods with these features in 2050 in the Blueprint scenario.

Mixed Use Development

The concept of mixing rather than segregating land uses has many manifestations, starting with locating jobs and housing near each other. The Sacramento region has three major employment centers, downtown Sacramento and two suburban centers. All three of them have far more jobs than nearby housing, an imbalance that the Blueprint strives to remedy with much more aggressive housing growth in these areas in the future. As a further sign of the fast implementation of the Blueprint, by 2008, 25,000 of the 40,000 new housing units projected near the Sacramento jobs center were either built, under construction, approved for development, or in the application stage.

Mixing land uses means more than the location of jobs and housing. Only 15 percent of all auto trips are commuter trips. Multiple worker households and other considerations mean that it will never be possible to have all workers living close to their jobs. Short connections to schools, shopping, services, parks, and other amenities are also important. The Blueprint focuses on the neighborhood scale by encouraging a mix of uses in both infill settings as well as in new, larger master planned communities. In the 2050 base case scenario, 26 percent of the people would live in areas with a good mix of housing, jobs, and other amenities, while in the Blueprint over twice that many people (53 percent) would live in these circumstances.

SACOG designed a transportation network to serve the Blueprint and base case growth patterns in 2050. The difference in travel performance was substantial. In the base case scenario, in 2050 vehicle miles traveled per household increased by 12 percent, while in the Blueprint scenario it decreased by 17 percent. Average daily travel time per household increased by 27 percent by 2050 in the base case and increased by only 5 percent in the Blueprint. The percentage of trips using transit was more than four times as high in the Blueprint (3.3 percent) compared to the base case (0.8 percent), and the percentage of walk or bike trips more than twice as high (12.9 percent) in the Blueprint than the base case (5.5 percent).

Other performance metrics were also favorable. Emissions of small particulates and greenhouse gases were 15 percent less in the Blueprint compared to the base case. Residential water demand is projected to be 33 percent less per household, largely due to smaller yards. The total cost of constructing infrastructure for water, transportation, sewer, flood control, drainage, and resource mitigation is $14 billion less through 2050 in the Blueprint compared to the base case.

Integrating Blueprint into the Metropolitan Transportation Plan

In 2008 the SACOG board adopted a new metropolitan transportation plan. The new MTP prioritized $42 billion in transportation investments through the year 2035. It was SACOG's first MTP to use a future land use pattern significantly influenced by the Blueprint growth principles, and a transportation investment portfolio purposely designed to serve a growth pattern that is more compact and has a stronger mix of land uses within the various neighborhoods and cities of the region.

Federal rules require that MPOs such as SACOG use a realistic land use pattern for their MTPs. In lay terms, the projected future land use pattern must represent what is most likely to be built, as opposed to a "visionary" pattern of what planners might prefer to be built. This meant that if Blueprint was to have a significant impact on the 2035 MTP, then SACOG must demonstrate that local governments were changing their policies and plans to encourage Blueprint style growth, and market performance must demonstrate that the growth pattern was shifting from base case to Blueprint. In a series of meetings with high-level staff at the Federal Highway Administration, the U.S. Environmental Protection Agency, and the California Air Resources Board, it was clear that there would be no latitude to claim air quality benefits unless SACOG could demonstrate these benefits were likely to occur. An active and constructive partnership with the Sacramento Air Quality Management District was essential to working out these issues. Also,

SACOG's commitment to extensive data collection, analysis, and state-of-the-art modeling tools was a critical component of persuading the federal oversight agencies that whatever travel and air emissions benefits SACOG claimed in the MTP from the Blueprint would be real and not illusory.

Since the 2002 MTP, SACOG staff embarked on a number of enhancements to its data and modeling capabilities. Most notably, staff developed parcel-level GIS data, including general plan and zoning designations, lot size, and ownership for all 800,000 parcels throughout the six-county region. For the first time SACOG used an integrated forecasting model, called MEPLAN. This land use/economic/ travel model uses economic costs, development policies (general plans), travel time, and household demographics to allocate future growth. The regional travel model, SACMET, was upgraded in a number of ways—most importantly, adding a postprocessing capacity called "4Ds." The 4Ds (density, diversity, design, and destination) are land use characteristics that influence travel behavior and are added to travel models to better understand the effects of smart growth land use design options on travel. The analysis uses elasticities, or percent change, to modify vehicle trips, vehicle miles traveled, and mode choices based on changes in the land use characteristics. During this same time period, the California Energy Commission contracted with a software development firm to create an Internet server-based processing and delivery system for the I-PLACE³S software. This system was an essential part of the project's success, enabling SACOG to use interactive planning technology in dozens of community meetings, as well as providing the kind of parcel-specific land use planning accuracy at a regional scale and real-time response speed.

I-PLACE³S, an Internet-accessed software program, is designed to achieve two primary objectives: provide sophisticated, objective technical information to illustrate the complex interrelationships between land use, transportation, and air quality issues; and provide that information in an easily understood and accessible format so that everyone—citizens, policy makers, stakeholders, and professional staff—can use it to develop informed opinions. SACOG improved and expanded I-PLACE³S to better serve the needs of regional and local decision making. The Blueprint process was designed to honor the simple precept that an involved and informed citizenry is an essential ingredient of a healthy democracy.

In the transition period between the end of the Blueprint process and the beginning of the 2035 MTP, SACOG committed to another round of enhancements to its data and models. Workshop capabilities were improved by embedding a somewhat simplified version of SACMET, the 2002 MTP regional travel model, into the I-PLACE³S software so that it could be used interactively to produce travel and land use information in minutes. This upgrade included the 4Ds land use sensitivities to better capture smart growth details. SACOG's overall analytical capacity was improved by shifting from the SACMET 4-step model to a new, activity-based regional travel model, SACSIM. Activity-based models are the next generation capability in regional travel modeling. These models analyze travel patterns in a fundamentally different manner than traditional four-step models. The four-step model segments travel into individual trips by purpose (home-based work, home-based shop, non–home-based, etc.). Activity-based models link trips into "tours" that begin and end at home or work depending on the list of activities associated with the tour. With this new approach the number and sequence of trips, the modes chosen, the time of day, and the total amount of travel time are internally consistent (less double counting of travel), which is not possible with four-step models. Also, SACOG built the SACSIM model to function at the parcel level to enhance the ability to capture the benefits of fine-grained smart growth planning options. Other activity-based models may still aggregate data into zones, sometimes several hundred acres each, causing data to be averaged within the zone, reducing resolution and accuracy. I-PLACE³S, with its parcel level land use planning capacity, is a perfect complement to SACSIM for detailed regional analysis outside of real-time workshop uses.

The net effect of the parcel specific I-PLACE³S and SACSIM modeling capabilities is like shining a bright light into a room that has been underlit; fine-grain relationships between specific land use choices and travel behavior are suddenly measurable. The prior models simply did not provide for sufficient detail to perform this level of analysis. SACOG's ability to understand the impacts and trade-offs between land use, transportation, and air quality choices improved dramatically because of these modeling tools.

In addition to the Blueprint growth pattern, the 2035 MTP has a different portfolio of transportation investments compared to previous plans. Leading the change is a 56 percent increase in bicycle and pedestrian investments and a 35 percent increase in smart growth programs. These new investments are made possible by reducing the demand for investment in options that serve only single occupant vehicles and allocating a larger share of flexible revenues to alternatives that meet the future set of mobility demands. The 2035 MTP also includes a 21 percent increase in transit funding and a 17 percent increase in road operations and maintenance funding to better optimize the existing system.

Increases in road capacity are also part of the 2008 MTP. Strategic road expansions include several carpool/bus lanes, largely in the inner areas of the region, and complete street grids that better serve local transit, bike, pedestrian, and auto travel. Through matching MTP investments with supportive Blueprint land uses and focusing on critical bottlenecks, congested vehicle miles of travel per household increase a modest 12 percent versus 60 percent projected in the last plan. By 2035 the projected vehicle miles of travel per household and air emissions are substantially lower than the prior MTP, while walk/bike and transit trips are substantially higher.

In 2006 California passed the Global Warming Solution Act, the toughest law in the nation for reducing greenhouse gas emissions. The state is still working out the details of how to reduce emissions to 1990 levels by 2020 and to 80 percent below 1990 levels by 2050. The California attorney general is already aggressively intervened with local governments, regional planning agencies, and developers to ensure that the greenhouse gas impacts of their plans are appropriately assessed and mitigated. The environmental impact report (EIR) prepared to address environmental effects of the 2008 MTP included a detailed analysis of greenhouse gas emissions through 2035. SACOG found that one benefit of the new land-use-focused 2008 MTP is that it is expected to reduce per capita greenhouse gas emissions by approximately 12 percent between 2008 and 2035 over the base case, and that CO_2 would be reduced by approximately one $MMTCO_2e$ compared to the prior MTP.

A few examples of SACOG's 2035 MTP investments that are targeted at creating synergies with the Blueprint growth strategy follow:

- Bridges. Downtown Sacramento, the employment center for the region, is surrounded the American and Sacramento Rivers. The Blueprint encourages more growth in the downtown, particularly housing, and in areas immediately across the rivers but otherwise adjacent to downtown. Two multimodal bridges, one over each river, will provide added connections and mobility to encourage this inward growth.

- Streetcars. Rail transit stimulates compact urban development by providing a viable option to the car and sending a signal to the private markets that the government is making long-term investments to promote growth in a particular area. Light-rail transit is an important part of the 2035 MTP, but lighter weight rail, commonly called streetcars, will be reintroduced to provide shorter-distance service. A starter streetcar line will be built to link inner West Sacramento and Sacramento across the Sacramento River, and a streetcar loop will be built to tie the region's second largest employment center in Rancho Cordova into the existing light rail line.

- Expanded bus service. While the plan expands the light rail system and reintroduces the streetcar, the largest increases in transit service miles come from enhanced local bus service and a significant expansion in the use of neighborhood shuttles.

- Complete streets. The plan focuses on multimodal road designs that promote transit, walking, biking, and smart growth land development along with auto mobility. The goal is not to eliminate the auto from the equation, but rather to ensure that all modes function well in the right-of-way.

- Targeted highway investments. While highways receive a declining share of funds in this plan, there are still important investments that improve traffic flow and reduce greenhouse gas emissions, including auxiliary lanes (particularly helpful in keeping delivery trucks off of local streets), interchange improvements, and expansion of the incomplete carpool/bus lane system.

Blueprint Implementation Strategies

SACOG, its member cities and counties, and its partners in the civic and private sectors are engaged in a variety of activities to help successfully implement the Blueprint.

- General plan updates. The fundamental document controlling future development patterns in each city and county is the general plan, which typically is updated every several years. Most cities and counties are integrating Blueprint growth projections and principles into their general plans as they move through their regular general plan update cycles. SACOG provides technical and sometimes financial assistance to support these efforts.
- Updated zoning codes. SACOG has prepared a form-based code handbook to help its members update their zoning codes to allow and encourage mixed use, higher density, pedestrian oriented development. A form-based code focuses on the function of an area rather than the uses and involves citizens in creating a more graphic-oriented and understandable code.
- Visual tools and citizen engagement. SACOG provides grants to its members who are preparing area, neighborhood, specific, or corridor plans and choose to use Blueprint style, information based, interactive citizen engagement processes. SACOG is also adding to its toolkit of modeling and graphic tools to support this planning, including 3D imagery with the land use modeling software, a series of visual before-and-after simulations to illustration how areas transform over time with Blueprint principles, and a large library of photos illustrating a variety of different Blueprint techniques suitable in various conditions around the region.
- Redevelopment districts. The primary redevelopment agency for Sacramento city and county is focusing on promoting transit oriented development around light rail stops. It established a new redevelopment district around one station and is dedicating funds generated through tax increment financing to infrastructure improvements that support higher density, mixed use development.
- Transportation funds for Blueprint growth. The 2035 MTP includes nearly $750 million of transportation funds to support Blueprint style growth through 2035. A competition is held approximately every eighteen months to solicit the best projects in the region that can leverage these funds for transportation infrastructure improvements like parking garages, street connectivity, and complete streets that will stimulate Blueprint growth.
- Rural-urban connections strategy. In January 2008 the SACOG board launched a major new project focused on promoting economic vitality in the rural areas of the region and helping people in the urban and rural areas to better understand how their interests are interconnected. The project includes many activities, including the following:
  - Enhancing the I-PLACE³S computer model to address the economic and other impacts of a variety of agricultural uses and rural development models.
  - Developing software to assist small cities and rural counties to analyze the economic impacts to their jurisdictions of different growth patterns (i.e., housing or jobs focused growth versus a balance of uses, higher density versus lower density growth patterns, faster versus slower growth rates).

- Researching the potential to improve the percentage of food produced locally that is consumed within the region and assessing the pros and cons of encouraging this.
- Assisting local governments to complete habitat conservation plans and other natural resource plans that are designed to sort out trade-offs between development and environmental protection on a larger subregional scale instead of with individual development projects.
- Determining what transportation investments are necessary in rural areas to support the needs of agriculture.

SUCCESSES AND CHALLENGES OF BLUEPRINT IMPLEMENTATION TO DATE

The first three and a half years of the fifty-year Blueprint growth strategy have, by and large, been very successful. As mentioned earlier, the product mix for the new housing stock has changed dramatically, with a much stronger emphasis on attached and small lot single family products. Significant infill and redevelopment is occurring in downtown Sacramento and West Sacramento as well as in many of the small, more suburban jurisdictions. Significant quantities of new housing are being built near the three largest employment centers in the region.

The most significant challenges are changing the growth patterns on the edge of the region from classic commuter bedroom growth to jobs-led growth that meets the needs of local residents. The rural-urban connections strategy is targeted at helping to address that challenge. The region also has significant natural resource issues in areas immediately adjacent to the existing urban footprint and targeted for greenfield growth in the Blueprint. The successful completion of the habitat conservation planning efforts will be important to avoid having growth pressures leapfrog over these areas to areas farther away from existing development.

Higher gas prices, rapidly changing demographics, increased public policy emphasis on reducing greenhouse gas emissions and other tailpipe pollutants, and the early market successes of Blueprint development projects all add to the momentum for Blueprint style growth in the future.

CHAPTER 13

ENVISION UTAH

BUILDING COMMUNITIES ON VALUES

Alan Matheson Jr.

Asked to describe the community we want for our children, most of us would paint a picture with common elements. We likely would want that community to provide good jobs; attainable housing; natural beauty and accessible recreational opportunities; safe, healthy, and active neighborhoods; a reasonable cost of living; strong schools; and evenings spent at the family dinner table rather than stuck in traffic. Although we generally know where we want our communities to be decades down the road, it is less clear how we get there. Utah tackled this problem in an innovative way, pioneering the process of regional visioning that today is guiding community form throughout the United States.

ENTER ENVISION UTAH

In the mid-1990s Utah faced unprecedented growth, and new worries emerged about how that growth would affect Utah's quality of life. The Governor's Office of Planning and Budget (GOPB) projected that the population of the Greater Wasatch Area (the ten counties around Salt Lake City) would grow from 1.6 million to 2.7 million by 2020, and to nearly 5 million by 2050. Residents worried about air quality, the tax burden imposed by multibillion-dollar water and transportation projects, increasing traffic congestion, housing that increasingly eluded the reach of many, development in beautiful mountain valleys treasured for recreation, and more.

Utah's conservative politics limited the options realistically available to address these challenges. Utahns strongly favor local control and have little appetite for regional government or increased regulation. They believe strongly in private property rights. In the early 1970s, voters soundly rejected a referendum to impose state land-use planning. Many openly resisted the notion of regional planning. The governor and the Utah legislature searched for ways to address the negative consequences of growth short of new legislation or regulation.

Under these circumstances, the model of a nonregulatory public/private partnership had appeal. The nonprofit Coalition for Utah's Future took the lead. Formed in 1987, the Coalition for Utah's Future had established its credibility in Utah as a community problem solver, having engaged diverse constituencies to work together, find common ground, and tackle long-term issues. Growth planning became the coalition's next target.

In 1995 the coalition formed the Quality Growth Steering Committee (QGSC), a special subcommittee to research the growth issue and make recommendations to the coalition's board on how to proceed. The QGSC, which included several prominent business leaders, GOPB, state legislators, urban planners, and local government officials, reached several conclusions:

- The coalition should undertake a regional visioning process that is ongoing, replicable, transparent, inclusive, and easy to update, with clear goals and established time tables.
- Residents must have an opportunity to be involved in a meaningful way in deciding how the Greater Wasatch Area should grow, and leaders should follow the public direction.
- The focus should be on finding practical solutions, not debating philosophies.
- The process must involve respected representatives of all key stakeholder groups, both public and private, who are willing to work toward a brighter future for all residents.
- The coalition should be an honest broker of real choices, presented through several alternative scenarios for future growth.
- Given good information, the collective public will make good decisions.
- The product should be a broadly supported vision of the region's preferred future.

To muster the community support needed for such an effort, the QGSC interviewed 200 community leaders to assess their level of support for a regional visioning effort. All but one agreed the effort was worthwhile and agreed to participate.

In 1995, at the recommendation of the coalition, Governor Mike Leavitt held a growth summit. The event was widely publicized by the media and well attended by members of the state legislature. The summit, which focused primarily on the "hot button" topics of open space preservation and transportation, was broadcast live on all local network affiliates. This served to raise awareness of growth issues and inspire public interest in finding solutions.

Building on momentum from the growth summit, the coalition worked with state agencies and legislators to obtain a $250,000 appropriation for GOPB to acquire Quality Growth Efficiency Tools—GIS data gathering and modeling tools to help the state better understand and project the implication of growth trends. In 1996 the coalition partnered with GOPB to build growth models and analytical tools.

Once a basic process had been defined, the coalition and the QGSC were ready to move forward with the formation of a public/private partnership. This partnership was officially launched in 1997 as "Envision Utah." Envision Utah's partnership involved all key stakeholders, including, by design, those originally skeptical of the effort. It included individuals of unquestioned credibility with power to effect change. All prospective members committed to share their expertise, leave their individual interests at the door, and reach consensus for the good of the community.

The geographical scope of Envision Utah initially encompassed the ten-county Greater Wasatch Area. This area includes ninety-four cities and towns and is home to 80 percent of Utah's population.

Leadership proved to be critical throughout the Envision Utah process. Robert Grow, the president and chief operating officer of Geneva Steel Company, became the first chair. He was succeeded by former U.S. ambassador to Singapore, Jon Huntsman Jr., who became Utah's governor in 2004 and later U.S. ambassador to China. These men, as well as the subsequent chairs, successfully negotiated the political shoals, calmed skepticism, and infused energy into an ambitious public process.

THE ENVISION UTAH PROCESS
A Foundation Built on Values

Quality of life cannot be advanced until it is defined. Therefore, as a foundational step, Envision Utah engaged Wirthlin Worldwide in 1997 to explore what residents value about living in Utah. Wirthlin had employed the technique of values analysis to help the world's major companies sell products. For the first time, they used the technique in Utah to help develop public policy. Detailed interviews and surveys of demographically representative residents led to an understanding of what people like and dislike about Utah and why. Envision Utah learned what residents want most out of life so it could plan a region that would satisfy those values. The values study also facilitated communication, allowing Envision Utah to speak to the public in terms of resonating values, not sterile policy. It helped diverse residents find common ground. Upon realizing that what they shared outweighed their differences, they worked together more constructively. The values research has guided all subsequent Envision Utah processes, materials, and workshops.

Scenario Planning

Another innovation pioneered by Envision Utah was using scenarios and public visioning to guide land-use planning. This approach allowed citizens to ask questions, explore options, and make informed choices as never before.

As a first step, Envision Utah created a baseline scenario—a projection of how the Greater Wasatch Area would grow if recent development trends continued through 2020. The baseline emerged from detailed technical analyses of critical trends, historic relationships, and local and national projections. Never in the state's history had a single entity attempted to gather and coordinate this quantity of information. More than 140 public and private entities contributed to its compilation. When the baseline was released in 1997, it served as a wake-up call to many Utahns. The results of "business as usual" clashed with the future they wanted. In particular, the public was shocked at the long-term costs of existing growth patterns. Recognizing that the current path led to a future inconsistent with their values, they were ready to explore alternatives.

Additional scenarios grew from ideas proposed by the public. At workshops, participants gathered in small groups around a map with people representing different interests and, through a "map game" exercise, collaborated to find agreement on development types and transportation routes. These exercises were small regional negotiations that required residents to open their minds, listen to differing perspectives, and find consensus. Their task was to solve a problem: how can the region best accommodate the projected future population in a way that maintains or enhances quality of life? There was no opportunity for pontificating; participants had to put themselves in the shoes of elected officials and find practical solutions to complex problems. Citizen-participants essentially built virtual futures with simple materials that realistically portrayed potential outcomes and highlighted the tradeoffs inherent in land-use decisions. Participants and sponsors described the process as enlightening and fun. Following the workshops, Envision Utah created computerized composites of the workshop maps that highlighted popular transportation routes, preferred land uses, and areas for development and land preservation. They posited interesting ideas and questions.

From the raw material of public input, Envision Utah developed three other scenarios, each presenting different ideas gleaned from the workshops and each exploring a distinct future development pattern. Using the Quality Growth Efficiency Tools, GOPB modeled the costs and benefits of each scenario twenty years into the future. The modeling showed how each scenario would perform relative to vehicle miles traveled, water consumption, land consumption, air quality, infrastructure costs, and other quality-of-life measures. The distinct impact of each projected growth pattern became clearer.

Quality Growth Strategy

In early 1999 Envision Utah undertook a massive effort to educate the public about the scenarios. The media provided extensive coverage. Nearly 600,000 residents received a four-page insert in their newspaper describing the scenarios and the modeling results. Through a mail-back survey, they identified preferred elements from the scenarios. Residents could also voice their preferences online or at one of fifty additional public meetings.

Nearly 20,000 residents voiced their preferences on how the region should grow, overwhelmingly choosing a scenario that included more walkable mixed-use neighborhoods and a robust public transportation system. The elements of that scenario formed the basis of Envision Utah's Quality Growth Strategy (QGS).

The QGS has six goals to protect the region's environment and advance its economic vitality and quality of life:

- Enhance air quality
- Increase mobility and transportation choices
- Preserve critical lands
- Conserve and maintain availability of water resources
- Provide housing opportunities for a range of family and income types
- Maximize efficiency in infrastructure investments

Thirty-two individual strategies support the QGS goals. A few examples of key strategies include the following:

- Promote pedestrian friendly/walkable communities
- Preserve critical land and open space through reuse, infill development, and conservation techniques
- Support the development of regional public transportation choices including bus, rail, and needed roads
- Create a network of bikeways and trails
- Foster development that supports transit by offering housing, work, shopping, and play near transit stops
- Encourage water conservation through conservation pricing, community education, and water efficiency

By design the QGS is not a master plan. It does not specify land uses on particular parcels. Such detail would have generated fierce opposition and threatened public support. Instead, the QGS touts principles in line with expressed public sentiment, generally directing new development into existing communities, favoring growth in the urbanized valleys and away from the agricultural mountain valleys in Summit County and Wasatch County. It contemplates contiguous expansion of existing communities and strongly discourages leapfrog development into surrounding rural areas. The QGS targets much new growth in mixed-use economic centers near areas of regional transportation significance. This pattern creates meaningful transportation and land use efficiencies and, importantly, is consistent with emerging and underserved market demand for greater convenience and affordability. By promoting fairly significant density increases in these relatively small geographical areas, the QGS expands housing choices and absorbs much of the region's growth while leaving existing neighborhoods largely unchanged.

The QGS has tangible benefits for the Greater Wasatch Area. For example, GOPB estimated that implementing the QGS over twenty years will, among other things, save $4.5 billion in future infrastructure costs and result in 171 fewer square miles of land being developed.

The QGS relies on local implementation and regional coordination. Without the force of law, the QGS will only be implemented to the extent local governments buy into the vision and adopt the necessary land-use ordinances. That support grows from the persuasive force of the modeled benefits and ongoing citizen involvement with local officials in land-use decisions.

IMPLEMENTING THE QUALITY GROWTH STRATEGY

Vision without implementation is hallucination. Envision Utah recognized that its success would be measured by on-the-ground results, not just a well-received plan. Consequently, Envision Utah worked to make the QGS the guiding tool for future development in the Greater Wasatch Area. Communities are built by elected officials, developers, lenders, and others operating in the market. To educate these key actors, Envision Utah created Urban Planning Tools for Quality Growth, a collection of model ordinances and ideas individual communities can draw upon to implement the QGS in a manner that makes sense locally. These tools echo the elements of early Utah communities, promoting close-knit neighborhoods, tree-lined streets, pedestrian-friendly walkways, and nature and farmland within reach of our cities. Subsequent "toolboxes" have focused on transit-oriented development, brownfield renewal, housing choices, regional and local economic development, and other topics. In addition, Envision Utah has held fourteen forums on topics such as workforce housing, local sales tax reform, street design, transfer-of-development rights, and transit-oriented development. In all, Envision Utah has trained over 3,000 local officials and developers in the use of these tools.

Ongoing public understanding and support is critical. Therefore, Envision Utah has conducted an annual media campaign addressing elements of the QGS. Local television and radio stations, as well as the print media, have assisted in sharing annual messages with the public. Envision Utah supplements this annual campaign with regular public presentations, community events, stories in the print and broadcast media, guest editorials, and educational materials addressing pressing growth issues and extolling the benefits of the QGS.

Beyond education, a good model is a powerful force for change. Therefore, Envision Utah, in tandem with the governor, created the Governor's Quality Growth Awards. Each year, Envision Utah selects projects from around the state that advance the QGS. Honorees receive the awards at an event hosted by the governor. The awards are publicized in the media and in booklets distributed to planners, developers, and cities throughout Utah. The projects honored to date demonstrate that Envision Utah's goals pass the critical test: success in the marketplace.

Most important, Envision Utah has facilitated over twenty subregional demonstration projects, each of which resulted in locally tailored approaches to advance the QGS. These projects have ranged in scale from neighborhoods to multicounty areas and generally follow the process used to create the QGS. Response from residents has consistently been enthusiastic as they gain a better understanding of the complex tradeoffs inherent in building a region and receive affirmation that their ideas matter.

For example, in 2004 the Utah Department of Transportation (UDOT) invited Envision Utah to serve as a neutral facilitator in developing growth scenarios for the Mountain View Corridor (MVC), a proposed second major highway connection between Salt Lake County and Utah County. The MVC project was perhaps the first process nationally to engage a state transportation agency and local communities in land-use planning as part of a National Environmental Policy Act review. Envision Utah ensured meaningful involvement from stakeholder groups and citizens of the affected cities. Ten jurisdictions, UDOT, and the Sierra Club signed the resulting agreement, which committed the jurisdictions to zone for more compact, mixed-use villages at proposed freeway interchanges and transit stops to enhance the viability of the proposed transportation corridor.

Building on the MVC experience, in 2005 Envision Utah initiated Wasatch Choices 2040, a partnership with the Wasatch Front Regional Council and the Mountainland Association of Governments, the state's two largest metropolitan planning organizations (MPOs), to explore how land use patterns could be changed to support a more efficient transportation system. Through public workshops, one thousand citizens in Weber, Davis, Salt Lake, and Utah Counties shared their opinions on future employment centers, roads, transit, and housing. Historically, transportation planners have gathered general plans from municipalities and built the transportation system around those plans. By contrast, Wasatch Choices 2040 explored new land-use patterns that would better coordinate with the transportation system and generated a set of growth principles agreed to by participants. A vision scenario provides a plausible illustration of how the region would grow if the growth principles were implemented. The vision results in 18 percent less congestion, 12 percent more transit use, and twenty-three fewer square miles of land consumption relative to the fully built-out 2030 long-range transportation plan. The MPOs have adopted the growth principles, thus institutionalizing them. The growth principles are the foundation and framework for developing performance criteria—such as environmental quality, economic growth, cost effectiveness, enhanced mobility, and safety—for new transportation projects.

In 2010 Envision Utah again partnered with the MPOs to refine the vision and secure its formal adoption by elected officials as the Wasatch Front's land-use and transportation goal. Now known as the Wasatch Choice for 2040, the vision serves as the foundation for the regional transportation plan and is the next evolutionary step in the QGS. With support from the U.S. Department of Housing and Urban Development (the Wasatch Front was one of only two regions nationally to receive the maximum initial livable communities grant), Envision Utah and other regional partners are working with municipalities, developers, and the financial community to implement the vision.

In addition to transportation, critical lands have also been a focus of Envision Utah's demonstration projects. The Great Salt Lake and its shorelands are an international flyway for millions of birds, but this treasure is threatened by encroaching development. Envision Utah facilitated three visioning efforts that encompassed most of the lake's eastern shoreline. Each plan identified natural areas to be protected and defined areas for parks, trails, and quality development. Community leaders continue to pass local ordinances and implement interlocal agreements in support of the plans. One resulting strategy for protecting the Great Salt Lake shorelands while respecting private property rights is transfer of development rights (TDR). With consulting help funded in part by Envision Utah, Davis County adopted a TDR ordinance. The new ordinance has not yet been put to extensive use.

Another example is Ogden Valley, which includes historic farms set in a critical watershed divided by clear mountain streams. Increasingly, it is a recreation destination with a growing system of trails, campgrounds, and ski resorts. Entitled development, however, will dramatically change the character of the valley. To respond to environmental, social, and economic concerns, Envision Utah helped facilitate a public process to determine how and where to accommodate the growth, and it introduced measures such as TDR. The Weber County Commission has adopted the recommendations as part of its general plan, including a fledgling TDR ordinance.

Envision Utah also took on the challenge of urban open space. The Jordan River, which divides the Salt Lake valley, has been neglected and in areas is quite degraded. On its journey from Utah Lake to the Great Salt Lake, the river flows through three counties and fifteen municipalities, dividing responsibility, which has hindered past efforts to revitalize the river corridor. Envision Utah involved 3,000 residents in creating the Jordan River Blueprint, a compelling vision for the future of the river corridor that emphasizes preserving natural areas, completing recreational facilities, and redeveloping blighted areas. With these marching orders, Envision Utah secured approval of the blueprint from nearly all jurisdictions along the river and guided creation of the Jordan River Commission, a new multi-jurisdictional authority charged with implementing the blueprint.

Envision Utah applied its efforts in a public-lands context in a project dubbed Wasatch Canyons Tomorrow. Rising majestically from the valley, the Wasatch Mountains provide much of Salt Lake City's water. They are the region's backyard; the place residents recreate and escape from the city. They are a significant economic generator. And they are under tremendous pressure from increased use. At the request of the governor, Envision Utah conducted a public education and survey process involving 16,000 people to assess what they value about the canyons and began gathering ideas for protecting those resources into the future. Wasatch Canyons Tomorrow generated a number of practical recommendations regarding future development, watershed protection, recreation, and transportation. Salt Lake County is using the recommendations to inform its update of the Wasatch Canyons Master Plan, and the transportation agencies have incorporated several of the transportation ideas into the regional transportation plan. These projects demonstrate that the Envision Utah process can effectively be adapted to address natural resource issues as well as urban development.

A strong central city is an important regional element. Salt Lake City's downtown is on the verge of a renaissance, with some $2 billion projected to be invested in the coming decade. In 2006, with a goal of shaping dozens of individual developments into a more cohesive visionary whole, the Salt Lake Chamber sponsored

Downtown Rising, a business-led public effort to explore the potential for Utah's capital city. The Salt Lake Chamber turned to Envision Utah to provide technical support, lead meetings, and conduct community visioning workshops and visual preference surveys. This effort identified six distinctive character districts that will continue to emerge and a number of individual signature projects—including a regional rail network, networks of parkways and trails, an international center, and university expansion—that will add immensely to the life and purpose of downtown.

In 2006 Envision Utah made its first foray off the Wasatch Front. One of the fastest growing regions in the country, Utah's Washington County wrestled with housing affordability, pressure on critical desert lands, water demand, transportation challenges, and a growing social divide over what to do about it. The Washington County Commission asked Envision Utah to help. Thus began Vision Dixie, an eighteen-month effort that included twenty-two public workshops, online surveys, a housing study, and community meetings featuring keypad polling that allows anonymous, real-time input from participants. More than 3,000 residents participated in the process, which resulted in a vision map and set of principles to guide future growth decisions. The county commissioners have adopted the principles and created a high-profile implementation committee to help local jurisdictions incorporate the principles into their plans and ordinances.

The success of Vision Dixie in a particularly conservative and less urban part of the state inspired several other rural Utah counties to ask Envision Utah for assistance with their growth challenges. In 2009 Envision Utah completed a regional vision for Morgan County, an emerald mountain valley under intense growth pressure. Envision Cache Valley—involving Cache County, Utah, and Franklin County, Idaho—was the first project to straddle a state line, reflecting the reality that regional issues are not constrained by political boundaries. Envision Cache Valley focused on solutions to preserving the valley's agricultural lands and heritage as the population doubles over the next thirty years. Encouraged by the results of Envision Cache Valley, the adjoining counties to the east—Bear Lake County, Idaho, and Rich County, Utah—engaged Envision Utah to undertake a similar project known as Bear Lake Valley Blueprint. Leaders are realizing that the Envision Utah approach to civic engagement can be just as successful in rural as in urban areas. Envision Utah is actively consulting with other states as they create their own versions of the organization.

DEALING WITH OPPOSITION

For an effort addressing broad regional issues that affect many people, Envision Utah has met with surprisingly little resistance. The general level of support can likely be attributed to four things: the strong effort to involve all stakeholders, including potential critics, early in the process; the focus on a long-term horizon (which tends to emphasize people's dreams and values), rather than on impending development decisions (which affect people's pocketbooks); the enthusiastic support of high-profile community leaders, gained through individual listening sessions; and the voluntary nature of the QGS.

There was some early skepticism from local elected officials, the Utah Association of Realtors, and a few in the media who perceived Envision Utah as the soft face of a hidden agenda to impose some form of regional government or growth restrictions. With time, it became clear that those fears were unfounded—Envision Utah has been the neutral facilitator that it professed to be—and that criticism has faded. In addition, a major homebuilder complained that Envision Utah was promoting housing types that wouldn't sell in the Utah market. In response, Envision Utah has organized a developers forum to facilitate conversation between developers and Envision Utah about market trends and challenges. That homebuilder has backed off its criticism, even asking Envision Utah for help, and is actively advertising the type of product it once said would not sell.

The Utah legislature has historically been dominated by rural interests, many of whom had a bias against planning. While not critical of Envision Utah, neither have they been particularly supportive. Envision Utah has addressed this situation by providing updates at legislative caucus meetings. In addition, some of Envision Utah's steering committee members have been elected to the legislature. Most important, the success of Envision Utah projects in rural counties has convinced rural legislators that the organization is relevant to their constituents. Recently, a committee chair who represents a rural district asked Envision Utah to share the Vision Dixie experience at a hearing and describe how it can serve as a model for other rural counties.

There remain some minor pockets of opposition. Periodically, there is a letter to the editor in the paper critical of Envision Utah. When warranted, Envision Utah responds with a public statement authored by a respected community leader. Otherwise, there is no overt public opposition to Envision Utah's work. Utah's mainstream media regularly support Envision Utah with enthusiastic articles and editorials.

The Impact of Envision Utah

As emphasized earlier, Envision Utah has no regulatory authority, and the QGS has no legal force. That raises an important question: can a regional vision that depends on voluntary actions by numerous local jurisdictions be successfully implemented in a state with a strong private property rights philosophy? Although the Envision Utah approach may not be the most effective path to change in all regions, in Utah it appears to be working.

Envision Utah's voluntary nature is a political necessity. Any more aggressive approach would have been widely opposed and lacked backing from key community leaders. The effort never would have taken flight. Beyond political expediency, the voluntary approach ultimately will be more effective than mandates. At the end of the day, no plan, regardless of its merits, will succeed without the support of the people. And the people generally will support only those plans in which they have ownership and perceive a personal benefit. Many well-intended regional planning efforts enforced by mandate are experiencing public backlash that divides the community and undermines worthy goals.

In Utah, by contrast, public support for the QGS appears to be growing. Research conducted by GOPB shows steady progress toward the QGS goals (e.g., increase in housing types and miles of transit available, and reduction in per capita vehicle miles traveled, average lot size, per capita water use, and land consumption). In marking progress on broad regional goals, causation is always an issue. It is difficult to determine how much of the change in the Greater Wasatch Region can be attributed to Envision Utah as opposed to other demographic, economic, or political forces. Nevertheless, there is widespread agreement in this region that Envision Utah has been instrumental in achieving positive change.

This is not to say that all Utah communities are equally onboard. While most jurisdictions have embraced the Envision Utah principles, some have not. Ignoring the impacts of growth, they cling to the development patterns of twenty years ago. Under a voluntary system, there will always be uneven results. Although the QGS will be implemented in some form, that form will be different from the idealized version on the original QGS maps. That, however, is preferable to the alternative: a mandated approach that would have been dead on arrival.

Envision Utah's effectiveness derives from the strong public voice and compelling technical analysis on which it is based. It also derives from strong partnerships. The governor, lieutenant governor, president of the senate, county mayor and many municipal mayors have served on the Envision Utah Steering Committee and support its efforts. The metropolitan planning organizations have partnered with Envision Utah to engage the public in developing our region's long-range transportation plan. Recognizing the tie between quality of life and economic development, the Salt Lake Chamber, Economic Development Corporation of Utah and other business leaders work closely with Envision Utah. Many environmental groups, such as the Nature Conservancy, promote Envision Utah and fund its projects (although some criticize Envision Utah for planning for growth rather than stopping it). Therefore, the QGS becomes a community goal, not an Envision Utah goal.

Beyond the examples described previously, Utah has accrued other benefits as a direct result of Envision Utah's regional visioning processes:

- Envision Utah worked directly with former Governor Mike Leavitt as he promoted the Quality Growth Act of 1999, which created a Quality Growth Commission, incentives for "quality growth communities," and state funding to preserve open space.
- In 2001 the Wasatch Front Regional Council, the Salt Lake area's metropolitan planning organization, released its draft long-range plan for 2030, with a heavy emphasis on roads. Envision Utah facilitated the formation of a committee, composed of transportation planners and mayors, to assess transit needs and recommend changes to the 2030 plan. The committee's revised plan increased

track miles from 150 to 291 and included the most aggressive bus rapid transit proposal in the country.

- Working behind the scenes, Envision Utah facilitated the purchase of 175 miles of existing railroad right-of-way for nine different potential transit corridors. This ensured the affordability of long-term transit expansion.
- A 2002 public awareness campaign that provided residents with information regarding the benefits of building out the public transportation system proved instrumental in the subsequent passage of a quarter-cent sales tax increase for the construction of the region's first light rail system. A similar measure had failed eight years earlier. Envision Utah is often credited with the turnaround.
- An independent University of Utah survey in 2003 indicated that 96 percent of local governments were aware of the QGS and that 97 percent were aware of Envision Utah's planning tools. Over 60 percent of local governments had incorporated elements of the QGS into their ordinances. More have followed since.
- Envision Utah developed iMPACS, a growth-cost model that allows developers and communities to quickly understand the costs and benefits of different development patterns and, therefore, make better land-use decisions.
- Envision Your Future, an educational package for grades five to twelve, correlates with core curricula and teaches students about the elements of community planning. It has been used successfully by more than 10,000 students.
- Envision Utah served as the only nonelected representative on the Wasatch Front Regional Council Executive Committee and was the driver behind WFRC's creation of the Regional Growth Committee, which promotes additional stakeholder involvement in long-range transportation planning.
- Kennecott Land Co., owner of half the remaining developable land in Salt Lake County, is developing 93,000 acres it owns into a series of mixed-use, pedestrian-oriented communities, tied together by a transit spine and surrounded by open space, which its former president asserted will be "an enduring legacy to Envision Utah's principles."
- Public attitudes about planning are much more positive, and a strong majority of residents now support walkable neighborhoods and more housing options for low- to moderate-income residents.
- Economic development agencies and business groups credit Envision Utah with helping to build Utah's thriving economy and attract new business by developing a plan to sustain our vibrant community over the long run, keep the cost of living in check, and establish a quality of life that attracts an active workforce.
- In 2007 Envision Utah commissioned Harris Interactive, the successor to Wirthlin Worldwide, to conduct a follow-up to the 1997 values study, and Robert Charles Lesser & Co. to conduct a market analysis. The purpose of these studies was to ensure that the values and priorities of residents continue to be reflected in the vision, strategies, and growth planning policies pursued

in the state and that growth plans are firmly rooted in market reality. This research revealed solid market support for Envision Utah's ongoing efforts to build mixed-use employment centers connected by a balanced transportation system.

A compelling indicator of Envision Utah's success is the recognition it has received outside the state. Envision Utah's cutting-edge approach has earned the nation's premiere planning awards, including the Urban Land Institute Award for Excellence and the American Planning Association's Daniel Burnham Award. In 2006 the *Washington Post* called Envision Utah the most cited example of regional visioning success in the nation. Because its process is inclusive, nonthreatening, transferable, and effective, Envision Utah has become a model emulated by dozens of regions around the country, including Los Angeles, Chicago, Austin, Orlando, Washington, D.C., Phoenix, and Sacramento.

CONCLUSION

Envision Utah will not be static. Through ongoing projects, Envision Utah keeps abreast of public opinion and market trends. Circumstances change. By listening and learning, the organization seeks regularly to update the QGS, keeping it relevant and compelling.

Leaders and residents increasingly recognize that their local decisions do not take place in a vacuum; local actions have regional impacts. With a bigger-picture perspective, decision makers increasingly pursue a course that unites, rather than segregates, the region. People in Utah and elsewhere are understandably concerned about the consequences of growth. That concern moderates, however, when they have a voice, a sense of ownership, in how growth occurs. They find comfort, even enthusiasm, knowing there is a plan in place to guide development decisions in a way consistent with their values and hopes for those who will follow. Quality growth—growth guided through a voluntary, market-based, civic process and based on sound technical analysis—can create the exemplary communities we want for our children. We can—and should—be optimistic. Working together, we can create beautiful, prosperous, healthy, and neighborly communities for future generations.

CHAPTER 14

REGIONAL PLANNING
IN FLORIDA

Charles L. Siemon

The Florida experience with greater-than-local resource planning and management is not easily described. A review of the Florida statutes suggests a robust set of greater-than-local resource planning and management programs—providing for a state comprehensive plan, regional planning agencies and strategic regional policy plans, regional water management districts, a regional transportation agency, local government comprehensive plans that are subject to state planning agency review and approval, community development districts, developments of regional impact, and areas of critical state concern. As is often the case, appearances can be deceiving, and understanding the Florida experience requires a very short history of Florida and its growth.

A Short History of Florida

In 1513 the Spanish explorer Ponce de Leon discovered Florida. Most early attempts to colonize Florida ended poorly, and by the mid-1800s the state was only sparsely settled (with a population of 1.6 persons per square mile) and largely agricultural. Starting in 1885, Henry Flagler got into the railroad business (to better serve a hotel he was building in St. Augustine) and progressively extended his railroad along the east coast of Florida, ultimately reaching Key West in 1912. During the first thirty years of the twentieth century, South Florida experienced an extraordinary, gravity-defying real estate boom. The boom collapsed under its own weight, pushed along by the stock market crash in 1929. The bust left South Florida to languish as a frontier until liberated by automobile access by way of the Interstate Highway System, the advent of jet aviation, and consumer access to air-conditioning. In 1950 the population of the entire state of Florida was 2.8 million people. In just twenty years, the state's population was 6.8 million and accelerating. In 2008 it stood in excess of 19 million.

Florida was an early pioneer in zoning, spurred by a special act of the Florida legislature and guided by a number of enlightened judicial opinions that rivaled the jurisprudence of other, more developed and mature states. Land use was not of much concern during the Great Depression and World War II. In the postwar period, Florida experienced modest growth in the late 1940s and the 1950s that accelerated in the 1960s. Florida did not have a standard state zoning enabling act until the 1960s, and as late as the early 1970s half of the counties had no zoning. Comprehensive planning was almost nonexistent, with few plans actually adopted and fewer still that were current. Like most states, Florida had had metropolitan planning organizations (MPOs) and regional planning councils to ensure eligibility for federal funding. However, the councils focused on transportation and were advisory and generally played no meaningful role in land use and environmental planning.

In 1971 South Florida experienced what was, at that time, the worst drought in recorded history bringing the implications of Florida's accelerating growth to the attention of the state: "Salt intruded into freshwater water supplies and Miami's well fields were threatened. Fires raged over 750,000 acres of dry saw grass and cypress. Alligators lost their watering holes. Vegetable crops 'dried up'" (Myers 1974). In response Governor Reubin Askew convened 150 leaders from around the state to address the land and water use issues facing the state. The results of the conference reflected a clear recognition of the importance of regional planning:

> There is a limit to the number of people which the South Florida basin can support and at the same time maintain a quality environment. The State and appropriate regional agencies must develop a comprehensive land and water use plan with enforcement machinery to limit population.... A state comprehensive land and water use plan would include an assessment of the quality and quantity of these resources. Moreover, it would set density controls on further development by regions and sub-regions. (Governor's Conference 1971, 2–3)

The following year Florida joined the "quiet revolution in land use controls" with the adoption of several statutes. The first was the Florida Environmental Land and Water Management Act of 1972, codified as chapter 380 of the Florida statutes, which was based on "Tentative Draft No. 3" of the American Law Institute's *A Model Land Development Code* project and created two greater-than-local land use controls: areas of critical state concern (ACSC) and developments of regional impact (DRI). The legislature also enacted the Florida State Comprehensive Planning Act of 1972, codified as chapter 186, which required the preparation of a state comprehensive plan in accordance with the long-range planning mandate of the Florida Constitution:

> The Executive Office of the Governor shall prepare a proposed state comprehensive plan which provides long-range guidance for the orderly social, economic,

and physical growth of the state. The plan shall be composed of goals, objectives, and policies that are briefly stated in plain, easily understandable words and that give specific policy direction to state and regional agencies. The goals, objectives, and policies shall be statewide in scope and shall be consistent and compatible with each other. The state comprehensive plan shall not include a land use map.

The state also created an Environmental Land Management Study Committee (ELMS), which was to consider additional resource planning and management programs. In 1974 the ELMS committee recommended a program of mandatory local government planning with state planning agency oversight. The following year, the Local Government Comprehensive Planning Act of 1975 (Planning Act or LGCPA) was adopted, which required each local government in the state to prepare a comprehensive plan with specified planning elements. When the plans were completed, the act provided that they be transmitted to the state land planning agency for formal compliance review and approval.

The Florida legislature had another busy year in 1985. The state comprehensive plan, which had been prepared by the Executive Office of the Governor, was reviewed by the legislature, and a series of goals and policies were adopted as the state comprehensive plan and codified as section 187.02 of the Florida statutes. The legislature also adopted the Omnibus Growth Management Act of 1985, a major overhaul of the planning act, which expanded the required elements of a local government comprehensive plan and required that local government land development regulations be updated to implement adopted comprehensive plans. The act also imposed an adequate public facilities mandate known as "concurrency" on a statewide basis. The concept of concurrency was that adequate public facilities should be available to serve the facilities demand of new growth before development is permitted. In addition, the act required regional planning councils to prepare regional policy plans and required that local government comprehensive plans be consistent with the state comprehensive plan and the regional policy plans. The Local Government Comprehensive Planning and Land Development Regulation Act has been amended several times to address specific concerns, including a serious tightening of the concurrency requirement in 2002.

An Assessment of Greater than Local Resource Planning and Management in Florida

Any assessment of greater-than-local resource planning and management in Florida should be grounded in an understanding of the metrics of Florida's growth, particularly in South Florida. Between 1960 and 2008, the population of the state increased by more than 14 million persons. During that period, slightly less than 4 million dwelling units were constructed in the state, most in sprawling suburbs at densities of two to four units per acre. In the face of the magnitude of change that was thrust upon the state, the challenge of planning for and managing growth was indisputably a daunting task. Indeed, a present-day visitor to Metro

Dade, Broward, or Palm Beach counties on the east coast and Hillsborough and
Pinellas counties on the west coast might not realize the extent and scope of
Florida's land use planning and regulation efforts based on how the landscape has
actually developed in these high-growth areas.

The Local Government Comprehensive Planning Act

Ironically, any assessment of regional planning in Florida starts with Florida's
mandatory local government comprehensive planning and land development
regulation program. That is so because the program is the center piece of the
state's top-down land use planning and management construct, which comprises
a mandated consistency of local plans and regulations with strategic regional policy plans, statewide planning rules, and the state comprehensive plan. In addition
to the consistency requirements, previously noted, review and approval of local
government comprehensive plans was made subject to administrative rules developed by the state land planning agency and ratified by the legislature. The purpose
of those rules makes it clear that the planning act is, to a considerable degree, a
greater-than-local planning program.

> This chapter establishes minimum criteria for the preparation, review, and
> determination of compliance of comprehensive plans and plan amendments
> pursuant to the Local Government Comprehensive Planning and Land Develop-
> ment Regulation Act, Chapter 163, F.S. This chapter establishes criteria imple-
> menting the legislative mandate that local comprehensive plans be consistent
> with the appropriate strategic regional policy plan and the State Comprehensive
> Plan, and recognizes the major role that local government will play, in accordance
> with that mandate, in accomplishing the goals and policies of the appropriate
> comprehensive regional policy plan and the State Comprehensive Plan.
>
> Rule 9J-5, Florida Administrative Code. The LGCPA requires local govern-
> ments to prepare and adopt a comprehensive plan that identifies future land uses
> within their jurisdictional boundaries and includes a capital improvement ele-
> ment to serve future development. The LGCPA also requires local governments
> to implement their comprehensive plans through land development regulations
> and only to approve development that is consistent with the adopted compre-
> hensive plan.

Local compliance with the requirements of the LGCPA was complicated by a
number of factors. As adopted, the LGCPA did not fully reflect the recommendations of the ELMS committee. Perhaps most notable was the failure to include the
funding and financial assistance necessary to support LGCPA's planning mandate,
a shortcoming that made the legislation more of a planning exercise than a true
plan of implementation. Though most cities and counties across the state updated
their comprehensive plans in accordance with the LGCPA over the course of the
next few years, most plans lacked vision and political commitment. Additionally,

the extent to which the LGCPA required local governments' land development regulations to be consistent with its comprehensive plan was not fully understood. As a result, some local governments updated their land development regulations, but most simply deferred any consistency determination until such time as a specific development application or rezoning request was pending.

Another difficulty was the absence of a meaningful state comprehensive plan, which meant that local comprehensive plan consistency was a matter of opinion as to what constituted "sound planning." The Florida legislature had adopted, in 1972, the Florida State Comprehensive Planning Act (FSCPA), which formalized the role of the state's regional planning councils and called for the creation of a state comprehensive plan. The 1970s passed, however, without the adoption of a state comprehensive plan. By 1983 the state of Florida still lacked a comprehensive plan, although the FSCPA was nearly ten years old. The following year, based on the recommendations of the second ELMS committee, the legislature pressed the issue by adopting the State and Regional Planning Act of 1984, which mandated the governor's office to prepare a draft state comprehensive plan by December 1, 1984. The act also required all state agencies to prepare and implement state agency functional plans consistent with the state comprehensive plan (once it had been adopted).

The draft plan was prepared and, after substantial revisions by the legislature, the state comprehensive plan was finally adopted in 1985 and codified in Florida statutes chapter 187. For the first time, the state of Florida had a single set of land use goals and policies that was intended to serve as direction setting with regard to growth and development throughout the state. According to the comprehensive planning act, "the State Comprehensive Plan shall provide long range policy guidance for the orderly social, economic, and physical growth of the state." The problem was that the policies and objectives were so broad and vainglorious—criticized by some as "motherhood and apple pie"—that they provided little or no guidance and have been honored mostly by being ignored. Importantly, the state comprehensive plan was "blind" to geography, despite the incredible environmental and geographic diversity of the state.

The logic of requiring adequate public facilities and concurrency was unassailable, but its application was problematic in a number of ways. Most significantly, as in most parts of the country, capital facilities generally lag behind the pace of growth—as tax revenues increase with new growth and development, new facilities are funded. In most parts of the country, that lag was inconvenient but tolerable. In Florida the pace of new growth and development overwhelmed available facilities, mostly roads, as the population of small towns increased from several thousand to tens of thousands in a handful of years. Even if funding was available, the time needed to acquire rights-of-way and construct the facilities resulted in a misalignment with regard to the availability of facilities.

There were a number of unintended consequences of concurrency. The first was that the program interrupted Florida's efforts to revitalize its coastal urban areas and transform them into transit friendly, compact, urban centers, because facilities in those areas were already at capacity. While the state ultimately allowed for concurrency exemption areas, many urban revitalization opportunities were lost, particularly where antigrowth sentiment prevented local governments from designating redevelopment areas (practically by definition "in someone's back-yard") as concurrency exemption areas. The situation in many areas that had grown rapidly in the 1960s, 1970s, and early 1980s was compounded by the state's imposition of a suburban level of service standard (LOS "D") as the default level throughout the state. This approach exacerbated the shortfall in transportation funding by reserving, from a regulatory perspective, approximately 25 percent of the road capacity. The second was that concurrency redirected growth and devel-opment away from the coast to undeveloped, often agricultural fields, where existing road networks had capacity. In a state already hampered by the legacy of decades of large land sales programs—literally millions of lots, many of them still vacant with little or no infrastructure other than thirty-year-old roads—the concurrency requirement has not generally achieved the goal of fostering good planning.

The irony of it all is that the results of concurrency displaced any sense of regional strategy or any effort to balance jobs and housing on a greater-than-local basis. The last and most problematic consequence of concurrency was that plan-ning, only recently recovered from years of neglect resulting from the triumph of the "city functional" over the "city beautiful" found itself in Florida once again subordinated to engineering, particularly traffic engineering.

Twenty years after the Growth Management Act of 1985, Florida's mandatory local government comprehensive plan program is the subject of considerable crit-icism. Local government comprehensive plans—with the exception of the future land use map—are largely ineffectual and are more often considered in litigation aimed at overturning a development approval than used as the guiding instrument of public policy. In part, the ineffectiveness of comprehensive plans is that they were produced inductively in response to detailed state rules that made the plan-ning and plan consistency process more of a checklist compliance exercise than a reasoned and embracing policy-making effort.

One of the most critical perspectives of local government comprehensive plans comes from a "home town democracy" movement that proposes that amendments to a local government comprehensive plan be subject to a referendum. The move-ment is grounded in several perspectives—that local governments are in the "pockets of developers" and that comprehensive plans do not really mean anything because they are being changed at developer request all the time. The culprit is not really local government and developers, but the system that produces formulaic, one-size-fits-all plans that are not practical in a complex environment, where multiple jurisdictions impact regional systems with no real regional oversight. Although the proponents of hometown democracy do not recognize it, the jury is still out, so to speak, on hometown democracy. But it is hard to see how a trial by neighborism plebiscite is more likely to produce reasoned, balanced merit-based policies than is the current system.

AREAS OF CRITICAL STATE CONCERN

The Area of Critical State Concern (ACSC) program also has a checkered career in Florida. Created by the Florida Environmental Land and Water Management Act of 1972 (FELWMA), the program is based on the concept that there are certain areas in Florida which, because of their location or character, involve resources or values of statewide significance. The idea of the ACSC was that the state would identify areas with resources and values that should be protected and establish principles for guiding development in those designated areas. After designation, local government land use decisions were subject to review and approval by the state land planning agency, and, if local governments adopted comprehensive plans and land development regulations that were approved by the state land planning agency, then the area would be de-designated.

The ASCS program also required that the governor and cabinet establish, as part of the designation process, certain minimum land use policies and standards, referred to as "principles for guiding development." All development in the designated area must be consistent with these guiding principles, and any local government with jurisdiction over land use in an area of critical state concern must amend its comprehensive plan to implement the guiding principles. If the local government fails to do so, then the governor and cabinet are empowered to prepare and adopt a local plan and land development regulations to implement the guiding principles. Additionally, development orders issued in an area of critical state concern are subject to an appeal by either the regional planning agency or state planning agency to the governor and cabinet sitting as the Florida Land and Water Adjudicatory Commission (FLAWAC).

When initially enacted, the FELWMA authorized the governor and cabinet to administratively designate areas of critical state concern (not to exceed a total of 5 percent of the state's land area at any one time). The statute was eventually amended after the Florida Supreme Court ruled that the designation process allowed the governor and cabinet to determine what resources were of regional or state significance and that such unfettered discretion violated the separation of powers and balance doctrines. See *Askew v. Cross Keys Waterways*, 372 So. 2d 913 (Fla. 1979). The FELWMA was thereafter amended to create a designation process whereby the governor first would appoint a resource planning commission (RPC) to perform a study of a proposed area of critical state concern. As amended, FELWMA provided that the RPC would determine whether a program should be adopted, under which local governments and other various entities would agree to address voluntarily the management needs of an area of concern. If a voluntary program were adopted, then the state land planning agency would monitor its implementation and effectiveness. If, however, the RPC determines that a formal management program should be adopted, then such recommendation would be forwarded to the governor and cabinet to decide whether a designation is appropriate. If the governor and cabinet agree with the designation recommendation, then the designation and guiding principles would be subject to a legislative confirmation during the next legislative session.

Two designations illustrate the implications of the ACSC program. The first is the designation of the Florida Keys as an ACSC. The Keys were first designated in 1978 and are still an ACSC in 2008, despite repeated efforts at the local level to convince the state land planning agency that the local governments in the Keys are protecting resources and values of statewide significance. The state land planning agency has repeatedly determined that the Keys should not be de-designated.

Another ACSC resource designation was an area comprising portions of multiple counties known as the Green Swamp. The Green Swamp was a prime recharge area for the Florida aquifer, which is the largest potable water source in the state. Concerns about growth in the recharge area and the potential impact on water quantity and quality led to the designation of the Green Swamp ACSC.

Both designations have been controversial, and there are as many opinions as to the efficacy of the ACSC program as there are observers. It is generally conceded that both programs have had a positive impact on the character, location, and magnitude of development; however, the ongoing tension between local and greater-than-local prerogatives remains contentious. The extended application of ACSC designations varies considerably from the expectations of the model code. One aspect of the ACSC program that has been particularly problematic is the issue of unfunded mandates. The ACSC program is by definition directed at resources of statewide significance, but the lion's share of the cost of managing those resources is born by local government. This misalignment between resource significance and financial responsibility is particularly problematic in the eyes of local officials.

DEVELOPMENTS OF REGIONAL IMPACT

The DRI program, another key element of the FELWMA, requires that developments which affect greater-than-local interests be subject to a regional impact review process. A proposed development is considered to be one of regional impact if its character, location, and magnitude will affect the citizens of more than one county. As an aid to the determination of the scale of impact, the Florida statutes establish thresholds for various land uses, and any project that exceeds 80 percent of the thresholds is presumed to be a DRI.

If a project is a DRI, the first step of the DRI review process is the submission of an application for development approval (ADA) to the appropriate regional planning council and local government(s) in which the proposed development is located. The ADA addresses a standard list of questions regarding land use, impacts on public facilities and the environment, project phasing, and economic and fiscal impacts. The process is commenced with a pre-application conference attended by state, regional, and local agency representatives to discuss whether any of the standard questions can be eliminated and to agree on an impact assessment methodology to be used in preparing responses to the DRI questions. The regional planning council reviews the ADA and is required to make a determination of "sufficiency" of the ADA within thirty days. If the regional planning council finds that the ADA does not sufficiently address all the issues, then the regional planning council specifies the additional information required to make the ADA sufficient. After additional information is submitted to the regional planning council, the council makes a second determination of sufficiency, and if the ADA is still not sufficient, the sufficiency cycle is repeated until the ADA is determined to be sufficient.

After the ADA is determined to be sufficient, the regional planning council provides a regional impact assessment to the local government that analyzes the proposed development's impact on resources of greater-than-local significance. The regional impact assessment includes a recommendation of whether the proposal should be denied, approved, or approved with conditions. The regional impact assessment is advisory and is not binding on the local government. The local government then conducts a duly noticed public hearing to approve, approve with conditions, or deny the proposed development. In the event the local government chooses to deny an ADA, the local government order must specify changes to the proposed development that would make the ADA eligible for approval.

The local government's decision with regard to an ADA is appealable to the FLAWAC by the developer, the regional planning council, or the state land planning agency. While appeals are encouraged to be based on the record created before the local government, the record of such proceedings often fails to satisfy the procedural requirements of Florida's Administrative Procedures Act. As a result, the administrative hearing officer usually conducts a *de novo* hearing in which each party makes an evidentiary presentation in support of its position. The hearing officer then considers the evidence presented and forwards a recommendation, including proposed findings of fact and conclusions of law, to the FLAWAC for a final determination on the appeal. The FLAWAC has plenary authority with regard to a DRI.

An approved DRI controls land use within its boundaries. The DRI development order confers vested rights to the landowner(s) that are subject only to the conditions specifically enumerated in the development order. With that being said, further regional review may be required if any changes to the approved plan of development are proposed and those changes amount to a substantial deviation from the original plan. The term "substantial deviation" is defined as any change "which creates a reasonable likelihood of additional regional impact or any type of regional impact created by the change not previously reviewed."

The DRI process has been much maligned by the private sector because of the time and cost of processing an ADA. On the other hand, it is generally conceded that DRIs are usually the best planned developments in the state. In some instances, the DRI process has been used to bring all of the regulatory agencies together to address the complexities of large-scale development—for example, complex community redevelopment projects. In some circumstances, the DRI process has been used to promote developments of regional benefit through the coordinated regional review process. There remains, however, significant opposition to the program—from developers because of the time and cost of the process and from environmentalists because DRIs are by definition large-scale developments and often involve large parcels that include environmentally sensitive lands.

As this summary of the planning and regulatory efforts in Florida on a regional basis indicates, there have been numerous efforts since the early 1970s to address regional issues in an effective manner. These efforts have had limited impacts and need to be examined and redirected to address the most important issues facing the state.

CHAPTER 15

REGIONAL PLANNING FOR LIVABLE COMMUNITIES IN ATLANTA

Rob LeBeau

The Atlanta Regional Commission (ARC) was created in 1947 by the Georgia General Assembly to serve as a regional planning and intergovernmental coordination agency for the Atlanta metropolitan area. For sixty years, ARC has helped to focus the region's leadership, attention, and resources on key issues of regional consequence such as aging services, governmental services, leadership development, research and mapping, workforce development, environmental planning, land use planning, and mobility and air quality issues.

Since the establishment of the first regional planning agency in Atlanta, the region has been a dynamic area for growth and development. In 1950 the population in the two-county planning area was 610,000. The current ten-county Atlanta region's planning area population surpassed the 4 million mark in 2007, after posting a 104,000-person increase between April 1, 2006, and April 1, 2007. The region is now home to 4,029,400 people, a population larger than that of twenty-four states. ARC is the metropolitan planning organization (MPO) for a twenty-county region that is home to 5,077,500 people.

The Atlanta region has historically been a diverse community with a strong mix of white and African American communities, and this diversity continues to expand. Some 75 percent of all growth since 2000 in the twenty-county region has come from nonwhites, with the African American population adding the most, followed by whites, Hispanics, and Asians. Between 2000 and 2006, the twenty-county Atlanta region added more than 371,000 African Americans, which is approximately 41 percent of all growth experienced during the period. The share of Hispanic population jumped from 7 percent in 2000 to 10 percent by 2006; African American share increased from 28 percent to 31 percent; and the Asian population went from a share of 3.3 percent in 2000 to 4.1 percent in 2006.

Atlanta has no natural physical boundaries to restrain development and is well served by three interstate systems that allow easy access to major employment centers. As such, the growth and development in the region has continued to expand outward, with many people moving farther away from the central city and town centers. The suburbs have opened up with numerous single family neighborhoods built in outer, once rural areas. This suburbanization is reflected in the conversion of undeveloped land to other uses. In 2001 the thirteen-county Atlanta region contained 1.28 million acres of primary, developable land (areas identified as agricultural or forested land). Between 2001 and 2007, approximately 214,000 acres of agricultural and forested land was lost to new development. During the same time, the region's population increased by 717,443 persons. If this rate of conversion continues, the region could exhaust its supply of developable land in twenty years. However, as available developable land becomes scarce, redevelopment and reuse becomes more prevalent and the developable land conversion rate slows significantly.

Growth has not always been distributed evenly, with much of the new development occurring north of the central business district. Although this trend has evened out recently, the prevailing patterns still remain, with more and higher value development being concentrated in the northern portions of the region.

The region's population is now spread among twenty counties, with the vast majority residing in the ten-county core planning area. Four of these counties boast populations greater than 600,000 people, while six counties have populations fewer than 100,000 (all but one of the smaller counties are outside the ten-county core planning area). The incorporated population is equally varied, the largest city being Atlanta, with more than 400,000 residents, followed by four other cities with populations over 50,000. There are numerous smaller cities as well, with several having populations under 1,000 people.

The Atlanta region has witnessed some remarkable events over the last fifty years, such as the evolution of the world's busiest airport at Hartsfield-Jackson Atlanta International Airport, the creation of Lake Lanier, the establishment of the Metropolitan Atlanta Rapid Transit Authority featuring a two-county heavy rail and bus transit system (and more recently the creation of three additional county-based bus systems), and the 1996 Summer Olympic Games that literally brought the world to the Atlanta region. However, this continually increasing population and disbursed development pattern has not been without its problems. The urbanized area has expanded significantly. The metro-Atlanta region is currently one of the least dense metropolitan areas in the United States, which results in one of the longest average daily work commutes. Natural resources, such as water and greenspace, are finite and must be managed appropriately. For example, Atlanta relies on surface water for 98 percent of its needs; however, the area is not located on a major body of water and is located at the headwaters of its rivers and streams, which limits available water flow and recharge rate. The region currently has nearly 170,000 acres of protected greenspace, which equates to 33 acres per 1,000 population. Since 2003, eight jurisdictions have voted to approve special ballot measures to tax themselves (valued at $216 million) for greenspace acquisition and protection.

THE ATLANTA REGIONAL COMMISSION

Cooperation among local governments in the Atlanta region is a long-standing tradition. ARC and its predecessor agencies have coordinated the planning efforts in the region since 1947, when the first publicly supported, multicounty planning agency in the United States was created. At that time, the Metropolitan Planning Commission (MPC) served DeKalb and Fulton counties and the city of Atlanta. Since then, ARC membership has grown to its current size of ten counties and sixty-seven municipalities. The Atlanta Regional Commission Board comprises officials from political subdivisions and private citizens within the region, with twenty-three local elected officials, fifteen private citizens (appointed by the twenty-three elected officials), and a representative of the Georgia Department of Community Affairs.

ARC serves multiple roles in the regional planning arena, and these roles cover different geographies as well.

- A regional development center (ten-county planning area) assists local governments in fulfilling the state's comprehensive planning requirements, including reviewing comprehensive plans, solid waste plans, and capital improvement elements; reviewing and determining compliance with state and regional goals for developments of regional impact; and preparing a regional land use plan with associated maps and policies.
- A metropolitan planning organization (eighteen-county planning area; forecasting for twenty-county area) develops regional plans and policies to enhance mobility, reduce congestion, and meet air quality standards through activities such as modeling, forecasts, and preparing short- and long-range transportation plans.
- The Metropolitan North Georgia Water Planning District (fifteen-county planning area) establishes policy, creates plans, and promotes intergovernmental coordination of all water issues in the district from a regional perspective, with a primary purpose of developing regional and watershed-specific plans for stormwater management, waste-water treatment, water supply, water conservation, and the general protection of water quality.
- The Area Agency on Aging (ten-county planning area) plans and provides comprehensive services to address the needs of the region's older population through a continuum of home and community-based services, including information and referral services, case management, transportation, home-delivered meals, senior centers, and legal services.
- The Atlanta Region Workforce Board (seven-county planning area) provides workforce solutions for dislocated workers, low-income adults and youth, and

businesses seeking qualified applicants. Services include training for in-demand occupations, business partnerships, youth programs, career resource centers, and rapid response activities to address plant closings and layoffs.

ARC is fortunate to be tasked with managing multiple issues around the region in one agency. This affords ARC the opportunity to offer programs and services that reflect strong integration among many of these issues.

In moving local governments in the region to conform their master plans and ordinances to regional plans, ARC relies on the use of collaborative planning and incentives. ARC has little power to require local governments to conform or participate. As the need to take a regional perspective rather than go it alone becomes more and more apparent to local officials, and the benefits of ARC's programs become apparent in communities that do participate, local governments in the region are joining the process.

In 1998 the Atlanta region suffered a major setback when a lapse in air quality conformity was determined by the Environmental Protection Agency (EPA). As a result, in 1999 the ARC sought to incorporate a stronger link between transportation investments and land use policies in the 2025 Regional Transportation Plan (RTP). One of these strategies was the creation of the livable centers initiative (LCI). The intent of this program is to encourage local governments in the Atlanta region to plan and implement strategies that link transportation improvements with development strategies, increase mobility options, decrease the dependence on the car, and, as a result, improve air quality.

The LCI program provides an excellent case study for a collaborative approach to implementing regional goals through local planning support and implementation assistance. The LCI program, along with the Envision6 process described later in the chapter, highlight two of the innovative approaches that the ARC takes in planning for a dynamic region.

LIVABLE CENTERS INITIATIVE: LOCAL IMPLEMENTATION OF REGIONAL GOALS AND POLICIES

Town centers, activity centers, and major corridors are vital to the Atlanta region's overall success. These areas are the traditional employment centers and shopping areas of the region but have typically lacked a strong residential component. Additionally, these areas are mostly built-out with significant investments in the supporting infrastructure. However, many of the infrastructure improvements—particularly related to the road network built over the past fifty years—have focused primarily on the automobile. Even in our traditional town centers, more recent road improvements have focused on moving vehicles through these centers, with little attention to internal multimodal circulation. The LCI program seeks a fundamental change in center and corridor development from a separation of uses and focus on the automobile to complete communities that contain a full mix of uses and accommodate multiple transportation modes.

Initiated in 1999 by the ARC, the LCI encourages local governments in the Atlanta region to plan and implement strategies that link transportation improvements with land use development strategies to create mixed use communities consistent with regional development policies. The LCI program has spurred cities, counties, and communities of all shapes and sizes to submit applications to ARC for 253 distinct planning studies during the past ten years for existing and new activity centers, town centers, and transportation corridors that bring a new level of livability to the region. LCI areas are typically characterized by significant infrastructure investments and provide a heavy concentration of commercial, retail, and office uses. This increased focus on redevelopment and small area planning has furthered a renaissance within the developed areas of the region. The heightened level of planning and awareness of urban development has been good for the economy in the LCI communities and the region. The fundamental concepts of the LCI studies include connecting homes, shops, and offices; enhancing streetscapes and sidewalks; emphasizing the pedestrian; improving access to transit and other transportation options; and expanding housing options.

Through the LCI program, federal transportation funds matched with local funds are used to provide planning grants to local governments and select nonprofit organizations. These plans link transportation improvements with land use strategies to enhance established communities and take advantage of the existing public and private assets already found in these communities. The primary goals of LCI are to encourage a diversity of mixed income residential neighborhoods, employment, shopping, and recreation choices; provide access to a range of travel options, including buses, roadways, walking, and biking; and engage the community's stakeholders in the planning, including groups not previously involved in community planning activities.

To participate, local governments submit an application for a study phase, and ARC reviews the application in light of the purposes of the program, including the community's ability to create a mixed-use, multimodal center. ARC then enters a formal contract with the local government that sets out the issues the municipality needs to address in the study, including a mixture of uses and a variety of transportation modes. In selecting transportation projects for the dedicated LCI money, ARC gives priority to those communities that have completed and approved the planning study and have independently taken local actions (including land use changes), as identified in the study's implementation plan, and to those transportation projects that meet the goals of the LCI program.

Some ninety-six LCI studies from 2000 to 2008 are now complete and being implemented in the eighteen-county Atlanta region. These studies have brought together citizens, officials, business leaders, and planners to create more than visions; they create great places. Out of the completed studies, 209 transportation projects developed from these LCI planning studies were submitted to ARC for transportation construction funding, with eighty-two of those selected to receive funding through the transportation improvement program from FY 2003–2011. The transportation projects feature new pedestrian and bicycle facilities, streetscapes, and intersection improvements to help reduce congestion, improve mobility, and encourage better land use in congested activity centers. They also transform downtown centers and activity centers into vibrant live, work, and play communities.

Genesis of the Livable Centers Initiative

ARC convened a land use task force in 1998 to review and refine the existing regional development policies for the 1999 regional development plan and support for the 2025 regional transportation plan. The task force especially wanted to clarify the definitions and desired outcomes of each major policy, believing that the policies would be effective only if local jurisdictions implemented them, and that implementation depended heavily on local planning officials actually understanding the policies. The task force realized that local jurisdictions needed real incentives more than they needed prescriptive or descriptive policies to catalyze a fundamental change in local land use planning that had typically focused on a separation of uses, with the automobile as the predominant, and sometimes only, transportation mode accommodated. The team wanted to create a demonstrable link between decisions about transportation infrastructure and land use.

ARC staff, along with the task force, believed that the best solutions would take the power that transportation investments bring forth to projects and use it to drive the local land use policies in the envisioned development patterns recommended through the regional development plan. The concept quickly took shape. ARC would allocate $5 million over the coming five years for local governments and nonprofit sponsors to produce plans defining strategies to develop town centers and activity centers and then allocate $350 million to fund transportation projects resulting from these studies. ARC adopted the policy to create and fund the LCI program when it approved the 2025 regional transportation plan (RTP) policies in May 1999. The ARC board further established the LCI program as a priority when it published the Regional Development Plan policies in October 1999.

Toward the end of 2004, ARC acknowledged the importance of planning corridors to incorporate the link between land use and transportation. In effect, the ARC board extended the LCI program to include another $5 million for five additional years of planning studies and added $150 million for priority funding of transportation projects. This funding commitment, included in the Mobility 2030 transportation plan, brought the ARC total investment in the LCI program to more than $500 million. To date, the 96 LCI communities have leveraged their seed money into $130 million in transportation projects alone to implement their plans.

During the summer of 2008, ARC engaged in an assessment of LCI implementation to comprehensively examine new development and local policies occurring in LCI communities. ARC distributed a survey to eighty-eight LCI areas, including all LCI study areas since the inception of the LCI program (excluding the 2008 studies that were not yet complete). The survey attempted to measure the progress of the LCI program through quantifying private developments and exploring land use policies that had changed since the implementation of the LCI plans.

Changing Local Regulations

Atlanta is the least densely developed region in the top fifteen U.S. metro areas. Many current zoning regulations restrict the development of diverse and affordable housing near jobs, forcing development further from these job centers and into single-use development patterns. This pattern can be detrimental to the region's long-term sustainability, as it limits a jobs-to-housing balance, increases traffic congestions, and creates the need to build new infrastructure.

The intent of the LCI program is to establish stronger mixed-use communities with access to a variety of transportation modes. Oftentimes the first step in implementing a community's LCI plan is to update its existing codes and ordinances to allow these innovative, mixed use projects to occur. With that in mind, as a component of the LCI implementation analysis, ARC gauged how the LCI communities were changing land use policies and regulations to accommodate new developments. The policy changes include updating or creating mixed use zoning districts, comprehensive plan amendments, and design guidelines.

There were seventy-eight LCI communities that completed the policy portion of the implementation survey. The findings show that progress has been made to update codes:

- 92 percent have adopted, or are in the process of adopting, their LCI study plan into their comprehensive plan
- 66 percent have adopted, or are in the process of adopting, special LCI zoning districts
- 56 percent have adopted, or are in the process of adopting, affordable or senior housing policies
- 83 percent have adopted, or are in the process of adopting, design guidelines that support the implementation of their LCI plan.

In essence, these local governments are changing their policies and regulations to incorporate higher density and a mix of uses, supported by a variety of transportation options, including cars, walking, biking, and transit.

LCI Developments

The survey also asked each study area to report on new development projects that were planned, under construction, or complete since the inception of their LCI study. The data sought to provide the development name, location, census tract, number of new residential units, type of residential unit, number of new hotel units, amount of commercial space, amount of office space, and construction stage.

Of the eighty-eight LCI study areas that received the survey, eighty returned completed surveys. There were nineteen LCIs that either reported they had no development or did not complete the development portion of the survey. The culmination of this survey found that significant development had occurred in these communities. Since the inception of the LCI program 1,148 development projects have been reported, including 762 projects completed by 2008. The 1,148 projects are anticipated to add the following:

- 84,500 residential units (with a range of building types including single family detached, townhomes, condos, and apartments consistent with the goals of creating mixed use communities)
- 12,000 hotel units
- 19 million square feet of commercial space
- 38 million square feet of office space

All these projects should support the goals of LCI because they are being built in designated LCI zones consistent with plans created and reviewed through the LCI program.

A regional comparison was conducted to determine the amount of development completed in LCI areas compared to new development in the region as a whole between 2000 and 2007. All of the LCI areas that responded to having completed development within their boundaries were located within a thirteen-county Atlanta region; therefore, the comparisons between the LCI areas and the Atlanta region were based on a thirteen-county geography.

The entire thirteen-county acreage is 2,450,762, and the LCI areas in these counties take up 83,224 acres, as shown in Figure 15.1. The LCI areas make up 3.4 percent of the total land area. The completed housing development for the LCI areas was reported as 36,645 units since the beginning of the LCI program. Since 2000 the housing development in the entire region has been 335,138 units. The LCI areas make up nearly 8 percent of the total housing development in this region.

The LCI areas reported 8,185,449 square feet of completed commercial development since the inception of the LCI program. The thirteen-county Atlanta region has reported 38,912,381 square feet of commercial development during the same period. As a result, the LCI areas contribute 21 percent of the total commercial development within the ten-county Atlanta region. The completed office development in the thirteen-county region was 32,016,187, and the completed LCI office

Development 2000–2005	Housing (units)	Commercial (sq ft)	Office (sq ft)
13-county	335,138	38,912,381	32,016,187
Land area: 2,450,762 acres			
LCI 13-county	26,645	8,185,449	21,411,504
Land area: 83,224 acres			
LCI % of 13-county development	7.95%	21.04%	66.88%
Land Area: 3.4%			

Figure 15.1. Atlanta Region Comparisons to LCI Areas for Completed Projects

development was reported at 21,411,504 since the inception of the LCI program. The LCI areas contribute a substantial 67 percent to the total thirteen-county office development.

LCI areas are capturing a large share of the regional commercial and office development. LCI areas continue to attract new residential growth but not at a rate equal to the share of commercial and office space. This trend continues as reported in the development tracking survey and shown by the regional comparisons. However, while there is a strong market and need for residential development in centers and corridors, housing development does not reflect a similar concentration in these areas. In many cases, the local codes and regulations do not allow for the inclusion of residential development in their town centers and activity centers. With the introduction of new mixed use codes, permitting higher residential densities, and approval of innovative projects, the residential share of development in centers and corridors should increase.

Two examples of LCI development illustrate how the program can work to foster the kind of development ARC is seeking to bring about.

Perimeter Activity Center. The Perimeter Activity Center is located just north of the city of Atlanta at the intersection of Interstate 285 and SR 400 and is home to one of the largest office markets in the southeast United States. This center developed in an intense yet suburban office pattern, with mid- to high-rise office buildings and retail shopping centers surrounded by surface and structured parking, but with each development disconnected from neighboring parcels. The Perimeter Community Improvement District led an LCI study in 2001 that focused on building on this strong retail and office market, but it also focused on bringing in a substantial residential component and providing opportunities for pedestrian connections and other nonvehicular activities. In 2008 the Perimeter Center LCI reported seventeen new developments planned, completed, or under way that would provide nearly 4 million square feet of office space, 1.5 million square feet of commercial space, 400 hotel rooms, and over 4,000 residential units. The majority of this new space will be contained in new fully integrated mixed use projects with strong urban design standards and enhanced pedestrian amenities. These pedestrian amenities focus on building wide sidewalks and crosswalks that comprise a complete network of pedestrian-ways to link homes, shops, and offices to each other and the three MARTA train stations in the area.

Woodstock Town Center. The city of Woodstock is a traditional railroad town located twenty-five miles north of downtown Atlanta with a current population of around 20,000 people. This city was developed along a railroad line with two blocks of one- and two-story commercial buildings on one side of the railroad tracks. When the city undertook the LCI study in 2002, there had been little development activity in the town center, and new residential developments were prohibited in the town center under the existing zoning codes. During the LCI study, the local citizens and elected officials came to the realization that a new development approach was needed to support the traditional town center. The completed LCI plan drew the interest of a local development company that assembled several parcels in the historic town center and designed a mixed use project that fully supported the plan and fit into the fabric of the existing town center. This new development encompasses thirty-two acres and includes about 100,000 square feet of retail and office space, 70 detached single-family homes, 125 lofts, 130 townhomes, and seven acres of park space.

Transportation Projects. As part of the LCI program, the ARC board committed $500 million in the regional transportation plan to fund transportation projects that are identified during the LCI planning process. The completed LCI plans identify hundreds of needed transportation improvements amounting to over $3 billion in improvements. These projects include a full range of transportation improvements, from pedestrian crosswalks and sidewalks to complete interchange improvements and new transit facilities. The LCI program transportation funding is not intended to fund all of these needs, but to assist communities with a few of these key projects.

The first year of funding for LCI transportation projects was in 2003, and to date approximately $135 million has been programmed for the preliminary engineering, right-of-way acquisition, and construction of eighty-two projects in centers and corridors around the region. Thirty-one LCI funded transportation projects have been completed, are under construction, or have been authorized to go to construction. Over 75 percent of these projects focus on enhancing the pedestrian environment through new sidewalks, bike lanes, crosswalks, pedestrian lighting, street furniture, and landscaping. These elements are essential to supporting the land use mix and establishing a strong pedestrian environment that attempts to follow the concepts of both "complete streets" and "context sensitive solutions." Examples of LCI transportation plans are the following:

Chamblee. The city of Chamblee completed an LCI study in 2000 for its MidCity District. This is an area surrounding a MARTA rail station and dominated by low-intensity industrial buildings. Since the completion of its study, this area has seen a tremendous amount of new residential development—primarily as apartments and condos—along with some supporting commercial services. Unfortunately, the existing transportation infrastructure was severely lacking in pedestrian accommodations, including a MARTA station that was designed primarily for vehicular access. The city of Chamblee has received $2.6 million in LCI transportation funding for projects that have focused on building new sidewalks with safe and clearly demarcated crosswalks that connect the residential developments and surrounding neighborhoods to the commercial areas and the MARTA rail station.

Midtown. Midtown Atlanta has traditionally had a strong office market, but it has also recently seen a significant amount of new residential, retail, restaurant, and other pedestrian supporting development. Peachtree Street is the primary artery in

Midtown and contains a tremendous amount of automobile traffic. However, the pedestrian infrastructure was inadequate to support the increased focus on street-front retail and residential developments, along with the increases in pedestrian activities. Midtown has received $9.1 million in LCI transportation funding for improvements along the primary corridors to enhance the multimodal character of the area. Improvements include features such as wider sidewalks, street trees, crosswalks, and pedestrian lighting.

The LCI program was established to help implement the regional transportation plan goals and regional development plan policies, which include focusing new development in mixed use areas with multiple transportation modes. The initiative is an innovative program to incentivize the implementation of these regional goals by encouraging local jurisdictions to take land use actions that create a greater mix of uses, including housing choices, in centers and corridors. The unique aspect of the LCI program, and the one that will ensure change in the region, is the ability to connect study funds and local land use initiatives with funds for transportation projects. Communities that independently implement portions of their completed plans receive priority funding for transportation projects in their study areas. LCI communities have over 1,100 new developments and eighty-two transportation projects planned or completed, with the majority of developments bringing a mix of uses and enhancing the multimodal environment in these areas.

Envision6: A Multidisciplinary Planning Approach

In 2005 ARC launched the Envision6 planning process to integrate regional land use and transportation planning initiatives used to support the regional transportation plan and regional development plan updates. Envision6 aimed to improve the regional vision, integrate local and regional plans, and better anticipate substantial population and employment growth.

During 2005, ARC met with all twenty counties included in ARC's transportation planning area. The purpose of the meetings was to review adopted future land use maps with elected officials, planners, transportation engineers, water and sewer staff, and school planners, and discuss current growth patterns and local aspirations for directing future growth. The results of the meetings were compiled into a Local Aspirations Land Use Map that would eventually be used to produce a regional map that reflects a balanced vision of future growth, land use, and public investments.

In addition to the Local Aspirations Map, ARC outlined other regional growth scenarios. To evaluate the alternative scenarios and associated forecast data, ARC staff used the MPO travel demand model to conduct land use sensitivity testing and also conducted land use scenario testing through geographic information system (GIS) based software known as INDEX. The scenarios evaluated included the adopted Mobility 2030 forecast, consolidated future land use maps from local comprehensive plans, and the draft Local Aspirations Map.

Both the land use sensitivity tests and the land use scenarios were run multiple times against the Mobility 2030 Travel Demand Model to analyze how changes in densities, jobs/housing balance, and access to transit impact Mobility 2030's performance. This component of the Envision6 process helped ARC better understand how changes to land use impact congestion levels, better anticipate growth, and make better choices with limited funds.

In order to receive additional input toward the development of plans for Envision6, ARC staff conducted charrettes with planning professionals and citizens. ARC conducted both statistical surveys on Envision6 topics as well as a web-based survey that was completed by over 1,000 individuals. Finally, ARC staff facilitated a focus group with a large contingent of real estate developers and market analysts to discuss future growth areas of the region and the likely development pattern and density associated with growth locations.

ARC's land use sensitivity testing included multiple tests of alternative land use forecasts against the Mobility 2030 RTP network. The tests exaggerated population and employment distributions by area to test the future network performance. The Mobility 2030 future network was held constant throughout the testing. The following three sensitivity testing forecasts bracketed the possible growth patterns for the Atlanta region and yielded the most desirable results relative to transit share, vehicle miles traveled, and hours of delay: concentrated population and job density, jobs closer to people, population and jobs close to transit.

The results of the sensitivity testing indicate that changes in land uses are not the silver bullets that will solve the region's congestion, but they do reveal a strong relationship between land use and transportation. Particularly important is the relationship of job locations to residential land use. As would be expected, the greater the distance that jobs are separated from residential uses, the higher the rates for automobile trips and congestion. ARC used the results of these sensitivity tests throughout the RTP planning process as bookends for further analysis and development of transportation and land use policies that work together. The purpose of this process was not to pick a specific land use scenario but to better understand relationships in the Atlanta region.

In May 2006 the ARC board took historic action by approving a resolution to support a unified growth policy map (UGPM), new regional development plan (RDP) policies, a place type and development matrix, and a regional strategic transportation system (RSTS) for metro Atlanta. These documents were the culmination of the year-long Envision6 public involvement and scenario development process. These plans are voluntary for local governments. ARC relies on the power of the vision to improve all communities, ARC's ability to direct transportation spending, and the financial and planning assistance incentives it can offer to local governments that buy into the process.

- The UGPM serves as the twenty-county future land use map, helps the region better understand growth patterns and the optimal locations for future population growth, and serves as a guide to RTP forecasts and investments.

In addition, local governments can use the Envision6 modeling and UGPM to better understand future land use relationships across county boundaries. The map seeks to direct growth into the existing city center, suburban centers, and corridors while preserving the region's outlying rural areas from intensive development.

- The place type and development matrix with supporting graphic illustrations delineates each of the land use categories in the UGPM and identifies the appropriate density ranges and use types for each category. The matrix seeks to relate the locations and infrastructure outlined in the UGPM to types and scale of future development and is used as a guide for both regional and local planners in development review and comprehensive plan decision making.
- ARC created eighteen RDP policies that approach land use from both a local and a regional perspective. Though the policies serve as recommendations rather than strict rules, they are all focused on a common goal: to integrate land use decisions with transportation, environmental, and other public investment decisions.
- The RSTS is a network of multimodal transportation facilities that accommodates the majority of travel in metro Atlanta. The facilities on the RSTS are given priority consideration in the allocation of federal and state transportation funding.

Envision6 was a groundbreaking review, discussion, and analysis of many options for growth of the Atlanta region in anticipation of another two million residents over the next twenty-five years, toward a population of nearly seven million people. Almost half of those new residents to the Atlanta region will arrive through natural increase of population alone. When considering the addition of new retirees and persons attracted to the region for jobs or business, it becomes clear that the region's growth must be managed wisely.

Envision6 brought together elected officials, developers, citizens, planners, engineers, and school administrators to consider where and how the Atlanta region should grow. Existing land use plans developed by local governments and new land use scenarios were evaluated. ARC and local governments made some important determinations from this process, such as: growth will continue in all counties of the region, insufficient public funds are available to meet infrastructure needs, land use decisions impact traffic congestion, and location of jobs in relation to housing is critical.

The Atlanta region faces many challenges in the coming years that will place greater demands on government finances. During 2005 Envision6 sought to establish a process by which the region collectively considers the consequences of growth that will occur in all counties of metro Atlanta, anticipate limited public funds for new infrastructure, and seek to make strategic decisions to best accommodate a larger population. While development will continue throughout the region, it is important to maintain and efficiently use the substantial public investments for infrastructure that have already occurred in the developed areas of the region. During the past several years, ARC provided resources to local governments to ensure that new development and transportation options occur in key economic and job centers. The LCI program is one example of an initiative undertaken by ARC to facilitate redevelopment in the major areas of commerce served by existing infrastructure. Programs like Envision6 and LCI are important ways for local, regional, and state agencies to cooperatively meet the region's challenges.

CHAPTER 16

FROM THE MOUNTAINS
TO THE SEA

MARYLAND'S SMART GROWTH PROGRAM

Richard Hall

Beginning in the 1990s, political leaders in the state of Maryland recognized that the dominant mode of low-density, single-use development spreading across the state was leaving some harm in its wake. Maryland was becoming one of many poster children for the negative impacts of sprawl. Accelerating loss of farmland and forests, excessive nutrients poisoning the Chesapeake Bay and its tributaries, traffic congestion, fiscal stress on governments trying to extend infrastructure to serve new population centers in former farmlands, and the exodus of people and investments from most Baltimore neighborhoods and other urbanized areas—and the certainty that these trends would only grow with time—created an overwhelming case for a statewide regional land use initiative to bring about smarter growth. From this recognition arose the Smart Growth and Neighborhood Conservation Act of 1997.

Already the fifth most densely populated state in the nation, Maryland has seen the third fastest growth per square mile since 1970 and the fourth fastest growth since 1990. From 1973 to 2002, the state's population grew 40 percent, from 4 million to nearly 5.7 million. The rapid population growth has been outpaced by even more rapid consumption of farms and forests by sprawling subdivisions and commercial districts. Between 1973 and 2010, more than half of the change in developed acres was in very low density residential. During this same period, the amount of developed land more than doubled, from 650,000 to 1.6 million acres.

The future is expected to bring more of the same. The number of households in many parts of Maryland is expected to grow 23 percent by 2035. Ninety-five percent of the state lies within the Chesapeake Bay watershed. The Bay and its tributaries are the defining natural resources of this region. The population in the Chesapeake watershed, which extends almost up to Utica, New York, was 16.7 million in 2005, and it is expected to grow to 18 million by 2020 and 20 million by 2030. This will bring further loss of open spaces, make it more difficult to create conservation lands, and put ever greater pressure on the quality of water in streams, rivers and the Chesapeake Bay.

Setting the Stage for Regional Planning

While Maryland is a home-rule state, the unit of local government in most of the state is the county. Incorporated municipalities range in size from the city of Baltimore (620,961 residents) to the town of Port Tobacco (13 residents). Although Baltimore is obviously a big city, relatively little land lies in incorporated munici-palities when viewing the state as a whole. This makes county government more powerful and influential than in most other Eastern home-rule states. Zoning powers, therefore, reside with county governments in most areas, and with munic-ipalities where they exist.

Maryland has twenty-three counties and Baltimore City, each having its own distinct zoning. In addition, many municipalities in Maryland also have zoning responsibilities. To be able to analyze zoning data statewide, the Maryland Department of Planning has created generalized zoning maps at a state scale.[1] These maps summarize each county's distinct zoning categories, as well as munic-ipal zoning (when available) into one of the three base generalized zoning cate-gories: resource protection, residential zoning, and other. The generalized zoning shows the predominance of lands classified as resource protection throughout the state, with these lands broken down into three subcategories: most protected, moderately protected, and least protected. These categories represent zoning rang-ing from relatively low-density development to permitted development densities of one home per twenty-acre lot. Generalized zoning for residential zones is broken down into four categories: very low density, low density, medium density, and high density residential. The map shows lower density zoning dominates on a statewide basis, encouraging sprawling development across the landscape. The final category includes commercial, industrial, municipalities (where zoning infor-mation is not available), other (e.g., military zones), and mixed use. The important fact here is Maryland's lack of mixed-use zoning.

Beginning in 1983, Maryland, Virginia, Pennsylvania, the District of Columbia, and the federal government have been working together through the Chesapeake Bay program to restore the Bay to its former glory as America's most productive estuary. The Chesapeake Bay program is a massive, long-term regional effort based on the recognition that land use—essentially suburban development and agriculture—represents the greatest source of excessive nutrients and other contaminants harming the Bay. In 1989, after studying the relationship between

[1]The Generalized Zoning Map is available at http://planning.maryland.gov/ourwork/ smartgrowthtrendsandanalysis.shtm/

development in the Chesapeake region and pollution of Chesapeake Bay, the Governor's Commission on Growth in the Chesapeake Region (the Barnes Commission) recommended ways to limit the impact of anticipated growth on the Chesapeake Bay watershed. To protect the Bay and Maryland's dwindling supply of open space, the Barnes Commission recommended legislation to designate certain areas in the state for growth and others for protection—that is, statewide zoning. The Maryland General Assembly, however, rejected this approach in 1991 and instead passed the Economic Growth, Resource Protection, and Planning Act of 1992. Central to the act were seven planning "visions" (later expanded to eight) that were to be incorporated into local plans and implemented by zoning and other regulations and program. Since then, Maryland has focused its Chesapeake Bay efforts on strategic land acquisition and implementation of pollution control measures, also known as best management practices (BMPs), to meet Maryland's obligations in the regional Chesapeake 2000 (C2K) Agreement, and most recently the 2010 Chesapeake Bay Total Maximum Daily Load (TMDL) promulgated by the U.S. Environmental Protection Agency. The debates of the late 1980s and early 1990s, however, set the stage for the more innovative growth management initiatives Maryland has pursued over the past decade.

Smart Growth and Neighborhood Conservation Act of 1997

The Smart Growth and Neighborhood Conservation Act of 1997 (Smart Growth Act) is Maryland's key sustainable development initiative. The act's goals are to bring about smarter growth at both the macro, statewide scale, and the local, town, and development scale, through a system of financial incentives and disincentives for both private developers and local governments. Because the earlier effort in 1991 to advance a smart growth agenda by shifting some land use powers from local government to the state had been soundly defeated, Governor Parris Glendening and his allies took that lesson to heart. They fashioned a very different approach.

The Smart Growth Act does not use direct regulation of land use and does not impose mandatory growth and conservation zones. Direct land-use regulation remains the jurisdiction of county and municipal governments using traditional planning and zoning tools. The act relies entirely on incentives and the strategic use of state funding to advance regional smart growth goals. The state program aims to move county and municipal governments to adopt plans and zoning that supports the Smart Growth Act's goals and strategies—and most have done so—but many elements of the program also give private developers reason to build consistent with statewide objectives, even where local zoning allows them to do otherwise.

The act, as its name was intended to show, is very explicitly a plan for growth. It recognizes and embraces the fact that more people and businesses are coming to Maryland. It seeks to direct and concentrate that growth in ways that will be more sustainable over the long run and do the least possible damage to the state's scenic and environmental resources. Unlike many regional land use plans, Maryland's Smart Growth Act does not include any new environmental regulations or standards. Instead, it aims to protect the environment by keeping development out of surviving natural areas through a combination of growth management incentives and strategic land acquisitions.

The Smart Growth Act includes five programs: The Priority Funding Areas Act, Rural Legacy, Live Near Your Work, Job Creation Tax Credits, and Brownfields Voluntary Cleanup and Revitalization Incentives. Of these, the Priority Funding Areas Act and Rural Legacy are the key regional initiatives.

Priority Funding Areas

The Priority Funding Areas Act is the best-known element of the program. The goal of the act is to bring about smarter growth at both the statewide and local level through a system of financial incentives and disincentives. The strategy is to use state infrastructure funds as a lever to achieve the desired landscape pattern of urban and rural lands, bring investment in and around already-developed areas, and achieve denser, more efficient land use. This policy does not prevent but only discourages building outside the priority funding areas. The act does not create or rely on a new source of money but instead uses the state's normal spending on transportation, sewers, and other infrastructure.

The act provides that, with stated exceptions, the state of Maryland may not provide funding for a growth-related project that is not in a priority funding area. Prior to the act, the location of a development played no role in its eligibility for state funding to build the infrastructure needed to support the development. Now location is supposed to play a critical, threshold role in directing major state investments.

Three key elements of the act's core mandate are the definition of growth-related projects, the delineation of priority funding areas, and the scope and impact of the exceptions to the rule restricting state investment to the priority funding areas.

Growth-related projects are defined to include major transportation projects, funding by the state Department of Housing and Community Development for new homes or neighborhood revitalization, funding by the Department of the Environment for water, sewer, and similar infrastructure, and a wide range of state government development activities. The act states that it is the policy of the state to direct state funding for school construction—one of the most important avenues of state capital spending—into priority funding areas, but it does not bar such spending outside the priority funding areas. While the range of state funding and activities that qualify as growth-related projects is broad, it does not encompass all state activities that come into play when private developments are proposed and carried out. The statute only works where a development requires significant new state infrastructure funding; otherwise, the act is irrelevant unless the county or town has independently shaped its zoning to support the overall geographic plan reflected in the map of priority funding areas.

Priority funding areas (PFAs) are defined both by geographic location and, in some cases, by density of development. Initially, PFAs include the following:

- Incorporated municipalities (remember that most of Maryland is not incorporated)
- Everything inside the Baltimore and the Washington, D.C., beltways
- Designated neighborhoods (a program under the state housing agency)
- Enterprise zones designated under state or federal law
- Areas designated by county governments because, for example, they are industrial or commercial zones served by public or community sewer

In addition to these categories, counties may also designate as PFAs communities that are served or planned to be served by sewer, as well as existing residential areas zoned for an average density of at least 2 units per acre and areas beyond the bounds of existing development if zoned for at least 3.5 units per acre. In order to designate new PFAs, counties are required to justify the designation through an analysis of the capacity of existing growth areas to accommodate growth and how much additional land is needed given the zoning densities in the county's master plan.

The goal, then, is to restrict PFAs to the preexisting cities, towns, and villages, with some allowance for extension so long as the land is served by sewer and is built at relatively efficient densities. PFAs are heavily concentrated inside the Baltimore and Washington beltways but also include many smaller cities and neighborhoods scattered around the state. Most PFAs were designated immediately after passage of the act, and their boundaries have changed little in the intervening years. Viewed from 50,000 feet, the pattern of PFAs leaves out the vast majority of Maryland's surviving farmland and mountain areas.

The act provides two mechanisms for government agencies to get exceptions from the rule. The Board of Public Works can grant an exemption to permit growth-related funding outside PFAs either upon a finding that extraordinary circumstances exist, requiring the exemption to avoid extreme inequity, hardship, or disadvantage, or for transportation projects that connect distinct PFAs or maintain the existing transportation system without significantly increasing highway capacity. Separate from the Department of Public Works, state agencies can fund projects outside PFAs if, for example, they are needed to protect public health or support an industry that has to be away from existing communities.

Rural Legacy

Created in 1997 as one of Maryland's Smart Growth programs, Rural Legacy provides funds on a competitive basis for counties and private land trusts to acquire permanent preservation easements on resource lands in locally designated rural legacy areas. A few properties have also been acquired through purchase. Rural Legacy is funded through a combination of Program Open Space dollars, general fund appropriations, and general obligation bonds from the state's capital budget. As of April 2011 through fiscal year 2008, Rural Legacy protected almost

70,000 acres. Every county has at least one Rural Legacy Area. The goals of the program are to "enhance natural resource, agricultural, forestry, and environmental protection while maintaining the viability of resource-based land usage and proper management of tillable and wooded areas . . . for farm production and timber harvests." The program is designed to do the following in order to establish a rural legacy for future generations:

- Leverage available funding
- Focus on strategic resources, including those resources threatened by sprawl development
- Streamline real property acquisition procedures to expedite land preservation
- Take advantage of innovative preservation techniques such as transfer of development rights and purchase of development rights
- Promote a greater level of natural and environmental resources protection than is provided by existing efforts

The state allocates funding to Rural Legacy sponsors through a competitive process. The Rural Legacy Advisory Committee, appointed by the governor and confirmed by the state senate, reviews all applications and makes recommendations to the Rural Legacy Board. The board then makes recommendations to the governor, and the legacy areas and grants for funding have to be approved by the Board of Public Works. Rural Legacy will pay landowners not only to relinquish development rights, but also for the active protection and stewardship of resources, such as the establishment of a permanent buffer alongside streams.

Created by legislation in 2001 to focus specifically on the state's green infrastructure, the Greenprint initiative seeks the permanent preservation of ecologically important natural areas through fee simple acquisition and purchase of development rights. The program specifically targets green infrastructure, including forests and wetlands of ecological, economic, and/or recreational value. Using computer modeling, the Department of Natural Resources actively identifies land that should be preserved in order to create a network of large natural areas linked by greenways or corridors.

How Has It Worked and Where Are We Going?

The Smart Growth and Priority Funding Areas Acts are now ten years old, and observers have begun to evaluate their impact on land use patterns. Recent studies by the National Center for Smart Growth Research and Education at the University of Maryland concluded that "the Act is not having its intended effect." In a 2007 report, the authors noted that state agencies have not always kept good records showing the geographic target of covered spending, but estimated that "growth-related capital and transportation spending covered by the Act amounted to about $1.1 billion per year between 1998 and 2007." While this is a small portion of the state's total annual spending, it represents 60 percent of the Maryland Department of Transportation's spending during those years and could provide substantial leverage to achieve the goals of the Priority Funding Areas program. The authors observed, however, that the share of residential housing permits issued for areas outside PFAs rose slightly from 28.6 percent in 1998 to 31.6 percent in 2004, suggesting that the act did not reduce sprawl in residential development during that period (Knaap and Lewis 2007). A second study published in 2009 found that "there is some evidence that PFAs do serve to concentrate urban development, job growth, and investments in wastewater infrastructure. The extent of concentration, however, varies by county, by industry, and by the extent to which local governments rely on state funds" (Lewis, Knaap, and Sohn 2009, 459). Altogether, the authors concluded that in their first decade, PFAs have not had the dramatic effect on growth patterns they were intended to bring.

It is not clear, however, that PFAs have failed to have an important impact on development patterns, since we do not know how much development would have gone outside the PFAs were it not for the act. In a context of rapid sprawl, just holding the line on keeping the great majority of growth within the designated zones for growth is an achievement. Nevertheless, it is clear that sprawl has continued despite the Smart Growth Act. Between 1990 and 2006, new residential housing consumed more than a quarter-million acres of land at the rate of 342.3 acres for every 1,000 people added to the state's population during that time. Outside priority funding areas, average lot sizes were increasing, at least until 2005, and were much larger than the average lots within PFAs. While three-quarters of the parcels developed between 1990 and 2005 were inside PFAs, three-quarters of the land consumed by development fell outside PFAs.

These considerations point to a weakness in the Smart Growth Act that is common among these kinds of programs. The act set no quantifiable goals or measures of success. Nor did it establish or call for a unified process or mechanism to gather and report the data needed to judge the program's success. The success of PFAs, moreover, is limited by their insufficient integration into state planning law and local master plans and the fact that its financial incentives are not always powerful enough to sway development actions.

There is a good deal of anecdotal evidence that the Smart Growth Act, and the shift in philosophy it brought to state government, has had regional impacts. In the 1990s, Maryland was plagued with bitter controversies over proposals to build massive new freeways or beltways connecting outer suburbs and rural districts and bypassing existing cities. These bypasses would be fundamentally inconsistent with the philosophy and goals of the Smart Growth Act. In the spirit of using state funds and programs to further smart growth, the Maryland Department of Transportation in 1999 canceled five bypass proposals that had been in the works within the agency for years. They have not been revived. During Governor Glendening's administration, the state also used its power of the purse to persuade county and local governments to refrain from adopting aggressive growth zoning for rural areas. The administration also supported those counties, like Montgomery, that moved aggressively to protect farmland and natural areas through zoning and acquisition. The state itself began to practice what it preached by keeping its own facilities in existing urban areas. While it is true that Governor Glendening's successor, Governor Robert L. Ehrlich Jr., largely abandoned the goals and strategies of the Smart Growth Act during his four years in office, the program was embodied in statute and has survived essentially intact.

There is no question the Smart Growth Act has had an impact. The question is whether that impact is great enough. The continuing development of housing subdivisions in rural areas, the ongoing financial struggles of many urban areas, growing traffic congestion, and the persistent failure to restore the Chesapeake Bay to an acceptable state of health all suggest the state of Maryland needs to do more to manage growth and its consequences. The Smart Growth Act of 1997 is not the complete and final answer.

CHAPTER 17

RAISING THE BAR AT THE CHESAPEAKE BAY PROGRAM

Carlton Haywood

The Chesapeake Watershed stretches into six states, covers 64,000 square miles, and has a population of more than 16 million people. The Chesapeake Bay is the largest estuary in the United States, with a 4,480-square-mile surface area, an 11,600-mile shoreline, hundreds of species of fish and shellfish, and thousands of species of plants. The Bay accounts for 500 million pounds of seafood annually. But it is an ecosystem that has been in decline for decades. The fish and shellfish harvests are at a tiny fraction of their historical levels. The grass beds and wetlands are disappearing. At the same time, the human activities that caused this decline are accelerating as the Washington, D.C., and Baltimore metropolitan areas have been growing—and sprawling—rapidly.

In 1983 the Chesapeake Bay Agreement formed the Chesapeake Bay Program as a partnership of the District of Columbia, the states of Maryland, Virginia, and Pennsylvania, and the federal Environmental Protection Agency. Its purpose was "to fully address the extent, complexity, and sources of pollutants entering the Bay." The program identified nutrients as a principal problem in the Bay. An office was established in Annapolis with a staff of more than eighty by 2010, and state and federal agencies formed their own Bay programs. Congress made annual appropriations toward the Bay program in the range of $20–$25 million a year.

In 1987 the Bay Agreement committed the partners to reducing controllable nutrients and pollutants by 40 percent by the year 2000. In 1999 the Bay received a 303(d) listing, identifying it as a body of water impaired by pollutants and not meeting water quality standards. The Chesapeake 2000 (C2K) Agreement included over 100 commitments, including one to "delist the Bay by 2010." After 2006, as it became increasingly apparent that the Bay's water quality goals would not be met by 2010, the EPA and states began planning for a total maximum daily load (TMDL) analysis that would impose load allocations on pollution sources and also impose regulatory requirements to meet those allocations. In December 2010 that TMDL was issued by the EPA, and the states are now engaged in developing new watershed implementation plans to achieve the required nutrient and sediment reductions.

CENTRAL GOALS AND STRATEGIES

The Chesapeake Bay Restoration and Protection Plan developed in September 1985 stated the goal of the Bay program: "Improve and protect the water quality and living resources of the Chesapeake Bay estuarine system to restore and maintain the Bay's ecological integrity, productivity and beneficial uses and to protect public health. This is the consummate purpose of the Chesapeake Bay restoration and protection program."

The central hypothesis of the Bay restoration is that declining living resources and habitat are caused by poor water quality, which in turn is caused by too many nutrients and sediments entering the Bay through the streams and rivers—that is, the tributaries—flowing into the Bay. The program seeks to restore the Bay by focusing on the tributaries and implementing tributary strategies that aim to reduce delivered loads of nutrients and sediments, thereby improving water quality and restoring living resources. To measure the progress of restoration, the program will track implementation of the tributary strategies, estimate loads to the Bay, set numeric goals that measure attainment of water quality standards, and monitor the health of key living resource communities.

The program is pursuing a wide range of specific strategies to restore the Bay's water quality and biotic communities. The great majority of these strategies rely on the partner states and the District of Columbia for implementation. Not surprisingly, these different jurisdictions are pursuing the strategies in somewhat different ways and with somewhat different commitment of resources. All the partners, however, are carrying out programs aimed at restoring water quality, protecting forests and creating riparian buffers in the Bay's watersheds, managing fisheries, and providing effective public education.

The issue of nutrient pollution provides a good picture of how the Chesapeake Bay Program works. Based on extensive scientific research, the program recognizes that the single greatest factor in the Bay's decline is the addition of excess nutrients and sediment in runoff that flows into the Bay, both directly and through its many tributaries. Taking nitrogen as an example, 33 percent comes through atmospheric deposition of nitrogen released by vehicle engines, utility plants, and livestock, much of which arises outside the watershed; 26 percent comes from chemical fertilizers used in farming and on urban/suburban land; 19 percent from manure; 18 percent from municipal wastewater treatment; and only 4 percent from septic systems. Program scientists estimated the reduction in nitrogen loading needed to restore healthy ecological processes, and the partner states and agencies agreed, through a complex negotiation, on an allocation of loadings by jurisdiction and source that would collectively meet that goal. Each state has focused on persuading farmers to adopt best management practices to reduce nutrient runoff, upgrading wastewater treatment plants, and land preservation. These efforts have seen significant successes—more than 60 percent of efforts required to reach nutrient goals have been implemented—but their success to date has been partly offset by growing nutrient inputs associated with population growth and suburban sprawl within the Bay's enormous watershed.

Growth management has proven an even more difficult challenge for the program partners than changing agricultural practices or improving sewer plants. While there is no watershed-wide land use plan, and none of the member states has adopted mandatory statewide growth controls, the partner states are each working on their own quite diverse efforts to promote environmentally sustainable development. The program partners acknowledge that more needs to be done to restore the Bay, and in December 2007 they made renewed commitments to take on these challenges.

ORGANIZATIONAL CHART

The Chesapeake Bay Program is supervised by the Chesapeake Executive Council, which consists of the administrator of the EPA; the governors of Maryland, Pennsylvania, and Virginia; the mayor of the District of Columbia; and the chair of the Chesapeake Bay Commission. The council is supported by a Principals Staff Committee and a Management Board, which provides strategic planning and operational guidance for the program. Citizens Advisory, Local Government Advisory, and Scientific and Technical Advisory committees provide advice to the Executive Council and to the Management Board. Six Goal Implementation Teams each focus on accomplishing one of the major goals of the Bay program.

THE NEED TO MEASURE AND COMMUNICATE PROGRESS

Everyone involved in the Chesapeake Bay Program is trying to do what is necessary to achieve Bay restoration goals in the context of limited resources. They are committed to quality science and to sharing all information with the public. Measuring progress is a key element of the Chesapeake Bay Program. The public is investing billions of dollars in this effort, and the Bay plays many vital roles in the lives of millions of people. It is only right that the public, and its representatives in the state and federal governments, have clear objective measures of whether and how well the program is achieving its goals. Measurements of success are just as important to the hundreds of individuals working within the program: How can we achieve our goals for the Bay if we do not have a very good idea whether our current efforts are working the way we want them to?

In July 2004 a short spell of widespread anoxia, a deprivation of oxygen in the Bay, led to alarmist press releases issued by environmental organizations. An article in the *Washington Post* reported that progress on Bay pollution had been over-stated. And a congressional hearing concluded with a request for a review by the Government Accountability Office. What went wrong? Were the public, press, and politicians failing to understand what the Bay program was doing? Or was the program failing to communicate?

The problems in 2004 arose from the fact that confusing and incorrect messages were being received, and the Bay program often was not the primary source of information. If the program did not answer the public's questions, or took too long, others were ready to fill the information void. The Bay program realized it needed to do a better job at explaining how it measures success and why it uses the metrics it uses.

In the fall of 2004 the Indicators Redesign Task Force was formed to identify problems utilizing current indicators, develop a framework for new or redesigned indicators, and start the process for developing new indicators. The Bay program already had indicators in place, but there were a number of problems with the existing system, especially from a communications point of view. There were more than 100 indicators, which was simply too many. There were few overarching indices and no hierarchy of importance. The indices tended to mix "state of the Bay" and "state of the Bay restoration" messages. Storylines tend to be detailed, and it was hard to find quick answers in the indicators. Individual indicators some-times gave conflicting messages, and, presented in standalone style, they did not tell the complete story. Sometimes there was also a long gap between monitoring and indicator availability. And the indicators lacked spatial detail.

In November 2005 the Government Accountability Office (GAO) issued a report on the Chesapeake Bay program. The report said the Bay program did not have an approach for integrating the results of its measures to assess progress toward the agreement's goal of protecting and restoring the Bay's living resources. It also said the Bay program had recognized that it may need an integrated approach for assessing overall progress in restoring the Bay and acknowledged that a task force had begun working on this effort.

The GAO found that the state of the Chesapeake Bay reports are the primary mechanism for reporting the current health status of the Bay. However, these reports did not effectively communicate the Bay's current conditions. As a result, the public cannot easily determine whether the health of the Bay is improving or not. Moreover, the lack of independence in the Bay program's reporting process has led to negative trends being downplayed and a rosier picture of the Bay's health being reported than may have been warranted.

To more effectively communicate the Bay's health and progress toward a restored ecosystem, the new vision for the program's state of the Bay reports is to provide accountability and facilitate understanding and decision making regarding the restoration. To achieve this vision, the Bay program will do the following:

- Maintain scientific integrity
- Distinguish between restoration efforts and the health of the Bay

- Report status with respect to goals and provide history to indicate a rate of progress
- Organize indicators and use common formats to facilitate understanding
- Provide summary, Bay-wide measures for bottom-line program accountability
- Separately provide detailed indicators and access to data on the Web for scientists
- Provide indicators at multiple geographic scales

The new indicator framework examines the Bay and watershed restoration, stressors, and ecosystem health through a hierarchy of indices, with the three over-arching ones being the Bay ecosystem health index, the restoration progress index, and the ecological footprint index. For each of these indices there are three top-level indices, each of which has several reporting indicators and indices—that is, concrete, quantifiable measures. Numerous more detailed indices feed into these measurements of progress for each top-level index.

For each index there is an established goal and a methodology for measuring reality against these goals. This hierarchy of indices provides for building up aggregate goals and measures of progress against those goals for each index as one moves up to the highest level indices. The whole structure is summarized in figure 17.1.

Reflecting the complexity of the ecosystem's problems and their causes, the goals for each reporting level indicator were arrived at through different processes. In general, draft goals are developed by teams of technical experts; the management level committee that supervises implementation of the restoration effort, and which is comprised of all the state and federal partner agencies, then approves each goal. Some of the water quality goals, specifically dissolved oxygen and clarity, were developed through state regulatory processes and have been adopted as state water quality standards. The habitat, lower food web, fish, and shellfish goals were developed after extensive data analysis and represent the best current understanding of what the biological communities of a restored Bay would look like. Restoration goals for nutrients and sediment were developed using the Chesapeake Bay Water Quality Model and the Chesapeake Watershed Model. These models showed by how much pollutants must be reduced in order to meet water quality standards and how much reduction should be assigned to each category of pollutant sources (e.g., point sources, agriculture, urban nonpoint, etc.). Restoration goals for habitat and harvest indicators were influenced as much by an assessment of what is possible as by what is needed. In a few cases—for example, menhaden and shad population levels—quantitative goals were not agreed upon in 2005, but the indicators remain in the framework as placeholders because of their importance. Efforts are under way to fill those gaps.

Progress for ecosystem health indicators is measured with data collected by monitoring programs, while progress for most restoration indicators is tracked with data provided by agencies that report acres of wetlands restored, grasses planted, BMPs installed, and so on. The Chesapeake Watershed Model is used to estimate nonpoint source nutrient and sediment load reductions for areas not covered by monitoring stations.

Overarching indices	Ecosystem health index			Restoration progress index			Ecological footprint index		
Top-level indices	Water quality	Habitat and lower food web	Fish and shellfish	Land and loads	Habitat	Harvest	Loads	Land use	Harvest
Reporting indicators and indices	– Dissolved oxygen – Chlorphyll-a – Clarity – Chemical contaminants	– SAVs – Wetlands – Phytoplankton – Zooplankton – Benthic community – Forage fish	– Crab – Oyster – Rockfish – Water Bird – Migratory fish	– Agricultural BMPs – Urban BMPs – WWTP plant upgrades – Air quality controls – Preserved lands	– SAVs – Wetlands – Reefs	– Fish passage – Oysters – Fisheries Management	– Nitrogen – Phosphorous – Sediment – Flows	– Impervious/ Pervious – Land uses	– Crab – Oyster – Fish
Diagnostic – detailed indicators	More detailed indicators			More detailed indicators			More detailed indicators		

Figure 17.1. Chesapeake Bay Indicators

These indicators have many different units of measure. Some examples include mg/l dissolved oxygen (DO), miles of buffer strips, acres of grasses, kg oyster biomass, tons/year sediment, and pounds/year nitrogen and phosphorus. To aid in communicating progress across the range of health and restoration measures, the Indicators Redesign Task Force decided to normalize all of the indicators to a single scale: percent of goal achieved. With this common scale, the reader, whether a relatively uniformed member of the public or a senior government manager, can scan across the range of health and restoration indicators and quickly determine which areas are relatively closer to the goal (good progress) and which are relatively far from the goal (poor progress).

The Indicators Redesign Task Force met for the first time in November 2004, and in April 2005 the Bay Program Implementation Committee approved the indicators redesign plan. A standing indicators workgroup was created and proceeded to explain the redesign plan to every Bay program committee. Over the course of several months, the indicators workgroup and relevant subcommittees held a series of iterative discussions on individual indicators. After each of the state governments was briefed, the 2005 Chesapeake Bay Health and Restoration Assessment (2005 State of the Bay Assessment) was released in March 2006 and was updated in the 2006 State of the Bay Assessment.

2006 STATE OF THE BAY ASSESSMENT

The State of the Bay Assessments seek to determine if the Bay is improving and if the restoration efforts are making progress. These assessments embody the new indicator framework and show how the system works. In order to meet the need for clear communications to the public and policy makers, the State of the Bay Assessments are structured to reflect the hierarchy built into the assessment framework, with summary messages and graphics, detailed analysis of each index, and the data on which the assessments are calculated. Summary information is widely distributed via print and electronic files, and the Chesapeake Bay Program website provides background and diagnostic information in more detailed articles and graphics.

The 2006 health assessment used thirteen indicators to study three priority areas: water quality, habitat, and fish and shellfish. It also assessed Bay stressors—river flow and nitrogen load—and water quality standards. The restoration assessment used eighteen indicators to examine five priority areas: reducing pollution, restoring habitat, managing fisheries, protecting watersheds, and fostering stewardship. The indicators for the Ecological Footprint Index are, as of 2006, still a work in progress. The intent for this group of indicators is to show the impact on Bay health of stressors other than pollutant sources. For example, annual stream flow has a major impact on the delivery of nutrients and sediments and should be considered when one compares the number of BMPs installed to the measured annual loads of pollutants delivered. Similarly, the harvest of key fish species has an impact on populations, just as water and habitat quality do. Workgroups at the Bay program are struggling with the best ways to tell this story.

The 2006 health assessment concluded that, overall, the ecosystem health remained degraded. While restoration efforts have offset the effects of rapidly growing population and land use change within the watershed, and modest gains have been made in some areas, the actions taken have not been sufficient to restore Bay health.

Looking at water quality, an aggregate measure of progress indicates that Bay health stands at 29 percent of the goal for dissolved oxygen, midchannel clarity, chlorophyll-a, and chemical contaminants. Habitats and lower food web measures have reached 35 percent of goals, and fish and shellfish have reached 42 percent of goals. Within the fish and shellfish index, for example, there is a wide range of achievement aggregated within that 42 percent measure, with blue crab abundance at just under 60 percent of goal and oysters at less than 10 percent.

The restoration element of the 2006 assessment concluded that, in light of the findings of the health assessment, restoration efforts need to accelerate if the Bay is to recover, especially in light of the continued growth in population and development within the watershed. The restoration assessment indicated that about half of needed pollution-reduction efforts have been undertaken over the past two decades, but this aggregate measure results from very widely differing progress on the more specific elements that make it up. For example, urban and suburban (nonpoint) nitrogen reduction efforts have fallen backward and gotten worse, while wastewater treatment plant (point) sources of nitrogen have exceeded 75 percent of goal. Habitat restoration efforts (bay grass planting, wetlands and fish passage restorations, and oyster recovery plans) have reached about 44 percent of goal, while protecting watersheds (planting forest buffers, adopting watershed management plans, and preserving land) achieved 69 percent of goal.

Following Up

Through 2006 the Bay program planned a peer review of all indicators, and workgroups continued to improve tracking methods, reduce data turnaround time, and develop missing indicators. Since 2006 the Bay program's reporting of progress in the Bay restoration has undergone continual improvement. There is an agreed-upon annual schedule for agencies to provide data to the Bay program so that a health and restoration report can be released at a public event each spring. Some indicators missing from the 2006 report have been added, particularly watershed health indicators. In addition to a printed report, the power of websites for providing more information to individuals with diverse interests and backgrounds has been harnessed by providing, with the indicator charts, links to maps, data, interpretive narratives, and links to related websites.

Graphics, while maintaining most of the design elements used in 2006, have undergone progressive polishing to improve reader comprehension. Three kinds of graphics are used in the assessment reports. The first shows the current status for key indicators, with status shown as a percentage of the goal in a bar chart. The second graphic charts a rate of progress for each key indicator, using the Y-axis for the percentage of the goal and the X-axis for time. Maps comprise the third graphical element, showing spatial patterns in status of restoration efforts and health of the Bay and its watershed.

The Chesapeake Bay Program experience suggests that such a large-scale program, which cuts across so many layers of government and affects so many industries and communities, requires sustained public and political support, and it can only maintain that support if it can objectively demonstrate progress in meeting clearly defined goals. For this reason, it is a key element of the Chesapeake Bay Program to develop and track indicators that relate to goals and are quantitative, measurable, measured, and timely. These indicators provide an accountability framework to keep the Bay restoration focused on key objectives and to provide leaders and the public with objective, quantifiable, and understandable measures of progress.

To keep these indicators relevant and ensure they communicate the program's mission and progress, we have found it is essential to consult frequently with stakeholder groups. That means meeting with agency managers at the beginning of the process, as their buy-in provides the authority to motivate the bureaucracy to change entrenched ways of collecting and reporting information; meeting often with scientists who collect and analyze the data, as they have to agree that what the indicators show is justified scientifically; and consulting with citizen and nontechnical constituencies from the beginning to ensure that indicators and messages are understandable and responsive to their concerns.

CHAPTER 18

THE POLITICAL DEAD ZONE
IN CHESAPEAKE BAY

Howard R. Ernst

Disputes over regional management of the Chesapeake Bay and its tributaries predate American independence. One of the longest running political feuds in American history, three hundred years old and running, involves a dispute between Virginia and Maryland over which state rightfully controls the Potomac River and its considerable resources (Clemons 2003). In the early spring of 1785, commissioners from the states of Virginia and Maryland met with George Washington at his Mount Vernon home to discuss their differences. The stated purpose of the meeting was to adopt "liberal and equitable regulations concerning said river as may be mutually advantageous to the two states" (Clifford n.d.). The meeting, known as the Mount Vernon Conference, failed to resolve the differences between the two states but did lead to a second meeting in Annapolis (i.e., the Annapolis Convention, 1786), which in turn led to the Philadelphia Convention (1787), which eventually produced the U.S. Constitution and gave birth to the federal government.

While it can be said that a dispute over a tributary of the Chesapeake Bay helped give birth to the federal government, the birth of the federal government did little to resolve conflicts over Bay resources. Regional competition for Chesapeake Bay resources turned violent by the mid-eighteenth century. It was during this period that the Bay's infamous oyster wars stained the banks of the Bay and its tributaries with the blood of watermen (See Wennersten 1981 on the oyster wars). Competition between Virginia and Maryland, as well as competition among watermen within the two states, led to armed skirmishes that eventually resulted in the state of Maryland creating its oyster navy in 1868. The state's oyster navy included six sloops, four schooners, two steamers, and an iron-hulled ship

This chapter is based on a chapter of Howard Ernst's *Fight for the Bay: Why a Dark Green Environmental Awakening Is Needed To Save the Chesapeake Bay* (2009) Lanham, MD: Rowman & Littlefield.

(Mountford 2003). Even with this impressive fleet, the violence continued into the twentieth century.

The decline of the oyster fishery, once known as Chesapeake Gold, eventually put an end to the oyster wars. By the early twentieth century the Bay's oyster harvests were in a rapid decline (Horton 2003, 167), leading would-be resource managers to focus their energies on other resources. In September of 1924, the governors of Maryland and Virginia planned a historic meeting to discuss Bay-wide management of the blue crab. The gathering was scheduled to take place aboard Virginia's state police steamer, anchored in the disputed waters of the Potomac (Ernst 2003, 107–108), but was postponed after Maryland's governor fell en route to the meeting and broke his arm. Two months later, when the meeting finally occurred in Annapolis, Maryland's conservation commissioner warned the governors that "the great industry may yet be saved for the watermen in both states," if only the states would act aggressively and in unison.

Unfortunately for the blue crab, resource managers in Maryland and Virginia have yet to agree on a common management strategy for their common resource, and as a result the crab industry is now severely degraded.[1] Other failed attempts at regional management for the Bay include a 1933 conference that was held in Baltimore and attended by resource managers from Maryland, Virginia, Delaware, and the District of Columbia, as well as representatives from the U.S. Bureau of Fisheries. At this conference, participants unanimously agreed to create a multi-state committee for the purpose of coordinating and promoting preservation efforts. While the need for coordinated management was clear, the committee was never created, and the participants returned to their individual states to pursue resource management in the usual manner (Chesapeake Bay Authority 1933, 165–168).

In the mid-1960s, the U.S. Army Corps of Engineers launched what at the time was one of the most ambitious attempts at regional management and planning that the country had ever undertaken. The $15 million project was designed to coordinate the research efforts of the region's leading scientific institutions, as well as the work of federal, state, and local governmental agencies. The project had three major goals: assess the existing state of the Bay and its resources, predict the likely future condition of the Bay in 2020, and recommend solutions to the Bay's existing and future problems. In 1973 the Corps fulfilled its first goal when it published a seven-volume inventory of the Bay's health (U.S. Corps of Engineers 1974). In 1976 the Corps fulfilled its second major objective when it published its twelve-volume study, *The Chesapeake Bay Future Conditions Report* (U.S. Corps of Engineers 1977.) But when it came to turning knowledge into action, the Corps' work, like the earlier attempts at regional management, came up short.

[1] Virginia and Maryland have attempted two bistate working groups to manage the blue crab (one in the 1980s and one in the late 1990s). In both cases, the groups were disbanded after their proposals proved controversial within the respective states. The 2006 Bay-wide harvest of blue crabs was one of the lowest on record (National Oceanic and Atmospheric Administration 2007).

The Corps of Engineers concluded its studies of the Bay prior to publishing its policy recommendations, the third goal of the project. In the late 1970s, the Corps was replaced by the newly created Environmental Protection Agency as the lead agency coordinating Bay policy. Rather than build on the Corps' considerable work, the EPA launched its own study of the Bay, which cost an additional $27 million and seven years to complete. Not surprisingly, since many of the EPA's research partners were the same research institutions that had partnered with the Corps in its earlier studies, the EPA's findings, released in 1983, were similar to the findings released by the Corps a decade earlier.

By the time the EPA completed its study, nearly sixty years had passed since the Maryland and Virginia governors had first met to discuss the Bay's rapidly declining resources (1924), fifty years had passed since the idea for a regional management authority had been lauded in Baltimore (1933), a decade had passed since the Corps of Engineers issued its assessment of the Bay (1973), and yet no meaningful regional planning body had been created to address the rapidly deteriorating ecosystem.

THE MODERN BAY BUREAUCRACY

The first major component of what has come to be known as the Chesapeake Bay partnership, otherwise known as the Bay Bureaucracy, came into existence in 1980, with the creation of the Chesapeake Bay Commission.[2] In its current configuration, the commission includes representatives from Maryland, Pennsylvania, and Virginia. The commission meets four times per year, rotating between the three states and Washington, D.C., and issues an annual report, as well as various special reports. The twenty-one member commission includes five state legislators from each state, each state's director of natural resources, and one citizen representative from each state. The Chesapeake Bay Commission has no regulatory powers but instead operates in an advisory capacity. The purpose of the commission is to advise the three state legislatures and to serve as a liaison to the U.S. Congress.

In 1983 a second major element of the Bay partnership took shape with the creation of the Chesapeake Bay Executive Council. Though its composition has changed over time, membership on the Executive Council now consists of the governors of Maryland, Pennsylvania, and Virginia, the administrator of the U.S. Environmental Protection Agency, the mayor of the District of Columbia, and the chair of the Chesapeake Bay Commission.[3] Like the Chesapeake Bay Commission, the Chesapeake Bay Executive Council has no independent regulatory powers. The Executive Council holds an annual meeting to discuss Bay policy and periodically adopts what have become known as the Chesapeake Bay Agreements.

[2] For more on the Chesapeake Bay Commission, see http://www.chesbay.state.va.us/index.htm.
[3] For more on the Chesapeake Bay Executive Council, see http://www.chesapeakebay.net/exec.htm.

The Bay Agreements themselves are the third major component of the Bay's bureaucratic structure. They are nonbinding documents that are intended to provide direction to the states but carry no legal weight. Article 1, section 10, of the U.S. Constitution prohibits states "without the consent of Congress . . . [from entering] into any agreement or compact." Since the Bay Agreements are voluntary and not enforceable, they do not require congressional approval and have never been approved by Congress, nor have they been approved by the state legislatures of the signatory states. As nonbinding documents, the Bay Agreements provide no consequence for failing to meet their stated goals and no basis for legal action should the states fall short of their commitments. Following the initial Bay Agreement in 1983, the Executive Council signed two additional Bay Agreements. The first Bay Agreement, little more than a paragraph in length, was a broad statement of intent to address the Bay's mounting problems. The 1987 agreement established thirty-one commitments (goals), and the 2000 agreement established 105 commitments (goals).

The fourth major component of the Bay Bureaucracy is the Chesapeake Bay Program, which was created as an outcome of the initial Bay Agreement in 1983. While the Chesapeake Bay Program is considered the implementation arm of the Bay Agreements, it was granted no regulatory powers. The nonregulatory Bay program was not given the authority to limit pollution, to restrict development, or even to manage the Bay's living resources. In sum, regional management for the Bay includes two advisory councils, a series of nonbinding agreements, and an environmental agency that has been provided no regulatory powers, hardly the recipe for success.

At this time, the Bay restoration effort has no comprehensive or even coordinated land use or growth management authority. This is particularly troubling given the fact that the Chesapeake Bay has one of the largest land-to-water ratios of any inland body of water on earth (Horton 2003, 5), making it highly susceptible to environmental problems related to land use. Moreover, even in its severely degraded condition, 90 percent of the Bay's 40 million acre watershed remains undeveloped (Horton 2003, 206). As population growth increases and the pressure for new development also continues to grow, it is clear that the fate of the Bay hinges on effective land management practices.

The current land management laws in place for the Bay are applied at the state and local level and generally only apply to a narrow strip of land that has immediate contact with the Bay and its tributaries. Both Virginia and Maryland have laws that restrict development within a 100-foot buffer of the Bay, but both states regularly issue variances to the restrictions, and both states allow farming to within twenty-five feet of the Bay and its tributaries. Pennsylvania, the state with the greatest amount of land in the watershed, does not have a similar set of laws. Most of the land management authority in Pennsylvania rests at the municipal level, with more than a third of the state's municipalities having no zoning laws and more than one-half of the municipalities having no comprehensive growth plans (Horton 2003, 208).

The state of Maryland was once considered a model for land protection. In a program that dates back to the late 1960s and predates the creation of the Bay program, the state instituted a transfer tax (i.e., a tax on the sale of property), which generates money for the preservation of open spaces. In recent years the fund has been raided by the general assembly to cover shortfalls in the state's general fund. A recent front-page story in the *Washington Post* alarmed area residents with the finding that millions of dollars of projects funds had been used to replace grass fields with Astroturf ball fields, a far cry from what the fund was created to protect (Fahrenthold 2007).

While the Bay program has been touted as "America's leading bay and river restoration program" and promotes itself as "a national and international model for estuarine research and restoration programs," it is important to keep in mind that this experiment in voluntary, cooperative management has not been success-ful.[4] While the restoration effort has produced a few success stories at the state and local level (e.g., recovery of striped bass, removal of several dams that once blocked fish spawning areas, and the protection of some forested buffers), the overall effort has not been successful. To date, the Bay program has failed to meet the pollution reduction goals specified in the Bay Agreements, most of their secondary goals, and the basic water quality standards of the Clean Water Act.

A comprehensive study of the Bay program, completed in 2005 by the investiga-tory arm of the U.S. Congress (Government Accountability Office), concluded that despite receiving more than $3.7 billion dollars in direct federal funding for Bay restoration projects over the previous decade and an additional $1.9 billion in indi-rect funding during this same period, the Bay restoration partners have failed to develop "a comprehensive, coordinated implementation strategy." The GAO study also found that the Bay Program's reports did not provide "credible information on the current health status of the bay" (Government Accountability Office 2006). In short, the Bay program has failed to meet its most important goals, has failed to effectively report the status of its progress, and, as a consequence, the Chesapeake Bay has not systemically improved. In light of the recent criticism, the Chesapeake Bay Program has had little choice but to acknowledge its shortcomings:

> Although there are a number of smaller-scale success stories, the overall ecosys-tem health of the Chesapeake Bay remains degraded. For more than twenty years, restoration efforts have managed to offset the impact of the region's growing population while making modest ecological gains in some areas. Major pollution reduction, habitat restoration, fisheries management and watershed protection actions taken to date have not yet been sufficient to restore the health of the Bay. (Chesapeake Bay Program 2006)

In its current configuration, the Bay program lacks the regulatory powers to achieve its goals coercively and the resources that would be necessary to achieve its

---

[4] While these claims are found in numerous Chesapeake Bay Program publications, for one example see "A 'Who's Who' in the Chesapeake Bay Program: 2003," 1, available online from the Bay Program, http://www.archive.chesapeakebay.net/pubs/whowho_2003.pdf.

goals voluntarily through environmental incentives. After more than a hundred years of struggling for effective regional management for the Bay, what the area now has are hollow agreements instead of enforceable laws, goals instead of pollution limits, a bureaucracy that lacks regulatory powers, and a severely impaired ecosystem that shows no sign of systemic improvement. The most startling fact is that the restoration program, the very program that has overseen one of the greatest man-made disasters in American history (i.e., the slow death of the Chesapeake Bay), appears able to perpetuate itself indefinitely, despite the mounting evidence that it adopted an ineffective management approach.

COMING TO TERMS WITH POLITICAL ANOXIA

With the benefit of hindsight, it is clear that the modern regional management effort for the Chesapeake was built on a series of assumptions—a paradigm that now permeates every layer of the Bay's bureaucracy. The cornerstone of this paradigm is the belief that voluntary environmental goals, produced in an inclusive manner and based on sound science, can supersede politics, litigation, regulations, and the confrontational system on which American politics is founded. It is based on the belief that local and state government officials and their partners in the business community want to do the right thing but require a scientific justification and moral arm twisting to head them in the right direction. This approach, often viewed as an alternative to the contentious environmental politics of the 1970s–1980s, has gained tremendous popularity in recent years and has been accepted with little question in the Chesapeake region.

The overarching paradigm of the voluntary-cooperative approach to environmental management is based on the assumption that nonbinding goals provide long-term direction to the restoration effort and can direct environmental decisions, regardless of who happens to hold office at any particular point in time. The inclusive-collaborative approach to setting restoration goals provides all stakeholders an opportunity to participate and stresses consensus. While this approach might take more time than other approaches, it increases the chance of buy-in and in turn increases the chance of success. Another assumption is that the key to environmental policy is building partnerships between environmental advocates and industry leaders (i.e., stakeholders) as these partnerships develop trust, increase capacity, and fuel environmental innovation.

After more than twenty-five years of pursuing this approach, with very few tangible environmental results, a meaningful critique of this approach is long overdue. It might very well be that the "old paradigm" (the environmental rights paradigm of the 1970s), which produced the Clean Air Act, the Clean Water Act, and created the Environmental Protection Agency, is more effective than the paradigm embodied by the Chesapeake Bay Program. The old paradigm suggests that the carrying capacity of nature (set by natural conditions and identified through scientific evaluations), not the desires of stakeholders (what the old paradigm referred to as special interest groups) should determine the necessary course of action. The old approach is based on the central assumption that environmental protection is a legal right and that the necessary policies should be put into place, even if they are expensive and inconvenient, to protect this right. It is based on the idea that people have a right to clean water, clean air, and vibrant natural resources in their public spaces. It also posits that no person or industry, no matter how profitable, has the right to degrade these conditions. The rights-based approach leads to several specific criticisms of the voluntary approach to environmental management:

1. Overreliance on the collaborative approach can result in a situation in which science is viewed as just another stakeholder perspective.
2. Pursuing consensus among stakeholders (special interest groups) can lead environmental managers to avoid addressing hard issues on which consensus is unlikely, if possible at all (e.g., addressing the Bay's number one source of pollution, agricultural waste).
3. Pursuing consensus among stakeholders replaces the polluter pays concept with the public pays concept, as polluters are almost always well represented in such systems, but the general public is typically not represented at all.
4. The inclusive approach can lead to an explosion of environmental goals, goals that put lesser concerns like environmental education on the same level of essential goals like pollution reduction.

This critique does not suggest that there is no place for voluntary-collaborative measures. It does suggest, however, that voluntary measures treat environmental protection as a luxury rather than a right. It also suggests that overreliance on the voluntary-consensus based approach has fostered a culture of complacency among Bay restoration managers and their public and private partners. Like the nutrients that feed a healthy Bay under normal conditions but that rob the Bay of life-supporting oxygen when delivered in excess, overreliance on the voluntary-collaborative approach to restoration has created a political dead zone for the Chesapeake Bay (Ernst 2009). The political dead zone is a place were big ideas go to die. What survives in the dead zone are a lesser species of policy, public policies that might help to reduce the speed of the Bay's decline but that are insufficient to reverse the general downward trend.

Taking a closer look at one of the Bay program's long-time restoration partners, the Chesapeake Bay Foundation, can help illustrate how the political dead zone works. The Chesapeake Bay Foundation is the largest environmental interest group dedicated to the restoration of the Chesapeake Bay and one of the most successful regional environmental groups in the county. The group has been in existence for over forty years and currently has an annual operating budget in excess of $20 million. It has over 100,000 dues paying members and a professional staff of more than 100 full-time employees. The organization's "Save the Bay" bumper stickers, which have been produced since 1967, are now ubiquitous throughout the Bay states.

Despite its organizational prowess and the fact that the organization markets itself as a watchdog group, the Chesapeake Bay Foundation is completely removed from electoral politics. The group has never endorsed or donated money to a Bay-friendly candidate, never advertised the voting records of elected officials, has no political action committee, and until very recently has shied away from pursuing its environmental cause through legal action. As a partner in the Bay restoration effort, the Chesapeake Bay Foundation, like virtually every Bay-specific group in the watershed, has adopted a 501c3 (tax-exempt) tax status that prohibits them from participating in electoral politics and severely limits their ability to engage in basic lobbying activities.

In exchange for sitting out the political game, groups like the Chesapeake Bay Foundation are free from federal taxes and are eligible for various grants, like those available from the Chesapeake Stewardship Fund.[5] This program (itself a partnership between the National Fish and Wildlife Foundation, Chesapeake Bay Program, federal agencies, charitable foundations, and corporate donors) has allocated more than $16 million in small watershed grants to 277 groups since 1999 (National Fish and Wildlife Foundation 2010). Many of the grants are small, less than $50,000, and serve as the lifeblood for many of the small environmental groups that receive the funding.

While $16 million in grants over a seven-year period is not enough to make a substantial impact on the quality of the Chesapeake Bay (the Chesapeake Bay Commission estimates that it would cost $12.8 billion in additional funding for the states to meet their commitments under the 2000 Bay Agreement [see Chesapeake Bay Commission 2003]), the modest funding is sufficient to keep the environmental advocacy groups busy and to help direct the nature of the advocacy-government relationship. Programs like these form a partnership between would-be advocates and the government agencies that they purport to hold accountable, as well as the corporate entities that contribute to the grants.

Groups like the Chesapeake Bay Foundation, which have traded in their most powerful advocacy tools for a beneficial tax status and grant money, are left on the sidelines of the policy process. Yes, they cheer on the players and occasionally boo and hiss when the game does not go their way, but they remain safely out of the political action. A recent "Action Alert" from the group reveals the ineffectiveness of this approach. An email blast dated February 16, 2011, warns the group's supporters that, "shockingly," a House appropriations bill threatens "deep cuts" to restoration programs and that Virginia Congressman Bob Goodlatte has proposed a legislative amendment that would halt the enforcement of the Clean Water Act's water quality standards. But in 2010, when Representative Goodlatte asked his Virginia constituents to return him to Congress for yet another term, the Chesapeake Bay Foundation had nothing to say and no resources to offer his

[5] Section 117(g)(2)(A) of the Estuaries and Clean Water Act of 2000 states that the only non-governmental groups eligible for the grants are nonprofits. For more information on these grants, see the Chesapeake Bay Program (http://www.chesapeakebay.net/smallwatergrants.htm) or the National Fish and Wildlife Foundation (http://www.nfwf.org/AM/Template.cfm?Section=Chesapeake_Bay_Stewardship_Fund&Template=/TaggedPage/TaggedPageDisplay.cfm&TPLID=46&ContentID=7547).

opponent, despite the fact that environmental groups like the League of Conservation Voters had given him failing marks for over a decade. The Chesapeake Bay Foundation's action alert concludes with a plea for supporters to send Congress an email. The problem, of course, is that polluting industries do more than clog the email inboxes of congressional staffers. While the region's leading environmental advocate for the Bay made no noise when it mattered most, during the election season, agribusiness found a way to contribute more than $150,000 to Congressman Goodlatte's 2010 campaign.

Conclusion

From the recent history of regional environmental management of the Chesapeake, it is hard to conclude anything other than that the voluntary-collaborative approach is currently sucking the air out of the advocacy community and robbing the restoration effort of the political will that ultimately makes meaningful action possible. The approach was well designed to resolve environmental conflict but does a poor job addressing the substantial funding and regulatory needs the Bay now requires.

As the Bay restoration effort moves into its next phase, the regulatory phase required by the Clean Water Act, it will likely require a more hard-line approach. Meaningfully addressing the Bay's problems will result in winners and losers and will inevitably spur conflict. Industries, like the Bay's agricultural industry, will require substantial regulations, and they will resist oversight. Other programs will require substantial public funds, which can only be acquired from increased taxes or cuts to other programs, which will also be resisted. It is very likely that the future of the Bay depends more on the actions of lobbyists, lawyers, and political action committees than the results of nonbinding Bay Agreements. The road ahead will be defined by conflict, which should be acknowledged as a normal part of the political process rather than something to overcome. And groups that desire to be meaningful players in the process should adopt a legal status that allows them to play the game. Ultimately, advocates for the Chesapeake Bay will need to establish that the public has a right to clean air, clean water, and vibrant natural resources, or risk losing what is left of the once mighty Chesapeake Bay.

CHAPTER 19

REGIONAL PLANNING AT A COUNTY SCALE IN LANCASTER COUNTY, PENNSYLVANIA

Ray D'Agostino and Mary L. Frey

As a commonwealth, Pennsylvania is a home rule state in which municipal governments, rather than counties or state agencies, control land use decisions through their local master plans and zoning ordinances. Regional or countywide zoning is authorized if municipalities agree to work with the county and one another, but they cannot be compelled to do so. There are currently no mechanisms that allow regional tax sharing for municipal finance, schools, and many other government services.

Given this context, it may not be hard to understand that growth management was late in coming to Pennsylvania. Lancaster County and several other counties in the southeastern portion of the state influenced the adoption of growth management legislation in 2000. Under Pennsylvania's Municipalities Planning Code, county and local agencies are authorized to designate future growth areas, public infrastructure areas, and rural resource areas. The county and local governments may also use growth management tools, including multi-municipal planning and zoning, specific plan, traditional neighborhood development, transferable development rights, and development of regional significance and impact.

Lancaster County, about forty miles west of Philadelphia, covers 950 square miles and has a population of approximately 500,000. Its sixty municipalities include the city of Lancaster, eighteen boroughs, and forty-one townships. The county is still largely rural and a popular tourist destination. The county is known for having the most productive nonirrigated farmland in the country. It is a place where Plain Sect (e.g., Amish) communities maintain their traditional way of life. But the county has seen accelerating suburban sprawl and conversion of farmland into subdivisions, though to a lesser extent than comparable counties in Pennsylvania. Traffic congestion has increased and some deterioration of its urban center in Lancaster City has occurred; however, in the last decade that has turned around. These trends have been accompanied by a public perception that the county is experiencing more crime and drug problems. Community leaders are aware of these perceptions and are working to address the issues.

As growth pressure mounted during the 1980s and 1990s, Lancaster County leaders and those in the sixty municipalities that make up Lancaster County realized that on their own they could not ensure success in preserving those characteristics that make Lancaster County a special place in the country. With this realization, regional planning in Lancaster County has flourished over the past ten years. In 2006 and 2007, two groundbreaking and award-winning regional comprehensive plans were adopted in Lancaster County.

Adopted by the county in 2005 and 2006, Envision Lancaster County is a series of documents developed to enhance and sustain the county for the next twenty-five years and beyond. Its purpose is to support balanced growth into the future by strengthening and sustaining the county's urban and rural communities, its diverse economy, choice of housing types and affordability, and natural and cultural heritage. Envision is Lancaster County's smart growth strategy.

In 2007, Growing Together, the largest multi-municipal planning effort to date in Pennsylvania, was adopted by the Lancaster Inter-Municipal Committee (LIMC), a council of thirteen municipal governments that have joined together to cooperate on government activities. Growing Together is a multi-municipal vision and comprehensive planning process for Central Lancaster County. Eleven of the thirteen LIMC members participated in Growing Together; one township chose not to participate and instead developed its own municipal comprehensive plan. One borough was not a member of the LIMC at the time of plan development.

Envision Lancaster County and Growing Together complement one another and together serve to create a coherent approach to long-term land use planning for the county and its municipalities. Both plans received the Outstanding Planning Award for a Comprehensive Plan from the Pennsylvania chapter of the American Planning Association in their respective years of adoption. Envision also received a U.S. EPA National Smart Growth award.

Envision Lancaster County: A Comprehensive Plan for Lancaster County

As the county's comprehensive plan, Envision Lancaster County guides the County Planning Commission's work. The plan consists of three components: a policy element entitled Revisions; a growth management element entitled Balance; and a series of functional elements that include detailed plans for housing, green infrastructure, cultural heritage, tourism, transportation, and water resources.

Public comments gathered by the County Planning Commission in the development of Balance show a great deal of public support for regional solutions to these challenges. County residents want farmland and open space preserved, development managed and concentrated in appropriate areas, revitalization of Lancaster City's downtown, and tax reforms. Recognizing that the County Planning Commission cannot make this plan a reality on its own, the commission has sought to build a public-private coalition to support the plan and its strategies. Through an extensive consultation and public review process, the County Planning Commission developed Envision Lancaster County to address these issues. The plan focuses on regional approaches through cooperation among the municipal governments, as well as the private sector.

HOME AND HERITAGE

Choices, the update to the housing element of the comprehensive plan, provides a strategy to ensure that all county residents have options for a place to call home. The goal is that an adequate supply and diversity of housing opportunities will be available in Lancaster County to give residents greater choice in housing type, location, price, and tenure—rental or ownership.

A market study found that Lancaster County is following a national trend in demand for more compact forms of housing, fueled by 82 million baby boomers in the process of downsizing, 72 million "Millennials" entering the market, and changing household characteristics. While more than 80 percent of new construction is for large single-family detached units, the market study projected 43 percent of households will prefer single-family attached units. Choices aims to achieve its housing goals through a collaborative effort by the county, municipalities, private sector, and nonprofit sector. By creating consistency between municipal ordinances and the policies of Envision, the mix of housing type and tenure will be expanded. By working with municipalities, 85 percent of new residential growth will be targeted to urban growth areas that have a full range of infrastructure, allowing for smaller lot sizes and greater housing density. The county will also work with municipalities and the nonprofits and the private sector to implement housing affordability programs.

Heritage, the cultural heritage element of the comprehensive plan, is designed to help residents discover, interpret, preserve, and celebrate the county's heritage resources. More than focusing on preserving buildings and structures, this element also celebrates the county's people. It is a blueprint for action across all levels of government and all sectors of the community: public, private, and nonprofit. This plan element identifies a number of actions that should bring these goals to fruition. For example, the plan recognizes that the use of urban and village growth boundaries should have a positive impact on preserving the vitality and assets of historic villages and structures, as well as helping protect farmland and open space outside the growth boundaries. Heritage recommends municipalities adopt ordinances and financial incentives that will facilitate the adaptive reuse of historic buildings and properties. Recognizing the role that aesthetics plays in preserving cultural heritage, Heritage recommends the use of historic district designations and development design reviews to perpetuate community character.

Sustaining the county's success as a tourist destination requires strong community and government support, quality leadership, continuous marketing efforts, and the ability to build on the region's strengths and resources. Tourism is the element of Envision Lancaster County that addresses the goal of building on the county's historic commitment to tourism and developing new, sustainable, and authentic tourism products. The overall objective is to increase the economic, social, and environmental benefits of tourism in Lancaster County.

BALANCING GROWTH

Balance, the growth management element of the comprehensive plan, establishes the overall direction, tools, and strategies by which municipalities and the county can work together to realize Lancaster County's aspirations. The theme of Balance is managing growth while preserving the county's natural and historic resources and unique sense of place. It is designed to shape land use patterns in the county by identifying areas appropriate for urban growth and areas appropriate for long-term agricultural and natural resource uses. The plan affirms the concept of urban growth areas set out in prior county growth management elements, proposes the designation of rural areas, and recommends strategies and a smart growth toolbox to shape growth to achieve desired patterns of development and preservation.

The rural strategy, a new and innovative component, has been the missing companion piece to the urban growth areas. It is not just about saving farmland. It is about promoting and expanding agriculture, agribusiness and the rural economy, reducing conflicts between development and farming, and protecting natural resources.

In developing Balance, the county conducted an extensive public involvement process. More than 3,000 people participated in meetings and surveys and the review of draft documents. There was also extensive media coverage of the planning process. The process consisted of three multipart community forums. The first set focused on existing conditions and trends; the second part examined alternatives for balancing growth and preservation; and the third series identified a preferred growth management framework for the county.

The first series of community forums reaffirmed the direction that the county has taken for managing growth over the past fifteen years:

- 79 percent of survey respondents said recent growth trends should not continue into the future
- 95 percent said farmland preservation should be a priority
- 95 percent said the rural character of the county should be maintained
- 87 percent said higher density development in growth areas should be encouraged
- 50 percent said there should be opportunities for expansion in growth areas

Citizen input clearly showed strong support for continuing the current growth management strategy (designating and supporting urban and rural areas) and strengthening farmland preservation efforts. The County Planning Commission created a map depicting a combination of the two complementary strategies. This Growth Management Framework Map serves as the basis for the continued implementation of urban growth areas and the establishment of rural areas. The map also shows village growth areas, municipal boundaries, crossroads communities, core reinvestment areas, general reinvestment areas, concentrated building areas, general building areas, designated agricultural areas, designated natural areas, and designated agricultural with natural areas.

The Urban Growth Area Strategy is based on the premise that the existing urban growth areas (UGAs) contain sufficient land to accommodate growth through 2030. The strategy includes these enhanced targets for growth: 85 percent (versus the previous 80 percent) of all new development should occur inside UGAs at a net density of 7.5 dwellings per acre (versus the previous 5.5 gross); 66 percent of all new acreage used for employment uses will be within UGAs.

Together with directing new development into designated growth areas, the plan advocates for a number of strategies that are supportive of existing communities. The plan focuses on adapting and reusing historic and characteristic buildings through appropriate zoning standards and incentives built into the permit review process. The plan calls for using traditional neighborhood design concepts and creating mixed use developments that integrate new housing and commercial development into an easily traveled network of schools, parks, and other public facilities. Since many of the county's existing communities have traditional character that should be preserved and exploited, the plan points out that new housing developments should be designed to fit into the pattern, character, and scale of existing neighborhoods.

Lancaster City and several smaller boroughs are the county's original livable communities, with walkable neighborhoods and a diversity of people, events, and businesses. The success of these urban places is critical to the success of the preservation plans for farmland and natural areas. Parts of these towns need revitalization. Reinvestment therefore plays a major role in Envision: 55 percent of new jobs and 12 percent of new dwellings should be located in reinvestment areas, which are the city of Lancaster, the eighteen boroughs, and currently developed areas of the townships.

A key goal of the Rural Area Strategy is the establishment of designated rural areas where rural resources, rural character, and a rural way of life are sustained and incompatible development is precluded. Four rural designations are proposed, and they will need to be established cooperatively with municipalities in a process similar to the one used to establish the existing forty-plus urban and village growth areas. The four rural designations are agricultural areas, agricultural with natural areas, natural areas, and rural centers. The rural centers are broken down into village growth areas, crossroads communities, rural business areas, and rural neighborhoods.

Agriculture is Lancaster County's leading rural industry sector. It makes up 63 percent of the land base and provides 11 percent of the economic output and 20 percent of the jobs. More than this, it is the bedrock of the county's heritage and a cornerstone to its sense of place. It should then be no surprise that many of the goals, objectives, and strategies throughout Envision in some way come back to preserving that which makes Lancaster unique, its agrarian culture and the land and people that compose this culture. A number of strategies are proposed to specifically support this vital industry and way of life that will require the cooperation of the county, municipalities, and landowners. These strategies fall into the following broad categories:

- Using zoning to protect farmland and supporting the practice of farming as well as the farmer
- Building coalitions and partnerships to advise farmers and public officials in new industry practices, market trends, and public policies that will support and strengthen agriculture
- Elevating agriculture by including agriculture in the discussion of all other elements of planning: transportation, economic development, housing, etc.

The growth management element update of the county's comprehensive plan provides a vision and the tools for achieving the balance the community desires in managing growth while preserving Lancaster County's natural and historic resources and unique sense of place.

Implementation

In order to implement the plan, Lancaster County must work cooperatively with the municipalities. The county does not provide infrastructure and does not control land use. So implementation depends on local officials. The Lancaster County Planning Commission has developed an Envision partnership program that will be the basis for working with municipalities on the implementation of Balance as well as the other elements of the county's comprehensive plan. Municipalities are the key to the implementation of countywide, regional, and local planning. The Lancaster County Planning Commission will strengthen its working relationship with municipalities through the Envision partnership. This partnership will accomplish the following:

- Help the County Planning Commission and municipalities agree on common priorities for implementation of county, regional, and local plans
- Help the County Planning Commission establish a work program and budget that supports the implementation of planning at the local level
- Allow the Lancaster County Planning Commission to target staff and financial resources to the implementation of these priorities
- Achieve the countywide vision for the future as identified by Lancastrians in Balance as well as the identified regional and local visions for the future.

The outcomes expected from the Envision partnership process are the following:

- A list of common goals and objectives between the local or regional plan and Balance
- A commitment for the county and the municipalities to work together on implementation of county, regional, and local plans
- Setting the stage for municipalities to do a self-assessment based on a series of Envision guidelines for implementation of Balance at the local level
- An understanding of the general concepts contained in Balance

Growing Together: A Comprehensive Plan for Central Lancaster County

While to some it may seem redundant to have two plans, one that covers the entire county and another that covers an area encompassing half its population, the two complement each other and are important to one another's success. Growing Together provides more specific recommendations and localized strategies, while Envision provides the broader framework; they are complementary and fulfilling at the same time. The same can be said of the relationship between Growing Together and local municipal plans.

With Central Lancaster County encompassing approximately 169 square miles and a population of approximately 200,000 residents (40.0 percent of the county total) and steadily growing (10.6 percent from 1990 to 2000), it can easily be said that this area represents the urban core of the county. As of July 2003, Central Lancaster County had a total of 108,077 acres, with 49,355 acres, or 45 percent, within the urban growth boundary. In 2000 Central Lancaster County's largest industries, in terms of employment, were manufacturing, education, health and social services, and retail trade. It is also easy to see that this particular area and Growing Together are central to the success of Envision.

The planning process began in 2002, when members of the LIMC board developed the idea of Growing Together and set up a steering committee to make it happen. Funding for the project has come from the Commonwealth of Pennsylvania ($150,000) and Lancaster County ($150,000).

The public participation process of Growing Together began in August 2003 with an opportunity for participants to hear about the plan and express their preliminary ideas and concerns about the future of Central Lancaster County. In January 2004, a stakeholder workshop brought together municipal officials, special interest groups, planning staff, and citizens to address critical questions related to elements of the plan.

Four public meetings, four classroom workshops in urban and suburban schools, and a focus group with African American and Latino participants were facilitated in January and February 2004. In September 2004 a Community Vision Summit was held to present an update on the project and report on the "Strong Places, Weak Places" mapping exercise. Participants reviewed goals and objectives drafted from ideas collected in the public meetings and small group discussions designed to address future development patterns for the area. Three public forums were offered in March 2005 to review goals and strategies and to recommend priorities. A final public forum in December 2005 was used to present the complete draft of the plan. In the summer of 2007, all eleven municipalities adopted Growing Together. Including the eleven municipalities involved in Growing Together, a total of forty-four of the county's sixty municipalities are involved in regional comprehensive plans.

DIRECTIONS AND GOALS

The Growing Together plan has eighteen goals, 115 objectives, and more than 300 strategies. There are four overarching key directions in the plan.

1. Expand regional cooperation: The plan recognizes that cooperation among municipalities is a precondition to success. Implementation of a majority of the objectives and strategies of the plan will require strong partnerships among municipalities, public agencies, special interest groups, businesses, and the public. Growing Together recommends that expanding regional cooperation should be approached in a flexible manner at the regional or subregional level. It also recommends that municipalities seek cooperation on issues that cross jurisdictions and in cases where the implementation of cooperative strategies can lead to more effective solutions. The plan specifically calls for cooperative funding (such as tax sharing) and shared, harmonized regulations to implement regional strategies of the plan.

2. Use land resources more efficiently: The Growing Together plan addresses future growth in several ways:

   - It recommends that 100 percent of growth in the next twenty-five years be inside the urban and village growth areas designated by each municipality. This recommendation is intended to stem development outside the growth areas and to reaffirm the special character and economic value of the agricultural land outside of these areas.

   - Future growth should occur in the form of integrated, mixed use development. The overwhelming majority of development in Central Lancaster County in the past twenty years has been in the form of development that segregates land uses. Growing Together recommends that future development strive to integrate land uses as much as possible to promote efficient use of developable land and improve mobility.

   - Growing Together identifies thirty-five areas with similar characteristics as growth opportunity areas within the aforementioned growth areas. They are undeveloped, within sewer and water service areas, next to major roads and bordered by development.

3. Enhance the support role of LIMC: Many of the objectives and strategies in Growing Together suggest a leading role for LIMC in their implementation.

The committee is positioned as a broker and convener of municipalities and organizations around issues, as an awareness-builder and communicator, and as a facilitator for specific strategies under the direction of the eleven municipalities. This increased role for LIMC will require changes to its funding and organizational structure.

4. Strengthen the economic role of Central Lancaster County: The economic activity within the LIMC municipalities drives the county's economy. So several of the objectives and strategies in Growing Together aim at ensuring that Central Lancaster County maintains its economic competitiveness. Goals and strategies in the land use element of the plan recommend providing an adequate supply of land as new development, redevelopment, and infill to accommodate future economic growth, particularly in priority areas identified by the county planning commission.

IMPLEMENTATION STRATEGIES

The plan includes elements addressing land use, housing, transportation, community facilities, parks and open space, natural resource protection, historic resource protection, utilities, and implementation. The land use element speaks to strategies for mixed use development and creating community character while also setting out exactly what the Growing Together towns are trying to achieve in each kind of land use area, whether agricultural preservation, growth management, redevelopment, and infill or urban core. For example, the urban core section of the land use element seeks to revitalize Lancaster City and other identified urban areas. Recognizing the positive role that urban areas can play for the entire region, the plan calls for the region to share the responsibility of revitalizing these urban communities through collective planning and funding.

The housing element focuses on promoting the development of diverse housing choices for both rental and ownership. Growing Together utilized the county's residential market analysis from Choices to determine market trends. The analysis indicates that an aging population will drive demand toward smaller, more compact housing designs, including attached houses and apartments, as the county absorbs nearly 18,000 additional residential units through 2030. The Growing Together plan calls for the participating municipalities to create a regional program of economic and development incentives to ensure there are affordable housing options for all residents. The plan also outlines ways to use zoning to encourage the creation of mixed use developments and diverse housing options. These options include reforms such as allowing such development where it is currently discouraged or excluded and providing economic incentives for affordable housing construction.

The transportation element aims to promote mobility by creating new, often small, relief routes connecting various parts of the existing transportation corridors. This part of the plan addresses vehicle transportation, public transportation, and alternative transportation (i.e., greenways, paths, and street use by pedestrian and bicycle riders). Residents accurately perceive that congestion is getting worse, with most traffic having to use a limited number of major roads with few inter-connections. The region provides few public transportation options. These issues are exacerbated by the design of most newer subdivisions, which force motorists into collectors and arterial streets, where they compete for space at the same peak periods. The plan includes numerous road improvement proposals, calls for requiring more connections between new and existing developments, and advo-cates the creation of a truly regional public transportation system.

The natural resource protection element aims to strengthen and regionalize policies to protect air quality, soils, water quality, aquifers, streams, and wetlands. Recognizing that natural resources do not adhere to our political boundaries, the plan calls for the adoption of uniform and consistent natural resource protection policies and regulations across all municipalities as the best way to protect these resources. Examples include proposals to evaluate and shape new developments in terms of their impact on the aquifers that are recharged by the land in question, reform stormwater management standards to require at least two forms of pretreatment before stormwater is discharged into surface or ground water, and preserve natural areas and corridors through land use controls, transfer of development rights, land acquisition, and adherence to the growth area program.

The success of Growing Together will depend on citizens and leaders of Central Lancaster County maintaining a high level of commitment to the project—a com-mitment directed by a more regional and cooperative way of thinking about prob-lems and opportunities. Everything about the plan—its statement of the problems, its objectives, its strategies, and its implementation—are framed in regional terms and require cooperative action among municipalities and other agencies, as well as NGOs, businesses, and citizens in order to succeed.

The plan calls for the creation of a Growing Together Implementation Committee, representing agencies, organizations, and citizens and consisting of a number of subcommittees tasked with implementing the strategies contained in the plan. Everyone involved will become accustomed to a new way of decision making that considers more than individual municipal needs and priorities but focuses on those of the region as a whole.

Parts of the plan are already moving forward. For example, the county in con-junction with the LIMC has developed a handbook on transfer of development rights (TDR), which includes intermunicipal TDR strategies. Neighborhood design ordinances are being considered within the region that could serve as models for the towns throughout the county.

The main focus, however, is to create a process and structure that will advance the plan as a whole. As of July 2008, all eleven municipalities have adopted an implementation agreement and formed a land use advisory board. The agreement is critical to making the plan a reality, and since key decisions will continue to be made by municipalities through their local land use ordinances, a central piece of the agreement is the land use advisory board, which will provide guidance to municipalities on ordinance and master plan consistency with Growing Together.

CHAPTER 20

LAND USE AND INFRASTRUCTURE PLANNING IN THE GREATER PHILADELPHIA REGION

Barry Seymour

Regional boundaries are often hard to define with precision. Philadelphia, the sixth largest city in the country with almost 1.5 million people, is located in Pennsylvania but adjoins New Jersey across the Delaware River. The state of Delaware and the city of Wilmington are located just fifteen miles to the south. Philadelphia is also midway between New York City and Washington, D.C., and may be considered part of the larger megaregion that has grown together along the East Coast. Linked by Interstate 95 and frequent high-speed train service via Amtrak, the New York–Philadelphia–Washington corridor increasingly operates as an integrated economic unit.

While recognizing these different scales and definitions of the region, the Delaware Valley Regional Planning Commission (DVRPC) defines the Philadelphia metropolitan area as part of two states, nine counties, and 352 local municipal governments. With over 5.5 million residents and almost 2.8 million jobs, the Philadelphia metropolitan area is the sixth largest region in the country. For comparison, the economy of the region is larger than those of Hong Kong, Norway, or Poland.

These boundaries guide the commission's core programs, but also enable and require that we work with our neighbors to coordinate planning across these regional boundaries. Philadelphia is not competing with Washington or New York, but it is competing in a global marketplace. Companies and workers can now locate anywhere, and regions are the geographic areas of competition. It is DVRPC's mission to plan for the orderly growth and development of the region and ensure that the region offers a skilled labor force and a high quality of life in order to stay competitive in the new economy.

DVRPC is the federally designated metropolitan planning organization (MPO) for the region. Created in 1965 through an agreement between Pennsylvania and New Jersey, DVRPC has the responsibility and mandate to prepare a long-range transportation plan for the region and to allocate state and federal funding for transportation improvements that are consistent with that plan. DVRPC also seeks to advance other regional initiatives, such as a regional open space plan, an economic development strategy, an air quality improvement plan, and a regional climate change action plan. The DVRPC board includes representatives from the two states, nine counties, and primary cities of the region.

There are a variety of challenges in coordinating regional transportation and land use planning in this part of the country. A strong home-rule tradition exists in Pennsylvania and New Jersey, and small municipalities have more influence and authority over land use than larger, regional agencies. The region is characterized by many declining cities and older suburbs but must also deal with suburban sprawl and growth pressures in rural areas. The small local governments (many with less than 10,000 residents) have the land use authority, but they have limited staff capacity and tend to defer to private property rights claims, which are enforced by the courts in both states.

In addition, both states have traditionally divided land use planning (decided at the local level) from transportation planning (decided by state agencies). While New Jersey has a state plan (there is no state plan in Pennsylvania), land use authority is still vested primarily at the local level, reflected in the individual comprehensive or master plans and zoning ordinances in each of the region's 352 local municipalities. The State Departments of Transportation control and manage the primary roadways in the region, but historically they have sought to respond and serve the local land use patterns and growth rather than seeking to direct or manage that growth.

Planning in the metropolitan area occurs on several scales. There are comprehensive land use plans and zoning ordinances established by each municipality and transportation plans created by the state transportation agencies. DVRPC tries to bridge the gap between the municipal and state planning agencies, working at both the regional and local levels.

In 1930, the Philadelphia metropolitan area had 222,000 acres developed and a population of 3.3 million. In 1970, 641,000 acres had been developed, and the population was 5.1 million. By 2000, 920,000 acres were developed, while the population had only grown to 5.4 million. The rate of land developed has increased at five times the rate of population growth over the past seventy years.

From 1970 to 2000, development and population trends were a recipe for sprawl. The rate of development was more than one acre per hour, accelerating over the past decade. This sprawling land use pattern has resulted in changing travel patterns. Commuters from the suburbs of Pennsylvania and New Jersey into the city of Philadelphia stayed about the same or decreased from 1980 to 2000, and commuters from the city to the suburbs increased slightly. More jobs are locating in large, suburban office parks, so the metro area is experiencing an increase in reverse commuters.

But the largest numbers of commuters now travel from suburb to suburb, and those numbers are growing. The region has extensive regional rail service, but it was developed at a time when most commuting went from the suburbs into the central city, and it is not well equipped to serve suburb-to-suburb travel. Thus, the number of drivers who travel alone has increased, carpooling is decreasing, and use of public transportation is declining.

REGIONAL INFRASTRUCTURE INVESTMENTS

The transportation infrastructure of the region has been stretched thin. State and county roads and bridges require a significant maintenance investment and are difficult to expand to carry heavier traffic flow. The existing transit system also requires extensive funding to maintain, with limited resources for system expansion. Choices must be made and priorities set to direct regional investments.

In order to plan for the future, DVRPC has identified four different planning areas that reflect the diverse character of the region: core cities, developed communities, growing suburbs, and rural areas. Each of these areas is facing different pressures, which require different types of policy responses and infrastructure investment. These areas should be supported by local governments with incentives, grants, technical assistance, and infrastructure investments while preserving surrounding open space and farmlands. These different planning areas form the framework for DVRPC's 2030 long-range plan, which in turn becomes the basis for the creation and administration of the Transportation Improvement Program (TIP), which directs funding for transportation improvements.

The long-range plan anticipates that we will spend upwards of $50 billion over twenty-five years for transportation system improvements. Given the age and condition of our infrastructure, the vast majority of that spending will be directed to system maintenance, repair, and reconstruction, with less than 10 percent allocated to new capacity. Approximately half of the funding will go into our transit systems, and half toward the roadway network. Investments are consistent with the regional land use plan, with priority given to support the existing systems in core cities and developed communities.

The TIP identifies the first four years of investment. Over $5 billion will be spent on transportation improvements under the current TIP, again with approximately half of that funding allocated to transit system improvements and the other half to highway improvements. In addition, over $140 million is allocated in the current TIP to bicycle and pedestrian system improvements.

The region's partners work together to establish the policies and priorities of the plan and the TIP. Each of the nine counties in the DVRPC region has its own unique character and needs. The core city of Philadelphia relies most heavily on the transit system. Suburban counties such as Montgomery or Camden utilize transit but also must address congested roadways. Developing counties such as Gloucester or Chester seek new investments and capacity to handle their growth. But all the member governments recognize that they must share the limited financial resources and that they must plan together for a single integrated regional system.

Linking Land Use and Transportation

It is the pattern, density, and mix of land uses that generate people and trips—the source of travel demand for transportation services and facilities. Designing transportation facilities without considering land use implications will cause future problems and inconsistencies as new capacity and services induce growth. At the same time, making land use decisions without considering the need for transportation facilities and services will lead to other problems in the future, such as congestion or safety problems. Planning for land use and transportation must be compatibly linked, in coordination with other principles and goals.

DVRPC has embraced smart growth and linked it with smart transportation as a way to influence regional development through infrastructure investment and planning. Current commission efforts to link land use and transportation focus on the following five areas:

1. *Create a Regional Policy Framework.* For the 2030 long-range plan, DVRPC staff worked with our regional transportation partners to develop a structure to link specific transportation investments to each of the four planning areas of core cities, developed communities, growing suburbs, and rural areas. In the core cities, the policy goal is redevelopment and renewal, with targeted infrastructure investments, asset maintenance, and rehabilitation of existing systems. In developed communities, the goal is stabilization and revitalization, with preventive maintenance, economic development, and streetscape and signage programs to reinforce locational and physical advantages. In the growing suburbs, the priority is growth management and community design, to support a more concentrated development pattern with higher densities that can support new transit service and alternatives to the single-occupant automobile. For rural areas, the policy goal is preservation and limited development, including limited expansion of infrastructure systems, preservation of a rural lifestyle and village character, and protection of natural resources.

For each of these four areas, policies were defined regarding where and when to maintain and improve transit, provide new transit capacity, maintain and improve highways, provide new highway capacity, or create bicycle and pedestrian facilities. In addition, regional agreement was reached on the overall allocation of funds for roadway reconstruction, bridge restoration, safety or operational improvements, new capacity, and other improvements, such as intelligent transportation systems. This policy framework provides guidance for future investments but also serves to avoid future conflicts over the allocation of funds and the selection of projects.

2. Corridor, or Multi-Municipal, Planning. With a large number of small communities in the region, the roadway network is the common thread that links communities and provides an opportunity for multi-municipal planning and cooperation. Since many of the major roads in the region are under the control of the state or county, DVRPC is in a unique position to build connections between communities, and connections between local land use planning and state transportation planning. DVRPC utilizes a comprehensive approach to these corridors, integrating land use, economic development, the environment, and transportation in a single plan. Corridor studies can help identify safety, access, and congestion problems but also lead communities toward changes in their local zoning or comprehensive plans to better manage growth or focus economic development efforts.

For example, a corridor study of eight growing suburban communities along Route 202 in Chester and Delaware counties in Pennsylvania focused on land use strategies and techniques to manage growth, including updates to local zoning ordinances, use of an official map to guide future road improvements, and use of access management tools to oversee the placement of new driveways. In contrast, a corridor study of five inner-ring suburban municipalities and an area of West Philadelphia focused on economic development opportunities along the corridor, including design guidelines for infill development, streetscape designs, and recommendations for transit-oriented development around existing train stations. While very different in character and needs, each of these studies allowed the communities to see the common interests of their neighbors and plan collectively to address common goals.

3. Multimodal Planning. DVRPC seeks a comprehensive approach to its transportation planning, which integrates transit, highways, and bicycle and pedestrian facilities to serve all needs. This is accomplished through the regional policy framework and the corridor plans described above, which seek to develop "complete streets" that serve cars, trucks, transit, bicycles, and pedestrians. This approach is further implemented through the TIP. The long-range plan identifies projects and allocates funding for highway and transit improvements but also includes a regional vision and plan for intelligent transportation systems (ITS), for bicycle and pedestrian facilities, for a regional trail network, for port and freight facilities, and for airports and aviation facilities. The TIP directs funding to implement the vision of the plan.

As a regional planning agency, one of DVRPC's key strengths is its ability to bring together the many stakeholders from throughout the region in a regional forum. To support multimodal transportation planning, DVRPC has created a series of regional advisory committees that convene to share information and ideas and to formulate policy recommendations for the full DVRPC board. Thus, there is a regional Goods Movement Task Force to consider freight issues, a Regional Aviation Committee to coordinate funding for airports, a Regional Transit Committee that brings the different transit agencies together, and a Regional Transportation Committee that seeks to integrate all the modes.

4. Context-Sensitive Planning. Roadways form the framework and backbone of a community, but modern roadway design too often ignores the character of the community and its current and planned land uses. DVRPC has been working with PennDOT and NJDOT on a new approach called "Smart Transportation," where transportation investments are tailored to the specific needs of each project. The different contexts—financial, community, land use, transportation, and environmental—determine the design of the solution. The best transportation solutions arise from a process in which a multidisciplinary team, considering a wide range of solutions, works closely with the community. DVRPC has worked directly with communities such as Burlington City, New Jersey, and Pottstown, Pennsylvania, in implementing context-sensitive design. The solution in Burlington City was the introduction of curb bump-outs and bike lanes to slow down traffic in a commercial district. Pottstown had similar traffic-calming needs on a wide main street. Planners and the community decided to introduce a unique back-in angled parking design on either side of the road, bicycle lanes, and a middle turning lane to reduce the number of lanes. The changes encourage people to stop, park, and shop while creating a safer environment for drivers, bicyclists, and pedestrians.

5. Community Development. While good transit service and transportation facilities are not always sufficient to support revitalization and redevelopment in older communities, they are a necessary element. In 2002 DVRPC created the Transportation and Community Development Initiative (TCDI) to provide planning grants to cities, boroughs, and older townships for design and feasibility studies to support infrastructure and redevelopment projects. Many of the projects leverage public grant monies with private investment; ninety-nine projects so far have used a $6 million investment to leverage billions. DVRPC has also worked with communities and developers to support and promote transit-oriented development (TOD). Although many of the communities in the Greater Philadelphia region were initially built around train stations, new development has moved away from these transit hubs. To support new TOD investment, DVRPC prepared a regional inventory of TOD opportunity sites, examining the level of service available, ridership, access, parking, land uses, zoning, patron amenities, and development potential. The inventory report was used to publicize those sites for the development community. A series of marketplace meetings were held where communities could promote their sites and meet with developers. DVRPC has also worked with selected communities to develop detailed local TOD plans.

The TCDI planning grants and the local TOD plans have created a new avenue for DVRPC to interface with and influence the many local governments and neighborhood organizations in the region. With land use control powers vested at the local level in Pennsylvania and New Jersey, regional agencies must seek other means to influence land use and development patterns. Regional policy, advocacy, and education are important, but ultimately advisory if communities do not choose to act. The allocation of infrastructure funding and projects is important but not always sufficient to change local land use decisions. Using direct funding to communities through the TCDI program has enabled DVRPC to directly implement our regional goals via local action, and the availability of that funding has brought greater recognition and participation in the regional forum by local governments.

OTHER REGIONAL INITIATIVES

Regional planners must continually look for creative ways to engage their local partners and stakeholders to build a regional identity, form regional partnerships, and engage in regional cooperation. As the designated regional metropolitan planning organization, DVRPC has a defined membership and the authority to bring the region's representatives together around transportation planning and funding. But in order to promote other regional goals, DVRPC must work with a wide variety of partners, including other public, private, and nonprofit regional and local organizations, to find common interests and opportunities for collaboration. In addition to our core transportation planning responsibilities, DVRPC has established a variety of other regional initiatives and engaged a variety of different partners.

Strategies for Older Suburbs

Philadelphia as a city was first established in 1682 and soon grew outward. Many of the suburban communities surrounding Philadelphia were established as towns or boroughs soon thereafter. These older suburbs (sometimes called first suburbs) face challenges of decaying infrastructure, older housing stock, and commercial districts that must compete with the newer malls or big-box retail. They also suffered in recent decades from a weak market in the central city and have limited staff or financial resources to take action. To assist these older suburbs, DVRPC provides technical and financial assistance in the form of peer-to-peer training programs, regional conferences, the TCDI grant program, and economic development market studies and action plans. The William Penn Foundation has been a key funding partner of the program. Through these actions, local capacity, knowledge, and collaboration have increased throughout the region.

Classic Towns of Greater Philadelphia

A new program is currently under development to help promote some of the older suburbs and city neighborhoods of the Greater Philadelphia region. These "classic towns" may face some of the challenges noted here, but they also provide a true Main Street shopping experience; a variety of housing types with a strong architectural heritage; local amenities such as parks, playgrounds, and libraries; and a walkable environment and sense of place that is often lacking in newer suburbs. DVRPC is helping to promote and market these communities through an umbrella campaign that will include a website, shared graphics, advertising placement, and assistance to the individual communities for their own marketing efforts. Each of the participating communities will contribute toward a common website and advertising.

GreenSpace Alliance

The Philadelphia region has a strong legacy of land conservation, with a variety of local and state agency funding programs and a number of nonprofit land conservancies. They have collectively preserved many thousands of acres but have not always coordinated their efforts. DVRPC worked with the Pennsylvania Environmental Council to help establish the GreenSpace Alliance, which brings together the state funding agencies with the local area land conservation organizations. DVRPC's regional open space plan was endorsed by the alliance and became their common framework for land conservation priorities in the region. DVRPC also works with our public and private partners in the New Jersey portion of our region as well to identify priority ecosystems, landscapes, and recreational facilities for acquisition and preservation.

Delaware Valley Smart Growth Alliance

DVRPC was a founding member and continues on the board of the Smart Growth Alliance, which includes representation from the region's real estate, environmental, conservation, and planning communities. The members of the Smart Growth Alliance worked together to establish a set of criteria to define smart growth projects in our region and to administer a jury program that reviews development applications on a voluntary basis to determine if they meet the criteria. If they do, they receive an endorsement from the alliance, and members will support the project as it moves through the permitting process. The Smart Growth Alliance is a true collaboration that brings together a diverse set of stakeholders to promote and support higher quality development at appropriate locations within the region.

Climate Change Action Plan

In 2007 the City of Philadelphia and Montgomery County, Pennsylvania, each prepared and adopted a climate change action plan, with recommendations for action at the city and county level. As other counties and local governments within the region began to also discuss potential responses to the climate change challenge, many looked toward DVRPC to develop a coordinated response and strategy at the metropolitan scale. The DVRPC board and staff responded and have begun to coordinate action across the region, beginning with a regional greenhouse gas emissions inventory and methodology that can be used and shared by local governments. They will also work together with our partners to develop a shared action strategy for the region. Results of this initiative will provide recommendations for action for businesses, local governments, and utilities in the region, and they will also inform DVRPC's ongoing infrastructure investment decisions in its long-range plan and TIP.

Each of these initiatives—economic revitalization, community marketing, open space preservation, smart growth promotion, and climate change—could be addressed at the local level but are more effectively addressed at the regional scale. Regional organizations such as DVRPC are uniquely positioned to view the metropolitan area as a single entity, to facilitate a shared forum to learn and exchange ideas, and to bring together a wide set of stakeholders that might not otherwise have joined forces. Regional planning is the mechanism to create new alliances and lead local interests to a shared agenda and shared actions that together are stronger than the sum of their parts.

CHAPTER 21

REGIONAL PLANNING FOR THE DELAWARE RIVER

Carol R. Collier

There is nothing static about managing a river system. A river, actually any natural system, is dynamic, always providing you with a new problem to solve. Just when you finalize a management plan for drought conditions, the river will have three years of major floods. Just when you negotiate a contentious flow allocation and reservoir release program, a new study will be released on ecological flow needs or an endangered species will be found. Just when you think the water quality of the river has improved to meet all criteria, analytical methodologies improve and you find new threats at lower detection levels. These parameters might include a persistent bioaccumulative toxic like PCBs or emergent contaminants including pharmaceuticals and endocrine disrupters. All these scenarios are happening in the Delaware River Basin. In addition, climate change provides new uncertainties that must be evaluated.

In a large river system, especially one with transboundary issues, there needs to be a mechanism to assist multiple authorities in dealing with these changing conditions. In our basin, the Delaware River Basin Commission (DRBC) provides such a mechanism and serves as the forum to plan and respond to change. In my time with DRBC, I have come to understand the following truths about water management:

- Water does not respect political boundaries.
- Water should be managed on a holistic, watershed basis.
- What happens on the land affects streams and rivers. You can not manage the water without managing the land.
- There is only one water system. A drop of water can be drinking water, in stream habitat or flood water. We must consider ground water and surface water, stormwater, water supply, and wastewater integrated as one system.
- We need to provide information about water availability, quality, and flood hazard areas so industries and local governments can make educated decisions on siting new facilities and accommodating residential growth.

- Downstream water supplies are dependent on the actions of other users.
- When establishing a water allocation and reservoir release program, one must consider water supply, instream flow needs, and flood mitigation both downstream and upstream of the dam.
- Floods will occur. We cannot stop the flood waters, but we can reduce the losses and damages from flooding. A floodplain is a natural extension of a river. Strategies need to consider upstream solutions, as well as keep people out of harm's way and warn them of impending floods.
- The Delaware River system is sensitive and can change quickly. We need to base our decisions on the range of conditions, not averages.
- There is not enough water in the basin to support all uses in another drought of record.
- We do not know all the answers. We need a stronger base of science to support the decision makers.
- Water management is not unilateral; it is a collaborative process. We need to engage all levels of government, including municipal government and local stakeholders.
- The management system of a river must be adaptive. Changes occur in the underlying science, management alternatives, and regional priorities. A river basin commission provides the forum for adaptive management.

THE DELAWARE RIVER BASIN

In the eastern United States, the Delaware is the longest undammed river, extending 330 miles from the Catskill Mountains in New York state to the mouth of the Delaware Bay, where it enters the Atlantic Ocean. The river is fed by 216 tributaries and drains 13,539 square miles, draining parts of the states of Pennsylvania, New Jersey, New York, and Delaware. Approximately 200 miles, or two-thirds of the river length, is nontidal.

The river and its surrounding land uses are very diverse. The upper basin is known for its natural beauty, world-class trout fishery, and rural communities. Three-quarters of the nontidal river—about 150 miles—has been included in the National Wild and Scenic Rivers System. The system was established by Congress in 1968 to preserve the character of rivers with "outstandingly remarkable scenic, recreational, geologic, fish and wildlife, historic, cultural or other similar values" and to ensure that designated river stretches remain free-flowing (P.L. 106-418, 106th Cong.).

While this area was formerly used mostly for vacation retreats, it is now feeling the pressure of significant growth and new home construction. This change in land use and the cutting of forested areas are affecting stream water quality and changing the stream hydrology, creating lower low and higher high flows. The headwaters are often considered the most important areas of a river system, and the headwaters of the Delaware are currently undergoing rapid change.

The lower, tidal portion of the basin is quite different, as it is largely developed with major population centers and ports. The Delaware River Port Complex is the largest freshwater port in the world. Philadelphia, the nation's fifth largest city with 1.3 million people, is located on the Delaware River. While it is a working river, the bay still has a ring of brackish and saltwater marshes providing vital habitat, nursery, and spawning areas.

The Delaware is a relatively small river with a large responsibility. Even though it drains only 0.4 percent of the total continental U.S. land area, the Delaware River Basin provides water for nearly 15 million people (5 percent of the nation's population), including 8 million living outside the watershed's borders. New York City draws half of its drinking water supply through an out-of-basin transfer from the Delaware.

While there were major pollution problems in the past due to untreated sewage and industrial discharges, the river now has good water quality, and people have found the recreational value of this "backyard" river, flocking to its waters in canoes, kayaks, motorboats, and sailboats. People are paying high prices to live near the river. Old port and shipyard facilities are being converted to multiuse river centers with residential condominiums and lofts, marinas, incubator industries, port-related commerce, and ship building/repair centers. Although the river is much cleaner, there are still concerns over water supply and allocation, and changes will be needed to address climate change.

FLOW ALLOCATION AND RESERVOIR RELEASE PROGRAM

Even though the Delaware River Basin receives approximately forty-five inches of precipitation annually, there are issues of water allocation due to the large and growing demand. Prior to the 1960s, the Delaware River Basin was an arena of interstate conflict and costly litigation over water rights. The U.S. Supreme Court had to resolve these disputes on more than one occasion during the 1900s, most recently in 1954. The basic issue in the conflict was the balancing of out-of-basin diversions to New York City with the in-basin needs for potable water and water supply for industry, power generation, and agriculture. In addition, and equally important, there must be enough freshwater flowing down the Delaware River to keep the salty waters of the Delaware Bay from inching upstream into industrial and potable water intakes in the Wilmington/Philadelphia/Camden urban area or infiltrating freshwater aquifers.

The water allocations in the 1950s were based on the human uses of water with little regard for instream needs to protect the fisheries and the aquatic community. In the past ten years, there has been more emphasis on the science of ecological flow needs. In addition, within the last four years there have been three major floods on the Delaware River, creating a demand to use reservoirs that were built for water supply for flood mitigation as well.

In 1954 the Supreme Court allowed New York City to divert a total of 800 million gallons per day (mgd), on average, from its three large reservoirs built on Delaware River headwater tributaries, with the condition that enough water be released into the Delaware River to meet a flow target of 1,750 cubic feet per second (cfs) at Montague, New Jersey, approximately eighty miles downstream of the uppermost reservoir. This flow target is based on a formula of 0.5 cfs per square mile of drainage area above the gage point. A river master (a hydrologist with the U. S. Geological Survey) was assigned to determine releases necessary to meet the Montague flow target. In addition, the Supreme Court decree allowed the State of New Jersey to divert up to 100 mgd out of the basin to service growing areas in the central part of the state.

A flow target of 3,000 cfs was set for the Delaware River at Trenton, which is the head of tide for the river, in order to safeguard the ability of New Jersey and Pennsylvania to draw sufficient, potable water for the downstream urban areas of Philadelphia and Camden through the "good faith" negotiations among the parties in the 1980s.

Recognizing the need for long-term water resources management and wanting a different mechanism than litigation, President John F. Kennedy and the governors of Delaware, New Jersey, Pennsylvania, and New York for the first time signed, in 1961, a concurrent compact legislation creating a regional body with the force of law to oversee a unified approach to managing a river system *without regard to political boundaries.* The members of this regional body—the Delaware River Basin Commission (DRBC)—are the governors of the four basin states and a federal representative appointed by the president of the United States. The five members appoint alternate commissioners, with the governors selecting high-ranking officials from their state environmental agencies. Each commissioner has one vote of equal power with a majority vote needed to decide most issues. Exceptions are votes on the commission's annual budget and drought declarations, which require unanimity. Each state and the federal government have relinquished a portion of their sovereign authority to come together and manage water resources on a watershed basis.

The Delaware River Basin Compact grants DRBC broad powers to plan, develop, conserve, regulate, allocate, and manage water resources in the basin. Unlike the strongly contested rights of first use in the western United States, the premise of both the Supreme Court decisions and the Delaware River Basin Compact is the doctrine of equitable apportionment. The 1961 compact states that "the Commission shall have the power from time to time as need appears, in accordance with the doctrine of equitable apportionment, to allocate the waters of the basin to and among the states signatory to this compact and to and among their respective political subdivisions, and to impose conditions, obligations and release requirements."

DRBC functions by vetting ideas through a number of advisory committees, which expands the sphere of stakeholders. The recommendations of the committees are then brought to the commissioners for action. It requires not only scientific and engineering expertise, but much time building trust among the stakeholders. Experience has shown time and again that it is very important to have a plan in place before an extreme event occurs. In the midst of an emergency is not the time to work out a complex response.

There are nearly forty river basin commissions or interstate water management agencies in the United States, but they all have different missions and authorities.

A limited number have congressional authorization. Some such as DRBC and the Susquehanna River Basin Commission have regulatory authority for both water allocation and water quality. Some just deal with water quantity issues; others, such as the Ohio River Valley Sanitation Commission (ORSANCO), just water quality. Many, such as the New England Interstate Water Pollution Control Commission (NEIWPCC), have only planning, education, and coordination authorities.

DRBC's first challenge came with multiple years of drought in the 1960s. The drought of record ran from 1961 through 1967. It was soon obvious that in drought conditions New York City could not withdraw 800 mgd and still have enough water left in the system to release to the Delaware River to meet the Montague Target of 1,750 cfs.

There were two choices—the parties could make a litigious attack and return to the U.S. Supreme Court or they could test the value of the Delaware River Basin Commission to develop an equitable solution. Luckily, they chose the latter alternative. Management schemes were tested in the drought of the 1960s and, in 1978, a series of interrelated management steps were developed through "The Good Faith Negotiations" to respond to changing conditions in the basin.

A Drought Operating Program was developed that is triggered by declining storage in three New York City reservoirs at the headwaters of the Delaware River. One key aspect is a drought rating curve with trigger points for drought watch, drought warning, and drought emergency. As water levels in the reservoirs decline, there is an agreed-upon plan of water use reductions. Reductions tied to a drought warning and drought watch are implemented as soon as the triggers are crossed; they do not require additional resolutions or commission action. Declaring a drought emergency, however, requires a unanimous vote by the DRBC members. This is one of the built-in checks and balances of the compact, because in drought emergency the DRBC is given additional authority to call for storage and releases from private, state, and federally owned reservoirs. Under this additional authority, DRBC manages an additional 69 billion gallons of storage.

During the drought of 2001–2002, 500 million gallons of water were conserved per day through use of the Drought Operating Program. This water was saved by reducing reservoir releases, since river flow targets and diversion amounts were lowered. Voluntary and mandatory conservation requirements for industrial, commercial, and residential users set by DRBC and the states also significantly lowered water demand. Use of the Drought Operating Program has reduced uncertainty in the management of water supply during periods of drought.

Incorporating Instream Flow Needs and Flood Mitigation

In the early years of basin flow management, instream flow necessary to support fisheries and healthy aquatic communities was largely ignored. Changes occurred in the 1980s and 1990s that promoted attention to river ecosystem health:

- With the construction of the New York City reservoirs and mandatory bottom releases of cold water to the Delaware River, a once largely warm water fishery was changed to a world-class cold water trout fishery. The fishery became an economic driver for the rural areas of the upper basin and is classified as one of the top ten trout fishing streams in the United States.

- A federally listed endangered species—the Dwarf Wedgemussel—was found in the Delaware River and a few of its headwater tributaries.
- As pollution in the river was abated, people wanted to fish and took more notice of fishery impacts. There are more people recreating on the river, demanding that instream flows for fish and boating be a recognized issue.
- When the economically valuable oyster populations of the Delaware Estuary declined due to parasites and disease, researchers also started to question the impact of changing freshwater flows to the estuary and the potential impact on oysters and other estuarine species.
- The general public has greatly increased its level of environmental knowledge and interest in protection of natural systems.

With this public demand, DRBC was again asked to facilitate the development of a management program that balances the court dictated out-of-basin diversions (New York City and New Jersey), the in-basin human water needs—drinking water, industry, power generation, agriculture (and increasingly golf course irrigation)—and flows for fisheries.

Because of the past history of flow allocation solely for human uses, DRBC's advisory committee dealing with flow issues was composed mostly of hydrologic engineers, with minimal representation of aquatic biologists and fisheries interests. As the demand for sound fishery science continued to grow, DRBC, with the help of The Nature Conservancy, created a Subcommittee for Ecological Flows (SEF) to assess the scientific requirements of the basin fishery and aquatic communities and initially prioritize the needs of the cold water trout fishery and endangered Dwarf Wedgemussel in the Upper Basin. Working with the U.S. Geological Survey and universities, DRBC initiated a number of studies to assess aspects of flow on the fishery, including average flow rate, flow variability, impact on bottom habitat, critical life stages, and impact on prey species. A decision support system (DSS) model has been developed to test different flow scenarios on habitat conditions.

In addition to small operational changes, such as ramping of reservoir releases that require minimal additional water, there was a desire to develop an operational program that better mimicked natural flows, such as providing more releases when there is more water in the reservoirs.

There had not been a significant flood on the Delaware River since 1955, yet we had three major floods in less than two years in 2004–2006. Our priorities are changing. Many mitigation measures are being considered, including requiring void space (freeboard) in the reservoirs to catch the floodwaters. These reservoirs were built and managed for drinking water supply for New York City and not as flood control dams for the Delaware River communities. There is significant controversy over the management of the dams. It is agreed that the primary function of the reservoirs is water supply, but that a void space could be created when there is a certainty of refill. New York City has instituted a "snowpack program" that lowers the reservoir levels based on the assumption that 50 percent of the water equivalent of the snow pack above the reservoir will reach the reservoir when it melts. There is also a separate spill mitigation program that calls for releases to create a void based on water levels in the reservoir and probability of refill depending on season of the year.

A Flexible Flow Management Program (FFMP) has been developed that mimics natural flows, incorporates the flood mitigation programs, and is based on adaptive management principles. A framework has been established that not only spells out the current reservoir release requirements, but also includes placeholders to reevaluate the flow regime as new scientific information becomes available or human water demands change. This includes a placeholder to reevaluate the system as new data about freshwater flows to the estuary become available.

Adapting to Climate Change

Scientists indicate that changes in climate may have significant impacts on our Delaware River Basin water systems. Projections indicate the following potential changes:

- Greater intensity of storms
- More precipitation in winter months and less in summer
- Increasing temperatures
- Decreasing snow pack
- Changes in forest species
- Sea level rise (up to a two-foot increase by the end of century)

If these forecasts come to fruition, we will experience increased droughts, as well as an increase in floods (working at the extremes). Water quality will be impacted by increasing temperatures and suspended sediment; stream and river buffers may change, and both terrestrial and aquatic biological systems will be vulnerable to invasive species.

The increasing sea level will negatively affect existing fresh and saltwater marshes that ring the estuary, and flood low-lying areas, and can have a detrimental effect on water supply. Water supply intakes in northeast Philadelphia and New Jersey, as well as water supply aquifers, may be compromised by saltwater, affecting millions of people.

How do we adapt to these potential changes? All levels of government, businesses, and individuals will need to change in some way. Just a few examples:

- Flood hazard areas along streams and rivers will likely increase, needing changes in mapping, local ordinances, and potential buy-outs or structural elevations.
- To protect the water supply intakes in the estuary, either DRBC will need to store additional water in upriver areas to release during dry times in order to

keep the salt line downstream of the intakes or the water purveyors will need to move their intakes upstream.

- Water quality may likely be compromised by increasing temperatures, increased sediment loads due to storms and erosional factors, and changes in algal species. Do we change the water quality standards to account for these climate-caused changes, or do we try to modify the situation by requiring more stringent thermal controls on wastewater and cooling water discharges and release additional cold water from reservoirs? Each approach has major consequences associated with it.
- As the climate changes, the vegetative species along river systems will change. Forested stream buffers are critical for the protection of stream water quality and reducing instream temperatures, especially in headwater areas. As the current vegetation species die, new species, potentially many invasives, will take their place. What will this do to terrestrial and aquatic systems?

It is very difficult to plan for extremes, especially with the current level of uncertainty. It is important that the organizations involved with natural resource management address these issues now and plan adaptive strategies for these changes.

River Basin Commissions: The Forum for Adaptive Management

Management of water systems is fraught with changing circumstances and is in fact a messy business. No one agency can effectively manage the resource, especially if a river or aquifer crosses multiple political boundaries. River basin commissions provide the mechanism to bring the parties to the table to work through the problem so that management and implementation plans that serve the needs of all jurisdictions and populations, as well as ecological values, can be developed and implemented.

One area that needs increased attention by the planning community is the integration of water management and land use decisions. Land use changes have impacts on all aspects of water system sustainability. While agencies such as DRBC can set environmental targets such as flow requirements and water quality standards and provide information to others, most decisions on what happens on the land are made at the municipal level. The next step in better resource management requires changes in three areas: taking water needs, impacts, and safety (flooding) into account when citing land uses and establishing local or regional zoning (municipal); requiring site controls that conserve water, infiltrate storm water, and reduce contamination (municipal); and accounting for future water needs of the municipalities in a watershed when setting water allocations (state or river basin commission).

CHAPTER 22

PLANNING FOR SUSTAINABLE AGRICULTURE, FORESTRY, AND BIODIVERSITY IN MAINE

Elizabeth Hertz

A unique partnership of state, federal, and nongovernmental agencies has worked together since 2001 delivering maps, data, information, and technical assistance to land trusts and municipalities to help ensure that Maine's landscape continues to support its current suite of plant and animal species well into the future. Beginning with Habitat (BwH) is the state of Maine's initiative to promote the protection of habitat for native species of plants and animals on a landscape scale by delivering the state's best available habitat and related data sets for the benefit of local governments, as well as land trusts and other NGOs. The data is designed to guide land use and conservation planning, acquisition, and management decisions. Maine is a home-rule state, and as such, local governments make critical land use decisions for much of the state's land area through their comprehensive plans and ordinances. BwH is voluntary; it requires municipal buy-in and local implementation to be effective.

Maine's landscape approach was developed by the University of Maine's Cooperative Fish and Wildlife Research Unit under the direction of the Department of Inland Fisheries and Wildlife (MDIFW). The program now involves a number of additional partners, including the Maine Department of Conservation, Maine State Planning Office, Maine Department of Transportation, U.S. Fish and Wildlife Service, Maine Audubon Society, The Nature Conservancy, and Maine Coast Heritage Trust. Building on the original landscape work done by the Cooperative

Fish and Wildlife Research Unit and MDIFW this partnership has developed and implemented the Beginning with Habitat Program.

BwH uses geographic information system (GIS) technology to create maps that show data layers in a format that citizen boards and municipal staff can easily understand and use. BwH relies on three primary data layers and a series of additional supporting data layers. The primary layers of BwH are water resources and riparian habitat, high value plant and animal habitat, and undeveloped, large habitat blocks. These are the building blocks the program uses for creating a landscape that supports clean water and wildlife.

Why take a landscape view of wildlife habitat? Because landscape-scale processes are vital to the long-term health of wildlife populations and other natural functions such as the protection of biodiversity and water quality. Maine recognizes that native habitats have to be viewed and protected on a landscape or regional basis. Even the best-intentioned local planning will fail to sustain habitats within a town's boundaries if these habitats are not connected to larger contiguous lands; if they are within a watershed whose headwaters are degraded through inappropriate land uses; if the town omits critical habitat areas from its conservation planning; or if neighboring towns make conflicting land-use decisions. Managing habitats on a landscape scale makes it easier to serve multiple and overlapping values, ensure adequate habitat for a range of species with differing needs, and accommodate private landowners' objectives.

As of the end of 2010, BwH had delivered maps and presentations to 308 Maine towns. The goal is to map Maine's 446 organized municipalities, keep the maps up to date, and provide technical assistance to support implementation of this planning approach at the local and regional levels.

The Methodology

1. *The Beginning with Habitat Maps.* The three primary BwH maps focus on water resources and riparian habitat, high value plant and animal habitats, and large habitat blocks, which the program defines as follows:

- Water resources and riparian habitat encompass the transitional zones between aquatic habitats and wetlands, on the one hand, and dry or upland habitats, on the other. This category therefore includes the banks and shores of streams, rivers, ponds and lakes, and the upland edge of wetlands. Analysis done by the University of Maine's Cooperative Fish and Wildlife Research Unit predicts that with adequate protection of these riparian habitats well over half of the state's vertebrate species would have sufficient habitat.
- High value plant and animal habitats include a series of defined habitat types based on the presence of particular categories of plants, animals, and natural communities, such as rare plants or animals (species listed as endangered or as species of special concern); rare or exemplary community types; essential

habitats designated for certain rare wildlife species; significant wildlife habitat for species such as deer, waterfowl, and wading birds; and U.S. Fish and Wildlife Priority Trust Species.

- Undeveloped habitat blocks are mapped by using roads and development as fragmenting landscape features. These large blocks provide essential habitat for plants and animals that require large ranges, such as fisher, as well as habitat for area sensitive nesting bird species. The large blocks capture much of the riparian and high value plant and animal habitats. They also tie together a diversity of habitat and community types, so they tend to support higher biodiversity than small blocks. Finally, planning in terms of large blocks provides more opportunities to accommodate existing human uses of the land within a viable habitat landscape.

By using this array of land characteristics, this planning approach seeks to capture the most ecologically valuable habitats and the connections between them, even though there is never perfect or complete information covering the landscape.

2. Focus Areas. In addition to these three map layers, Beginning with Habitat has also developed a series of focus areas of statewide ecological significance based on specific criteria that include the rare natural *communities*, the rare *species*, and/or the *contiguous habitats* present in an area. Focus areas are designed to bring attention to areas with high concentrations of known rare and significant plant and animal habitats. Focus areas provide a mechanism to help prioritize conservation targets, and provide an impetus for adjacent towns to work together to conserve significant natural resources. The criteria for choosing a focus area are whether an area contains the following:

- A rare natural community ranked S1, S2, or S3 by the state's Natural Heritage Program
- An A-ranked, pristine natural community
- A B-ranked, very good natural community and/or one or more significant wildlife resources
- A globally rare plant or animal species, ranked G1, G2, or G3
- Any viable population of a rare animal, ranked S1, S2, or S3
- Three or more viable populations of rare plant species, ranked S1, S2, or S3
- A large undeveloped block with at least one B-ranked common natural community, a significant wildlife resource, or two or more viable populations of rare plant species

The state (S1, S2, and S3) and global (G1, G2, and G3) species rankings, and the community rankings (A and B) of rarity and imperilment are applied by the Maine Natural Areas Program using the universal ranking system developed by The Nature Conservancy and tracked by Nature Serve (Nature Serve 2009).

3. Implementation. Using the BwH maps as guidance, local governments, state agencies, and NGOs working independently and cooperatively can deploy a

number of tools to protect important habitats and, equally important, connect
them to one another. Local governments are encouraged to use the maps in a
number of ways:

- Riparian regulation: Under state law, towns are required to protect most
  riparian habitat by adopting the state's shoreland zoning ordinance, which
  provides 75-foot buffers for second order and larger streams, and a 250-foot
  buffer around rivers, lakes, ponds, and nonforested wetlands greater than ten
  acres.
- Local zoning: Towns have substantial powers through their zoning authority
  to direct development away from important upland habitats. Towns can use
  very low density zones, transfer of development rights, clustering
  requirements, and mandatory dedication of open spaces for conservation to
  manage new development. (The BwH maps are not suitable for specific permit
  decisions on individual parcels because they are not rigorously field tested on a
  parcel-level scale.)
- Infrastructure planning: Since development follows infrastructure such as
  sewers and roads, public agencies can use Beginning with Habitat maps to
  place infrastructure in areas most suitable for growth and to control density in
  other areas. On a state level, Maine has created a Habitat and Transportation
  Working Group to integrate transportation priorities and actions with
  conservation goals, using the Beginning with Habitat philosophy of regional,
  landscape-based habitat protection.
- Site review: Local ordinances for review of development applications can
  require consultation with the appropriate regional office of MDIFW when a
  proposal potentially conflicts with a mapped resource.
- Impact fees: Develop and adopt an impact fee program with funds allocated at
  least in part to protecting open space.
- Land acquisition: Land preservation efforts can be informed by BwH, since the
  maps identify the key habitats for water quality and plant and wildlife
  protection. Many communities in Maine are passing bond issues in support of
  land acquisition. BwH maps have been used to help identify priority areas for
  those programs.
- Undeveloped habitat blocks: Towns can work within their own jurisdictions
  and cooperatively plan with neighboring towns to protect large habitat blocks
  identified on the maps. The state urges towns to protect at least several blocks
  of 250–500 acres and, where they still exist, larger blocks of 1,000 acres or
  more. By working together, towns can collectively protect much larger blocks
  of 5,000 acres or more.

BwH initially concentrated on getting maps and technical assistance out to individual municipalities and land trusts. The effort has shifted to include increased
effort on regional and watershed level projects in order to support the preservation
of landscape level functions such as wildlife habitat, connectivity, and water quality protection. Since 2001, BwH has created maps and datasets for 157 watershed

groups, land trusts, and other regional entities. In order to reach the BwH goal of preserving a landscape that will support the full suite of plant and animal species for generations to come, planning will have to take place on a scale beyond the town-by-town efforts that have been Maine's historical planning model.

THE SAGADAHOC EXAMPLE

The Sagadahoc Region Rural Resource Initiative (SRRRI) is an example of regional planning to protect natural elements of the rural service center. The SRRRI project area includes the twelve towns surrounding Merrymeeting Bay in midcoast Maine. The area has a central service center made up of three towns. The southernmost part of the region is a series of coastal peninsulas, while the northern extent still supports working farms and forestland. Merrymeeting Bay is a focus area of statewide significance supporting rare tidal marsh plants, high value waterfowl and wading bird habitat, grassland bird habitat, and rare animals.

In January 2004 the Sagadahoc County regional planner convened a meeting of the twelve towns to determine what planning issues could benefit from regional cooperation. The most common response was preservation of open space. A self-selected group representing eleven of the twelve towns continued to meet and discuss components of the region's open space, including the working rural landscape, wildlife habitat, and significant natural and recreational resources. They also discussed ways to identify critical landscape linkages and strategies to protect the rural character of the region.

Service center communities are those towns or groups of towns in which most of the jobs of an area are found and where residents shop, go to the doctor, and go to school. The rural area that complements the service center provides different yet equally important elements. The rural service center provides those places where people fish, canoe, and hike in their leisure time, take their children to pick fruit, and purchase produce from local farmers. The working farms and forests of the rural service center provide regional benefits and in fact help to define and support the quality of life and character of a region. These landscapes also support plant and animal biodiversity and water quality.

What is unique about the SRRRI project is its regional focus on planning to sustain the elements critical to support the rural service center areas of the region. A two-tiered approach was taken. The first step was to identify and map significant rural resources, including BwH data for the region, and prioritize their regional value. The second step was to review existing municipal comprehensive plans to determine how towns are currently proposing to address areas identified through the first step; the areas of conflict between proposed land uses and identified resources; the areas of conflict between towns arising from rural/growth areas and resources that cross town boundaries; and to identify ways that towns can work individually and cooperatively to address these issues.

Participating in the project were the affected towns, the Midcoast Council for Business Development and Planning (in the form of the regional planner), the

Maine Coastal Program, Maine State Planning Office, Maine Natural Areas Program, Maine Audubon, The Nature Conservancy, Bowdoin College environmental studies student interns, and the Beginning with Habitat Program.

The mapping process proceeded in four steps:

1. Identification of key landscape elements necessary to support native plants and animals using BwH data, riparian habitat, the high value habitats, and large habitat blocks
2. A GIS analysis to identify and prioritize regionally significant habitat
3. Identification of connections between these habitat areas
4. A combination of these map layers with scenic and cultural assets maps to create a regional vision

The prioritization of habitat areas used a decision support system that focused on riparian habitats and undeveloped lands. For example, high value wetlands had a score of 3, and all other wetlands had a score of 1. The most rare plants and animals had a score of 4, while other rare species had a score of 2. Fields of seventy-five or more acres had a score of 3; fields of five to thirty acres had a score of 1. Undeveloped blocks were classified by size, and habitat values and habitat acres were calculated and mapped for each block. The scores were additive, and the GIS system maintained the individual and total scores for each data cell.

Connectivity among undeveloped blocks plays a major role in the habitat analysis. Why is connectivity important? Because animals and plants need to move to feed and breed, respond and adapt to environmental and seasonal changes and disperse away from their parents. The long-term survival of many species depends on genetic flow among various local populations inhabiting different habitat blocks. Ecological systems also depend on factors such as hydrology, nutrient cycling, and water and air quality, which flow among or across habitat blocks. These systems may be degraded or lost in one block if not protected in others, as when contamination upstream pollutes downstream aquatic and wetland habitats.

In planning for open space preservation and biodiversity protection, the Sagadahoc region initiative strove to maintain larger habitat blocks and the connections between them, minimize fragmentation, preserve riparian habitat and upland/wetland connections, and focus efforts on habitats of special concern. The process led to the creation of a regional conservation blueprint that can be used in support of intermunicipal shore land zoning and other land use agreements. The process has generated regional support for preservation of the working and natural landscape and is developing regional best practices for activities like road building and subdivision design. The opportunity to share experiences and expertise between towns and work together toward common goals has created a strong foundation for regional cooperation on a whole range of issues. A regional trail project along the Kennebec River developed from this work, and as of 2010 it has completed a feasibility study and received funding to build the first section of the trail.

The morals of the SRRRI story are proving valuable as state and local agencies look to protect habitat and water quality on a landscape scale elsewhere in Maine:

- The natural landscape provides common currency. It binds people and communities together.
- The natural landscape does not honor geopolitical boundaries.
- Working farms and forests offer regional benefits.
- Comprehensive planning on a town-by-town basis cannot preserve Maine's rural resources and character.

Town-by-town comprehensive plans do not protect cross-boundary resources. Even with the best local planning, habitat will become fragmented, water quality compromised, and public access limited. Still, in Maine most decisions about land use and resource protection are going to be made locally for the foreseeable future. It is vital to provide tools and incentives for use by local governments in managing cross-boundary and shared resources. The Sagadahoc Region Rural Resources Initiative is a start down this path of regional planning and cooperation.

PART III

SOCIETY, ECONOMICS, AND REGIONAL PLANNING

CHAPTER 23

REGIONS FOR CLIMATE RESILIENCY

Robert D. Yaro and David M. Kooris

Mounting evidence of the reality of climate change has shifted public debate away from arguments over whether climate change will happen and steered it toward discussions of how best to respond to it. Governments around the world are working to determine the most appropriate planning scale to mitigate the degree of climate change and adapt to its inevitable impacts. Because of the time lag of even the most ambitious mitigation attempts, a continued rise in global average temperatures and some local climate impacts are inevitable. We must simultaneously work to limit these effects while adapting to those most likely to occur.

In order to freeze the global temperature rise at two degrees, a level identified by global scientists, economists, and corporate leaders as that which is necessary to avoid the most catastrophic effects of climate change, the nations of the world will need to reduce carbon output by 60 to 80 percent below 1990 levels by 2050 (International Panel on Climate Change website; Stern 2007; U.S. Climate Action Partnership website). Nationally, the United States needs to reduce its emissions of greenhouse gases by 33 percent below 1990 levels by 2030 in order to meet the necessary targets for 2050, but as of 2008 America was emitting 16 percent more than it was in 1990 (U.S. Energy Information Administration 2008). Current trends are working dramatically against these goals, but regional planning for climate change mitigation and adaptation presents an opportunity to achieve the scale of action potentially most effective to reverse a significant portion of these trends.

The global scale of climate change threats calls for action at the international level, but smaller-scale climate change planning is also vital to reducing carbon emissions. Climate change mitigation efforts must be built into policy making at the local, regional, state, and federal levels in order to achieve reductions in carbon emissions that would be, cumulatively, significant at the global scale. In the United States in 2005, 34 percent of emissions from energy consumption were generated by residential and commercial buildings, 28 percent by transportation, and the remainder by industry and agriculture (Pew Center 2006). Our built environment—settlement patterns and mobility systems—has a significant impact on emissions by determining energy demand, directly in the building and transport sectors and indirectly in the electricity generation sector. The policies and infrastructure investments of all levels of government across the nation have a profound impact on where we live and work and how we move around. Through careful planning, each level of government can use that influence to reduce carbon emissions and help to mitigate and adapt to global climate change. While many policies will necessarily be implemented at the state and municipal levels, coordinated land use and transportation planning at the regional scale can be most successful at achieving economic growth in an age of carbon constraint.

REGIONAL CLIMATE PLANNING:
THE NECESSARY SCALE FOR ACTION

Even as the challenges of climate change gain relevance, there has existed a vacuum of policy solutions at the federal level. The national government has provided no leadership in promoting land use patterns and mobility systems needed to shape mitigation strategies. In response to this lack of national leadership, many state, county, and municipal governments have begun implementing their own climate action plans. Realities on the ground, however, rarely correspond to the centuries old legacy of political boundaries that stretch from the Atlantic to the Pacific. Controlling emissions from the building and transport sectors most often requires coordinated planning between clusters of states or localities to achieve the critical geographic and economic mass necessary to most accurately reflect real estate markets and commuter sheds, the scale at which land use and transportation planning decisions have impact.

Overall, community desire and political will has been demonstrated by the bipartisan and widespread action on climate change across this nation. As of the summer of 2008, seventeen states had set statewide emissions reduction targets, including several that have adopted targets that exceed the Kyoto accords (Pew Center 2008). Over 800 municipal leaders have adopted the U.S. Conference of Mayors Climate Protection Agreement, over 1,000 have associated themselves with the similar Cool Cities initiative of the Sierra Club, and over 400 municipalities and counties are working within ICLEI's Cities for Climate Protection Program to assess their emissions and create action plans to tackle climate change in their communities (ICLEI–Local Governments for Sustainability website; Sierra Club Cool Cities website; U.S. Conference of Mayors 2007). Aiming to meet or beat the Kyoto targets within their communities, these local governments have committed to at least a 7 percent reduction below 1990 levels by 2012.

Governors and state agencies have been focused primarily on emissions reductions in the power generation sector through renewable electricity generation and efficiency targets. As of the summer of 2008, twenty-five states and the District of Columbia had binding renewable portfolio standards for electricity generation (U.S. Department of Energy 2009). States can and must play a role in reducing emissions from the power generation sector, but groups of states working together can attain even greater effectiveness in carbon reduction. More than a dozen states have now joined multistate climate compacts to limit greenhouse gases from the power generation sector through the Northeast Regional Greenhouse Gas Initiative (RGGI) and the Western Climate Initiative. We are witnessing regional planning for controlling power plant emissions at the scale at which the challenge presents itself: a geographic scale falling between that of the state and that of the nation.

At the other end of the spectrum, local leadership to tackle climate change is necessary and has, over the past decade, served to dramatically elevate the national discussion about this issue. Yet the focus has been almost exclusively on reducing municipal emissions through efficiency measures in public buildings, vehicle fleet, public works, traffic lights, and other elements within local government's direct control, not on communitywide strategies. While reductions within the municipal corporation will have a quantifiable and significant impact on a community's carbon footprint, it cannot possibly be of a great enough magnitude to reach the necessary reduction targets by 2030 and 2050 to prevent global warming's most severe impacts. In an attempt to influence the emissions of the greater community, many municipalities have implemented green or energy efficient building codes, logically managed at the scale of local government.

State and local governments, then, are actively filling a national policy void and tackling those emissions drivers that occur at the geographic scales they respectively control: power plant emissions and building energy demand. At the megaregional scale, few partnerships have emerged that explicitly link transportation infrastructure investment or settlement location policy to climate mitigation. Local governments must create partnerships with bordering communities to achieve the geographic mass necessary to influence transportation emissions through settlement patterns and mobility systems. To reach the necessary reduction levels by 2050, we must transition our existing communities to reduce energy consumption and carbon production while at the same time ensuring that new development is also designed around these goals. Simultaneously, we must take steps to adapt both old and new communities to anticipate the effects of climate change that are the inevitable result of past emissions.

TACKLING EMISSIONS BY COORDINATING LAND USE AND TRANSPORTATION

The transport sector accounts for one-third of all emissions from energy consumption in the United States. This commanding share is directly attributable to our nation's reliance on the single passenger vehicle for the majority of work and leisure trips. While transit ridership is growing, nearly half of total U.S. ridership is in the New York metropolitan region alone, indicating that the vast majority of the country is almost entirely automobile dependent. Fuel efficiency and alternative fuels are cited by many as the key to reducing the nation's oil dependence and transportation emissions. Yet as recently demonstrated in *Growing Cooler*, an

Urban Land Institute report, growth in vehicle miles traveled (VMT) per capita negates these benefits even if CAFÉ standards continue to increase as the carbon content of fuel steadily declines (Ewing et al. 2007). *Growing Cooler* demonstrates that even with the nation's automobile fleet 30 percent more efficient than today's, and fuel carbon content reduced by 10 percent by 2030, growth in VMT ensures that carbon emissions from automobiles will still be nearly 15 percent higher than 2005 levels. This is a significant distance from the reductions necessary to halt the most severe impacts of climate change. The question, then, is how to reduce VMT. The answer lies in regional cooperation to foster development patterns that are significantly less automobile dependent than late twentieth century sprawl and to create alternatives to the automobile to serve both new and existing settlements of the country.

Locating Development Sustainably

The magnitude of new development necessary to accommodate the nation's population and economic growth by midcentury makes the prospects of retrofitting the American spatial development pattern all the more promising. Between now and 2025, our nation is anticipating significant job and population growth of 20 percent and approximately 15 percent, respectively. Looking out further to 2050, the United States is anticipated to reach a population of 420 million, an increase of 40 percent over today's level. To accommodate this growth, a massive amount of the built environment will be replaced or newly created. Half of all development on the ground in 2025 will not have existed in 2000 (Nelson 2006). An even greater share will be new by 2050. Now is our greatest opportunity to reduce our future energy needs related to the built environment and mobility.

The changing tastes and needs of a changing population will help planners create more sustainable and climate-friendly communities. Demographic trends indicate that our nation will have greater amounts of those groups for whom a single family house on a large lot is not the most desired option—childless households, young singles marrying later, and retirees—and even groups that have traditionally preferred suburban living are showing growing preference for compact and mixed-use developments. The United States already has enough single family houses on large lots to meet demand expected by 2025; instead, we will need more small lot and attached residential and compact mixed-use development (Nelson 2006). Even the preferences of American society today demonstrate pent up demand for a more sustainable development pattern. Over half of the respondents to the National Survey on Communities conducted for Smart Growth America indicated that they would prefer a compact walkable community to a sprawling one; and over 60 percent of respondents thinking about buying a house in the next three years answered in favor of smart growth (Ewing et al. 2007). Ensuring that the next generation of development will take place in a way that is less carbon intensive and more sustainable requires only harnessing the changing trends in public preferences and housing needs.

So-called "Euclidian" zoning, however, which predominates across the country, makes it difficult to meet these changing demands. Euclidean zoning strictly separates land uses and densities, creating single use districts separated by large distances that leave few alternatives to the automobile. To achieve energy and carbon reductions, walkable nodes of activity are necessary, linked to one another with bus rapid or rail transit, and creating a deliberate link between land use, development intensity, and transportation is needed to enable alternatives to the single occupancy car. While zoning control lies in the hand of local government, municipalities and even counties rarely cover the geographic scale necessary to impact daily travel patterns. In the New York metropolitan region, only New York City itself, at 301 square miles and with a massive transit network, can coordinate mobility options with land use within its borders. The other 780 plus municipalities in the tri-state metropolitan area average at only 17 square miles in geographic area. With many members of the workforce employed in a different municipality, county, or even state from that in which they live, coordinating land use and transportation to enable alternative forms of mobility is clearly a regional challenge and requires planning and coordination at that scale.

Providing Mobility Alternatives

To effectively meet the mobility needs of politically balkanized metropolitan regions, transportation planning must also take place at the regional scale, since very few municipalities encompass entire commuter sheds, retail markets, or leisure catchment areas. Further, in the dozens of metropolitan areas that cross state boundaries, not even individual states encompass the entirety of these places. Not only does the geographical range of transit networks necessitate regional partnerships, but the financing of these systems cannot be supported by any single community alone.

At a geographic scale between the state and the nation, sustainable mobility options are needed as megaregions—linked networks of metropolitan regions, with shared economies, infrastructure, and natural resource systems—emerge as building blocks of the global economy. Sprawl along the metropolitan fringe has resulted in greater integration of job and housing markets between previously distinct metropolitan regions, resulting in a pronounced rise in trips between these areas. In the Northeast, the fastest growing commuter class is workers traveling between metropolitan areas. Between Boston and Washington, D.C., this class grew by 37 percent between 1990 and 2000 to 650,000 people. Given congestion on our nation's roads and runways and the climate impact per capita of automobiles and airplanes, these trips will have to shift to intercity rail in order for this trend to be sustainable. With the only higher speed rail service in the nation—Acela—the Northeast should be poised to shift trips to Amtrak, which is 18 percent more efficient than air travel and 17 percent more efficient than an automobile (Davis et al. 2009). If this shift is to be realized, however, it will require a level of investment in the megaregion's rail infrastructure and capacity that has not taken place for generations. The congressional delegations, state governments, and civic and business leaders from Maine to Virginia are beginning to coordinate their planning and advocacy for this shared resource through the Business Alliance for Northeast

Mobility (America 2050 website). Across the nation, ten other megaregions in addition to the Northeast currently exist or are emerging based on their economic interdependence and integrated mobility systems. Only through similar coordinated planning for intercity mobility at the megaregional scale in every corner of the nation will our economy be able to reap the benefits of metropolitan agglomeration without increasing the risks associated with global warming because of the emissions from intercity travel.

The majority of work and leisure travel takes place between localities within metropolitan regions. Some regions in the Northeast and Midwest have been handed a legacy of transit systems that will enable them to meet the mobility needs of their populations in a carbon constrained future. Others along the West Coast, Midwest, and Mid-Atlantic have created systems in recent decades that are seeing ridership that greatly exceeds projected demand. Even the most sprawling regions of the nation, including most notably Charlotte, Houston, and Phoenix, are building regional transit systems that will position those cities and their suburbs for another generation of growth. The effort to create and maintain these transit systems requires a regional framework, as does the process of organizing future growth around these assets. Projects ranging from the least capital intensive bus line to a new commuter rail route cannot be supported by entirely local funding sources. Transit networks that correspond to regional mobility patterns require equally spatially expansive funding and management mechanisms. The nation's most successful metropolitan planning organizations (MPOs) and transit agencies have demonstrated that providing alternatives to the automobile requires a regional policy and investment framework.

REGIONAL COLLABORATION FOR ECOLOGICAL CLIMATE ADAPTATION

Preserving undeveloped land can have pronounced mitigation benefits and is a primary component of successful adaptation measures; however, sustaining these ecological resource areas requires regional collaboration. Forested lands have carbon locked within their biomass that, if developed, would be released into the atmosphere. Preserving the riparian and coastal zones of our regions helps avoid some of the inevitable property damage resulting from changing weather patterns and sea level rise. Wildlife migration corridors will be essential enablers of animals' and plants' ability to remain in their adapted habitat. A coordinated and cumulative regional approach is essential for ecological integrity for climate mitigation and adaptation.

The roots, trunks, branches, and leaves of the forest are a visual representation of sequestered carbon. A forested acre in the Northeast contains, on average, seventy-five tons of carbon (Perschel et al. 2007). Releasing this carbon into the atmosphere would be roughly the equivalent of burning 30,000 gallons of gasoline (Farmer 2007). Existing and new urban and rural forests continue to absorb carbon dioxide annually as they grow, though this amount diminishes over time. It is estimated that new forests can sequester up to three tons per acre per year, declining to up to one ton per acre per year as they mature, and reaching saturation between the ages of 90 and 120 (U.S. Environmental Protection Agency 2007). Urban canopies can have a pronounced ongoing impact in offsetting emissions at the regional scale directly through sequestration and indirectly through the mitigation of urban heat islands.

Even with robust mitigation attempts, changes to the world's climate are now inevitable, and costly impacts can be anticipated. While the magnitude of sea level rise is unknown, some change is certain, and coastal impacts during storm events will increase. In the Northeast and several other regions, there will also be more frequent and severe rain events that will increase the need to manage stormwater. The combined sewer and water infrastructure typical of older communities necessitates innovative strategies to enable water retention and rising rivers to avoid pollution overflow. Paramount to this effort is the need to limit impervious surface in all watersheds and all development in floodplains. One-hundred-year-old floodplains in New England and New York could experience flooding at a frequency of every two to ten years (Frumhoff et al. 2007). Flood risk is directly linked to the integrity of the entire river corridor, requiring regional coordination across political borders.

With global warming, ecological zones will spatially shift according to changing temperatures and precipitation. Plant and animal species will need to migrate to remain in the environmental conditions to which they are adapted (Collingham and Huntley 2000). This forced migration will be impeded if sprawling metropolitan development fragments habitat and migration corridors. Priorities to preserve migration corridors differ from those based in island biogeography for biodiversity protection. North-South oriented linear reserves bridge more ecological zones than circular reserves designed to limit distances. Where protected landscapes are fragmented, linking corridors are essential for migration between reserves as climates shift (Pearson and Dawson 2005). These practices are embodied in the European Centre for Nature Conservation's designation of continental target corridors. Megaregional planning is necessary to link migration corridors across North America.

Achieving Climate Resiliency through Regional Planning

Critics have decried the potential mitigation value of coordinated land use and transportation planning because new development inevitably, they say, results in more emissions than present regardless of the magnitude of the net increase. These criticisms miss the fundamental ability that regionally planned new development has to change the travel behaviors and reduce the vulnerability of the existing built environment. The intensification of an arterial strip or new mixed use activity in a declining town center coupled with bus or rail service enables nonmotorized and transit trips for not only the residents and workers of the new development, but also for those in the adjacent suburban landscape. Regionally planned new sustainable development can, therefore, result in a net decrease in total emissions from the transportation sector by incrementally transitioning an existing built landscape to one that provides more mobility choices to all residents and workers. Despite the amount of new development that will be required to meet population and economic growth, there will continue to be historic communities that cannot be served by transit, have densities too low to support walking, and/or cannot be redesigned to mitigate expected climate impacts. In these cases, regional strategies could be employed to reduce threats to these places—for example, by using regional transfer of development rights systems to promote relocation of vulnerable communities to safer places. Flood prone communities, for example, could be relocated through this and other techniques to higher, safer locations, incorporating standards designed to make them more transit and pedestrian friendly. The coming decades present an opportunity to harness the demands of a growing population both to retrofit existing communities to be less energy intensive and to incrementally undo the most unsustainable development decisions of the past. Through coordinated planning at the regional scale most appropriate for each challenge, we can continue to grow and prosper while reducing our carbon emissions and ecological footprint.

CHAPTER 24

MEGAREGION PLANNING
AND HIGH-SPEED RAIL

Petra Todorovich

On April 16, 2009, President Obama stood before an audience at the Eisenhower Executive Office Building and made an announcement that signaled a new era of passenger rail in the United States. Months before, the American Recovery and Reinvestment Act (ARRA) had provided $8 billion for a new program at the Federal Railroad Administration (FRA) to issue competitive grants to states to make capital investments in high-speed and conventional passenger rail. Little did the president know that providing the single largest boost for intercity rail planning in this country in a generation had also motivated a sudden and giant leap forward in planning and governing megaregions. Luckily, regional planners had been studying emerging megaregions for the previous five years, in affiliation with the New York–based Regional Plan Association's (RPA) America 2050 program. Again and again, the planners had identified high-speed rail as the key transportation investment to serve megaregion economies. But high-speed rail was a distant dream. That all changed with the passage of ARRA at the nadir of the Great Recession. Now a federal program exists to support high-speed rail planning and implementation. Making that program a success will largely depend on the ability of multiple actors at the local, regional, state, and binational levels to come together as megaregions to coordinate and leverage federal rail investments.

REVISITING MEGALOPOLIS: RPA RESURRECTS THE MEGAREGION IDEA

As if planning for the Tri-State New York metropolitan region was not sufficiently complicated, in 2005 the Regional Plan Association launched a national program called America 2050 that focused on the emergence of a new urban scale: the megaregion. This was not actually a new concept for RPA. In 1967 a volume of the *Second Regional Plan* documented the emergence of "The Atlantic Urban Region," an urban chain stretching 460 miles from Maine to Virginia (Regional Plan

Association 1967). Earlier that decade, French geographer Jean Gottmann had coined the term "Megalopolis" to describe the same region in his 1961 book, *Megalopolis: The Urbanized Northeastern Seaboard of the United States* (Gottmann 1961). The Northeast's more or less continuous urbanization from the northern suburbs of Boston to the southern suburbs of Washington, D.C., had attracted the attention of Gottmann and RPA. But in 1967 RPA observed that while this chain of settlements containing 42 million people surely derived some benefit from their mutual proximity, the larger form of the Atlantic Urban Region was still composed of more or less independent metropolitan regions.

By 2005, when RPA revisited that larger form, the autonomy of the Northeast's metropolitan regions was starting to wane. Rapid, low-density sprawl was erasing the formerly distinct boundaries between the New York and Philadelphia metropolitan regions, and between Philadelphia and Wilmington. The term "extreme commutes" had been coined by the U.S. Census to describe road warriors traveling more than ninety minutes each way to their jobs, with many of them located in the Northeast. And intercity business travel within the Northeast was also growing. The four most congested airports in the country were located in New York City, Newark, and Philadelphia. With 251 daily flights taking place among the Northeast's major airports, and 40 percent of Amtrak's rail ridership taking place on the Northeast Corridor, a Northeast Megaregion was moving from a spatial construct to reality (RPA 2007).

But at the dawn of the twenty-first century, the forces making the Northeast Megaregion a more cohesive and integrated megaregion were also threatening its demise. Growing congestion in its roads, rail network, and airports; rising house costs; loss of open space; and threats to clean drinking water all contributed to imperil the Northeast's future as an economic competitor and healthy and pleasant place to live. In other words, the Northeast was (and is) heading toward the dystopian vision of Megalopolis—a region of continuous sprawl with infrastructure systems that are too crowded and too deteriorated to function efficiently, a high cost of living, and a natural environment that has suffered the impacts of an aggressive human footprint. As Regional Plan Association's president, Robert Yaro, frequently remarks, "The Northeast has all the disadvantages of being the most expensive, densely populated, and congested region in the country—and none of the advantages." The subtext of this statement is that we need to flip the equation around and capture the benefits of having the most population density, the most expansive rail transit network, and the largest concentration of skilled workers in the nation. To do so, RPA set out to understand the larger phenomenon of megaregions and how they were playing out around the country.

SCALING UP: AMERICA'S EMERGING MEGAREGIONS

In 2004 Robert Yaro, Armando Carbonell, and Jonathan Barnett led a graduate planning studio at the University of Pennsylvania called Plan for America. The Plan for America studio traveled to Europe on spring break to meet with Sir Peter Hall at

University College London, where students and professors alike were inspired by the European Spatial Development Perspective (ESDP), a 1999 policy statement on balanced growth in the European territory. The imaginative spatial planners behind the ESDP had identified large urban agglomerations in Central Europe like the Pentagon and the Blue Banana (Faludi 2002). Also called "global integration zones," these networked cities and regions in the EU were supported by open border policies among EU member states and strengthened by EU investments in the Trans-European Network and high-speed passenger rail. Adopting a similar spatial perspective on urban networks in America, the Penn students identified a series of possible "supercities," which were later redefined by RPA as megaregions.

RPA launched its America 2050 program after the Penn students issued their final report in spring 2004. The RPA prospectus on America 2050 outlined the case for adopting a megaregion perspective and national plan (RPA 2006). Generally, it argued that five major trends shaping the United States demanded a national planning and infrastructure strategy for accommodating future growth. They included the following:

- America's rapid population growth, about 130 million additional people by 2050
- Overburdened and deteriorating infrastructure systems
- The urgent need to mitigate climate change and reduce our dependence on fossil fuels and oil imports
- Growing social and economic disparities within and between regions
- And the emergence of a new urban form: megaregions

Megaregions are networks of proximate metropolitan regions, connected by transportation systems, natural systems, settlement patterns, and linked economies. Eleven emerging U.S. megaregions capture over 70 percent of the nation's population and jobs (see fig. 24.1). They present a new scale at which to plan and coordinate large infrastructure and natural systems—a scale at which there are few examples of governance models, let alone institutions capable of planning or financing complex systems like high-speed rail. Given this vacuum, America 2050 set out to address a planning void at two different scales: federal, where leadership would surely be required to help plan, finance, and facilitate partnerships needed to meet the challenges described here; and the megaregion, by conducting research, building coalitions, and identifying best practices for megaregion planning and coordination.

The first several years of the America 2050 program were spent building a base of research to underpin our understanding of megaregions and verify that this urban form was present outside the Northeast. All of the research that America 2050 assembled is located permanently on the America 2050 website in its research section. During this time, RPA began to think about megaregions as organized around specific relationships that present themselves at the larger scale—such as water resources in the Great Lakes Megaregion, intercity rail in the Northeast Corridor, a common coastline and vulnerability to natural and man-made disasters in the Gulf Coast, seaport and goods movement issues in southern

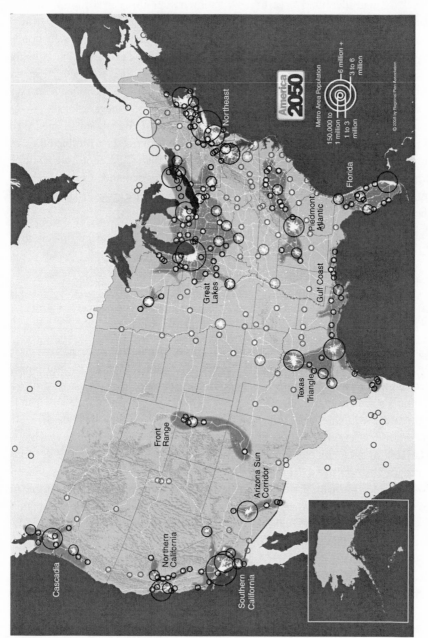

Figure 24.1. Emerging Megaregions of the United States

California, and urban sprawl in northern California. Recognizing these critical relationships was the key to unlocking interest by regional stakeholders in cooperating with each other. "You're in a megaregion; do something about it" was not a compelling opening line. However, they found that "working with your neighbors is critical to solving fill-in-the-blank" elicited much more interest.

From 2005 to 2008, megaregion studies were conducted in eight megaregions, mostly at or in partnership with graduate planning schools, including University of Pennsylvania, Georgia Tech, Portland State University, Arizona State University, University of Michigan, and University of Texas at Austin. In addition, several councils of governments in California (Sacramento Area Council of Governments, San Diego Association of Governments, and Kern County) published a study of the Southwest Megaregion, which led to their continued cooperation on goods movement and airport planning. In Florida, the South Florida Regional Planning Council prepared a study of the Florida Megaregion and convened a conference around it in 2006. In northern California, the independent planning and civic organization SPUR published a study of the Northern California Megaregion, stretching from the Bay Area to Sacramento. Following the SPUR study, transportation officials from across the megaregion came together to submit a joint application for a northern California freight program that was successful in securing $840 million from the California Transportation Commission, an achievement they regarded as a "coup" (Nelson 2008).

RAIL ADVOCACY IN THE NORTHEAST CORRIDOR

Back in the Northeast Megaregion, RPA helped revive a coalition of business groups that had previously advocated for Amtrak funding to form the Business Alliance for Northeast Mobility. With a reinvigorated membership of about thirty chambers of commerce and civic organizations from Maine to Virginia, the Business Alliance began lobbying Congress in 2006 for increased rail funding to bring Amtrak's Northeast Rail Corridor to a state of good repair. The Business Alliance focused on turning one of the key disadvantages of the Northeast's geography—fragmented governance among twelve states—into a political advantage—twenty-four U.S. senators and dozens more U.S. representatives. The Business Alliance held several rail advocacy events at the U.S. Capitol and at Union Station in Washington, D.C., in 2007–2008 with members of the Northeast Delegation. The strategy seemed to work. In 2008, after previous unsuccessful attempts, Congress passed the Passenger Rail Investment Improvement Act, which authorized approximately $13 billion in funding for Amtrak over five years and set up a new High Speed Intercity Passenger Rail program at the Federal Railroad Administration that provided competitive grants to states to invest in capital improvements for passenger rail. This new program was put to use immediately, by serving as the legislative vehicle for the $8 billion appropriation of high-speed rail funding in ARRA. The subsequent year, federal appropriators reaffirmed their commitment to the high-speed rail program with another $2.5 billion for the high-speed program.

With painful irony, a relatively small share of the money made its way to the Northeast Corridor. The Business Alliance had gambled on advocating for increased national rail funding, because about half of Amtrak's annual capital investments are typically made in the Northeast Corridor, Amtrak's largest rail infrastructure asset. And, indeed, approximately $706 million included in ARRA for Amtrak came to the Northeast Corridor in 2009, along with additional funding in the 2010 annual appropriation (Federal Railroad Administration 2010). But little of the $8 billion in high-speed rail grants came to the Northeast Corridor, for two frustratingly technical reasons. None of Amtrak's Northeast Corridor projects could be completed in two years—a statutory requirement of the stimulus bill— and the Northeast Corridor states had recently initiated a master planning process for 2030, which had triggered the need for a new, corridor-wide environmental impact statement (EIS). All of the high-speed rail grants from the stimulus bill required a completed EIS, and the Northeast Corridor's had yet to begin and would certainly take a minimum of two years. So after playing a role in securing rail funding for the entire country, the Northeast Corridor sat on the sidelines as the largest passenger rail grants in decades were doled out in California, Florida, the Midwest, and other regions.

On the bright side, being passed over seems to have acted as a wake-up call to transportation officials in the Northeast states, who have reemerged with greater motivation to better coordinate in the future for federal funding. In June 2010, eleven Northeast states submitted an application to the FRA for $18.8 million in planning funds to conduct a comprehensive planning study for the Northeast Corridor, building on the master plan. The new planning study would allow Northeast states to break out individual capital projects on the corridor with independent utility that could be funded through the federal high-speed rail program and complete the required EIS for the corridor for a doubling of ridership by 2030. Of most interest to this author, the planning study and EIS would also consider a true high-speed rail option of building two new dedicated tracks along the Northeast Corridor for high-speed trains, significantly increasing capacity and reducing trip times on the corridor—and competing with the other world-class high-speed rail systems being planned in California and Florida. Such an outcome could be the key to realizing the promise of an integrated Northeast Megaregion economy and act as the ultimate test for megaregion cooperation.

MEGAREGIONS AND HIGH-SPEED RAIL

High-speed rail is not just a test for megaregion coordination; it also promises great reward. In fact, it is likely that only with the fast and convenient ground connections provided by high-speed rail can megaregions realize the productivity benefits of their metropolitan economies acting as integrated units. This is the difference between the Northeast Megaregion's dystopian future and the desired path. High-speed rail could act as the main intercity transportation spine for an expanded megaregion-scale rail transit network, enhanced with transit oriented development. A Northeast megaregion (and other megaregions) linked by high-speed rail could potentially realize the following benefits:

- Increased productivity for service-based businesses gained by time savings and increased mobility. Faster, more frequent, and reliable connections that enable business trips among the specialized economies of the Northeast (i.e., education and health services in Boston; financial services and media in New York; government and professional services in Washington) can foster greater productivity for the megaregion as a whole.
- Expanding the scope of labor markets accessed by major employment centers. Faster rail connections between employment hubs and adjacent, smaller cities and residential areas can deepen labor markets, giving employers access to more workers and providing workers with more and cheaper housing options (Martin Prosperity Insight 2010).
- Bringing smaller and underperforming cities within two-hour commuting distance of major employment hubs (like Boston, New York, and Washington) can potentially benefit cities like Hartford, Worcester, and Philadelphia, which have been losing jobs steadily in recent decades. This could also take pressure off the housing market in larger cities, if workers can work in New York and live in Philadelphia, for example (Regional Plan Association 2007).
- Focusing development and real estate opportunities around stations. Rail passenger stations provide focal points for transportation-oriented development, such as new office, retail, institutional, and residential development. Focusing development around transportation hubs can reduce the need to drive, enliven and activate communities, and promote energy savings through transportation and building related efficiencies.

Regional planning must recognize and capitalize on the self-interest of local actors that make up a region in order to be successful. Megaregion planning is no different in its need to tap into the mutual self-interest of component metropolitan actors. Yet megaregion planning is even more difficult than regional planning because the megaregion scale is less connected to individuals' daily experiences than the metropolitan region. In light of these challenges, America 2050 has found that megaregion cooperation must be motivated by the promise of clear and tangible rewards to be gained by megaregion cooperation. Such rewards, in the form of federal high-speed rail planning grants, have recently brought megaregions together to develop corridor-wide rail plans and explore governance models for finance, construction, and rail service operations. These regions, particularly those that span multiple states and international boundaries, will need to establish formal partnerships to manage major procedures like procurement and financing. The greater promise of high-speed rail—increased productivity, access to larger job markets, promoting sustainable land development, and revitalizing cities—will require a broader regional planning perspective at the megaregion scale. In this way, high speed is providing a laboratory for megaregion planning.

CHAPTER 25

THE ECONOMIC BENEFITS
OF REGIONAL PLANNING

Christopher Jones

Economic influences are patently regional, extending beyond municipal, county, and state political boundaries. With widespread acknowledgment of the importance of metropolitan economies, it seems reasonable to assume that good regional planning results in improved economic performance. And yet hard evidence for this effect is scarce. In part, it is because there is no single definition of success. Is it increased jobs and incomes, more affordable housing, lower taxes? And is it just the totality of these benefits that should be the objective, or is their equitable distribution just as legitimate? Even with clear goals, it can be very difficult to quantify the impacts of regional initiatives. Not only is it difficult to establish causality, but there are few strong regional institutions to clearly demonstrate their influence over metropolitan economies.

Even with limited means for demonstrating the rate of return, it would be shortsighted for both public and private stakeholders to ignore the obvious impacts of regional economic dynamics and not to seek to turn these influences to their advantage. To do so, they need to understand how these dynamics operate at different geographic scales and what measures are most likely to succeed. An examination of a growing body of research and two successful case studies can provide some lessons for approaches that different regions can take.

WHEN IT COMES TO THE ECONOMY, PROXIMITY MATTERS

One of the paradoxes of globalization is that cheaper communication and transportation have reinforced the importance of place in clustering human capital and generating centers of innovation and value. And while an integrated global economy has narrowed many differences between regions, there is evidence that geographic proximity still has a strong influence.

In particular, research demonstrates the powerful effects of cities on the economies of their surrounding regions. For example, Michael L. Lahr's study,

"Is New York City Still Propelling Growth in Its Suburbs," analyzed employment and earnings growth rates from 1969 to 2000 for the thirty-one-county New York metropolitan region. It concluded that the suburbs rely on New York City for their economic well-being and found that growth in the city's financial industries clearly drove growth in the suburban counties (Lahr 2003). In "Do Cities and Suburbs Cluster?," William Goertzman, Matthew Spiegel, and Susan Wachter examined how closely urban and suburban housing markets were linked in four California metropolitan areas from 1980 to 1994. They found that housing price changes within the central cities were significantly more correlated with their own suburbs than with other central cities. And the connection between city and suburb is tighter than the relation of suburb to suburb across metro areas. A number of national studies have also verified the importance of the city-suburb relationships (Goertzman et al. 1998).

As metropolitan areas have grown, these relationships have become more complicated. Multicentered regions and overlapping housing and labor markets have resulted in new regional forms alongside of the traditional metropolitan area. Regional Plan Association (RPA) has focused on the emergence of "megaregions" in America—large areas such as the Northeast Corridor that have highly integrated and interdependent economies based on a network of metropolitan centers such as the cities of Washington, D.C., Baltimore, Philadelphia, New York, and Boston. In a study for the Regional Plan Association, Moody's Economy.com has found that both employment change and housing prices are more highly correlated—in many cases much more highly correlated—within the ten American megaregions than they are across the megaregions. Other work in RPA's America 2050 initiative is showing how these relationships are operating and evolving in several of these megaregions. The implications of these studies are that cooperation across local and state political boundaries makes economic sense; the central city-suburb relationship is still key to the economic health of both; and multicentric regions, overlapping labor markets, and economic homogenization are giving rise to larger aggregations that must also be considered in forming regional economic policy.

The tough part is showing how specific solutions lead to quantifiable economic benefits. Without translating policies into dollars and cents, and showing how these flow to different constituencies throughout the region, it is difficult to build the political consensus for specific initiatives. Two case studies demonstrate that this can be accomplished. One is a nearly forty-year-old experiment in metropolitan governance. The other is a more recent example of the type of consensus building that has been evolving through regional visioning initiatives over the past fifteen years.

REGIONAL GOVERNANCE TO ADDRESS FISCAL INEQUITIES

The Minneapolis–St. Paul region began to address its economic challenges on a regional scale when the state formed the Twin Cities Metropolitan Council in 1967, which expanded in 1994. The region covers 2.8 million people in seven counties, which have 187 cities and towns and forty-eight school districts. Minnesota's Fiscal Disparities Act of 1971 aimed to allow all cities to share in the region's growth, reduce competition for the tax base, and spread the benefits of regional public investments. As the name implies, its primary goal and driving force was regional equity. However, efficiency and growth were also part of the argument. The act promoted better planning by encouraging regional cooperation, providing extra resources for redevelopment, and encouraging environmental protection. Under this program, 40 percent of the growth in each jurisdiction's commercial and industrial tax collections go into a regional pool and is redistributed based on criteria linked to population and property wealth. A basic justification for this approach is that all communities in the region contribute to the creation of commercial and industrial wealth by helping finance infrastructure and providing homes for employees and customers, but without tax sharing only the community in which each business is located can benefit from the tax revenue that business generates.

The results of revenue sharing and regional governance in the Twin Cities region have been very positive, explaining the longevity of this very unusual system. A 2005 report by the Twin Cities Metropolitan Council reported the following results:

- A shared annual tax base of $273 million
- Reduced tax base disparities, from 13–1 to 4–1, for towns with more than 9,000 people
- More net financial gainers (129 municipalities) than losers (52 municipalities)
- Gainers and losers change over time
- A reduced ratables chase

While the impact of tax sharing on overall economic growth is unclear, the Twin Cities region has been economically successful over the past thirty years, and the program has achieved its fundamental objective of greatly reducing fiscal disparities among the region's cities and towns.

BUILDING A CONSENSUS FOR GROWTH ON THE WEST COAST

A critical first step toward regional planning is recognizing that one is indeed part of a region. The counties and municipalities of southern California have taken that step and are working through the Southern California Association of Governments to plan for a projected population growth of 6.2 million people, to reach a total population of 23 million, by 2025. That is like adding two cities the size of Chicago to an already heavily populated region. In response, the metropolitan communities have developed the Compass Blueprint 2% Strategy as a vision to guide this growth in a manner that will provide for better mobility, livability, prosperity, and sustainability. This blueprint for growth management seeks to focus new development within existing cities and suburbs and major transportation corridors, promote extensive development of mixed use and walkable communities, bring growth around existing transit stations, and preserve remaining open space.

The blueprint provides for achieving these goals while changing current land use regulations on only 2 percent of the region's total land area—a threshold intended to show it does not require wholesale revision of all current municipal and county regulation. By focusing on a relatively small portion of the region's total land mass and altering the planning approach in those targeted areas, the entire region can reap tremendous benefits. The Compass Blueprint has identified and mapped the "2% Strategy Opportunity Areas" where new planning, zoning, and transportation infrastructure would accommodate anticipated population growth while providing better access to jobs and an improved jobs/housing balance, conserving open space, and renovating urban cores, thereby creating wealth through increased property values. The opportunity areas generally consist of major residential and employment zones, city centers, neighborhoods with railway stations and other rapid transit facilities, industrial centers, certain residential infill areas.

As the metropolitan planning organization (MPO) for six very large counties (Imperial, Los Angeles, Orange, San Bernardino, Riverside, and Ventura), the Southern California Association of Governments has significant influence but limited coercive powers over land use in the counties and municipalities within its ambit. The association is implementing the Compass Blueprint through a voluntary process of cooperative planning. A central feature is developing a compelling analysis of the economic return on investment for potential redevelopment areas. The result has been a growing number of places with both the potential and political will to accept new housing and commercial development. As of 2005, major redevelopment projects were under way in five communities, with plans proceeding in twelve more. The lessons learned from these studies and strategies are the following:

- The impacts on distribution can be as important as impacts on aggregate growth. Regional policies can address regional inequities as well as efficiency and, if successful, bridge some of the social divides that weaken prospects for collective action.
- It is important to understand and address the issues of winners and losers. Demonstrating the aggregate benefits to the region are necessary but not sufficient. An upfront appraisal of who will and will not benefit is needed to evaluate the public benefits and address sources of opposition.
- State or federal intervention and incentives are nearly always needed. Both the Twin Cities and southern California case studies require state action— enabling legislation in the case of Minnesota, and incentives for infrastructure investment in the case of California. Fiscal incentives, planning grants, and environmental regulations are all means by which states and the federal government can encourage regional cooperation.
- Local ownership and public participation are essential. The recent success of regional visioning efforts like the Southern California Compass project points to the importance of including municipalities and the public throughout the planning to overcome local resistance.

- The approach and geographic scale should fit the goal. Efficiency—in land use and services—can be gained on several geographic levels. Greater equity requires a large area, at least the size of a metropolitan region. But transportation and environmental objectives need to go beyond the metropolitan scale.

CHAPTER 26

SERVING THE
ENVIRONMENT AND
ECONOMY THROUGH
REGIONAL PLANNING

Paul D. Gottlieb

Economy vs. Environment?

How do economists make the case for regional planning? First, perhaps, they need to convince themselves. Many economists believe there is likely to be a trade-off between the objectives of environmental planning and economic welfare. Even if one grants that planning to protect environmental resources suppresses growth, this position relies on a conventional, and incomplete, view of what economic welfare means.

In 1992, for example, the Center for Urban Policy Research (CUPR) at Rutgers University studied the economic impact of the newly established New Jersey State Plan. This work was mandated by the state legislature and completed under state supervision. One section of the CUPR report estimated that the state plan would reduce statewide infrastructure costs by $1.3 billion due to its encouragement of compact development and growth in areas with excess infrastructure capacity. "With less construction spending," the report argued, "there will be fewer construction jobs and, through the multiplier, fewer jobs in industries that are related to construction" (Burchell et al. 1992, 43). The authors went on to estimate that the state plan would lead to 9,000 fewer people, 11,000 fewer jobs, and $1.7 million less personal income in the year 2010 when compared to trend development.

In an economy the size of New Jersey's, these numbers are not all that significant. Nor is it obvious that the report's authors—let alone its readers—viewed these projected plan impacts with alarm. Too often, however, calculations like these are used to argue that a given environmental or planning regulation will exact a penalty in the form of reduced economic growth. This kind of argument relies on a very narrow understanding of economic welfare. The concept of economic welfare should include not only the income opportunities that become available through growth and spending, but also the aesthetic, recreational, and quality-of-life benefits of open space. The fact that it is difficult to put a price tag on these latter kinds of benefits does not make them any less real. Indeed, the free market's failure to take such benefits into account could well mean that the higher, trend growth scenario is the "wrong" one, while the more sluggish planned growth scenario forecast by CUPR represents the true social optimum.

In an article that makes clear he is no tree hugger, urban economist Jan Brueckner makes precisely this point. He argues that farmers are unable to charge for the open space and anticongestion services they provide unwittingly to their residential neighbors. These services have genuine economic value; but without any obligation to pay for them, the neighbors behave as "free riders." Any introductory economics textbook can tell you the result of such a situation. The economic good—scenic open space, in this case—will be *underprovided* relative to the universal standard of welfare to which all economists subscribe. Brueckner concludes that some regulation of urban sprawl may be justified in order to retain open space benefits (Brueckner 2000, 167).

This argument about the quality-of-life benefits of open space is frequently extended to the provision of so-called ecosystem services that support human life in a more fundamental way. Perhaps the most famous domestic example of land preservation passing a cost-benefit test on grounds of ecosystem services is the Catskills Memorandum of Agreement. Under this agreement, the City of New York supposedly agreed to buy $1 billion worth of land in the Catskills watershed to provide the same drinking water protection services that would otherwise require the construction of a $6–$8 billion filtration plant (Chichilnisky and Heal 1998, 629–630).

In a challenge to the conventional wisdom on this case, environmental ethicist Mark Sagoff argues that there is no historic or scientific relationship between land development in the Catskills and the city's water quality. Undeveloped land and the filtration plant were *not* substitute forms of capital. Instead, he argues, the Memorandum of Agreement ended a legal fight between the city and the federal government over a new EPA filtration mandate while providing a useful cover story for the acquisition of open space that environmentalists wanted to set aside for other reasons. In practice, real estate development in the Catskills has been negligible, and a clear-eyed calculation of its own interest in water supply has caused New York City to invest far more in the Catskills physical plant than in land set-asides since the memorandum was signed (Sagoff 2002, 16–21).

Notwithstanding this tarnishing of an example that has achieved legendary status among environmentalists, the Catskills case still has several lessons to impart to regional planners. The first lesson is that providing effective ecosystem services to humans frequently requires a *combination* of natural and human-made capital. This assertion should be second nature to regional planners, who understand that there is a lot more to regional planning than simply preserving vacant land. With this principle in mind, of course, the cost-benefit analysis of regional planning becomes even more challenging because of the enormous number of partially engineered landscapes that a planner (as opposed to a water agency facing a federal ultimatum, for example) must consider.

A second lesson of the Catskills case is that, in contrast to the job of water filtration, the quality-of-life benefits of scenic open space are self-evident and are recognized by a large segment of the local community—as well as by environmentalists and tourists who live farther afield. So it turns out that the free-rider problem noted above exists alongside significant open space purchase programs, as well as regulatory restrictions that have similar effects on preservation, but which do not involve compensation to landowners. These latter programs are of course controversial, but one fact is beyond dispute: Citizens' perceived gains and willingness to pay for the quality-of-life benefits of regional planning are substantial and can presumably be tapped in more creative ways. Such benefits can also exist at a considerable distance from the place where the regional planning actually takes place.

One example may be found in the New Jersey Highlands Act. This regional planning program will attempt to use transfer of development rights (TDRs) to compensate large landowners facing development restrictions in the plan's preservation area. A tax on drinking water has also been proposed as a funding source for purchasing land or development rights in the Highlands. This is one of the few proposals regarding the Highlands on which environmentalists and farmers find themselves in complete agreement (Chambers 2004). The water tax would put part of the burden of preservation on a large group of state residents living outside the Highlands. The argument for the water tax seems to rely on an analogy to the Catskills case: "If we do *not* buy this land, New Jersey's water users will have to pay that much more for treatment infrastructure later on. Better a small investment in land now than a large capital expenditure down the road."

Even if we agree with Sagoff that the water supply benefits of undeveloped land are overstated, the idea of a broad-based tax for land preservation still makes a great deal of sense. For one thing, preserved open space generates flood control benefits that are more straightforward than the supposed water supply benefits. Here the choice of buying land now or expanding culverts and storm sewers later (not to mention rebuilding washed-out infrastructure) looks like a real one. In addition, as argued above, the recreational, scenic, and quality-of-life benefits about to be delivered by the Highlands plan are significant. I suspect that day to day, the typical New Jersey voter thinks more about these kinds of benefits than about the official rationale for a piece of legislation that carries the title "Highlands Water Protection and Planning Act."

In economics, one common solution to a free-rider problem is to coerce payments out of those who value the service but do not pay for it. There appears to be ample justification in this case for a tax that goes beyond water users to include citizens throughout the state and even nonresidents, perhaps through charges on campsites or other services likely to be used by tourists.

NET BENEFITS OF PLANNING

For better or worse, most regional plans in America do not seek to control population growth directly. Instead, they seek to design and redistribute growth so that the low-density residential landscape we have become accustomed to is replaced by a more diverse mix of open space and higher-density towns, cities, and villages. This raises the question of which type of landscape is actually the optimal one from an economic point of view. Regional planners should perhaps be a bit less smug about the superiority of their own peculiar design vision. For one thing, the frequent claim that high-density suburban centers will permit mass transit flies in the face of mountains of evidence on Americans' attachment to the automobile. That having been said, it is virtually impossible for an economist (or anyone else) to define the economically optimal landscape with confidence. All we can say is that there are reasons to believe that a landscape planned at a regional scale will be an improvement over one that is not.

The most basic question to ask is, "What is the regional plan replacing?" It is *not* replacing a set of unconstrained free-market choices that reflect "what people and businesses really want." Instead, regional planning is imposed on a landscape that is already highly regulated at the local level. The shortsightedness and outright selfishness of much local land use regulation has been discussed by a number of planning scholars and practitioners over the years. I have made this point in defense of regional planning before (Gottlieb 1999, 51–64). The critique of local planning and zoning also seems to be picking up steam among those who are directly in charge of training local planners (see, e.g., Levine 2006; Pendall 2000).

The economic benefits of regional planning flow largely from the fact that many urban systems, like watersheds, commutersheds, and housing markets, exist at a scale much larger than the decision-making units of local government. This fundamental mismatch between the scale of impacts and the scale of decision making holds for individuals as well as for towns (driving and home buying being the main examples). It would be a remarkable coincidence indeed if a system with this many externalities and common property resources produced an optimal economic outcome.

That is the easy part of the argument. The hard part of the argument is deciding exactly how to move the system away from the status quo. This thorny problem is the main reason why economists prefer not to plan but to *price*. The benefit of simply increasing the price of activities with negative spillovers is that individuals remain free to choose their preferred lifestyles: these are not dictated by a central planner. A good example of a pricing solution to problems arising at the urban fringe is developer impact fees. It should be no surprise, then, that by-the-book economist Jan Brueckner favors impact fees as an antidote to urban sprawl (Brueckner 2000, 166–167). It must be acknowledged, however, that the precise calibration of the many impact fees that would actually be required to fix market failures in a complex urban setting is beyond the ability of policy makers, even regional ones. So regional planning, even if it is based on opinion surveys and outright hunches, becomes a useful second-best solution to market failure from the economist's point of view.

The discussion so far has been fairly theoretical, so let us return to the benefits of regional planning that can actually be measured in dollars. Most of these relate to the more efficient use of infrastructure caused by concentrating development at the large scale (central city redevelopment) or at the small scale (denser subdivisions). Turning to the small scale first, estimates of the infrastructure cost savings from compact development at the subdivision scale are typically in the range of 15 percent or so (Burchell et al. 1998). This sounds good until you realize that almost all the infrastructure within a subdivision is built by developers and then rolled into the cost of the homes. It follows that this kind of infrastructure is, in many ways, a private good for which homebuyers are more than willing to pay. What is the governmental interest in eliminating this 15 percent premium on the cost of the sewer pipe running down Fair Oaks Lane if homebuyers are happy to pay it to enjoy lower densities? If it can be shown that these extra costs are paid *in*voluntarily—the result of minimum lot size restrictions that skew the market— then we are back to our argument about the perversity of local land use regulations. Without this proof, however, the pure cost-of-sprawl argument stands on thin ice.

When it comes to off-site infrastructure, like schools, city roads, and wastewater treatment plants, the fiscal argument for regional planning is somewhat more compelling. This is cost-of-sprawl reasoning at the larger scale. Using a state-level infrastructure model that I helped develop for the New Jersey State Planning Commission, the Center for Urban Policy Research calculated that the 1990 New Jersey State Plan would save $740 million in state and local road costs and $440 million in water supply and sewer infrastructure costs over a twenty-year planning horizon (Burchell 1992, xiv–xv; Gottlieb and Reilly 1990; Reilly 1990). These savings are generated mostly by a projected redistribution of people and jobs across municipal boundaries, not within them. (Whether the people and jobs would go willingly is not addressed.) Interestingly, the CUPR team found no effect of the state plan on school infrastructure costs, commenting that "the oft-repeated scenario of significant excess capacity in urban and closer-in suburban schools, and deficient capacity in exurban and rural schools is, in reality, a myth" (Burchell 1992, xvi).

To put the CUPR numbers in perspective, at this writing the governor of New Jersey has just proposed massive budget cuts in order to close a $3.4 billion deficit in the state budget and possibly chip away at a level of debt that is roughly ten times this amount (Chen 1998). Even if we convert CUPR's estimate of planning's cost savings to 2008 dollars, the twenty years' worth of projected savings amount to only half of the state's annual budget deficit, and less than 1 percent of the state's outstanding debt—and the state is not the only governmental entity with fiscal responsibility for these infrastructure systems. So smart growth is certainly a start, but infrastructure savings from planning are not a panacea for solving the fiscal problems of a large urban state. That is why I return repeatedly in this essay to planning's quality-of-life benefits.

Making the Case

Over years of working as an economist with planners and planning advocates, I have frequently been troubled by a tendency to put the measurable dollar benefits of regional planning into a completely different compartment than the aesthetic, quality-of-life, and environmental benefits. Advocates who do this often look for hard numbers on the infrastructure side, hoping that such numbers will persuade the "hard-headed business community" of the advantages of smart growth planning. But as I have suggested, these numbers rarely amount to a grand slam, so calculating and reporting them separately is not exactly putting your best foot forward.

Through my association with the Land Policy Institute at Michigan State University, I have been involved in precisely these kinds of efforts to persuade business leaders of the dollar-and-cents benefits of smart growth, which Michigan governor Jennifer Granholm supports in principle. On the one hand, Michigan has fallen on hard times, so any policy designed to get more bang out of the public buck is welcome, even necessary. On the other hand, the easily measured benefits of smart growth planning are modest, while a conservative state founded on manufacturing finds it difficult to embrace anything that looks like a restriction on free enterprise. For obvious reasons, the negative effects of growth are less severe in Michigan than elsewhere and do not appear to be generating a tidal wave of complaints from the kind of affluent residents who drive the smart growth movement forward in other places.

In places like New Jersey and northern California, however, the problems associated with rapid growth have gotten the attention of the business community all on their own. Growth management and quality of life represent a significant portion of the mission of regional civic organizations, like Joint Venture Silicon Valley, that are chaired by the CEOs of large local businesses. The interest of businesses in local quality of life, which of course has an effect on recruiting, can be seen in the many regional data monitoring projects that emphasize amenity and infrastructure variables.

In central New Jersey I have been involved, as a subcontractor to the Regional Plan Association, with something called the Somerset County Regional Center Vision Initiative.[1] This project is essentially a design-oriented plan that tries to concentrate development and improve transportation infrastructure in a preexisting edge city. Somerset's planning goals are very much in line with those of the New Jersey State Plan.

What has struck me about the Somerset planning process is the active participation, at the board level, of the Somerset County Business Partnership, a chamber of commerce that advertises itself, interestingly, as a "Smart Growth Organization." My interaction with the leadership and my knowledge of this particular county (including down-zoning in a place called Hillsborough) lead me to believe that an

[1]See http://www.rpa.org/pdf/somersetvision.pdf.

implicit bargain has been struck in which the county's exurban residents are more than happy to funnel virtually all growth into the old, relatively poor city of Somerville, while the residents there are more than happy to accept it. Here is a smart growth consensus uniting the business community with regional planners and progressive social activists. It probably could not have happened as easily at a scale larger than a single county or involving cities as troubled as Newark or Camden. It is driven, admittedly, by the no-growth sentiments of affluent suburban residents—business executives acting in their role as homeowners as well as facility builders and corporate recruiters. The danger, of course, is that the residents of Somerville will be actively excluded from moving to adjacent suburbs; but for now I shall give the political power structure in Somerset County the benefit of the doubt.

I find myself persuaded that the "business case" for regional planning essentially makes itself—but only in fast-growing, congested areas where the amenity costs of growth are widely recognized. Furthermore, unless you attach dollars and cents to the aesthetic and environmental benefits of regional planning, it is not clear that the numbers will ever be persuasive. That remains a valid exercise. The framework of economics encompasses everything. Regional planning is either a net winner in economic terms or it is a net loser. It can't be both simultaneously. All factors cannot be easily measured, but that is no reason to be defensive about the modest fiscal benefits or the restriction on development opportunities that regional planning sometimes brings about. Not only are the benefits of regional planning likely to be substantial; they are also likely to be large enough to compensate the few who lose.

CHAPTER 27

PROMOTING FISCAL EQUITY AND EFFICIENT DEVELOPMENT PRACTICES AT THE METROPOLITAN SCALE

Myron Orfield and Thomas Luce

Metropolitan areas across the United States are struggling with sprawling development patterns and the unequal distribution of opportunity across regional landscapes. One important reason for this is the highly fragmented structure of local governance that exists in many U.S. metropolitan areas. Communities in highly fragmented systems face significant, often overwhelming, pressures to compete for development that will expand their tax bases. These pressures often drive local land use planning decisions, encourage sprawl, and increase economic and social disparities.

Localities pay attention to the net effect that any new development will have on local revenues and expenditures—on whether the proposed development "pays its way." To win the most profitable land uses, local governments may offer public subsidies or infrastructure improvements. But perhaps the most common approach is "fiscal zoning"—making land use decisions not based on the suitability of the land or the long-term needs of the region, but on the tax revenue a development can generate right away in a small part of the region. For example, many communities lay out great tracts of land for commercial development, regardless of whether it is the most appropriate use for the location (See Fischel [1992, 171–177] for a discussion of fiscal zoning and why it occurs).

This competition is costly in several ways. First, from the entire region's perspective, it is wasteful of public resources. Public sector time, effort, and money

Metropolitan area	Counties	Municipalities and townships	Total local governments	Local governments per 10,000 residents
Pittsburgh	6	412	418	1.77
Minneapolis–St. Paul	13	331	344	1.24
St. Louis	12	300	312	1.23
Cincinnati	13	222	235	1.23
Kansas City	11	171	182	1.06
Cleveland	8	259	267	0.92
Philadelphia	14	428	442	0.74
Milwaukee	5	108	113	0.69
Chicago	13	554	567	0.66
Detroit	10	325	335	0.62
Boston	14	282	296	0.51
Dallas	12	184	196	0.42
Portland	8	79	87	0.41
New York	27	729	756	0.38
Atlanta	20	107	127	0.35
Denver	7	67	74	0.32
Houston	8	115	123	0.28
Seattle	6	88	94	0.28
Washington, D.C.	33	125	158	0.22
Tampa	4	35	39	0.18
San Francisco	10	104	114	0.17
Miami	2	55	57	0.16
Phoenix	2	32	34	0.12
Los Angeles	5	177	182	0.12
San Diego	1	18	19	0.07

Figure 27.1. Fragmentation in the twenty-five largest U.S. metropolitan areas

is likely to be expended to affect the location of businesses that would have located somewhere in the region anyway. Second, the competition can contribute to vicious cycles of decline. If a business relocates from one municipality to another, the loser must either raise tax rates to maintain revenues or decrease the amount or quality of services, diminishing its attractiveness to businesses in the next round of competition. Third, such uncoordinated competition often makes the task of providing regional infrastructure more expensive than it has to be. Finally, local income and property taxes magnify the fiscal benefits to localities of business compared to residential development. This can lead to inadequate provision of housing, especially affordable housing.

Figure 27.1 shows the degree of local government fragmentation in the twenty-five largest U.S. metropolitan areas. The variation is enormous—from 1.77 local governments per 10,000 residents in Pittsburgh (or just 5,650 residents per local government) to 0.07 in San Diego (or more than 140,000 residents per local government). Older metropolitan areas in the Northeast and Midwest tend to

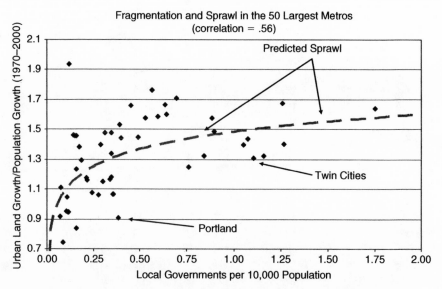

Figure 27.2. Fragmentation and sprawl in the fifty largest metropolitan areas

show the greatest degrees of fragmentation, with lower rates typically in the newer metros of the South and West.

Figure 27.2 shows the relationship between fragmentation and sprawl—the more fragmented the region, the greater its rate of sprawl in recent decades.[1] The sprawl measure varies from 0.74 to 1.93. (A value less than 1 implies that population grew more quickly than urbanized land; a value greater than 1 implies that urbanized land grew more quickly.) Interestingly, the two metropolitan areas with the most powerful regional planning organizations in the country—Portland Metro in Portland and the Metropolitan Council in the Twin Cities—are among the metros showing the greatest differences between their actual and predicted sprawl rates. Both show sprawl rates considerably lower than would be expected given their levels of fragmentation, indicating that strong regional planning is one way to combat the negative effects of local government fragmentation. Portland is the farthest below the line among less-fragmented metros, and the Twin Cities is the farthest below among highly fragmented regions.

Fragmentation is also associated with fiscal inequality in large metropolitan areas. Figure 27.3 shows this relationship—more fragmented metropolitan areas tend to show greater inequities in local tax bases.[2] As with sprawl, two of the metropolitan areas showing the greatest difference between actual and predicted sprawl rates are the Twin Cities and Portland, the two large metropolitan areas with the most extensive regional planning systems. In the Twin Cities, the fiscal disparities tax base sharing program further enhances the region's positive standing.

The implications of tax base disparities like those implied by the Gini coefficients in figure 27.3 are important. Municipalities at the low end of the spectrum face a very difficult choice between providing regionally competitive levels of local

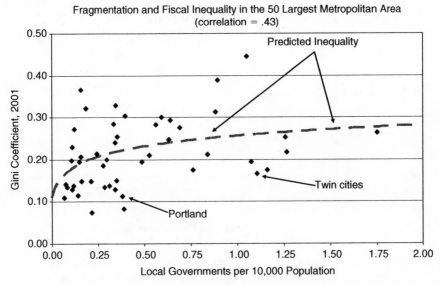

Figure 27.3. Fragmentation and fiscal inequality in the fifty largest metropolitan areas

public services like police and fire protection by assessing tax rates that are higher than their regional counterparts—sometimes much higher—and assessing competitive tax rates while providing much lower than average local services. Either combination puts them at a serious disadvantage when competing for new residents or businesses. Tax base disparities greater than ten to one are not uncommon in U.S. metropolitan areas (Orfield 2002, table 3-2, 56). Disparities of this magnitude clearly create the potential for vicious cycles of decline in low tax base places.

Tax base sharing (TBS) is one way to significantly improve both the equity and efficiency of regional fiscal systems. In such a system, a portion of local tax base (usually a percentage of growth) is put into a regional pool that is then redistributed back to local areas based on some criteria other than their contributions to the pool.

The formula that distributes the pool back to communities can take a variety of forms. It can be very redistributive—sending disproportionate shares of the pool to high-poverty or low-tax-base places, for instance. Or it can be relatively neutral—distributing the pool by population or household shares. It can also be designed to compensate local areas for extra costs of public services. The age of the housing stock—a good proxy for the age of infrastructure—could be used in this way. In any of these cases, because contributions to the pool are based on local tax bases, the system reduces fiscal disparities across the region.

If the contribution formula is designed properly, TBS can also improve the efficiency of local economies and fiscal systems. In the Twin Cities version communities contribute 40 percent of the increase in commercial-industrial property tax base to the pool, which is then redistributed with a formula based on population and local tax base. This reduces the incentives for communities to compete for tax base, because they do not keep all of the resulting revenues. However, because localities retain enough of the tax base to cover the costs of growth, the incentive is not so strong that local areas will be unwilling to allow new development within their borders. (For a more extensive discussion of tax base sharing, see Luce [1998b].) Since localities will spend less time and effort trying to lure businesses to their area, business activity will gravitate toward areas generating the greatest economic returns, improving the overall performance of the regional economy.

This means that there is potential for individual communities to benefit from TBS in several direct and indirect ways. Places that contribute less tax base than they get from the distribution formula receive an obvious fiscal benefit—more tax base that allows them to increase public services, lower tax rates, or both. However, other indirect benefits accrue to both net receivers and net contributors. Reduced competition for tax base will mean that fewer public resources (spending and other incentives) will be devoted to the "ratables chase," freeing up local resources for other purposes in all types of communities. A more efficient regional economy should grow more quickly, increasing local tax bases and the regional pool beyond what would exist without TBS.

Other indirect benefits of TBS that apply to both net receivers and net contributors involve the potential effects of enhanced interlocal or regional cooperation for economic development and planning. TBS ensures that all share in the benefits of regional growth and reduces the stakes for individual jurisdictions in the location of specific economic activities. This lowers barriers to cooperative economic development programs, enhancing the entire region's growth prospects.

These TBS outcomes also reduce opposition to regional planning efforts that can affect local tax bases, including affordable housing initiatives and environmental protection. Housing initiatives designed to enhance the economic opportunities available to moderate and low income families by locating affordable housing in areas with strong job growth often face local opposition because of the potential effects on local tax base. TBS can be a central part of an incentive structure that reduces these fiscal disincentives.

Regional efforts to protect environmental assets, like open space, lakes, streams, and clean air can face local opposition for many of the same reasons. Because of the amenity value, land near sensitive natural areas often represents very valuable local tax base. This means that costs of protecting such areas—in the form of forgone tax base—are often highly localized, while the benefits are much more diffused across the entire region and beyond. As a result, local governments do not face the proper incentives to conserve sensitive areas. They will do too little because the purely local benefits from protection—low because benefits are so diffused—do not outweigh the highly concentrated costs. TBS eases these difficulties by reducing the fiscal incentives to develop sensitive areas and by facilitating regional environmental planning efforts that weigh all of the costs and benefits. In sum, TBS can thus be designed to serve several purposes. It can:

- Reduce the incentives for localities to compete with each other for tax base
- Reduce inequalities in tax base, tax rates, and local public services

- Encourage joint regional or multijurisdictional economic development efforts
- Complement regional land use planning efforts
- Provide insurance against future changes in growth patterns—no part of a region can count on being a regional growth leader forever

THE TWIN CITIES FISCAL DISPARITIES PROGRAM

The Twin Cities Fiscal Disparities Program is the best existing example of regional tax base sharing. The program covers the seven core counties of the Twin Cities metropolitan area. There are 192 municipalities, 50 school districts, and more than 100 special districts covered by the program. In existence since 1971, it pools 40 percent of the growth in commercial-industrial tax base and redistributes it based on population and total local property tax base per capita. If a municipality's property tax base per capita is less than the regional average, it receives a portion of the pool greater than its share of the region's population; if its tax base is greater than average, it receives a portion less than its population share (see Hinze and Baker [2005] for a complete description of the formula).

As of 2004, 32 percent of the region's commercial-industrial tax base was in the pool, and 64 percent of the region's population lived in municipalities that were net beneficiaries of the program. The program reduces tax base inequality in the region by about 20 percent, as measured by the Gini coefficient (representing a decline from 0.21 to 0.17). The effects are even more pronounced at the extremes of the distribution. The program reduces the ratio of the highest to lowest tax base per household from 25–1 to 8–1, and of the second highest to second lowest, from 10–1 to 4–1.

The region's two central cities are affected in significantly different ways. St. Paul, with much of its prime real estate devoted to state office buildings and other nonprofit purposes, is a major beneficiary of the program. Its average tax on a homesteaded residence is about 9 percent lower than it would be in the absence of the program (Hinze and Baker 2005, 26). Minneapolis, on the other hand, has had periods when it contributed more to the pool than it received from it and other times when it has been a net receiver.

Figure 27.4 shows the geographic distribution of net gains in tax capacity from the Minneapolis–St. Paul region's Fiscal Disparities Program.[3] Net contributors to the program—municipalities that contribute more tax base to the pool than they receive from the pool—are largely middle ring suburbs that fall along the interstate highway system, including the ring-roads (I-494 and I-694), I-35W, I-35E, and I-94. The pattern shows very clearly the impact that highway investments have on the distribution of tax base within a region. Net receivers of the program—municipalities that receive more tax base than they contribute—are a combination of central cities, inner suburbs, and outer suburbs.

Figure 27.4 clearly suggests that the Twin Cities regional planning system and the Fiscal Disparities Program moderate the impacts of the region's highly fragmented local government system. The degree to which this remains true depends

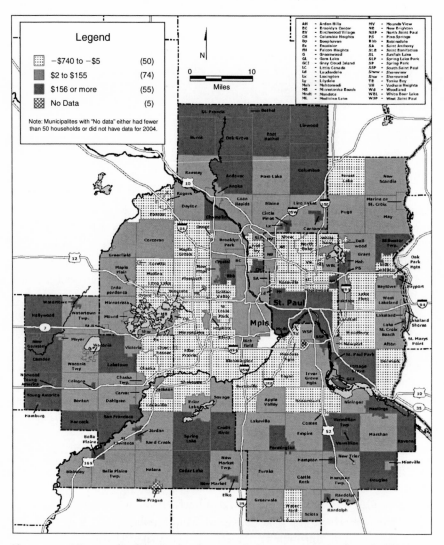

Figure 27.4. Minneapolis–Saint Paul region net gain in tax capacity per household by municipality, 2004

to some extent on whether both institutions are expanded to reflect the region's growth. When the Metropolitan Council and the Fiscal Disparities Program were formed in 1971, the seven-county boundary used for both contained the entire regional economy. Since then the region has expanded to include four "collar counties" to the north and west in Minnesota and two to the east (in Wisconsin).

Much of the region's growth is now occurring in these collar counties. Between 2000 and 2005, 32 percent of the growth in the region's eleven Minnesota counties occurred in the four Minnesota collar counties—Chisago, Isanti, Sherburne, and Wright. If regional institutions are to continue to effectively counterbalance the negative effects of fragmentation, these counties must eventually be added to the Metropolitan Council and the Fiscal Disparities Program.

On its surface, expanding the Fiscal Disparities Program into the four Minnesota collar counties should be relatively noncontroversial. Each would stand to gain significant amounts of tax base by joining the system. Simulations of net distributions assuming that the four counties were included in the program from the beginning show this clearly. (The simulations were performed by the Research Office of the Minnesota House of Representatives. A map of the results is available at http://www .regionalplans.com.) Nearly 90 percent of the municipalities in the collar counties— seventy-seven out of eighty-eight—would be net receivers in the program. These cities and townships represent 80 percent of the population in the four counties. In many cases the fiscal benefits would be substantial.

OTHER TAX BASE SHARING PROGRAMS

The Twin Cities Fiscal Disparities Program is the only full-scale regional TBS program in the United States. However, there are other smaller-scale examples in New Jersey, Ohio, and Minnesota. In addition, other county or regionwide programs have been proposed.

The New Jersey program operates in the area surrounding the Meadowlands Stadium complex. The New Jersey Meadowlands Commission has overseen a TBS program since 1970 that collects 40 percent of the growth in property tax revenues in portions of fourteen Bergen and Hudson county communities. The revenues are redistributed annually based on the share of the Meadowlands district that falls in each community. Because all participating communities share in revenue generated by development no matter where it takes place, the commission, which oversees land use planning in the district, is able to plan for both conservation and development where they are most needed.

The seeds of an equity-based tax-sharing program are also in place in the Miami Valley of Ohio. Montgomery County—the county containing Dayton—has established what it calls the Economic Development/Government Equity (ED/GE) program to "share some of the economic benefits . . . resulting from new economic development among the jurisdictions of Montgomery County" (Montgomery County 2001). The program creates an annual countywide funding pool for economic development projects, as well as a government equity fund that shares a portion of growth in municipalities' property and income tax revenues each year. All thirty communities in the county, including the city of Dayton, participate in the voluntary program.

Minnesota also has a second TBS program, initiated in 1996. Established on the Iron Range in northern Minnesota, the program covers all or parts of five counties, including the city of Duluth. The program was set up to work exactly the same way as the Fiscal Disparities Program, except that it uses 1995 as the base year. The first year of implementation was 1998. By 2004 the program had grown to include 8 percent of the commercial-industrial tax base (1.6 percent of total tax base).

Another prominent example of a regionwide tax base sharing proposal occurred in 2002 in Sacramento. The program would have pooled local sales tax revenues from new commercial-industrial development in the region. One-third of the pool would have been redistributed to the cities in the region based on population; another third would have reverted to the city where the development occurred; and the final third would also have gone to the host city if it met certain smart growth goals involving affordable housing, infill development, and open space conservation. (Simulations showed that more than 60 percent of the region's residents would have been in places that were net receivers.) The proposal passed both houses of the California legislature, but the two bills were never reconciled because of a threatened veto by the governor. California is potentially fertile ground for proposals of this sort because the local sales tax, the most important local tax in the state, generates such strong incentives for interlocal competition for commercial developments like auto malls—the holy grail of local economic development programs in California. (Simulations of sales tax base sharing for fifteen California metropolitan areas implied that two-thirds of the regions' residents lived in places that would have been net receivers.)

Simulations of Tax Base Sharing in Other Regions

Other research has shown how effective TBS can be in reducing fiscal inequality. Simulations for the twenty-five largest metropolitan areas show that programs with designs and scales similar to the Twin Cities Fiscal Disparities Program would be more efficient than existing state aid systems in reducing inequality (Orfield 2002, 107–109). The simulations, which created regional pools equal to 10 percent of total regional tax bases, reduced inequality (measured by the Gini coefficient) by 20 percent on average.

A comparable, more detailed study of the Twin Cities, Chicago, Philadelphia, Portland, and Seattle shows similar results and illustrates two other important characteristics of TBS (Luce 1998a). First, contrary to what one might expect, central cities are not always the major beneficiaries of TBS. Although three of the seven central cities in these metros (St. Paul, Philadelphia, and Tacoma) experienced tax base gains of more than 10 percent, two others (Minneapolis and Chicago) gained much less (2 and 7 percent, respectively), and the final two (Portland and Seattle) were net contributors. Second, equity effects of tax base sharing were greatest at the extremes of the tax base distributions. In all five metropolitan areas, TBS reduced a measure of inequality at the extremes of the distributions (the ratio of the ninety-fifth to fifth percentiles) by proportionately more than the Gini coefficient (which is affected most by differences in the core of the distribution).

Ameregis, a consulting firm specializing in metropolitan studies, has simulated the effects of TBS in many metropolitan areas.[4] These studies highlight other features of the approach. In principle, TBS can be employed with any local tax. In most states, the property tax is the most important local tax. But in some states income or sales taxes are as (or more) important. Simulations in Lexington,

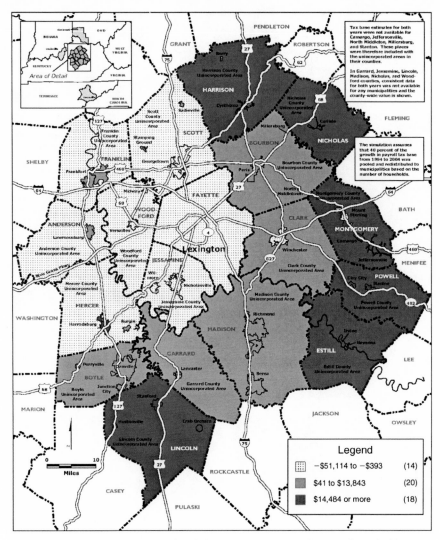

Figure 27.5. Bluegrass region: Simulated change in property tax base per household resulting from a property tax base sharing program, 1994–2004

Kentucky, Cleveland, Ohio, and Sacramento, California, illustrate that TBS can be just as effective with taxes other than the property tax.

In Kentucky, both property and income (or payroll) taxes are important local revenue sources (Ameregis 2006). Figures 27.5 and 27.6 show the results of simulations of the effects of tax base sharing with these two bases in the Lexington region. In each case, the maps show the net distribution (contribution minus distribution) per household for municipalities and unincorporated areas if a tax base sharing program had pooled 40 percent of the increase in tax base between 1994 and 2004 and redistributed it to municipalities based on the number of households in each place.

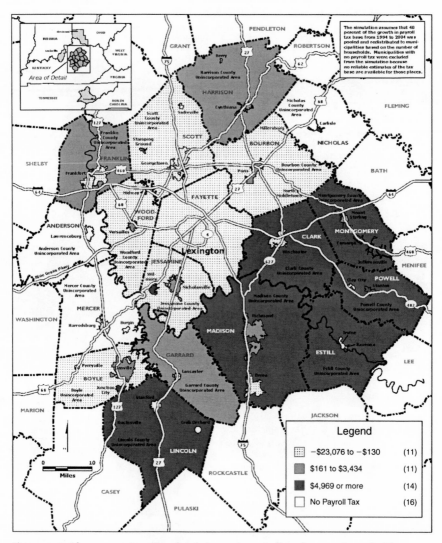

Figure 27.6. Bluegrass region: Simulated change in payroll tax base per household resulting from a payroll tax base sharing program by municipality and unincorporated county, 1994–2004

In the simulation for the property tax (fig. 27.5), tax base sharing would increase the tax base available in thirty-eight of the fifty-two municipalities and unincorporated areas in the region—areas serving 65 percent of the households outside of Lexington. Lexington, itself, would have been a small net contributor to the system. Its total property tax base would have been roughly 2 percent lower in 2004, or by about the amount its base grew in six months during the period.

The payroll tax simulation (fig. 27.6) yields similar results. In this case, tax base sharing would increase the tax base available to twenty-six of the thirty-six localities included in the simulation. The net receivers represent 68 percent of households in the included municipalities outside of Lexington, while Lexington would essentially break even. (Lexington's net contribution would have been less than 1 percent of its base.)

Overall, net contributors to the regional property tax pool (municipalities that would have contributed more property tax base than they received) would have had about 4 percent less tax base in 2004 than their actual base. Net contributors in the payroll tax simulation would have had about 5 percent less tax base in 2004 as a group. However, if tax base sharing had actually been in place, municipalities and counties would have had much more incentive to engage in cooperative economic development activities. If these incentives had led to just four- or five-tenths of a percent faster growth per year in their tax bases (depending on the tax base), the resulting tax base in these places would have been greater in 2004 than it was without the program.

Recent simulations for an area in northeastern Ohio significantly larger than a single metropolitan area show similar results. Performed by the Center for Housing Research and Policy, Cleveland State University, the models use commercial-industrial property and income tax base changes from 1996 to 2006. A sixteen-county region including the Cleveland, Akron, Canton, and Youngstown metropolitan areas plus six adjoining nonmetropolitan counties were included in the analysis. For each of the taxes, contributions from each locality were 40 percent of growth in tax base, and distributions were determined by the share of regional households and the age or housing stock (a proxy for the age of infrastructure).

In the results for the property tax, 366 of 487 communities in the region, including Cleveland, were net receivers of tax base in the simulation. Comprised of the region's central cities, inner suburbs, and outlying areas for the most part, net receivers represented 69 percent of regional population. Most net contributors were clustered around the interstate highway system in the second and third ring suburbs of Cleveland and Akron. The program would have reduced commercial industrial property tax base disparities (measured by the ratio of the average for the top 10 percent to the bottom 10 percent) by about 10 percent (from 5.3 to 4.8).

The results for the local income tax were different in interesting ways. Only communities that currently use the tax were included. The net beneficiaries were 113 of 190 communities, representing 62 percent of the regional population. Net contributors included Cleveland and many of the suburbs between Cleveland and Akron. In this case, tax base disparities (measured by the ratio of the top 10 percent to the bottom 10 percent) were reduced by 38 percent (from 13.6 to 8.5). Maps of the results of these simulations are available at http://www.regionalplans.com.

The final example shows the geographic flexibility of TBS. Figure 27.7 shows the results for simulations performed in New Jersey. The region shown—South Jersey—represents one of the three regions used in the work which, combined, make up the entire state of New Jersey. Many of New Jersey's municipalities are part of metropolitan areas not centered in New Jersey—Philadelphia and

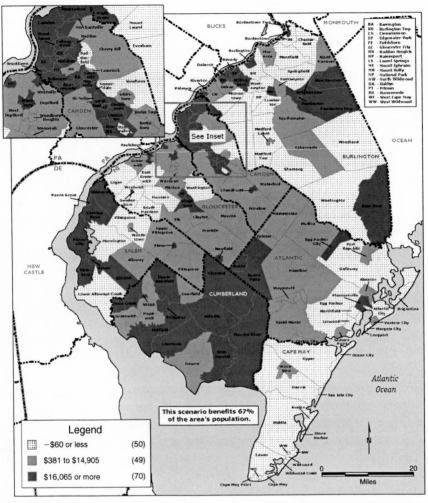

Figure 27.7. Southern New Jersey: Simulated change in property tax base per household as a result of redistribution of 40 percent of tax base growth according to number of households, 1993–2003

New York. As a result, none of the regions used in the analysis are a single metropolitan area or combination of entire metros. The south Jersey region includes a large number of Philadelphia suburbs, resort areas along the Atlantic shore, and the rural and exurban areas around them. Communities that were net receivers in the simulation are clustered in the Philadelphia suburbs along the Pennsylvania/New Jersey portion of the Delaware River and in outlying areas. Sixty-seven percent of the region's population is in these cities and towns. Net contributors are largely in resort areas along the Atlantic shore and in suburban areas around the New Jersey Turnpike (which parallels the Delaware River).

Summary and Conclusions

Highly fragmented local government systems encourage sprawl and foster fiscal inequality. TBS programs can ease both of these problems by reducing incentives for inefficient competition for economic activity among local governments and redistributing local tax base from high-capacity to low-capacity communities. The record in the Twin Cities with the Fiscal Disparities Program and simulations in a variety of metropolitan areas show that a properly structured program can achieve both of these goals.

TBS also complements other components of regional policy making. By ensuring that all parts of a region share in the tax benefits of new economic development, TBS encourages multijurisdictional and regionwide cooperation on development planning. Spreading the rewards of new developments also supports regional planning efforts by reducing the intensity of the competition for land uses with the greatest fiscal rewards, easing the tradeoffs facing regional decision makers. This also reduces barriers to regional approaches to issues like affordable housing and environmental protection that often face local opposition because of their local fiscal outcomes. Indeed, in the Twin Cities, the Fiscal Disparities Program was part of a quid pro quo that led to concurrent implementation of regional planning and tax base sharing (Orfield 1997, 124–125).

The simulations show how flexible TBS can be. It can be used with any local tax, not just the property tax. Indeed, local income taxes (especially if they are paid in one's place of work) and sales taxes create incentives distorting regional economies that are at least as strong as property taxes. TBS can also be applied to a variety of geographies—to part of a metropolitan area (as in Dayton or the Meadowlands); in an entire metropolitan area (as in the Twin Cities and Sacramento); to megaregions comprised of a number of linked metropolitan areas (as in northeast Ohio); and to diverse combinations of suburbs and nonmetropolitan communities (as in South Jersey).

The simulations also show that, regardless of the tax instrument or the geography, the characteristic outcomes of TBS provide political ammunition for its proponents. Because of the way that economic activity tends to cluster, TBS almost invariably provides tax base benefits to large majorities of regional populations. In most cases, roughly two-thirds of residents are in areas that are net receivers. And because many central cities are still competitive in regional markets for commercial-industrial tax base (the target of most TBS schemes), TBS proposals can often avoid the pitfalls of antagonisms that dominate city-suburb relations in many metropolitan areas.

In sum, tax base sharing enjoys a unique place in the hierarchy of economic policy making. It is a policy that avoids one of the most famous trade-offs in economics. Arthur Okun's famous essay, *Equality and Efficiency: The Big Trade-Off*, argued that policies designed to improve the efficiency of the economy almost invariably worsen equity outcomes and that equity-enhancing policies typically reduce the efficiency of the economy (Okun 1975). Tax base sharing can do both. It enhances the efficiency of regional economies by reducing wasteful competition for tax base and improves equity outcomes by redistributing tax base from high-capacity to low-capacity places.

NOTES

1. Sprawl is measured by {(urban land in 2000 / urban land in 1970)} / {(population in 2000 / population in 1970)}. Urban land is defined as a census tract with a housing density of more than one unit per four acres, the density currently used by the Census Bureau to define urbanized land at the fringes of metropolitan areas. The "predicted sprawl" line shows the simple regression line between the log of the sprawl ratio and the log of the fragmentation measure for the fifty largest metropolitan areas. The log-log relationship is the strongest specification, with a simple correlation of 0.56 (significant at the 99 percent confidence level). If the lone outlier (New Orleans, the high outlier in the upper left quadrant) is removed, the correlation increases to 0.64. The positive relationship between fragmentation and sprawl remains statistically significant when metropolitan population, population growth, dummy variables for coastal locations, water constraints on development, and the existence of a strong regional planning organization are added as independent variables.

2. Fiscal inequality is measured by the Gini coefficient. The Gini coefficient measures the difference between the actual distribution of tax base and a perfectly equal distribution. It varies between 0 and 1, taking on a value of 0 if the distribution is perfectly equal (all jurisdictions have the same tax base per household) and 1 if the distribution is perfectly unequal (one jurisdiction with only one household has all of the tax base). The "predicted inequality" line shows the simple regression line between the log of the Gini coefficient and the log of the fragmentation measure for the fifty largest metropolitan areas. The log-log relationship is the strongest specification, with a simple correlation of 0.43 (significant at the 99 percent confidence level). The positive relationship between the Gini coefficient and fragmentation remains statistically significant if metropolitan population, population growth, and a dummy variable for the existence of a strong regional planning organization are added as independent variables.

3. In Minnesota, the primary local tax instrument is the property tax. State law sets the rate structure for different types of property. The rate per dollar of assessed value is greater for commercial-industrial property than for owner-occupied residential property, for instance. A particular locality's mix of property types then determines how productive its tax base is (in terms of revenue generated per dollar of property values). This is the locality's "tax capacity." Local governments then determine their overall tax rate by varying the percentage of tax capacity that they tap.

4. Ameregis studies on more than thirty U.S. metropolitan areas and states are available at http://www.ameregis.com. Many of the studies include tax base sharing simulations.

CHAPTER 28

BUT WHERE WILL PEOPLE LIVE?

REGIONAL PLANNING AND AFFORDABLE HOUSING

Alan Mallach

The provision of housing for a region's low and moderate income households lies at the heart of the principles of smart growth and sound regional planning. From a regional planning perspective, affordable housing strategies are not merely a matter of ensuring that people have a place to live somewhere—although that goal is often not achieved—but that where they live reflects sound principles of growth and social equity. Providing affordable housing opportunities throughout a region or metropolitan area, and doing so in a way that relates housing to job opportunities and transportation is not simply a matter of equity, important as that is. It is a critical element in building a healthy region that permits individuals to live near their work, allows regions to grow in an environmentally responsible fashion, and begins to undo the concentration of poor people and racial minorities into urban ghettos that still characterizes so many American metropolitan areas.

Yet, in today's regional planning landscape, affordable housing remains a largely underdeveloped area. The regional planning framework for affordable housing is limited and uneven. To the extent that it exists at all, it is largely limited to research and data collection, hortatory goal statements, and technical support for local actions. Largely, but not entirely. Fair share strategies grounded in regional planning considerations exist in a few jurisdictions, while an even smaller number have gone beyond numerical allocations to embrace proactive strategies and incentives for regional solutions. Even regional agencies that play an advisory or supportive role, however, can add significant value to how affordable housing issues are handled within their region, as well as focus the attention of local governments and civic leaders on the regional nature of the issue.

Still, there is little question that housing lags behind other areas such as environmental management and transportation in the extent to which decisions are animated by a regional perspective.

AFFORDABLE HOUSING AND REGIONAL PLANNING TODAY

Regional strategies for affordable housing include a small number of fair share plans, a still smaller number of proactive strategies, and a far larger number of other efforts that take various forms, all advisory or supportive in nature.

Fair Share Plans

Fair share plans allocate the regional need for affordable housing—or, in California, housing for people of all economic levels—across the local jurisdictions of a region on the basis of a formula designed to foster a rational distribution of affordable housing throughout the region. The first such plan was adopted by the Miami Valley Regional Planning Commission for the Dayton, Ohio, region in 1970. Although not legally binding on the municipalities of the region, it led to significant production of affordable housing throughout the region over the course of the next decade as a result of the sustained efforts of the commission (Listokin 1976, 118–126). Continued local opposition, and changes in regional priorities, however, led the commission ultimately to abandon the effort, which is no longer being pursued.

A number of statewide efforts to foster fair share approaches have taken place over the years, beginning with the Massachusetts "anti-snob zoning" law enacted in 1969. The Massachusetts law simply imposes a uniform standard on all municipalities in the state. Unless 10 percent of a town's housing inventory is affordable housing, a developer seeking to build affordable housing (or a mixed-income development containing a minimum percentage of affordable units) who is thwarted by local action may appeal to a state housing appeals board, which can reverse the municipal action and order the project approved (General Laws of Massachusetts, chap. 40B). This statute has spawned progeny in Connecticut, Rhode Island, and Illinois. While at least moderately effective as a way of generating affordable housing production, these efforts can hardly be considered to be regional planning in any meaningful sense.

The two state fair share statutes that bear some relationship to regional planning are those of New Jersey and California. Under the New Jersey Fair Housing Act, enacted in response to the state supreme court's *Mt. Laurel* decision, the state Council on Affordable Housing (COAH) was charged with developing a methodology for determining each municipality's share of the regional need for affordable housing (New Jersey Statutes Annotated, 52:27D-301 et seq., adopted 1985).[1] During its first two fair share cycles, in 1986 and 1993, COAH used criteria that bear some

---

[1] Regions are defined somewhat arbitrarily in the statute, as an area encompassing two to four contiguous counties. Outside the Pinelands and Highlands, New Jersey lacks a sub-state regional planning framework beyond individual counties.

relationship to regional planning, including vacant land and employment growth. Specifically, COAH used a surrogate for employment growth in the form of non-residential ratable growth. (For a detailed discussion of the COAH formula, see Meck et al. [2003, 35–37]).

Subsequently, however, COAH has largely jettisoned planning considerations and adopted a growth share methodology that requires affordable housing to be provided as a set percentage of ongoing residential and nonresidential development taking place in the municipality. Under the current rules, which represent a revision of earlier rules that were invalidated as a result of a court challenge, every municipality must provide one affordable housing unit for every five market-rate units constructed, and one affordable housing unit for every sixteen jobs created. The latter is based on a formula that derives added jobs from the square footage of new nonresidential construction. While there are legitimate reasons for this change in policy, it is nonetheless a step backward from an attempt, however uncertain, to link affordable housing to larger regional planning considerations.

Legislation enacted in 2008, however, may add a significant regional planning dimension to New Jersey's fair share law. Under the 2008 amendments, a number of existing regional planning agencies in the state—collectively covering a substantial part of the state's area—were given the mission to "identify and coordinate regional affordable housing opportunities in conjunction with municipalities in areas with convenient access to infrastructure, employment opportunities, and public transportation" (N.J. Statutes Annotated 52:27D-329.9(c)(2)).[2]

It is far from clear what will result from this legislation. The agencies and their constituent municipalities have only begun to grapple with the implications of the law, while neither COAH nor any other state agency has offered these agencies, particularly those with limited or no housing planning track record, any constructive guidance. Still, over the course of the next few years it may lead to some important new developments in integrating regional planning and affordable housing.

California law provides, at least potentially, for a closer relationship between fair share allocation and regional planning. Under the statute, each regional Council of Governments (COG) must design a formula for allocating housing needs by income range to all of the cities or counties within the COG's region (California Government Code Sec. 65584). The COG is given broad discretion, within an overall statutory framework, to choose its allocation criteria. The statute, in addition to calling for increasing "the mix of housing types, tenure and affordability in all cities and counties . . . in an equitable manner," calls for promoting environmental and

---

[2]Agencies designated include the New Jersey Meadowlands Commission, the Pinelands Commission, the Fort Monmouth Economic Revitalization Planning Authority, the Highlands Water Protection and Planning Council, and the Casino Reinvestment Development Authority. These are, to put it mildly, a mixed bag of regional agencies, ranging from two (Pinelands and Highlands) with both broad geographic reach and planning scope under existing law, to the CRDA, which had never exercised any planning-related authority prior to the enactment of this legislation.

agricultural resources, the encouragement of efficient development patterns, and an improved intraregional relationship between jobs and housing (Id. Sec. 65584d).

Once the COG has made its allocation, each city or county must incorporate the fair share into its housing element and take affirmative steps to further production of those units, including use of inclusionary zoning, density bonuses, and other provisions. The COG, however, has no power to enforce compliance. Although the results have been substantial, they have, perhaps inevitably, fallen well short of the goals set by the various plans. A study of the San Francisco Bay area found that between 1988 and 1998, area communities produced only 32 percent of the affordable housing mandated by the allocation, but 117 percent of the "above-moderate-income" housing allocated (Meck et al. 2003, 54). Ultimately, enforcement, to the extent that it exists, is driven by advocacy and litigation by nongovernmental supporters of affordable housing. The fact that a number of such cases have been brought, and have succeeded, has been a significant factor in promoting compliance with the law (Pindell 2005, 8–11).

Proactive Regional Strategies

For a regional agency to take more than an advisory role in furthering a regional strategy for affordable housing typically requires enactment of state legislation, a step that is rarely forthcoming. Two notable examples are found in Portland, Oregon, and in the Minnesota Twin Cities. Although neither explicitly mandates housing performance by local jurisdictions, both provide strong direction for a regional strategy to incorporate affordable housing into the land use planning process.

Portland Metro, the regional body responsible for growth management in the Portland Metropolitan area, was created by a voter referendum in 1992 and is governed by an elected council. It exercises strong regional planning and land use authority through a Metro Code adopted by the council. Title 7 of the Metro Code incorporates affordable housing provisions as an integral part of the regional urban growth management strategy. Section 3.07.730A of the code provides that "cities and counties shall ensure that their comprehensive plan and implementing ordinances address: 1) diversity; 2) maintaining the existing supply of affordable housing and increasing new dispersed affordable housing; and 3) increasing affordable housing opportunities for households of all income levels" (Portland Metro 2004). The ways in which they do so are at the municipality's discretion; they must, however, at a minimum consider a variety of strategies and tools set forth in Metro's Regional Affordable Housing Strategy and report periodically on their progress. In addition, municipalities were encouraged to adopt Metro's voluntary affordable housing production goals "as a guide to measure progress towards meeting the affordable housing needs of households with incomes between 0% and 50% of the regional median family income."

The results of Metro's efforts outside the city of Portland, which has had a long-standing commitment to affordable housing, appear to be limited. Only three of the twenty-seven cities or counties within Metro formally adopted Metro's goals, while eight formally declined to adopt them. In most of the others, the affordable housing goals were still being discussed or considered four years after having been proposed (Portland Metro 2005).

The Minnesota Livable Communities Act was enacted in 1995. (Minnesota Statutes 473.25 through 473.254). It provides the Twin Cities Metropolitan Council, a body covering a seven-county area, with the power to levy a tax surcharge across the region, which is used to create three funding pools:

- The Tax Base Revitalization Account, used to finance environmental cleanup of contaminated sites, to be used to create and/or retain jobs and affordable housing
- The Livable Communities Demonstration Account, used to finance development and redevelopment projects that link housing, jobs, and services
- The Local Housing Incentive Account, used to provide incentives for the development of low and moderate income housing.

In 2007, the Council expected to distribute $16.55 million from the three accounts.

Municipalities within the region are eligible to receive money from these accounts only after they have negotiated housing goals with the council. Municipalities are given a further incentive both to negotiate goals and to actively pursue their implementation under the council's policies to give priority for infrastructure funding, including Federal TEA-21 monies, on the basis of housing performance (Meck et al. 2003, 88–90).

Regional Support Roles

By far the most common role of regional agencies in housing is neither regulation, fair share allocation, nor proactive strategies, but one of providing noncoercive support for local housing activities within their region. Such activities do not threaten what may be perceived as local prerogatives, nor do they, as a rule, require that state legislatures enact potentially controversial legislation. They nonetheless offer real promise as vehicles to promote, albeit in a gradual and arguably modest fashion, regional cooperation and engagement around affordable housing strategies. A few examples will illustrate this point.

While the Metropolitan Washington Council of Governments sponsored a regional fair share allocation plan in the 1970s, it no longer pursues that route (see Franklin et al. 1974, 167–168, for a short discussion of the Metro Washington fair share allocation plan). Today it focuses its attention on supporting local activities and fostering more regional interaction on a voluntary basis. The COG houses and provides staff support to the Washington Area Housing Partnership, which actively promotes affordable housing development throughout the region, while conducting other programs to foster a more balanced dispersion of Housing Choice Vouchers (formerly known as Section 8 vouchers) around the region and providing information and support for local efforts.

The Atlanta Regional Commission sponsors regular regional housing forums to inform and educate decision makers within the region about affordable housing issues generally, housing needs in the Atlanta region, and specific strategies that can be pursued to address those strategies. The Greater Bridgeport Regional Planning Agency, in southern Connecticut, fostered the Greater Bridgeport Affordable Housing Compact, a voluntary program under which the region's municipalities agree to participate in a regional strategy to increase the supply of affordable housing. The compact does not, however, appear to have led to significant results.

The Metropolitan Area Planning Council, which serves the Boston area, defines its role in affordable housing as creating and disseminating housing data; drafting housing-related publications and articles; addressing housing needs through the production of planning documents, including MetroPlan (a regional vision plan that is entirely advisory in nature), local comprehensive and community development plans, as well as model bylaws; and exploring pressing issues and devising housing solutions through forums and workshops. Their role can be summarized as that of a regional information clearinghouse, which is likely to be useful largely to those within the region who are already prompted to address affordable housing issues for other reasons.

The question, of course, is whether these activities actually change the framework in which decisions are made about affordable housing and lead to a broader and more balanced regional focus on the issue, or simply provide employment for planners and consultants. There is a constant risk that meetings and publications can be seen as a substitute for action, and even dissipate momentum for action by allowing those participating in them or producing them to believe that they represent substantive steps toward change. At a minimum, however, the willingness of regional agencies to provide rhetorical endorsement for regionally oriented local actions may add credibility to the work of local officials and advocates.

REGIONAL PLANNING AND AFFORDABLE HOUSING: AN UNDERDEVELOPED RELATIONSHIP

Not only is affordable housing a significantly underdeveloped part of the regional planning framework in the United States, but there is little evidence of any trend toward a growing formal regional planning or land use role in this area. While there is evidence of broader regionwide concern with affordable housing issues in many parts of the United States, that concern has not been translated into regional planning initiatives. Important recent policy steps that have a strong de facto regional impact, such as the high-density, mixed-income development incentive programs enacted by both Massachusetts and Connecticut, have no regional planning framework and provide no role for those states' regional planning bodies.[3]

---

[3]Massachusetts Smart Growth Zoning Districts (Chapter 40R enacted in 2004) and Connecticut Housing Program for Economic Growth (Sec. 38 of HB1500, enacted 2007). Both programs provide incentive payments to municipalities that zone suitable areas for high-density as of right development, with additional payments when developments are approved in those areas. Chapter 40S in Massachusetts also provides compensatory payments to school districts to reflect the additional school enrollment, if any, resulting from the zoning changes.

Notwithstanding the compelling rationale for treating affordable housing as a regional issue, this situation should come as no surprise. The ability to regulate the use of land within the municipality, and to make decisions about sensitive and controversial matters such as affordable housing, is arguably the single most cherished prerogative of American local government. Decisions about land use in general, and about affordable housing in particular, are seen as affecting the most fundamental social and economic values of a community's residents; as Danielson wrote, over thirty years ago, "the use of local powers over land, housing and urban development to promote local social values and protect community character are widely viewed as the most important function of local governments in suburbia" (Danielson 1976, 28). This sentiment is particularly pronounced in the small suburban and exurban boroughs, villages, and townships of the typical metropolitan area, many of which came into existence largely to separate themselves from nearby central cities.

Further, although affordable housing may have a clear regional dimension to planners and economists, that regional dimension is not particularly compelling to local officials and their constituents. On the contrary, the nature of the housing that is or is not built in the community—and the characteristics, real or imagined, of those who will live in it—is seen as the most local of concerns. This perspective contrasts sharply with transportation and many environmental issues, where local officials and their constituents are more ready to recognize the inherently regional nature of such things as public transportation networks and watersheds. Moreover, those issues do not trigger the same intense response that is prompted by affordable housing developments among suburbanites preoccupied with the value of their homes and the size of their property tax bills. Indeed, many suburbanites are likely to feel that regional environmental and transportation initiatives add value to their homes and enhance their quality of life. The fact that some of the concerns those same suburbanites feel with respect to affordable housing may be illusory or readily mitigated does not lessen the intensity with which they are felt and their significance as a basis for demanding to retain local control.

Toward Incremental Regionalism

All of this does not mean that affordable housing is any less a regional issue, or that there is no role to be played by regional bodies. What it does mean is that regional bodies, while exercising no authority—now or for the foreseeable future—over affordable housing matters, can and should adopt incremental strategies to foster a regional approach to affordable housing on the part of the region's local jurisdictions. While recognizing the political pressures that may constrain their efforts, regional bodies can nonetheless often go beyond the largely passive role of information provider and cheerleader from the sidelines to become active participants in the processes and debates taking place within their region. The Metropolitan Washington Council of Governments is not the only regional body to do so; organizations such as SANDAG, the San Diego Association of Governments, and the Thomas Jefferson Planning District Commission, serving the region surrounding Charlottesville, Virginia, have also taken active roles in bringing parties together and advocating for regional housing solutions. There are a number of specific steps that regional bodies can take toward this end:

- Recognize explicitly not only the regional nature of the affordable housing issue but also that affordable housing is part of the regional body's mission.

Even without explicit powers, regional planning agencies should acknowledge that they have a responsibility to offer a regional perspective on affordable housing and set forth a direction for the region, even if they have no authority to compel others to follow that direction. While few of the state statutes, compacts, or other processes by which regional agencies have been created may require them to engage in affordable housing activities, even fewer—if any—preclude such a role.

- Develop strategies to promote greater awareness of affordable housing as a regional concern and encourage greater focus on regional strategies to address affordable housing issues.

Regional agencies have a strong role to play as conveners, bringing people together from not only the many local governments that make up the region, but also from the private sector, including major employers, institutions and nonprofit organizations within the region that are concerned with affordable housing issues from a variety of perspectives. Regional agencies can support private-sector driven regional affordable housing strategies, similar to the Metro Washington COG's support of the Washington Area Housing Partnership, or help bring such entities into being.

In this framework, and arguably only in this framework, developing informational materials such as need assessments and model strategies for implementation by local governments within the region can be valuable. Indeed, where such documents are produced without being part of such a proactive outreach or consciousness-raising strategy they are likely to be of little value and end up largely sitting on the regional agency's bookshelf (or, as is more likely to be the case today, hibernating in .pdf format on the agency's website).

- Identify and foster awareness of linkages between affordable housing and other regional issues.

The relationship between the provision of affordable housing and the location of key transportation improvements such as bus rapid transit or light rail lines is a powerful one. Transit-oriented development provides the best opportunity for multifamily building in many places, and proximity to transit is particularly valuable to those needing affordable housing. Regional planning agencies should integrate thinking about affordable housing into transportation planning. Where a regional planning agency serves as the metropolitan planning organization (MPO) for purposes of allocating federal transportation funds, it should incorporate affordable housing criteria into its allocation process. Although the linkage is often not as direct, affordable housing is equally interwoven with environmental issues, from wastewater planning to open space preservation.

• Advocate for state measures to build regional affordable housing strategies.

State efforts to promote affordable housing have grown since the beginning of the 1990s, with states such as Illinois, Florida, Washington, Connecticut, and others enacting laws requiring municipalities and counties to address affordable housing needs in various ways. With increasing affordability pressures being experienced in many parts of the country, and growing numbers of public officials as well as business leaders recognizing the importance of affordable housing to their state's economic future, these efforts are likely to continue. Regional planning agencies should not only support those efforts but also bring their regional perspective to bear, helping to frame state affordable housing initiatives in ways that are linked to larger regional planning and development frameworks.

In conclusion, affordable housing is a regional issue and will continue to be one, whether it is explicitly acknowledged as such by a region's local governments or regional planning body. As such, it is the responsibility of any credible regional planning or growth management entity to address it, working as effectively as it can within the political constraints with which it must contend.

PART IV

LAND ACQUISITION AND REGIONAL PLANNING

CHAPTER 29

ECOREGIONAL CONSERVATION

A COMPREHENSIVE APPROACH TO CONSERVING BIODIVERSITY

Mark G. Anderson and Bob Allen

Biodiversity conservation has evolved in recent decades, fueled by the activities of practitioners supported by new research in ecology and conservation biology. Scientists have increasingly recognized shortcomings in the single species approach to conservation and are accordingly emphasizing the conservation of ecological communities and ecosystems. Coupled with this emphasis has been an increased appreciation for natural processes and landscape-level factors that sustain these communities and ecosystems.

These developments have led The Nature Conservancy (TNC) to evolve new principles for conservation planning. The mission of The Nature Conservancy is the long-term conservation of all biodiversity present in all ecoregions. This broad objective encompasses every living thing, from rare salamanders or large carnivores to whole ecosystems such as oak-hickory forest with all its associated species diversity, along with structural components and ecosystem functions. In broadening the scope of its work, the Conservancy has shifted toward protecting landscapes on an ecoregional scale. Planning by ecoregions, or areas that are unified in climate, topography, geology, and vegetation, is more sensible ecologically than planning within political boundaries such as states or provinces.

Ecoregional conservation, or selecting conservation areas within ecological areas, expands the traditional approach of protecting rare species and terrestrial communities by including common ecosystems that are representative of each ecoregion. Protection of viable examples of these representative ecosystems can serve as a "coarse filter," protecting a broad diversity of both common and rare species. The New Jersey Pine Barrens, for example, falls within the North Atlantic coast ecoregion.

Landscape-scale conservation, a finer-scale strategy, determines what actions need to take place in each of these areas. Within New Jersey, for example, TNC has completed four landscape-scale conservation plans, including ones for the Pine Barrens and the Delaware Bayshores. The intent of these efforts is to develop a scientific context and a flexible strategy for successful conservation in each ecoregion.

A MULTIPLE-SCALE MODEL FOR CONSERVATION AREAS

The overall goal of ecoregional conservation is to assemble a portfolio of public and private conservation areas that collectively conserve the full biological diversity of an ecoregion. Each portfolio is meant to encompass multiple examples of all native species and ecological communities in sufficient number, distribution, and quality to ensure their long-term persistence within the ecoregion. In the Northeast and Mid-Atlantic United States, the portfolios have focused first on terrestrial ecosystems, defined using a standard classification system. Freshwater aquatic systems have been integrated into the portfolios as scientists develop new analytic techniques and richer data sets. The terrestrial ecosystems occur at three basic size scales: matrix-forming, large patch, and small patch.

Matrix-forming ecosystems in the eastern United States are dominant forest communities delineated by large intact areas of forest on the scale of thousands to millions of acres. Conservation areas must be big enough to absorb and recover from infrequent but catastrophic regional-scale disturbances such as hurricanes, tornadoes, fire, and insect outbreaks. They must also be large enough to ensure that multiple breeding populations of forest interior species have the habitat they need to survive. Conservation of the matrix forest is particularly important to the biological integrity of the ecoregion. In the North Atlantic coast, we identified forest blocks of 10,000 acres or greater.

Large patch-forming ecosystems are associated with environmental conditions that are more specific than those of matrix forests. Examples include red maple swamps, riparian river systems, and fire-dependent pine barrens. Conservation areas may be an order of magnitude smaller than the matrix-forming ecosystems, but they must still be large enough to contain the many species that associate with them, usually 50 to 1,000 acres. In the case of the North Atlantic coast ecoregion, we identified natural areas of 100 to 1,000 or more acres.

Small patch-forming ecosystems form small, discrete patches of cover and often contain a disproportionately large percentage of species that associate with very specific ecological conditions. Examples from the North Atlantic coast include maritime forest, coastal plain ponds, beach-dunes, and coastal salt ponds.

The protection of many rare species, such as the best remaining populations of a rare dragonfly and its supporting habitat, may be accomplished by protecting patch-forming ecosystems. Other focal species, such as piping plover, that we believe cannot be adequately conserved by protection of ecosystems alone but require explicit conservation attention, whether because they are globally rare, in decline, native to the ecoregion, or designated as threatened or endangered by state or federal agencies, are designated "fine-filter" conservation targets. Explicit conservation attention, for example, may include targeted direct management such as closing portions of beaches where plovers nest.

THE IDEAL CONSERVATION AREA

When examining a landscape, it becomes immediately clear that patch-forming ecosystems nest within matrix-forming ecosystems. By definition, this way of grouping systems recognizes a spatial hierarchy. For example, a large area dominated by pine-oak forest (a matrix-forming system) may, on close examination, reveal a network of hardwood swamps and marshes (large patch systems). These may contain even smaller settings of reedgrass savannahs and coastal plain ponds (small patch systems). Accordingly, the highest priority action will be given to those places where matrix, large, and small conservation targets are co-located at the same site. Nesting and clustering targets together increases their individual and joint viability and is cost effective. Thus an ideal reserve consists of a mosaic of viable matrix, large and small patch communities, and rare species populations.

What Is a Viable Example of a Matrix or Patch Ecosystem?

A viable example of an ecosystem is one that has the integrity in structure, composition, and internal and external processes needed to persist for over one hundred years without serious degradation. As this is difficult to evaluate directly, we measure three indirect factors, the size, current condition, and landscape context of each example and use the information to make judgments about viability.

For patch communities, landscape context is of primary importance as these communities typically depend on landscape level processes, such as intact hydrology or fire cycles, that operate beyond the actual acreage.

Size is particularly important for matrix-forming ecosystems. For example, based on historical records, hurricanes tend to create a mosaic of disturbance with patches of total destruction ranging up to about 1,000 contiguous acres. From this we estimate a reserve would need to be at least four times that size (4,000 acres) to remain viable with respect to hurricanes (so that no more than 25 percent of the reserve was disturbed at any one time). We can do similar calculations to ensure sustainable population sizes for species such as the black-and-white warbler. For instance, in order to ensure enough suitable forested habitat for twenty-five pairs of black-and-white warblers, we would estimate our reserve to be at least 250 acres.

A variety of observable features affect the condition of an ecosystem. Primary among these features are fragmentation by roads, trails, or land conversion, invasion by exotics, and human manipulation, such as cutting, grazing, mowing, altered soils, and altered natural processes, usually reflected in changes in vegetation structure and composition. Positive features such as signs of historical continuity or the development of biological legacies—critical features that take generations to develop (e.g., fallen logs and rotting wood in old-growth forests)—are evidence of good condition.

To allow for change and guard against unexpected attrition, viability also implies conserving replicate examples. Exactly how many examples of each type of ecosystem we need to conserve is not known with any precision. However, based on evidence from minimal viable population studies, we have generally set an initial minimum of twenty examples for small patch communities. For a widespread community type, examples can be spread throughout its native range, and protection can occur in several ecoregions. Conversely, if the community is completely restricted to a single ecoregion, then all twenty examples must come from that ecoregion. For instance, when we selected the piping plover as a target for the North Atlantic coast ecoregion, we first determined piping plover to have a limited distribution (the bulk of their population is along the eastern coast of the United States), and thus we would like to see at least ten viable occurrences within the North Atlantic coast ecoregion. We then divided the ecoregion into subsections (e.g., southern third, middle third, northern third) and determined if there were at least three viable occurrences in each subsection. The results of these types of analyses can then lead to the identification of new threats and potentially new site-specific strategies.

Placement of Conservation Areas

How do we select these conservation target examples to ensure that the full ecological variability of the communities and of the ecoregion is represented? To answer this question we turn to the geography and ecology of the ecoregion itself. Using maps and digital information we ask questions such as Where are the steep slopes, summits, ridgetops, valleys, floodplains, and wetlands? Which of these are underlain by resistant granite and which are constructed on sandstone? Where is the elevation change rapid and where is it slow? We summarize this information in a set of ecological land units (ELUs), which are unique combinations of elevation, bedrock, and topographic features. On this geographic framework we overlay all the viable examples of communities and species that have been located and evaluated by the State Natural Heritage Network, our long-term partners in biodiversity conservation. The Natural Heritage programs maintain an ongoing inventory of each state's flora, fauna, and communities. We then select replicate examples of each target from each of the different subregions to ensure that we conserve examples in a variety of ecological settings. At this stage we also identify gaps in our knowledge. This information is channeled back to our Heritage partners as recommendations on which areas and which targets need more inventory attention.

Selection of matrix-forming ecosystems and stream networks involves additional data analysis. With respect to the former, in recent years, a variety of methods have been developed to assess the location and condition of large unfragmented pieces of forest. The method we have used to delineate matrix forest examples in all northeast plans is based on roads, land cover, and expert interviews using geographic tools and data. Using road-bounded blocks to delineate matrix examples has practical advantages. The core idea behind the road-bounded block, however, was not practicality but that roads have altered the landscape so dramatically that their presence provides a useful way of assessing the size and ecological importance of remaining contiguous areas of forest.

By combining potential forest blocks with ELUs in an ecoregion, we identify forest-landscape combinations. Experts review the forest-landscape groupings to ensure that they indeed capture the range of diversity within the ecoregion, and then, within each grouping, prioritize the matrix-forming areas based on their relative biodiversity values, the feasibility of protection, and the urgency of action. A similar approach is used for delineating critical watersheds. We evaluate watershed condition by examining additional features, such as dams, road-stream crossings, and proportion of agriculture or developed land.

Landscape-Scale Conservation Planning

After viable examples have been identified and selected, conservation areas must be designed to ensure their long-term viability. Like the ecoregional assessment, landscape-scale designs revolve around a series of questions.

- How is the landscape constructed and what is the condition of the forest?
- Where are the identified ecoregional targets and where are other potential ecoregional targets?
- What do we want these ecosystems and focal species populations to look like over the long term?
- What attributes of the landscape maintain these targets over the long term?
- What are the current and potential activities on the landscape that might interfere with the maintenance of those attributes? What can we do about those activities to prevent or mitigate them?
- Where, on the ground, do we need to act and what kinds of actions are necessary to accomplish our goals? Can we do enough to succeed in our goals?

Careful attention to these questions forms the basis for a site conservation plan. This plan is the foundation of our future stewardship and protection activities.

The Nature Conservancy completed a second iteration of its ecoregional plan for the North Atlantic Ecoregion in 2006, and this plan provides a good example of what ecoregional planning means in practice. The 2006 assessment sets out an agenda for preserving both the broad landscapes and specific sites where the region's surviving biological diversity can be found and saved from the threats they face due to human impacts. The assessment describes the region's ecology, maps large and small-scale ecosystems and the land use context in which they are found, and identifies and ranks priority areas for conservation. Finally, the assessment makes specific recommendations for conservation actions on the ecoregional scale that can be used by public and private agencies.

Taking coastal stream systems as an example of the many ecosystems addressed by the assessment, the plan focused on streams and tidal creeks flowing directly into the ocean. Size 1 rivers (those with <30 sq. mi. drainage areas) were classified into nine types based on their salinity and watershed size, because salinity is the key factor distinguishing the natural communities living in these streams and size is a key element of ecological viability in a context of human impacts. Within each of these nine categories, each stream within the ecoregion was ranked for viability of its natural communities based on factors such as hydrologic regime, water chemistry and the percentage of land within the watershed and stream buffers that still had natural land cover (as opposed to development), the stream's degree of connectivity to upland habitats, and plant community structure. (The lack of consistent data for all streams required the analysis team to use proxy attributes in some cases.)

An initial screening process based on the context and condition of each stream was used to narrow the population of potential priority streams. Each stream was ranked using GIS data on land use and impervious surface impacts, connectivity and dam impacts, pollution point source impacts, presence of rare species, and similar criteria. The rankings were used to assign an estimated portfolio category of "yes," "maybe," or "no" to each watershed. Conservancy scientists interviewed local experts to gather additional information, not represented in this GIS analysis, to verify these initial portfolio recommendations. Incorporating all this information, the assessment designates final "yes" and "maybe" watersheds. These sites were then mapped on the ecoregional scale and compared with the recommendations from other, overlapping elements of the North Atlantic Coast Assessment, such as salt marshes, beaches, wetlands, forest patches, and species elements.

The assessment's final recommendations for inclusion in a conservation portfolio are designed to include the most viable watershed examples that are geographically well distributed and include all types of coastal stream ecosystem types in the ecoregion. The recommended portfolio includes 349 watersheds. These represent 21 percent of all watersheds, 25 percent of all direct-to-ocean connected examples in the ecoregion, and more than 10 percent of each of the nine types. The majority of the portfolio tidal creeks suffer to some degree from the impacts of human activities. Fragmentation by dams and roads' impervious surfaces, agriculture, riparian buffer conversion, and/or point sources of pollution can be found in many of the watersheds. Nevertheless, the portfolio watersheds demonstrate sufficient integrity to believe their preservation will save the native biodiversity of the ecoregion's coastal streams. The assessment includes a similar analysis and set of portfolio recommendations for each of the other ecosystem types within the ecoregion.

Beyond the identification of priority sites for conservation, the assessment analyzes the threats facing the ecoregion and makes recommendations for regional conservation action planning. The assessment focuses on the threats presented by habitat loss and fragmentation, the alteration of natural hydrology by withdrawals and dams, the interruption of natural succession processes like wildfire, nutrient enrichment and other forms of water pollution, invasive species and pests, recreational activities, and climate change and sea level rise. In light of these threats, the assessment recommends ecoregional-scale conservation planning, particularly the protection of functional landscapes that encompass a wide range of natural communities and habitat types. Such functional landscapes are generally going to be bigger and more diverse than individual parks, making them more resilient to future impacts. The assessment recognizes that effective planning does not just mean buying land but also requires management of the land to protect and restore its natural communities and public education to develop a broad appreciation for each distinctive ecoregion and win support for its conservation.

The Nature Conservancy is convinced that ecoregional conservation represents an efficient and effective strategy toward our mission of biodiversity conservation. In the northeastern United States, the Conservancy has completed ecoregion plans for all terrestrial ecoregions and is now embarking upon a marine ecoregional plan. The latest version of the North Atlantic coast ecoregion plan identified 352 matrix and large patch natural area blocks and 145 small patch ecosystems and species examples. With an agenda this ambitious, we expect both challenges and opportunities.

CHAPTER 30

SAVING THE CHESAPEAKE BAY THROUGH REGIONAL LAND CONSERVATION

Rob Etgen

The Eastern Shore Land Conservancy (ESLC) is a regional nonprofit organization that serves six counties on Maryland's Eastern Shore of the Chesapeake Bay. Founded in 1990, ESLC's mission is to sustain the Eastern Shore's rich landscapes through strategic land conservation and sound land use planning. The organization's vision for 2050 is an Eastern Shore where towns are vibrant and well defined; farms, forests, and fisheries are thriving; and scenic, historic, natural, and riverine landscapes are maintained.

For over three centuries Maryland's Eastern Shore has been an idyllic landscape of farms and quaint small towns. Today, however, the area is rapidly losing its rural character and small town charm. Counties face development proposals on their rural lands, while towns face proposals along their edges that would double, triple, and even quadruple their current populations. Left unchecked, this unprecedented growth pressure will forever destroy the rural legacy that makes the region an exceptional place.

According to the Maryland Department of Planning, about 160,000 new residents will make the Eastern Shore their home by 2030—adding more than 70,000 new houses and consuming an additional 215,000 acres of farms and forests. This equals approximately 450,000 total acres of forest and farm land that will be forever lost to roads, subdivisions, malls, and parking lots. That's a loss of open space bigger than Queen Anne's county—equal to all the tillable farmland in Kent, Caroline, and Cecil counties combined.

STRATEGIC LAND CONSERVATION

ESLC's land conservation programs have been preserving land using conservation easements, its Land Rescue Revolving Fund, and other easement and estate planning programs. Through these strategies, 254 farms on over 50,000 acres have been permanently preserved directly by ESLC. The organization targets greenbelts around towns and significant resources, such as the Harriet Tubman Underground Railroad Corridor, the Chesapeake Country National Scenic Byway, and Blackwater National Wildlife Refuge. But land protection alone is not enough to save the Eastern Shore.

The second focus of ESLC is promoting sound land use planning. In 2000 ESLC began working in response to accelerating threats posed to the region by development pressure. ESLC launched a set of activities to build leadership and provide education to help communities make the best decisions on behalf of the Eastern Shore. The campaign included raising public awareness through newsletters, a website, research papers, and a planning awards program. Professional training was provided at an annual planning conference and local workshops. ESLC also supported local leaders and the public with research and pursued preservation and planning funding. The research included studies of downzoning impacts on landowner equity and transfer of development rights prescriptions for counties. Investments were made in the regional Rural Legacy preservation program and federal funds assisted the Delmarva Conservation Corridor. Economic development targeted farms, forests, and fisheries.

EASTERN SHORE 2010—A REGIONAL VISION

The flagship of ESLC's planning work is Eastern Shore 2010: A Regional Vision. Eastern Shore 2010 is an intercounty land use agreement that sets the highest expectations for the care of the Eastern Shore landscape proposed in spring 2002 by ESLC with the guidance of a steering committee chaired by congressman Wayne Gilchrest and former governor Harry Hughes. Following extensive regional discussion about the agreement, the six Middle and Upper Shore counties passed resolutions of support for Eastern Shore 2010 and agreed to work cooperatively toward its goals. The four important land use goals of Eastern Shore 2010 are preserving land, encouraging resource-based economic development, curbing sprawl, and improving regional transportation choices.

The effort began in 2002 with a public opinion poll and drafting of the agreement by ESLC and an advisory committee. That spring, briefings were presented to individual boards of county commissioners. That summer, a public dialogue was conducted to obtain individual endorsements of the agreement.

Polling revealed support for the concept of Eastern Shore 2010 by 82 percent of the public; 88 percent supported their county entering into Eastern Shore 2010; and 78 percent supported "reasonable investments" of tax dollars to achieve the goals outlined in Eastern Shore 2010. Presentations were made to a regional association of county governments, farm bureaus, community groups, and towns. County meetings were held that fall to review and revise the program. County signatures were collected in the winter, and the ESLC launched implementation in spring 2003.

Implementation involved forming a set of regional task forces to seek innovative strategies and resources. Each task force developed a white paper of implementation options for each goal, including the review of literature, recommendations for action, and an analysis of costs and resources. ESLC coordinated the task force issue of land protection; American Farmland Trust coordinated working landscapes; and a local consultant coordinated growth areas and sprawl control. The issue of transportation was coordinated by ESLC with support from a local consultant and an Advisory Committee of regional experts.

In 2006, facing only modest progress toward the goals and even worsening development pressure throughout the region, ESLC proposed an upgrade to Eastern Shore 2010. The updated agreement revises the four original goals to make them more aggressive and more finely tuned to practical realities of facing development pressure on the Eastern Shore. Five of the six counties eventually endorsed the updated agreement.

The following is a summary of each goal from the 2002 version of Eastern Shore 2010, progress to date on that goal, and a summary of the changes made in 2007.

Goal 1: Protecting Land

Goal 1 of the original Eastern Shore 2010 called on county governments to protect half of all open space outside areas specifically designated for growth by 2010. Meeting that goal would permanently preserve from development 578,277 acres from Cecil to Dorchester. That is 900 square miles, nearly equal to all of Kent, Queen Anne's, and Talbot counties.

By 2007 the six counties were halfway to the goal, with more than 283,000 rural acres protected. But none is on track to hit its 2010 target, and shortfalls in each will likely range from 15,000 to 25,000 acres. Collectively, the shortfall amounts to 113,740 acres, or 178 square miles. That's like a mile-wide swath of potentially developable farm and forestland, running virtually the full length of the Delmarva Peninsula.

To help meet the goal of protecting 578,277 acres by 2010, ESLC proposed counties dedicate an amount equivalent to at least 1.5 percent of their annual budgets to preserving land. Caroline County proves it can be done by a rural Eastern Shore county. In Fiscal Year 2007, Caroline budgeted $1,140,000 for land preservation, an amount equivalent to 2.5 percent of its budget. A variety of revenue sources are available to counties, including impact fees, excise taxes, transfer taxes, bond funds, and funds from the county budget. Some 78 percent of voters say they would support "reasonable investments of public funds" to attain such a goal— and this support ranged from 69 to 82 percent across the six counties.

Goal 2: Maintaining a Working Landscape

Goal 2 called for promoting the Eastern Shore's traditional occupations—agriculture, forestry, and fishing—by incorporating them into county economic development plans by 2005. The counties have achieved this goal, and many other private and public efforts are under way to add economic value to these traditional ways of making a living. Two of the Upper Shore counties, Cecil and Queen Anne's, have gone beyond the Eastern Shore 2010 commitment by dedicating full-time staff to marketing and promoting agriculture and other natural resource-based industries.

The updated goal calls for implementing the economic development incentives called for in the original goal. This is already happening in some counties, including Queen Anne's, which recently created an office of agriculture and economic development. Caroline, Dorchester, and Talbot are working jointly through the Mid-Shore Regional Council to, among other things, create a full-time position to focus solely on the economic development of resource-based industries in the three counties and investigate the feasibility of a barley-based ethanol plant.

Goal 3: Curbing Sprawl

Goal 3 committed county governments by 2005 to guide at least half of new growth into areas already planned to accommodate it—where communities already exist and where state and local money is directed for public water, sewer, roads, and schools. All six counties met this goal starting in 2004. Across the Upper Shore, however, it is a qualified success, achieved largely by more development *inside* growth centers. The problem is that large building lots are the norm outside growth centers—more than five times the size of lots inside, on average, across the Shore. In Upper Shore counties, less than half of new homes—those outside growth centers—are consuming close to 90 percent of all open space lost.

In 2006 this goal was significantly upgraded. This portion of the agreement calls for counties to annually guide at least 80 percent of growth into designated growth areas; establish a maximum annual residential growth rate, and include a work-force housing element in the county comprehensive plan. Polling showed 87 percent of voters are concerned about sprawl and 85 percent agree with promoting and investing in existing communities.

The updated Eastern Shore 2010 agreement raises the goal for directing growth to growth areas from 50 to 80 percent. This will save tens of thousands of acres, because development outside growth areas consumes four to nine times the land per household (depending on the county) as development in higher-growth zones. Zoning is critical: both to accommodate growth where it is planned and to restrict it where rural landscapes are desired. Rapid population growth can undermine the best county programs for preserving their rural nature. The Eastern Shore, which took from 1607 to the 1980s to reach 300,000 people, is on a pace to nearly double that by 2030.

Goal 3 includes an objective for setting an upper limit to annual growth. The precise growth rate is left up to the counties. Making growth pay its full costs, planning for the population that current residents want versus what is forecast, and requiring that adequate schools, sewers, and roads be in place first are ways to slow growth. To ensure people can afford homes in counties where they work, this goal commits local governments to make such housing a part of their development plans. Currently, only Queen Anne's County requires new subdivisions to include a certain percentage of modestly priced homes.

Maryland ranks as the nation's fourth least affordable state for housing, according to a League of Women Voters report. Marylanders now endure the second longest commute times in the nation—thirty minutes one way on average—and one cause is workers driving farther from their jobs to afford the home they want. The state last year passed HB 1160, creating up to $10 million a year in grants for counties and towns. To qualify, local jurisdictions must commit to creating a workforce housing element in their comprehensive plan in state-approved growth areas.

Goal 4: Planning for Transportation as a Region

Goal 4 proposed development of a regional transportation plan, including alternatives to the automobile. This is critical because automobile use continues rising three times faster than population throughout the Chesapeake region. The impacts of this go beyond congestion and strains on county budgets. Transportation and land use are inseparable issues. A constantly expanding road network, especially one responding to piecemeal, county-by-county pressures, inevitably sets the stage for more sprawl development, which in turn raises demand for more roads.

The Upper Shore counties have made little progress toward the kind of regional planning needed to break this cycle. A few laudable transportation alternatives exist, such as Upper Shore Take a Ride, County Ride, and the Dorchester Developmental Unit Specialized Transportation. Other efforts include a Delmarva bike map of quiet back roads connecting Shore communities and Vienna's plan to ensure walkable, bikeable connections between new development and the existing community.

Goal 4 repeats the call for Upper Shore governments to develop a regional transportation plan by 2010 and adds a call for devising alternatives to a third bay bridge. With continuation of current driving trends, linked closely with current development trends, a third bay bridge becomes all but inevitable. By 2025, an average day's traffic on the existing twin spans will be nearly as bad as on a weekend day now—and twelve-hour delays at peak weekend times would be common, according to a recent state Bay Crossing Task Force report. Another span would bring irreparable changes to the farms, historic communities, and rural way of life on the Shore, with major impacts on presently undeveloped tidal shorelines.

Combined with this would be automotive impacts beyond the obvious traffic congestion and smog. Paved surfaces in the Bay region are growing five times faster than the population, and the roads, driveways, garages, and parking lots account for more than half of it. Small wonder that stormwater runoff, which is worst where large areas are paved over, is the Shore's fastest-increasing source of water pollution and a major force degrading streams throughout Maryland.

Fortunately, the grim Bay Crossing task force projections show only what will happen if nothing is done to reshape growth and transportation. Alternatives exist to stretch the capacity of the existing bridges. The Upper Shore counties must immediately engage state government in discussing beach-oriented rapid transit buses, variable tolls to smooth congestion peaks on the bridges, ride-sharing, telecommuting, and other alternatives. Better balancing jobs and housing on both sides of the bridge could reduce commuter traffic. This could avoid gridlock on the current bridges and major change to the Shore from another car crossing, and provide time for exploration of a mass-transit bay crossing by ferry or rail.

THE FATE OF THE EASTERN SHORE?

The sobering projections of runaway development overwhelming the Eastern Shore are not destiny. They are based on assumptions that trends of the recent past will continue. Our lands and waters are under assault, but far more remains than has been lost. Eastern Shore counties possess the knowledge and the tools to do better. And by broad and solid margins, their citizens demand it. Of all the generations in all of human time here, this one uniquely has the power to alter irrevocably—or sustain—the Shore as an island amid the sea of East Coast development. On our watch it will be largely decided whether or not our "Eden" gets sliced and diced by development, served up with a steaming side of asphalt. Swift and strong action is needed to manage growth on the Shore that maintains our heritage and quality of life. We are all responsible for what will or will not happen.

CHAPTER 31

CREATING SYNERGY WITH REGIONAL PLANNING AND CONSERVATION EASEMENTS

John Bernstein

Conservation easements have become one of the premier conservation strategies in America. In a 2005 report the Land Trust Alliance and Trust for Public Land estimated that over 5 million acres of land had been placed under conservation easement in the United States, with the State of Maine alone having well over one million acres under easement. As experience with easements has grown, so has our understanding of how easements can be deployed most effectively in achieving conservation goals. The most important insight we have gained is that conservation easements can and should be used as part of an integrated, regional conservation strategy that combines land use planning, regulation, and easements. Without such a comprehensive scheme, easements may create only a patchwork of protected lands amidst a sea of development.

While they vary in terms and details, all conservation easements are legal restrictions recorded on real property in order to protect natural, scenic, agricultural, or cultural resources by specifying permitted and forbidden activities on the land—especially with respect to subdivision and development. They are usually permanent and are generally donated, sold, or given in exchange for some form of government land use permit. Conservation easements are usually granted to a public agency or private nonprofit whose mission is conservation, while the land itself may be owned by anyone and may be freely sold or given to others—but the legal restrictions of the easement are attached to the land and survive to bind all successors in ownership. In many cases, a public agency contributes money toward the acquisition of land by another agency or a nonprofit and receives the right to enforce the easement in exchange. In farmland preservation easements, private landowners retain and use their land while selling or donating an easement that restricts future uses to farming or ranching. The easement gives the public or private conservation organization the right (and indeed the obligation) to enforce its terms. The restrictions embodied in an easement need not be static: Easements often include management plans specifying allowable uses on the protected property that are reviewed and updated every few years; other easements permit the landowner to make changes to protected land or structures after review and approval of the easement holder.

There are three basic ways of looking at the use of conservation easements: What can and can't be done with conservation easements alone, what can and can't be done using regulation alone, and what can be done using a synergy of both techniques.

Utilizing conservation easements alone or in isolation from planning and regulation almost always results in a patchwork landscape. Such patterns are acceptable only where there is little pressure for land conversion. As there is no way to ensure that all communities and landowners will participate, the use of easements alone can lead to a "free rider problem." Easements can be an expensive tool when they are used over large areas, and it is difficult to plan a pattern of easement acquisition on a large scale. Easements also entail ongoing costs for perpetual monitoring and enforcement.

On the other hand, the use of regulation can get a lot done at once, but regulation has its own disadvantages. Politically, stringent land use regulations are usually difficult to achieve. Municipal zoning rules suffer from the same problems as easements when different towns take different, conflicting approaches to nearby lands. Given constitutional and societal views of individual property rights, traditional land use regulation may not be able to protect all resources and address unique features of properties. And, of course, regulations may change as time goes on and political winds shift.

Synergy is a form of hybrid planning, an impure technique that combines features of both acquisition and regulation. It is important to recognize that such hybrid systems do not necessarily come about as a single plan or government program. Hybrid systems can evolve as government imposes growth management restrictions and the private and public sectors develop land acquisition programs over time, often in parallel. A typical program of hybrid planning uses effective rural zoning, funding for the purchase of conservation easements, transfer of development rights (TDR) and incentives such as tax credits and property tax rebates for donating conservation easements. The funding for the purchase of easements need not be sufficient to buy them on all land zoned for low density: Bond funding typically looks to buy easements over 30–50 percent of the land over twenty to thirty years. Private land trusts play a key role in leveraging public funding from state and local government for easement purchases. In practice, the use of low-density rural zoning has not reduced the value of donated or purchased easements excessively. Most landowners retain enough development opportunities that their remaining rights in the land are very valuable.

A hybrid system makes regulation more palatable because the funding for easement purchases provides some compensation for the (real or perceived) lost equity of affected landowners. The hybrid approach increases the rate of easement

donation in the short run when landowners see land use is stabilized through regulation, and government is supporting land conservation with effective zoning.
The system also stabilizes land use in the long run as a group of landowners with
land in easement is developed. These landowners have a vested interest in the continuance of effective zoning to control what can happen on non-eased land in their
neighborhood; later up-zoning could destroy the economic value of their restricted
land, both by making it difficult to farm and by degrading the scenic value of a
rural area. The hybrid system has led to the creation of massive blocks of easement-
protected land.

WHERE HYBRID PLANNING WORKS

Regions and communities can look to excellent examples of successful hybrid planning using conservation easements and regulation on the state and county levels.

The Adirondack Park

In the Adirondack Park, early and rigorous state land use regulations are now reinforced by extensive use of conservation easements, which now protect more than
750,000 acres. The regulations are administered by the state's Adirondack Park
Agency under the authority of the state's Adirondack Park Agency Act, and these
regulations impose highly restrictive rural zoning across large portions of the park.
This framework has stabilized the pattern of land use so effectively that The Nature
Conservancy, the Adirondack Land Trust, and the State of New York have all purchased or received significant conservation easements; many easements have been
donated, and many have been very large.

California Coastal Commission and Coastal Conservancy

Another example of hybrid planning has been used by the California Coastal
Commission, a state agency created by voter initiative in 1972 to manage development and other human uses of California's coastal zone (excepting San Francisco
Bay, which has its own coastal zone management agency). The commission has
broad regulatory powers, and it has integrated easement programs into its overall
regulatory structure. Development in the coastal zone requires a coastal permit
from the commission or local government pursuant to detailed regulatory standards. Counties and municipalities are required to create land use plans in the
form of local coastal plans (LCPs) for their coastal areas. Once an LCP is approved
by the Coastal Commission, individual permit decisions generally fall to the local
government. Even where permitting decisions are made at the local level in the first
instance, many county and municipal permit decisions can be appealed to the
Coastal Commission. Coastal zoning in high value resource areas can vary from
one unit per 60 acres to one unit per 640 acres.

Within this overall land use management structure, easements play an important role. The Coastal Commission has created two distinct easement programs:
public access and agricultural easements. Further, many nonprofit partners, such
as the Trust for Public Land and the Peninsula Open Space Trust, have taken

advantage of the conservation-oriented coastal zoning to engineer major private conservation transactions. As part of the approvals for many developments, the Coastal Commission requires developers or landowners to provide an offer to dedicate a public access easement (OTD). The justification for this requirement is that such OTDs compensate the public for the impact of private developments on public rights and values, such as the blocking of paths, harming viewsheds, and increasing traffic. The Coastal Commission program is unusual in that the OTD means nothing until some public agency or nonprofit land trust agrees to accept the easement. While the program has succeeded in creating many OTDs, the commission reported that as of 2007 only 19 percent of 1,269 OTDs had been accepted, and some of this 19 percent had not yet been opened for public access. Most OTDs expire after twenty-one years, unless they are accepted and recorded.

The Coastal Commission actively seeks private land trusts to take on easements, and some coastal land trusts have been created to accept OTDs. Other groups, as noted earlier, are very active in private land conservation transactions. Strict regulation stabilizes land use and allows the trusts to compete in areas of intense development pressure. There is strong popular support for the easement holding groups. The state has created the California Coastal Conservancy to provide funding for easements, and significant financial contributions have also been made by coastal jurisdictions, especially Santa Cruz, San Mateo, Marin, and Sonoma Counties, which all enjoy dedicated sources of conservation funding. Total state and local funding for easements is in the hundreds of millions of dollars.

New Jersey Pinelands

In New Jersey the hybrid system has operated to conserve both agricultural and natural lands. Through the state's Pinelands Protection Act and Comprehensive Management Plan (CMP), the New Jersey Pinelands Commission places severe restrictions on development over several hundred thousand acres by designating large management areas with specific use and intensity limits. Two agricultural zones, totaling 106,000 acres, permit only farming and farm-related structures, while forest and wetland conservation zones restrict development in another 540,000 acres. The Pinelands CMP includes a large-scale TDR program that gives landowners in the most heavily regulated agricultural and preservation zones transferable rights that developers must purchase for many activities in the Pinelands regional growth zones. When a landowner severs such a Pinelands Development Credit, the land is automatically and permanently deed restricted, and the state receives an easement to enforce these development restrictions. As of the end of 2007, this program had resulted in deed restrictions on 50,000 acres.

In addition to the TDR program, the State of New Jersey and private land trusts like the New Jersey Conservation Foundation have obtained easements through purchase and donation on tens of thousands of conservation acres. The most notable recent example was the purchase by the New Jersey Conservation Foundation of the former DeMarco family cranberry farm to create a 9,400-acre nature preserve in the heart of the New Jersey Pine Barrens. The State of

New Jersey contributed $3.5 million toward the $12 million purchase price, receiving both an undivided 30 percent interest in the property and a conservation easement that enables the public to ensure the land is preserved in perpetuity. In many cases, developers are required by the Pinelands Commission to place easements on land, such as threatened or endangered species habitats, as a condition of gaining approval for development projects. Although the total number of acres deed restricted through regulatory processes, purchases, and donations has not been compiled, it surely numbers in the tens of thousands.

Baltimore County, Maryland

In Maryland, most undeveloped and farmed lands are not incorporated, so counties, rather than municipalities, play the leading role in land use planning and regulation. In Baltimore County, Maryland, early planning was conducted by the firm of Wallace and McHarg Associates for the Valleys Planning Council, a pioneering land trust in the area. Ian McHarg's Plan for the Valleys, created in 1963, was one of the very first to call for agricultural preservation on prime soils. The county recognizes the smart-growth benefits of combining land use planning and regulation with acquisition of land and easements. The county sees this comprehensive approach as not only preserving agricultural landscapes and natural resources, but also as helping sustain Baltimore and other existing communities while promoting more efficient land use and community design.

By 2000 the county had created several resource conservation zones designed to protect both natural areas and farmland from sprawl development. In agricultural areas, residential development was permitted only at densities of one unit per twenty or fifty acres (depending on the zone), and other forms of new development restricted to certain agricultural and recreational activities. State and private land trusts have simultaneously pursued the acquisition of conservation easements. There are now five land trusts operating in the county and over 40,000 acres in easement.

LESSONS LEARNED

In areas where conservation easements and land use regulation have been used in a synergistic approach, the following effects have been observed:

- Easement purchase has increased the political acceptance of needed regulations.
- Effective rural zoning has increased the rate of easement donation by providing landscape-level stability and may lower the cost of acquisition.
- When a critical mass of easements is attained, the zoning is stabilized, because a large number of landowners benefit from retention of existing regulations.

Conversely, where effective zoning is not in force, the following may be true:

- Easements may be less effective and more subject to legal challenges.
- Easement-protected lands may become surrounded by development, and the easements may no longer serve their original function.
- Fewer easements are donated, and those that are sold are often expensive.

PART V

ENVISIONING
THE REGION

CHAPTER 32

CREATING A REGIONAL
VISION FOR REGIONAL
PLANNING

Gerrit-Jan Knaap

Reality Check is an approach to crafting a shared vision for how a region should manage future growth in population and jobs. My collaborators and I have developed and applied this approach in Maryland, and similar efforts are taking place in other places around the country. Reality Check provides an effective model for reaching shared visions for future growth that can guide policy, motivate public support, and thus help shape landscape change to achieve critical social and environmental values.

Reality Check *Plus* was a statewide effort to raise awareness and initiate critical thinking about the level, pace, and distribution of growth in jobs and housing coming to Maryland over the ensuing twenty-five years. The word "Plus" was added to the title to convey the intention of organizers to go beyond the visioning exercise to a stage in which the development pattern in the state and the policies that govern it would actually be improved. Organizers also used the project to encourage both the public and elected officials to think regionally or even on a statewide basis about how best to accommodate this new growth. This process was carried out through visioning exercises held in 2006 in each of four regions of the state: the Eastern Shore and southern, central, and western Maryland. More than 850 political, business, environmental, real estate, and civic leaders participated in these exercises. The exercise is, in a sense, extremely simple—participants decide where they would like to see new jobs and housing go by placing representative plastic blocks on a table-top map—but the exercise at once captures key values that should drive detailed planning for growth, a regional point of view that integrates economic, social, and environmental values, and a recognition that the single most powerful tool government has in land use planning is the ability to direct *where* new development and conservation are placed on the landscape.

Intentionally designed as a nongovernmental initiative, Reality Check *Plus* had no government funds or control but was carried out by private organizations and funded by charitable foundations and private businesses. It was not intended to produce a state plan or detailed development and conservation map, but instead to create a statewide set of guiding principles and indicators for how Maryland's citizens believe new growth should occur. The process also *began* the task of figuring out how to implement these principles and development directives—a plan created by laymen that would look very different from today's patterns of growth in the state.

The planning exercises described here were not aimed at replacing detailed professional planning and normal political processes at the state and local levels. They were instead aimed at building a consensus and constituency to do that planning well, based on truly regional thinking, and to move those political processes forward to positive, sustainable outcomes. In this sense, Reality Check *Plus* and similar efforts elsewhere are a beginning and a motivator for, not an alternative to, sound government planning.

The initiative was led by the National Center for Smart Growth Research and Education at the University of Maryland, the Baltimore District Council of the Urban Land Institute, and 1,000 Friends of Maryland. The largest individual funders were the Home Builders Association of Maryland and the Lincoln Institute of Land Policy, although the largest percentage of the initiative's budget was raised through a variety of contributions from nonprofit foundations. The initiative was organized by a statewide leadership committee and four regional committees for the Eastern Shore and central, southern, and western Maryland.

The motivation for developing Reality Check *Plus* was a recognition that Maryland is already one of the nation's most densely populated states and is expected to continue growing at a rapid pace. The U.S. Census Bureau predicts that Maryland will grow from its 2000 population of about 5.5 million to 7.0 million by 2030—more than half a million more people than the state itself projects over that period. In these circumstances, Maryland is faced with some critical, urgent questions:

- Where will these new residents—and the millions more to follow them in subsequent years—live and work?
- What will be the cumulative effect of such an increase in population and development on the state's transportation network, housing costs, taxes, and the health of the Chesapeake Bay and its tributaries?
- What, ultimately, will be the effect on the quality of life for all Marylanders?

REGIONAL PLANNING EXERCISES

The regional sessions brought invited participants together for a briefing session on trends in each region, then an extended exercise in planning for growth within the region. The regional committees spent a great deal of effort on their invitation lists, as the balance of those invited to participate in this exercise is critical to the project's credibility. Regional committees took great pains to include a representative sample of the region's economic, political, geographic, and ethnic diversity. Farmers, business owners, developers, environmental activists, community leaders, and local, county, and state government officials were all represented. While elected officials and other government employees took no part in organizing Reality Check *Plus*, together they made up nearly one-third of the invited participants. In the afternoon of each session, results from each table at the morning exercise were presented, and the meeting was opened to the general public for a review and discussion of the morning's actions.

The heart of Reality Check *Plus* is the planning exercise in which participants collectively planned where to place the growth anticipated for their region through 2030. For this process, the forecast growth in jobs and housing was taken as a given with which they, as representatives of their own and the public interest, must deal.

At each regional session, participants were divided into groups of eight to ten people representative of the various interests and points of view at the session. Each group worked at a table on which a large, detailed map of the region was spread. The maps used colors to represent existing population and employment density and included major roads and transit lines, parklands, rivers and water bodies, floodplains, major public facilities, and other key infrastructure. To encourage regional thinking and discourage parochialism, the maps did not include political boundaries of counties and municipalities. Each table had a facilitator and a computer operator/scribe.

Participants first were asked to reach consensus on a set of general principles to guide their decisions about where on the map to place expected growth—using ideas such as protecting open space and natural resources, making efficient use of existing infrastructure, and balancing jobs and housing. Once they had created a set of guiding principles, participants were given Lego blocks of four different colors, each color representing jobs, higher priced housing (the top 80 percent), lower priced housing (the bottom 20 percent), and low density housing (exchangeable for the other housing pieces on a ratio of 4:1). Each group was given a number of pieces in each color representing the anticipated amount of jobs and housing currently projected for the region through 2030. The maps were overlaid with a grid, with each square the size of a Lego piece and representing about 1 square mile (depending on the scale of each region's map). Participants planned where to put growth by stacking pieces on each square. Stacking all jobs or housing pieces on a block produced single-use neighborhoods; stacking mixed pieces produced mixed use districts. Participants were required to use all of their blocks. They could not put them in another region, a neighboring state, or their pockets!

After they had placed their Lego pieces to their satisfaction, the members of each group discussed a series of questions:

- How does the group feel about the amount of growth projected for the region?

- Given that some level of growth is inevitable,
  - What policies do you think state and local governments should adopt in order to accommodate the additional growth, yet maintain the region's quality of life?
  - What are the implementation tools required to achieve the envisioned growth pattern and maintain or improve quality of life?
- Based on your knowledge of the region, what infrastructure improvements would be required to achieve the envisioned growth pattern?

National Center for Smart Growth Research and Education staff and graduate assistants collected and analyzed the guiding principles, Lego distribution decisions, and responses to the post-planning questions from each group in order to report to all the participants and the public during the afternoon portion of each program.

Using the average allocation of jobs and housing from all the groups, staff produced a composite regional map for every table at each session and later produced a composite map for the state as a whole. After the exercises were over, the center also analyzed the Reality Check plans by comparing them against current forecasts of growth distribution by the Metropolitan Washington Council of Governments and the Baltimore Metropolitan Council, and a statewide build-out scenario based on current zoning. Organizers also compared the participants' job and housing distributions with existing distribution within Maryland's current priority funding area boundaries, inside the Baltimore and Washington beltways, and near existing transit stations. Finally, the center estimated the amount of new impervious surface, the increase in lane miles of highways and roads, the impacts on the state's green infrastructure, and the degree to which participants mixed or segregated higher and lower priced housing.

OUTCOMES OF THE REGIONAL PLANNING EXERCISES

It is impossible to capture all of the ideas, dialogue, and learning that take place at events such as the Reality Check visioning sessions. Nevertheless, the discussions gave rise to a number of important consensus principles for guiding future growth:

- Adopt stronger measures to protect farms, forests, and environmentally sensitive areas.
- Concentrate new development in existing communities or designated growth areas.
- Give priority to new development where infrastructure already exists.
- Provide more housing for families of modest incomes.
- Locate housing and jobs closer together.
- Preserve the rural and/or historic character of Maryland's small towns.
- Provide more transit services in all four regions of the state.
- Encourage greater regional cooperation.

While these principles may now seem obvious to many, it is valuable to enable leaders across a region and across a range of interests and societal roles to generate such principles through their own dialogue. In doing so, the process builds genuine commitment among diverse constituencies for shaping public policies to achieve these principles.

Several indicators showed that the participants wanted development to occur in ways that are different from current trends and policies. Participants placed a higher percentage of new growth inside Maryland's designated growth areas (the priority funding areas) than is the case today, and a far higher percentage than zoning currently allows. By the same token, participants provided greater protection for the state's green infrastructure land—the ecologically significant lands outside designated growth areas—than current patterns and zoning. Central Maryland participants placed enough growth inside the Baltimore and Washington beltways to keep the percentage of houses and jobs in those areas about the same as they are today, even with all the anticipated population growth for the state.

Participants favored denser development than typical current patterns and zoning allow—regimes that have often led to significant low-density sprawl. Even in the traditionally conservative and home-rule-oriented Eastern Shore, participants suggested the use of urban growth boundaries and state-sponsored management to preserve the rural hinterlands. The Central Maryland participants also placed more jobs and considerably more housing closer to transit stations than is forecast today.

Of course, not all participants were of one mind. In the Western Maryland session, for example, different perspectives appeared to reflect the amount of new growth each area had already seen: participants from high growth areas, such as Frederick, more strongly favored growth controls, while those from areas that were still very rural, such as Allegany County, were often more concerned about generating new employment and improved infrastructure.

All four regions showed a fairly strong preference for locating housing for people of different income levels in the same places. All in all, the visions developed through Reality Check *Plus* would produce substantially less new impervious surface than permitted under current zoning.

IMPLEMENTATION

Reality Check *Plus* participants discussed the challenge of implementing their vision for Maryland's future, and a consensus arose around several basic strategies:

- Increase the education of public and elected officials on growth and related issues.
- New infrastructure must be coordinated with new growth and supported financially by the state.
- Efforts to protect the environment and other resources should be strengthened.
- Zoning and planning should be modified to permit improved development patterns.
- More transit and transportation options should be provided.

- Economic development incentives should be increased to support growth where it is wanted.
- Regional and intergovernmental cooperation should be increased.

SCENARIO DEVELOPMENT

The National Center for Smart Growth Research and Education at the University of Maryland is assuming primary responsibility for research projects associated with the development of future growth scenarios and policy recommendations. The center, working with the Maryland Department of Planning and Department of Transportation, is in the process of developing and analyzing alternative statewide development scenarios. These scenarios will be based on plausible stories about how various driving forces could affect development patterns in the state in the decades to come, but in ways that suggest decidedly different spatial distribution. Once those scenarios are developed, researchers will then compare their effects on such indicators as the creation of vehicle miles traveled, effects on watersheds, consumption of energy, or encroachment into environmentally sensitive areas.

Also with assistance from the Maryland Department of Planning and support from the Abell Foundation and the Chesapeake Bay Trust, the center is developing a Maryland Smart Growth Indicators Program that will offer periodic performance measures of land development, housing, and environmental trends. The center is also leading a multiorganizational effort to evaluate the efficacy of land use programs in five states that have established programs that are nationally prominent: Maryland, Oregon, New Jersey, Florida, and California.

SMART GROWTH @ 10

With the assistance of several organizations, the center hosted a conference in October 2007 titled "Smart Growth @ 10," timed to provide an update on the ten-year anniversary of the passage of Maryland's Smart Growth legislation. The center commissioned twenty-six papers from academic researchers and practitioners for this conference, which was held in Annapolis and College Park, Maryland.

The Urban Land Institute's Baltimore District Council, one of the original cosponsors of the Reality Check *Plus* effort, is providing educational programs related to growth issues in Maryland. The other partner, the statewide citizens' coalition 1,000 Friends of Maryland, is advocating change in policy at both the state and local levels. The National Center for Smart Growth and 1,000 Friends have also formed a new coalition, called PLUS (Partnership for Land Use Success) that includes the Baltimore Urban League, the Citizen Planning and Housing Association, the Maryland Municipal League, and the Home Builders Association of Maryland. The goal of this group is to try to harness their disparate views on land use issues into constructive consensus whenever possible.

CHAPTER 33

VISIONING SACRAMENTO

Mike McKeever

For the past decade, the Sacramento region has been deeply invested in the development, adoption, and implementation of integrated land use, transportation, and air quality planning. The effort is led by the Sacramento Area Council of Governments (SACOG), the metropolitan planning organization (MPO) for six counties (Sacramento, Yolo, Sutter, Yuba, Placer, and El Dorado), and the twenty-two cities within them. For measure, the Sacramento region had a population of 1,850,432 in 1999. By 2007, the population of this fast-growing region had increased more than 12 percent, to 2,268,620.

Since 1999 the SACOG board has adopted four major plans: the 1999 Metropolitan Transportation Plan (MTP), the 2002 MTP, the Blueprint long-range growth strategy (adopted in 2004), and the 2008 MTP. This case study examines the evolving technical, planning, process, and political aspects of each plan.

1999 METROPOLITAN TRANSPORTATION PLAN: THE LAST OF THE OLD-SCHOOL PLANS

As the MPO for the region, SACOG is required to regularly update its MTP in a manner that is consistent with federal and state requirements, including the Federal Clean Air Act. Since 1974 portions of the SACOG region have not been able to attain the standards of the Clean Air Act, requiring that each MTP meet conformity requirements to ensure that the region is making adequate progress toward meeting the clean air standards.

Like many regional agencies around the country, SACOG produced its 1999 MTP largely by combining the individual transportation plans of its member cities, counties, and various transit districts into what then qualified as the regional plan. While this approach had a certain perceived benefit to member agencies and partners, it did not optimize the regional travel performance of the transportation system or the air emissions.

The underlying projected land use pattern for the 1999 plan was worked out by SACOG staff with senior planning staff of the local governments, based on their existing general plans, codes, and development trends. There was no regional analysis or proactive behavior on SACOG's part, such as explaining how the trend in development patterns might damage or benefit regional travel patterns and air emissions. SACOG did not have parcel-level geographic information system (GIS) data for most of its region, so it was unable to analyze land use trends in a detailed manner. SACOG's regional travel model, SACMET, was a traditional four-step travel model with households and employment aggregated to travel analysis zones as the basic unit of analysis. Citizen and stakeholder involvement was limited to one town hall meeting in each county, making requested presentations, consulting with a standing SACOG committee of primarily senior public works staff from local governments, and a public hearing.

The plan was unanimously adopted by the SACOG board of directors; however, its projected performance in terms of congestion, vehicle miles traveled, and non–auto mode share was modest to disappointing. Soon after the plan was adopted the veteran SACOG executive director retired and a new executive director was hired. He was greeted with a lawsuit against the MTP filed by a Sacramento environmental organization. The group opposed several road capacity projects in the plan and challenged technical and process details of the air quality conformity finding. The suit was settled in SACOG's favor, with a commitment to a more extensive public review process for the air quality conformity finding in the next MTP cycle.

2002 METROPOLITAN TRANSPORTATION PLAN: THE FIRST STEP FORWARD

The SACOG board appointed a fifty-five-person transportation roundtable to oversee development of the 2002 MTP. The roundtable was broadly representative of the diverse interests in the SACOG region, from business and development interests to activists for environmental, housing, and social justice issues, as well as civic organizations and academia. Notably absent from the roundtable were senior public works staff from the cities and counties, and only one transit operator represented the thirteen transit operators in the region. These people were apprised of progress through other standing SACOG committees, but they clearly were not the focal point for input. The board appointed one of its members, the mayor of West Sacramento, to be its liaison to the roundtable. The mayor's leadership is a thread through this story: he chaired the roundtable, then chaired the board during adoption of the Blueprint in 2004 and chaired its Transportation Committee to develop the new MTP in 2008 that was based on the Blueprint.

Over a two-year professionally facilitated process, the members of the roundtable developed decision-making ground rules. To capture the broad range of ideas and opinions, the roundtable designed a range of transportation scenarios and asked SACOG to model the impacts of each, including one scenario that invested all of the available funds into road capacity enhancements, and one scenario that instead invested all of the funds into improvements to transit, walking, and bicycling systems. SACOG's technical capabilities had improved since the 1999 MTP. A regional GIS network was forming with cooperative working groups of the cities, counties, electric utility, fire services, and others in the region. After scenarios were created and modeled that emphasized road investments versus transit, walking, and biking investments, the group concluded that a balanced investment portfolio for all modes worked best.

Early in the roundtable's work, some SACOG board members, led by a veteran Sacramento County supervisor familiar with the Envision Utah scenario planning exercise, advocated for a scenario to be developed that emphasized what were coming to be known as smart growth principles (e.g., mixing land uses, growing more compactly, and using pedestrian and transit-oriented design principles). Environmental members of the roundtable were supportive. SACOG's senior staff, supportive in concept, believed that to address land use in a technically and politically effective way would require a greater effort than was possible in the final stages of the 2002 MTP cycle. It is interesting to note that, over a decade earlier, SACOG staff analyzed the travel benefits of a more compact future regional land use pattern. At the time, the board felt that land use was not an issue with which they wanted SACOG involved. The study's findings were, however, cited ten years later by some board members who were advocating for investigating land use. The board agreed with the slower approach recommended by the staff and asked the executive director to pursue funds to conduct a comprehensive land use study to inform the next major MTP update.

The 2002 MTP was unanimously adopted by the SACOG board, and although the environmental organization that filed lawsuit over the prior plan was still dissatisfied with some of the road investments in the plan, it did not litigate this time. Nevertheless, for all the broad-based work that went into the plan, its less-than-stellar projected future travel and air quality performance was of concern to the SACOG board, staff, and many members of the roundtable. This motivated many key people inside and outside of the government to get serious about a regional land use study. Maybe the problems were not solvable through a better supply of transportation improvements. Maybe there was something about growth patterns in the region that was creating a demand for transportation improvements that simply could not be met. It was this environment that led the SACOG board to launch the technically challenging and politically risky regional land use scenario planning project that eventually came to be known as Blueprint.

BLUEPRINT: A LAND USE STUDY THAT BECAME A GAME CHANGER

The first year of the thirty-month Blueprint planning process was spent designing the project, developing strategic partnerships, raising funds, hiring staff, and significantly upgrading the data and modeling capabilities of the agency. SACOG hired a planner to manage the Blueprint process who had recently relocated to

Sacramento from Portland, Oregon. His professional experience had included extensive involvement working with local governments on the development and implementation of the first regional land use plan in Portland, as well as work on integrated land use transportation planning with several regional planning agencies throughout the country. He was instrumental in the development of the I-PLACE³S (Planning for Community Energy, Environmental and Economic Sustainability) planning method and GIS software. The executive director made Blueprint the number one priority for the agency and instructed the new project manager to design the best regional land use planning project ever conducted.

Independently, regional business and civic organizations had decided that the Sacramento region badly needed a vision for its future. These organizations, the Metropolitan Chamber of Commerce, Valley Vision (a civic organization), and the local chapter of the Urban Land Institute, formed the core strategic partnership for the project. Others joined as the project progressed, including the local chapters of the Building Industry Association, American Institute of Architects, and the environmental organization that had sued SACOG over the 1999 MTP. A long-distance partnership with leaders of the Envision Utah project provided strategic and technical advice throughout the Blueprint process.

This strong base of support from nongovernmental organizations helped the Blueprint overcome its first challenge. A freshman local state legislator, with the support of many of the more urban local governments on the SACOG board, introduced a bill designed to change the way state sales tax revenues were distributed to local governments, to encourage communities to plan for sufficient housing, and not overbuild sales tax–generating retail stores. Debate over the bill created a significant fissure on the SACOG board. Weighted voting rules were invoked for the first time as the board deliberated whether it would oppose or support the bill. Neither side could muster sufficient votes to pass a motion. SACOG remained neutral.

The experience led to a major, and ultimately critical, change in the structure of the SACOG board. For several years, the board had fourteen members, causing many of the smaller cities to jointly pick a single representative. In 2003, the board amended its bylaws to expand the board to thirty-one members, providing every member with direct representation. A veteran board member from the fast growing suburban city of Lincoln in Placer County led the reform effort. In retrospect, many credit the broader board representation with creating the increased trust needed to pave the way for the development and adoption of the Blueprint.

As the board debated the controversial state legislation and reorganizing itself, SACOG staff embarked on a number of enhancements to its data and modeling capabilities, including developing parcel level GIS data; activating an Internet-based delivery system for the I-PLACE³S land use scenario building tool; installing an integrated growth forecasting model, MEPLAN; and adding a postprocessing capability to its regional travel model (the 4Ds—density, destination, design, and diversity) to enhance its sensitivities to land use changes that might influence travel behavior.

The first product of the effort was a base case scenario for growth through 2050 that assumed policy and market trend lines of the recent past would continue unchanged. The base case was developed by SACOG staff and consultants, with significant input from a first-in-the-region committee of the land use planning directors for SACOG's member cities and counties. A detailed projection for future growth in population, employment, and housing in the region was developed by a consulting firm specializing in projections for the California economy. A demographic forecast was also prepared, including changes to the age, household size, ethnicity, and incomes of the region's future population.

The performance metrics for the region in 2050 if the base case scenario materialized were very bad. Congestion, time devoted to daily travel, supply of affordable housing, conversion of farmland and natural resource lands to urbanization, carbon dioxide and particulate matter all were significantly worse than current conditions. It is not an exaggeration to say the region was stunned. The lead editorial in the *Sacramento Bee* the next day was titled "SACOG Shows Region the Road to Ruin." There was a quick and nearly unanimous consensus that the base case future was not what the region wanted. But if not the current trends scenario, then what?

Alternatives to the base case future were needed. These scenarios were designed to test the technical and political viability and the applicability of seven growth management principles, commonly known as smart growth principles, as follows:

- Provide a variety of transportation choices
- Offer housing choices and opportunities
- Take advantage of compact development
- Use existing assets
- Mix land uses and development types
- Preserve open space, farmland, and natural beauty through natural resources conservation
- Encourage distinctive, attractive communities with quality design

The principles were not assumed at the outset to be inherently good or bad but ideas of sufficient seriousness to be worth examining. The Blueprint tested these principles at three geographic scales: neighborhood, county, and regional.

The Neighborhoods

A series of thirty neighborhood-level workshops were held, at least one in each of twenty-seven of SACOG's twenty-eight member local governments. Multiple workshops were held in the two largest jurisdictions, Sacramento City and Sacramento County. To help reach out to communities across a large region, SACOG turned to Valley Vision, who was a full partner in executing the project. Valley Vision recruited and involved citizens and stakeholders in the workshops, and they formed advisory committees of key opinion leaders and stakeholders within each county to further recruit workshop participants. The goal, realized at most workshops, was to seat individuals from five to seven diverse interests at each small group table, including developers; local property owners and businesses;

citizens; activists from the environmental, housing, and other issue-specific communities; and public agency representatives.

Each host local government selected two case study sites to be the subject of their workshop, one an example of infill development opportunities and the other an example of greenfield (larger tracts of vacant land) development opportunities. Six to eight citizens sat at each workshop table and, after watching an introductory video and PowerPoint presentation about the Blueprint, the region's changing demographics, smart growth principles, and some details of the case study sites, they spent the balance of the evening designing a conceptual plan for one of the case study sites.

Project staff designed a series of interactive planning exercises for participants. In their small groups participants used context maps, pictures, and data, along with a map of the study area, and a menu of land use options to make decisions that were recorded by placing stickers on parcels to represent the land uses they wanted in their plan. Roving land use and transportation experts answered questions, and a trained facilitator guided the discussion.

A laptop computer and operator running the new web-based I-PLACE³S software via cell phone connection were available at each table to enter the plan as the citizens created it and, at various junctures, to tell them how it was performing on key metrics like jobs-housing balance, housing diversity, vehicle miles traveled, air emissions per household, and mode choice (i.e., percent of trips by car, transit, walking, and biking). An economic reality test included in I-PLACE3S conducts a planning level pro forma analysis on the proposed development ideas for every parcel. This return on investment function was used to test the profit performance and, thus, investment feasibility for private developers.

This citizen involvement process reflects a significant advancement from the days of asking citizens "what do you want?" and recording their opinions on flip charts. The entire workshop was designed both to empower the citizens by building their knowledge base and to reinforce the message that this was an information-based planning process, not one that had been precooked in some manner or was dominated by a particular planning philosophy. The technical results of these neighborhood workshops are summarized at http://www.sacregionblueprint.org. Every table's plan is saved on the SACOG website and can be viewed at any time.

Two important findings became clear to many SACOG board members. First, the innovative outreach method attracted large numbers of people to the workshops. Many were new participants in local land use issues. Second, there was a striking degree of agreement on the types of plans people supported, among the very diverse people at each table, among the tables at each workshop, and among the communities where the workshops were hosted. The smart growth principles of pedestrian and transit design, housing products that provided far more diversity than common in the current marketplace (in part to provide greater affordability, but also to meet the needs of the aging population), were supported throughout the region—whether they were from a low-income neighborhood in urban Sacramento or an affluent suburban jurisdiction.

It is worth noting that, of the other regional scenario planning exercises in the country at that time, none had conducted extensive neighborhood-scale planning this early in the process. SACOG was, in fact, pointedly advised by veterans of some of these other planning processes not to do neighborhood-scale planning early in the process because it would generate too much controversy, and the project would never be able to proceed to alternative regional scenarios. However, SACOG's approach to Blueprint from the outset was grounded in trying to find land use solutions that would work, would be politically supportable, and could be implemented at-scale quickly. The experience with too many planning projects at all scales is that enthusiasm, and therefore performance, falls off after the plan is adopted and moves to implementation. SACOG wanted to minimize the chances for what one representative from the U.S. Department of Energy (one of the funders for the development of the I-PLACE³S planning method) termed "stranded inspiration."

By the time the neighborhood workshop series was complete, it was clear that the Blueprint project had acquired legs. Many participants commented about how great the experience was. The development community, some of whom were initially skeptical of where the project was headed, gained confidence through seeing firsthand that a wide diversity of citizens supported growth on infill and greenfield sites alike in their communities.

The Counties

SACOG convened committees of senior land use planners within each of the counties and built three alternative county level planning scenarios for growth through 2050 to compare to the base case scenario. The planners started with the citizen input from the neighborhood workshops. They examined the results of the current-day housing market preference survey and the long-range demographic forecast to develop realistic targets for what portion of future housing construction should be planned for about eight different low, medium, and high density housing products. Current general plans and zoning codes were assessed to determine to what extent built densities were at or below allowed densities. The planner committees discussed ways it may be possible to change local policies and codes over the next five decades. Each county prepared three scenarios, all designed to use smart growth principles, but in different ways and to different degrees. The overall growth rate within the county also typically varied between the three scenarios. This method of building the county scenarios was designed to blend visionary planning with real-world local policies and market conditions—again, toward the goal of ultimately finding a preferred scenario that would perform well and would actually be implemented.

The county-level round of workshops was conducted with a minimum of one workshop in each county and several in Sacramento County. Modified but familiar maps, charts, and stickers seen earlier in the neighborhood workshops were used. But this time the participants had to first choose the countywide scenario they liked best, either the base case or one of the three alternatives. The scenarios were labeled A, B, C, and D (an idea borrowed from Envision Utah) to avoid biasing

people's opinions about their merits. Valley Vision again recruited and grouped
five to seven diverse perspectives at each table. The citizen planners examined large
posters with maps and performance metrics, comparing and contrasting the four
scenarios; agreed on the single scenario they liked the most; and then used the
stickers and felt markers to modify it to make it even more to their liking.

Again, laptop computers and operators were at each table to enter the changes and
give immediate feedback on how their changes would alter the performance of the
scenario for travel behavior, air quality impacts, jobs-housing balance, total growth,
and other impacts measured by I-PLACE³S. This time, the computers were connected
to the server via high-speed Internet, not cell phones, to transfer much larger data sets
resulting from more parcels in a county compared to a neighborhood.

The county workshop series was also well attended and built greater momentum and credibility for the project. People interested more in the environmental
protection side of the issue seemed pleased that there was so much support for scenarios based on smart growth principles. People interested more in the housing
supply and development side of the issue seemed pleased that the discussion was
focused on managing growth well, rather than the often-typical fast-versus-slow or
no-growth arguments. Following the county workshops, SACOG staff met with
the committee of planners within each county to review the public input and
decide which ideas that had been tested were supported by none or few, which
ideas were supported by most or all, and which ideas had divided opinion. Through
this process, a draft of three scenarios for each county fed into the creation of three
regional scenarios.

Back to the Region

Three alternative regional scenarios were created with the regional planners committee to compare to the base case future. The three scenarios were similar or iden-
tical for about 80 percent of the growth through 2050. In one scenario, that final
20 percent was located in small towns (and one new town) around the periphery of
the region; in another scenario, the final 20 percent was located in inner-ring suburban locations adjacent to existing urbanization, and in the final scenario, the
final 20 percent growth was placed into inner infill and revitalization areas.

The four regional scenarios (base case plus three new ones) were also labeled
A, B, C, and D and taken to a daylong regional forum attended by 1,500 people in
downtown Sacramento. Facilitators for each table were recruited, drawing from
local elected officials, senior local government staff, and staff from related state
agencies, transit, and air districts. The training the facilitators were required to
take, and their direct participation in the event, was an important element in building their understanding and support for what became the final preferred scenario.

Again, Valley Vision recruited and placed the participants at small group tables.
After hearing introductory video and PowerPoint presentations, each table spent
the balance of the day selecting the regional 2050 scenario they liked best and then
modifying it with peel-off stickers representing different land use types to better
meet their preferences. This workshop was so large that SACOG did not have

enough laptop computers for each of the 150 tables, so live computer analysis was conducted at only a few representative tables.

After the small group work, participants used individual keypad clickers to record both their personal preferences and the consensus preference of their small group. No tables voted for the base case scenario, and very few voted for the scenario that placed the final 20 percent growth in the cities the farthest away from the urban core of the region. The consensus votes of the tables favored the scenario that placed the final 20 percent in the inner suburban areas, while the individual votes favored the scenario that placed the final 20 percent of the growth in inner infill areas, an interesting divergence that turned out to be not particularly difficult to resolve. After analyzing each of the table's maps, SACOG staff prepared a draft preferred scenario that was a balance of the two most popular scenarios from the regional workshop.

Throughout the entire workshop process, SACOG board members were briefed and provided opportunities to give input and guidance on project progress at least monthly, both at committee meetings and at full board meetings. The input from the elected officials hit a crescendo, however, with the last big event of the Blueprint, a first-ever regional summit of all city and county elected officials. In preparation for the summit, a random-sample public opinion poll was taken to measure citizens' attitudes about growth and the principles that underpinned the draft preferred scenario (now modified and relabeled "Blueprint Principles"). A national polling firm conducted the survey, and its president, the primary pollster for governor and President Ronald Reagan, came to the summit to present the results personally. Among his key messages and advice to assembled local elected leadership of the region were the points that citizens were very nervous about growth, fearing that it would degrade a quality of life that they believed currently was very high; supportive of using the Blueprint growth principles to manage growth; supportive of regional cooperation for managing growth but skeptical whether their local officials would do it; and dramatically more positive in their attitudes about the positive aspects of growth if they believed their local communities would use the Blueprint principles to help them make planning decisions.

The elected officials used electronic keypads to identify what aspects of the draft preferred Blueprint alternative they liked and disliked. The draft alternative was very popular with the participants, and the few areas of concern gave SACOG staff fairly clear direction about the types of final refinements needed before taking the plan to the SACOG board for final action.

By the time the workshops and two regional forums had been conducted in April 2004, more than 5,000 individuals had used the modeling software and given input into the future vision of land use in the Sacramento region.

The Blueprint Decision

In December 2004 the SACOG board unanimously adopted the Blueprint growth strategy. By this point in the process SACOG had received many regional, state, and national awards for the project, including the Governor's Award for

Environmental and Economic Leadership, the Federal Highway Administration/ Federal Transit Administration Transportation Planning Excellence Award, the U.S. Environmental Protection Agency National Award for Smart Growth Achievement, and the Association of Metropolitan Planning Organizations National Award for Outstanding Achievement. A remarkable group of broad-based supporters, individuals, and organizations came to the SACOG board meeting to applaud the board's work, including the Building Industry Association and the environmental organization that had sued SACOG. Instead of suing, this same organization gave SACOG its Environmental Leadership Award for 2004.

The board's Blueprint adoption action included a conceptual map for growth through 2050, a set of Blueprint growth principles, and an implementation strategy. The implementation strategy included actions such as pursuing state legislative reform to amend the California Environmental Quality Act (CEQA) to better promote Blueprint-style growth, development of a rural lands and open space strategy for the region, technical assistance to local governments to help them amend their general plans and zoning codes to reflect the Blueprint, and pursuit of financial incentives to assist, in particular, with infill development.

MTP 2008: The Region's First Integrated Land Use, Transportation, and Air Quality Plan

Immediately after the Blueprint was adopted, SACOG went to work on the 2008 MTP. There were three main, related, technical and regulatory issues to address:

1. How could SACOG best employ the adopted Blueprint as its long-term land use plan for determining transportation needs in the MTP?
2. How would the MTP accommodate the new requirements in SAFETEA-LU, the reauthorized federal transportation bill?
3. How would the MTP address the new air quality plan (State Implementation Plan, or SIP) being prepared by air districts to meet the new, tougher eight-hour ozone standards the federal government had promulgated to replace the one-hour ozone standard?

SACOG, of course, wanted this MTP to be significantly influenced by the Blueprint; that is why the board had launched the Blueprint in the first place. SACOG also wanted to produce the new MTP using a stakeholder and citizen involvement process that met, or exceeded, the bar established by the Blueprint. A working committee to create an outreach strategy was established with SACOG's partner Regional Transportation Planning Agencies (RTPAs), the major transit operators, and the Sacramento Metropolitan Air Quality Management District, which had the lead role in developing the new SIP for the region. After the 2002 MTP, public works directors requested greater involvement in developing the next plan. A regional committee of local government public works directors was actively involved throughout the project.

The Analytical Tools

In preparation for both the public workshops and the technical work of the MTP update, SACOG committed to another round of enhancements to its data and models. A somewhat simplified version of SACMET, the regional travel model, was programmed into PLACE³S so that it could be used interactively to produce travel and land use information live in public workshops. SACOG's overall analytical capacity was improved by shifting from the SACMET four-step model to a new, activity-based regional travel model, SACSIM, which projects transportation behavior at the parcel rather than zonal level for the entire region. The net effect of the parcel specific I-PLACE³S and SACSIM modeling capabilities is like shining a bright light into an underlit room. Fine-grain relationships between specific land use choices and travel behavior are suddenly measurable.

The Process

SACOG and its partners designed a two-part workshop series to support the MTP update. A series of seventeen community workshops started the process. Valley Vision was reengaged as a partner and used Blueprint recruitment and workshop participant and table perspective diversity techniques. Nearly 1,800 citizen planners came out to workshops throughout the region between February and June 2006.

A transportation version of the Blueprint workshop program was designed, complete with menus, stickers, maps, and posters. This time, instead of planning for a specific number of new people, jobs, and houses coming to the region by 2050, participants were asked to design for mobility in 2035, and they were given a budget to spend. Federal law requires that MTPs only include transportation projects that can be delivered by revenues that are reasonably certain to be available. So the budget was important to keep the workshops focused on what was realistic, and not an exercise to produce a dream list of ideas.

SACOG staff worked with senior local government planning staff to develop a preliminary land use map to show growth through 2035, the planning horizon year for the MTP. The 2050 Blueprint preferred scenario map was the starting place for developing the 2035 map, with changes made both to reflect the shorter time frame as well as SACOG's best information on where local governments and the market were performing in ways consistent, or not, with the Blueprint. The preliminary land use allocation for 2035 was significantly refined over the course of the MTP planning process as more empirical experience became available with Blueprint implementation and SACOG staff had more time to work, in detail, with local government planning staff.

SACOG staff worked with its partners and local agency staff to design three alternative transportation scenarios for each county. Participants listened to a short video and a PowerPoint presentation explaining how the underlying smarter growth land use pattern for this MTP would create more need for investments in alternative modes to the automobile, and for shorter distance automobile trips. Ways to quantify differences in mobility performance among the scenarios were also explained.

Participants in each small group agreed on the scenario they liked best and then used stickers representing a variety of transit, pedestrian, bicycle, and road investments to modify the scenario to better match their preferences. Laptop computers again were used to show participants how their choices changed the performance of the scenario, for better or worse. This may have been the first time in the history of U.S. transportation planning that live feedback on regional travel performance was provided in a public workshop addressing an area this large.

The results of the county workshops were compiled, analyzed with the travel models at SACOG, and used to prepare three regional-scale transportation scenarios. SACOG deviated from the Blueprint approach to the large regional workshop for the MTP. Instead of inviting everyone to a single downtown location, eight simultaneous workshops were held throughout the region, linked by satellite video. The goal was to make it clear, by allowing more people to attend one of eight dispersed workshops, that this truly was a regional plan being developed and their input mattered. The event was cohosted by the local network television station with the highest ratings in the Sacramento region. One of the station's news anchors served as emcee throughout the evening. Presentations at the largest site, Memorial Auditorium in downtown Sacramento, were broadcast to all eight sites, along with prepackaged educational videos. The balance of the citizen's work was done locally at each of the eight workshop locations.

Again, a diverse range of workshop participants sat in small groups, chose which of three regional scenarios they liked the most, and used menus and stickers to refine the map to better match their preferences. As with the county workshops, a budget was imposed. Laptop computers were not used interactively at these workshops, although at the end of the workshop all participants used electronic keypads to record their opinions on key issues. Although there were temporary technical issues with both the satellite and keypad technology at this event, it was a significant success, attended by nearly 1,500 people at the eight locations, and extensive citizen input was provided to guide development of the draft MTP.

The final big public involvement event was an hour-long live television show sponsored by the station, replacing the regular 6:30 newscast on January 31, 2007. Forty studio guests, selected by the station, were seated in an in-the-round, town-hall-style studio and responded to questions posed to them by two news anchors. An online poll collected viewer feedback on several questions posed during the show. More than 56,000 viewers tuned in to watch this regional dialogue, and 1,300 gave immediate feedback responses in the interactive poll.

Significant public attitude research also was conducted. A regional telephone poll was completed to test attitudes on different transportation investment options. The poll was supplemented with four geographically representative focus groups of the general public and an online poll. A separate set of eight focus groups was conducted to focus in on environmental justice issues. In total, more than 1,500 individuals gave input through focus groups and scientific surveys. SACOG learned that all areas and groups of residents want a balance of highway/freeway improvements and public transportation expansion.

The Decision

On March 20 the SACOG board unanimously adopted the 2008 MTP—the first MTP to explicitly propose a range of policies and associated strategies specifically designed to integrate with a Blueprint-influenced land use pattern. The SACOG board's action also included the certification of the associated environmental document that includes meaningful mitigation measures to integrate the MTP's transportation plan with land use, air quality, and climate change concerns.

The MTP shows dramatically improved transportation performance compared to the prior plans, including less congestion; more transit, walk, and bike travel; and reductions in per household vehicle miles traveled. Its state environmental document also showed reductions in carbon emissions per household, a big issue in a state with the nation's toughest global warming law.

Conclusion

The story of these four major planning actions by SACOG traces a steady evolution to a new style of regional planning. The keys to success were commitments to the highest quality data and modeling tools—necessary to ground policy making in information; create meaningful citizen engagement; and focus on the connections and interactions between land use, transportation, and air quality planning issues.

FULFILLING THE PROMISE
OF REGIONAL PLANNING

Carleton K. Montgomery

The initiatives discussed in this book make the case that regional planning is a real, dynamic, and creative force in many parts of North America. With all we have seen of these programs, we are in a good position to judge whether regional planning really works, how to overcome the basic obstacles we find to the creation of regional planning programs, and why regional strategies are essential to solving the great environmental, economic, and social threats of the new century.

DOES REGIONAL PLANNING WORK?

We know fragmented municipal planning has brought, or permitted, many problems. So we have to ask, is regional planning proving itself able to solve these problems in practice? This is a critical but sometimes difficult question to answer. Many regional planning programs are still too young to evaluate fairly. Judging even long-standing programs is difficult given the range and ambition of their goals and policies. Most regional planning efforts are using simple metrics, if they are using any quantitative measures at all, and there is no common approach to measure success. The published scholarly studies applying rigorous metrics to regional planning programs are useful, but also few in number. In these circumstances, the contributors to this book cannot offer a definitive answer to the question of how well regional planning is working in all cases. Nevertheless, the evidence to date permits us to conclude that both mandatory and voluntary programs have begun to achieve real, if incomplete, success.

The range of established and evolving regional planning initiatives shows that regional planning has come of age. The regional approach is far from pervasive in the United States, and it faces many deep challenges. Yet regional planning is successful in a remarkable number of places. Regional planning is real, not merely aspirational; it is taking place in many parts of the country, not only in one or two places seen as the exceptions that prove the rule; and it is increasingly comprehensive, not restricted to single issue planning.

When a young person comes of age, he or she deserves the respect and is subject to the responsibilities of an adult—but has not yet fully matured. In this sense, too, regional planning has come of age. Genuine regional planning that actually shapes patterns of growth and resource use is still far too rare. In many places, it must overcome the power of municipal parochialism, attitudes about private property rights, and land development interests, as well as the simple weight of received ways of doing business.

The work described in this book shows that, in many places, mandatory regional planning programs have shaped the pattern of development across the landscape, concentrating growth in designated areas and dramatically reducing sprawl where the plans call for preservation of rural and natural areas. There is also evidence that some regional programs are successfully directing infrastructure investments to achieve better outcomes for the entire region, promoting the revitalization of cities, providing more efficient transportation options, and protecting essential water resources. Many are promoting the efficient and sustainable design of new developments within their regions. While it is difficult or impossible to disentangle the influence of changing market preferences and regional policies, we can at least conclude that new policies are harnessing and encouraging market changes for the better in some regions.

Academic research on particular initiatives is scarce and, in most cases, nonexistent. We often have to rely on regional agencies themselves for data on how well they are doing, and the data we find will depend on whether and how the agency has decided to measure its own work. Regional planning programs evaluate themselves in a wide variety of ways and in varying degrees of rigor. Only one program has built measures of success directly into its regulatory structure: the Tahoe compact requires the agency to develop specific, numeric environmental carrying capacity thresholds and to adopt a plan and regulations that will meet those thresholds. Its thirty-six thresholds adopted in 1982 cover issues such as lake clarity, wildlife habitats, vegetation, and scenic resources. No other has tied its rules directly to such measures as has the Tahoe program.

Mandatory Programs

A look at the mandatory plans with a sufficiently long track record shows they can shape regional land use change and, where this is part of their goals, influence infrastructure and financial resource allocations. The most essential measure of success for a mandatory regional planning program has to be whether it succeeds in directing the location and intensity of new development, and in this area they have the most success. Portland Metro's urban growth boundary (UGB) has kept the great majority of development within the boundary. While Metro has expanded the UGB since its original adoption, the agency can justly claim success in stifling sprawl and preserving rural landscapes in its environs. A number of studies have shown that nearly all residential and commercial development in the Portland region has taken place inside the UGB (see Chapman and Lund 2004).

The Pinelands Commission measures the impact of its work through evaluating landscape integrity and doing long-term monitoring of aquatic habitats, as well as annual economic monitoring studies. More than 90 percent of development since the Pinelands Comprehensive Management Plan was put in place has occurred inside designated growth zones, and the commission's recent Ecological Integrity Assessment indicates the plan has succeeded in maintaining very large areas of contiguous, largely unfragmented habitats—a picture we surely would not see but for the regional land use regulations. The commission's economic monitoring reports, moreover, have consistently found that communities inside the Pinelands perform as well as or better than those outside on a range of economic perform-ance measures.

The mandatory programs highlighted here also look to a variety of additional measures, such as lands acquired for conservation, transit infrastructure built, habitat restorations completed, housing prices, and other economic measures. Again, among the mandatory programs, the Tahoe Regional Planning Agency has the most formalized measures of environmental goals; while twenty-two of its thirty-six environmental thresholds were not attained as of 2006, the agency has made progress on challenging issues, such as returning the fabled clarity of Lake Tahoe to its natural state. In 2008, moreover, the agency announced results of research finding that while Lake Tahoe's clarity was still declining, the rate of decline began to slow down in 2001, which the agency attributes to policies that have significantly reduced runoff from urban areas and roads. The Meadowlands Commission has been highly successful in managing the land use control, landfill cleanup, and other efforts that have preserved several thousand acres of wetlands and brought them back to life. Portland Metro has succeeded in promoting goals like traffic improvement, walkability, bicycle friendliness, and open space preser-vation. Consistent with this picture, urban development in the most rapidly grow-ing part of the Portland Metro area was changing toward the desired community design, in terms of street design and circulation systems, density, land use mix, and accessibility to transit and other uses (Song and Knaap 2004; Chapman and Lund 2004). While there are no published analyses of the overall success or impacts of the Adirondack Park Agency and its regional plans, it is evident that the state's efforts over more than a hundred years to preserve very large contiguous forests and wetlands have succeeded so far.

Even with their mandatory regulatory powers, however, these programs may not achieve their ultimate goals, such as preserving or restoring native ecosystems, controlling pervasive impacts like water quality degradation, and fostering funda-mental change in transportation systems and the design of new development. Where they fail, the failures may arise from weaknesses inherent in their structure, from inherited problems that arose before regional management was put in place, and from the power of economic interests not aligned with the plan's vision and goals. The Cape Cod program, for example, has not solved the problem of con-tamination of groundwater and estuaries due to the Cape's historic reliance on septic systems. The Pinelands program has kept most development out of its large, designated conservation zones, but the region has seen a growing number of forest areas fragmented by very large-lot, scattered housing and the degradation of habitats by nonpoint source pollution flowing from developed headwaters into downstream preserved lands.

Voluntary Programs

One of the most pressing questions for regional planning is whether voluntary programs do, or can, work. As the essays on these programs show, there are important voluntary planning initiatives whose advocates believe that voluntary collaboration will prove to be not only the sole politically feasible approach but also the most effective. Voluntary programs in which municipal and county governments convene to devise and carry out regional plans have had some success. But most of these programs are still in their youth. It remains to be seen how far this approach will influence development and conservation patterns and whether such programs will have staying power over decades.

Though sometimes prodded by state or federal mandates, these are cases in which county and local governments have willingly entered a collaborative planning process because their political leaders recognize the potential value of innovative regional action. That does not necessarily mean change comes easily. Programs that lack the regulatory authority to manage development toward their regional vision depend on changing the minds of policy makers and their constituents. These programs, then, may have an even greater need for objective, public measures of success than do the regulatory programs. On the other hand, we see cases where such regional programs are changing the paradigm for land use change and are beginning to make a difference on the ground—and their advocates often plausibly argue their regions would never support or accede to a mandatory regional planning regime. (See McKinney and Johnson [2009] for more examples of collaborative regional conservation initiatives.)

A case study in the difficulty of using voluntary cooperation to address a tough regional problem is the Chesapeake Bay restoration effort. The challenge here is daunting, involving a vast and rapidly urbanizing watershed that stretches across four states and the District of Columbia. The Chesapeake Bay Program recognizes that setting clear, well-designed measures is critical to such an ambitious project that does not have mandatory growth management powers. When widespread anoxia hit the Bay in 2004, the program lost public and congressional credibility because its state-of-the-Bay reports now appeared to be too optimistic and inaccurate in light of the actual condition of the Bay. The program responded by rebuilding its science-based indicators of Bay health, making them simpler both to guide state actions and to communicate more effectively with the public. Results to date show that efforts by the states have kept overall inputs stable in the face of rapid urbanization within the watershed—but these efforts have not significantly reduced overall nutrient inputs into the Bay. The indicators provide a solid basis for concluding current efforts alone will not restore the Bay, but they also point to the kinds of land use policies that could achieve that goal.

Howard Ernst argues (chap. 18) that the effort to restore the Chesapeake Bay has developed a bureaucracy whose complexity is inversely proportional to its influence over the human activities that are poisoning the Bay. Observing that "the Bay restoration effort has no comprehensive or even coordinated land use or growth management authority," Ernst suggests that the network of compacts, committees, and collaborative planning agencies simply do not have the will or the power to do what needs to be done to stem the flow of contaminants from agriculture and urban/suburban development into the Bay. The creation of indicators and goals is not enough, for there are no consequences for states and local governments that do not meet the goals, or even implement policies calculated to meet them.

There is substantial evidence that statewide planning requirements are only as effective as the strength of the mandate on local governments. The Florida experience exemplifies the difficulty of achieving good planning simply by requiring that local governments do good planning, without a robust regional planning structure to tailor generic mandates and push local planning toward a substantial regional land use vision. Florida's use of concurrency requirements has not fostered regional planning but appears instead to have had the unintended consequence of promoting sprawl while discouraging infill and redevelopment (see chap. 14). Researchers like John Carruthers have reached similar conclusions in examining the statewide growth management programs of Florida, California, Georgia, Oregon, and Washington (see Carruthers 2002a and 2002b; see also Norton 2005; Edwards and Haines 2007). Carruthers concludes, for example, that Florida's planning "mandate has worked to *increase* the spatial extent of urbanized land" (Carruthers 2002a, 1975). In contrast, he finds, the Oregon and Washington programs are making a positive difference in combating sprawl because they mandate stronger regionalist controls—particularly urban growth boundaries.

Nevertheless, voluntary programs are beginning to have an impact in many regions. Sacramento is already beginning to see a significant change in the mix of housing types since SACOG adopted its Blueprint Growth Strategy and Metropolitan Transportation Plan. Maine's Beginning with Habitat program has captured the interest of local governments in many parts of the state. Elizabeth Hertz highlights the example of twelve towns around Merrymeeting Bay that have joined with state agencies and nonprofits to form a regional planning team that aims to preserve the region's natural and scenic resources by coordinating local land use controls on a watershed basis (see chap. 22). Envision Utah has built on the foundation it created through public education and visioning to work with state and local governments on a number of planning projects that link transportation with local land use controls and promote transit. The Atlanta Regional Commission's Livable Centers Initiative (LCI) aims to attract new development to centers identified through a collaborative planning process with local governments. Between 2000 and 2005, a high percentage of commercial and office development went into LCI areas, but they only attracted residential development equivalent to their share of the region's land area. Rob LeBeau attributes the failure to concentrate residential growth during this period, at least in part, to the fact that many LCI towns still had traditional zoning that barred mixed use residential construction, suggesting that the picture should change as local governments bring their ordinances into line with the program's goals (see chap. 15).

In sum, experience suggests once again that there is no simple answer to the question whether different approaches to regionalism are working or will work given time. In judging these efforts, it is important to remember that North America is still in the early stages of change in its dominant culture of land use management. The ability of any program, and especially voluntary ones, to survive and bring practical changes depends on many factors. Prominent among these are the nature and scale of the challenges to be met; the history and culture of a particular region that sets the context of regional identity, parochial loyalties, fear or trust, and sense of possibility among the public; and the regulatory or persuasive tools the program can bring to bear. Some challenges, such as restoring the Chesapeake Bay or controlling development in a crowded place like New Jersey, face such powerful economic and social forces that they do seem to require mandatory regional powers to succeed. Others regions and circumstances, however, are clearly open to making real progress through voluntary initiatives. Some voluntary programs will prove too weak to marshal local governments and economic forces toward a coherent outcome, while others will develop tools, like transportation or other infrastructure funding, that give them enough influence to tip the balance. Some initiatives will face a distrustful public that cannot get past fears of losing what they think local autonomy gives them, or what joining a broader effort may bring to their own neighborhoods, while others will be able to build a compelling vision that wins the loyalty of the region's residents.

CHALLENGES FOR REGIONAL ACTION

That regional challenges require regional strategies and structures is no longer a profound insight, yet robust regionalism is still an exotic and, to many, a dangerous innovation. Given the dramatic (if incomplete) success of several regional planning efforts, and the extraordinary promise this approach carries for the future, why isn't more of it happening in the United States? Why does so much of the country fiddle while Rome is burning, playing with half-baked, aspirational standards and processes that local governments can, and generally do, ignore? And why are even the most powerful regional planning regimes struggling to achieve some of their core goals?

Experience suggests there are no silver bullets for overcoming any of these obstacles. The two universal ingredients to successful innovation are political leadership and extensive public education on the vision of a better future these plans can bring. As we have learned so often, the best idea in the world goes nowhere without political and public support. Political leadership and public support also go hand in hand: leaders help move public perceptions, and public support makes it possible for leaders to lead. In every successful regional planning effort, advocates inside and outside government are taking on the responsibility of persuading their public of the benefits change will bring.

Tradition of Local Control

Long-standing regional government agencies such as those in the New Jersey Pinelands, Cape Cod, and Portland have won broad, resilient public support where they have taken hold. There is good reason to conclude that virtually all parts of the country could benefit from some form of regional governance, yet in most regions such agencies have not arisen in large part because municipal and county governments have proven fiercely jealous of their control over land use. There are several ways to explain the phenomenon. The defense of local government, like so much in American politics, flows in part from a narrative about local democracy and control deeply embedded in our culture—a "nostalgic preference for a small self-contained municipality" that "collides with the reality of the metropolitan land-scape" in which atomized local governments cannot control their own fates and there is very little participatory democracy at work (Reynolds 2007, 483). It is also true that the tenacious hold of municipal governance is built into the long-standing, and frequently the constitutional, structure of the states, and this structure gives the interests that benefit from it the tools to defend their powers and privileges (Briffault 2000). It must also be said that residents of suburbs and small cities see a real threat in being swallowed by central city governments, which they see as inefficient, corrupt, and self-serving; and in some metropolitan areas, minority residents of the center city equally fear being dominated and used by richer, more powerful suburbs (e.g., powell 2000).

Controlling growth in one place, moreover, can mean sending it somewhere else, and that somewhere else has its own residents and municipal leaders who often do not want to become the receiving area for the region's population growth. This phenomenon is certainly evident in the more heavily developed Northeast, where excessive dependence on property taxes has caused a political sea change over the past two decades, leading many municipal governments to fight residential growth for the school children, traffic congestion, and fiscal burdens it brings in its wake.

The programs discussed in this book adopt one of three basic approaches to overcoming localist opposition. The first approach is found where state and federal government simply impose a regional planning system and let the program's success over time in preserving values the public cherishes win over the opposition. This is the story, for example, of the Pinelands and Columbia River Gorge National Scenic Area. The second approach is seen where regional leaders recognize the need for regionalism and put a proposal to the voters. This is the story, for example, of Portland and Cape Cod. In some recent cases, Western voters have rejected such proposals to create regional planning structures, reflecting the difficulty in many regions of winning majority support for new government systems the region's public has never experienced and opponents brand as dangerous to their freedoms. The last approach is to first lay a groundwork of public support for voluntary regionalism through the kinds of intensive outreach and visioning processes that we see in Envision Utah, the SACOG initiatives, and Reality Check *Plus*. It is impossible to say which approach is better in general. Each can work with capable political leadership, funding, and time.

Environment vs. Growth

Sustainable economic growth demands environmental resources be preserved and improved, and many industries and business leaders are climbing on the regional planning train. In practice, however, many economic interests—particularly the construction and real estate industries—have fought regional growth management. Inevitably, any given region and plan will have opponents from one or more sectors that believe growth management means growth suppression. Any effective growth management is obviously going to prevent some development ambitions in some places, just as any meaningful zoning regime will do. It is critical, therefore, to distinguish between planning's effect on particular projects or sectors from its overall, long-term effect on the regional economy. It is critical to recognize, as Paul Gottlieb stresses, that a rational evaluation of the economic costs and benefits of regional growth management requires a comprehensive, rather than conventional, definition of economic welfare—one that also includes ecosystems services as well as aesthetic, recreational, and quality-of-life benefits. Similarly, to the extent the economic question is one of public finance and tax revenues, the indirect costs of different kinds of new development for infrastructure, schools, and other services have to be priced and included in the analysis. Unfortunately, this kind of comprehensive analysis has not yet been undertaken for any of our regional planning initiatives (Chapter 26).

Only one regional planning agency, the Pinelands Commission, has established an ongoing economic monitoring program. Set up to address the question whether Pinelands communities were seeing different economic results from other parts of New Jersey, the Pinelands produces annual reports on an evolving array of indicators of employment, municipal finance, and home values. As John Stokes and Susan Grogan explain, the results have consistently indicated that economic activity within the Pinelands equals or betters that outside (see chap. 6).

While regions are increasingly important in shaping economic factors like employment and innovation, Christopher Jones notes that there is little hard evidence on how regional planning affects regional economies. Given the tremendous diversity of regional economies and regional planning programs, the range of possible definitions of success, and the relatively small size of the sample available to study, it will always be extremely difficult to reach reliable scientific conclusions about the economic influence of regional planning as such. The economic case for regionalism has to be made by examining the benefits arising from particular regional planning projects such as those discussed in this volume.

It is prosperity that often creates the need for regional planning—as in Atlanta, Maryland, Puget Sound, Tahoe, Cape Cod—making it difficult to show that regionalism has also fostered strong economies once regional policies were added to the mix. In other cases—such as Portland and the Twin Cities tax sharing program—strong regional governance was in part a response to economic problems, as local leaders saw regional growth policies as a way to strengthen existing cities. In yet others—such as the Pinelands—economic growth was not a primary motivation for regional planning. The continuing health of the regional economies in all these examples suggests regional growth management is at least compatible with economic success.

Private Property Rights Ideology

A pervasive source of resistance to regional land use controls comes from the deeply rooted premise that people should be able to do what they like on their own land. While this principle has long ago been breached by all manner of development controls in virtually all parts of the country, it still exercises a braking effect on any new adventures in growth management. More often than not, the appeal to private property rights is a rhetorical screen for development practices that bring negative impacts stretching far beyond the landowner's parcel line. Indeed, Paul Gottlieb points out that, contrary to many a naive argument, regional planning does not replace unconstrained consumer choices, giving rise to a free-market landscape. Existing housing, job, and transportation choices that shape the built and natural environment are already heavily regulated—just at different scales ill-matched to the actual market, and with less coordination of various regulatory structures. Nevertheless, since the Supreme Court's *Kelo* decision in 2006, opponents of regulatory growth management have confused land use controls with the taking of land for private commercial use in order to take advantage of public anger at abuses of eminent domain (e.g., Ring 2006). Especially in the West, opposition to land use controls has become the single most important enemy of effective regional planning.

This is a large and constantly changing subject—too large and uncertain for detailed treatment here. I want only to point to the extraordinary recent history of property rights measures and countermeasures in Oregon. Oregon voters overwhelmingly approved Measure 37 in 2004, threatening to reverse all that Portland Metro had accomplished through land use controls. Measure 37 allowed property owners to make claims on government for the value they claimed to have lost due to land use regulations enacted after they came into ownership, or to receive a waiver from the regulations. Though delayed by a series of court challenges, Measure 37 resulted in the filing of thousands of claims, some for billions of dollars, against government agencies—including more than 2,000 in the Portland Metro region. Governments were overwhelmed with claims and were unable to make determinations on whether given regulations actually reduced property values and by how much. Naturally, it was easier to give waivers. Soon, however, the public began to have second thoughts, as inappropriate developments were approved, residents began to fear for their own neighborhoods. Builders, too, soon realized the downside to a building free-for-all and the benefits of good planning for the value of their own developments. In 2007 Oregon voters approved Measure 49, a complex new law that effectively repealed Measure 37. Measure 49 will continue to discourage new regulation but provides more limited development rights to claimants who have already received valid Measure 37 waivers. Also in 2007, voters in three states, including Washington, rejected a ballot measure modeled on Measure 37. It appears that, at least in parts of the West, the assault on growth management and environmental regulation may be slowing in the face of broader public recognition of their benefits, indeed their necessity.

Poverty and Segregation

It has been said that the poor will always be with us. No one claims sound regional planning will eliminate poverty. But regional planning is uniquely suited to address one of the great evils of poverty—namely, concentrated poverty and the racial and economic segregation associated with it in our society. While many factors play a role, the vicious cycle of middle class flight, disinvestments, and educational and economic failure are key forces in creating central cities, neighborhoods, and suburbs of concentrated poverty. Seeing an entire metropolitan area as a unit with common interests and needs is the basis on which government can deploy a series of policies that can begin to reverse local decline and concentrated poverty. At the same time, these very problems of economic and racial segregation can make it very difficult to find a regional identity and sense of common purpose that will support regionalist initiatives.

Essentially, regional strategies include policies such as revenue sharing among fragmented municipal governments, various approaches to providing affordable housing in all communities, and the creation or strengthening of transit options to link homes and jobs. Affordable housing has proven a very difficult challenge. By limiting housing options and promoting the physical segregation of housing types, sprawling growth has not only drawn capital and people from many center cities, it has also failed to bring affordable housing to the suburbs. Most of the regional planning programs in this book, moreover, came about because of rapid population growth, so it is not surprising that these regions have also seen rapid inflation of housing prices.

Housing for all segments of society is critical to the economic health of a region, and the great majority of regional planning programs include affordable housing in their planning and regulatory initiatives in some fashion and degree. For example, under legislation adopted in 2008, New Jersey's three regional planning agencies (Highlands, Meadowlands, and Pinelands) are now required to plan regionally for affordable housing, and it requires that 20 percent of all new residential developments be affordable units. How these new mandates will work in practice is an open question. Portland Metro's Code requires municipal master plans and ordinances to provide for affordable housing, and Metro sets housing density targets within its designated growth centers and requires zoning to permit accessory uses, in part to promote this end. Among voluntary programs, the Sacramento program is required by state law, as a council of governments, to plan for meeting the region's housing needs, including affordable housing, and its consensus Blueprint Growth Strategy seeks to limit large-lot development while encouraging inclusionary zoning and construction of multifamily units.

Setting Boundaries

A regional plan needs a regional boundary within which its standards and strategies are deployed. There must inevitably be an inside and an outside, however large the inside may be. Margaret Dewar and David Epstein have argued that, at least for megaregional planning, a "single boundary cannot serve for formulating plans for the range of challenges facing an area," so planning boundaries should be changeable and should vary depending on the task at hand (Dewar and Epstein 2007). This approach, however, would prove highly problematic if applied to an actual regional plan. It is hard enough to get any planning boundaries in place; it is virtually impossible to create multiple boundaries for different purposes; and it is extremely difficult to substantially change boundaries once established. Regional plans are strongest where they create settled and reliable expectations. On the other hand, fixed boundaries bring inherent difficulties of their own because they will leave important areas out, they are always fixed on the basis of imperfect information about natural and social resources, and the world changes around them.

Regionalism is based on the idea that institutions and policies need to be scaled to the problems they aim to solve. But we know that no political boundary can capture all the forces that determine the outcomes in our own place, and we often must work with the many jurisdictional boundaries we are given by history, geography, and received institutions. To take an example close to my own heart, it will not save the Pine Barrens treefrog if we stop global warming but develop all the treefrog's habitats; and it will not work to save the frog's habitats from development but lose them to climate change. Similarly, in the Adirondack mountains people have protected hundreds of lakes, but many of them have essentially died due to the acid rain caused by power plants in the Ohio Valley—far outside the Adirondack Park. There are comparable examples in every place where people are struggling to save natural resources. Every regional policy, whether on the environment, housing, employment, or transportation, faces this fundamental problem of being unable to control forces beyond its borders.

There plainly is no general solution to this problem. Every boundary will leave something important outside. Even where it is theoretically possible to expand a regional planning jurisdiction, it is not necessarily a good thing to do. As I have noted before, a great virtue of regional governance is precisely that it can be drawn big enough to cover critical forces shaping the region while still being small enough to benefit from local knowledge and a strong regional identity. Development pressure on Cape Cod is influenced by growth patterns in its neighboring counties and the region's big cities, but greatly expanding the program's geographic range would undermine the popular sense of a unique place on which the program's public support depends. Bigger is not necessarily better. This dilemma points to the fact that effective regional planning does not stand alone. It must be integrated not just with political institutions within its borders, but must also collaborate with state, national, and to some extent global efforts by public and private actors.

Climate Change

Global warming represents a universal and daunting threat to reaching the goals for which the regional planning efforts in this book are striving. For those focused on protecting a distinctive ecosystem, climate change threatens to eviscerate all their efforts by making the climate unsuitable for today's native natural communities. Climate change is already disrupting critical relationships among plant and animal species, accelerating the invasion of nonnative species, and submerging coastal habitats. Rising sea levels threaten to impose massive costs on coastal communities that seek to hold back the waters, and new precipitation and temperature regimes are projected to make water supply an even more difficult challenge than it already is in much of the country. Given that the causes are continental, indeed global, in scale, what can regional planning do to help reverse the trend and adjust to the climate changes that are coming? Land use patterns clearly play a role in the generation of greenhouses gases. We should expect, therefore, that regional initiatives can play a role as part of the broad range of actions at all levels of society needed both to reverse and to accommodate global warming.

Noting that the federal government has not, so far, provided effective leadership on climate change, Bob Yaro and David Kooris point out that the action in this field is now taking place at the state, regional, and municipal levels (chap. 23). States are working to bring about more efficient energy generation, and many municipalities are working on making their own operations more energy efficient. Regional initiatives among and within states provide a promising means of linking land use patterns and transportation systems to reduce CO_2 emissions. The same growth vision that has arisen to address preclimate change environmental, social, and economic goals should also reduce carbon emissions and help people and habitats adjust to the impacts of global warming. Reviving and returning to the cities, building compact, mixed use, transit-oriented development, and protecting large open spaces will, in combination, reduce greenhouse gas emissions compared to existing sprawl models of growth. The most important effect, and test, will be the reduction in vehicle miles traveled, hopefully both in absolute terms and when compared to alternative growth patterns. Concentrating and planning new development will also provide more room for natural communities to migrate and adjust to climate change. As weather cycles shift and most areas suffer more droughts, at least seasonally, conservation of aquifer recharge areas and efficient use of water for human needs will be ever more important.

The most significant initiative to link regional land use management and transportation in the cause of reducing carbon emissions is California's Senate Bill 375. The statute, adopted in October 2008, seeks to reduce greenhouse gas emissions from cars and light trucks through several new requirements that link transportation, land use change and design, and housing supply planning:

- Metropolitan planning organizations (MPOs) must include sustainable communities strategies in their regional transportation plans.
- The California Air Resources Board will develop new regional targets for the reduction of greenhouse gas emissions by cars and light trucks. MPOs will be required to quantify how their transportation plans will reduce greenhouse gases and whether their plans will achieve the new reduction targets.
- If there is a gap in achieving the targets, MPOs must develop alternative planning strategies that show how the targets can be achieved through

alternative patterns of development and infrastructure construction. The bill specifies, however, that these plans will not supersede or interfere in the existing control of counties and cities over land use decisions; nor does it require local land use policies to conform to the MPOs' plans.

- The bill encourages the construction of higher-density, mixed-income, transit-oriented development by reducing or eliminating certain state-mandated environmental reviews for projects that meet certain criteria, including consistency with the MPOs' smart growth plans.
- MPOs are required to update their regional housing needs assessments and housing allocations among local jurisdictions to be consistent with their new plans.

It is of course too soon to tell how this statute will influence land use planning, landscape change, and carbon emissions in practice. It does, however, represent an extraordinary advance in the thinking and culture surrounding land use and transportation. It is noteworthy that the bill arose out of the regional planning efforts of the Sacramento Area Council of Governments.

Keys to Success

The programs discussed in this book demonstrate that one size does not fit all regions, and there is no one right way to do regional planning. But experience to date does suggest strategies that help the most effective programs find success:

- Provide a clear legislative mandate. There should be a fundamental, overriding purpose that guides the regional planning agency or process. Planners, politicians, and the public should have a clear idea of this overriding purpose and what the regional planning agency or structure is expected to accomplish.
- Be comprehensive. Make sure the regional planning agency or process has sufficiently broad jurisdiction to succeed in achieving its purpose. Include regional landscape change, water resources, community design and infrastructure investment, transportation, affordable housing, and potentially other issues like property taxes.
- Build in effective means to conform local land use plans to the regional vision. Most regional planning initiatives will incorporate more local levels of government that hold land use regulation powers under long-standing state law. If there is no effective way to bring local plans into conformance, the regional plan will either have little effect on the real world or will evolve into a mere reflection of fragmented local plans.
- Insulate the regional structure from partisan politics. Regional plans will only work if they survive the vicissitudes of partisan political struggles, and to survive they must stand in some substantial way outside those struggles. Setting up a specialized regional planning body, giving it a professional staff, providing the members of its governing board to be chosen by more than one person or agency (such as the governor, legislature, counties, and tribes), and

cultivating a bipartisan culture of support for the program can provide the necessary insulation.

- Draw boundaries to capture critical environmental, economic, or political dynamics. No regional planning boundary can capture all important places and forces and remain regional, but poor boundary decisions can undermine a regional plan's ability to achieve its goals, and these boundaries are hard to change once they are first established.
- Use multiple boundary-crossing land use tools. We have seen there are many tools available for regional growth management and conservation—regional growth management maps, TDR, long-range transportation planning, and so on. Successful programs tend to use many of these tools in concert.
- Integrate land acquisition and planning. Both as a conservation measure and as a means of focusing development energies into compact communities, land acquisition is a central tool of regional growth management. But it is most effective when directed by a regional vision, so that scarce acquisition funds go to the most important conservation targets and do not undermine the regional vision for areas most appropriate for growth.
- Pay attention to *how* we build where we build. Inefficient, poor quality development created at random and without regard to transportation and other infrastructure will undermine the long-term integrity of a regional plan. If today's growth zones do not work as sustainable communities that efficiently absorb demand, then the pressure to continue spreading out, developing ever more forests and fields, will prove irresistible. Good growth is just as essential to growth management as setting boundaries to contain growth.
- Build in processes for changing the plan that provide flexibility without threatening the plan's stability and credibility over time. No regional plan will succeed unless the public, developers, and all levels of government believe it is there to stay. If the plan is too changeable, it will not guide the expectations and decisions of private industry and government. The mechanisms for change, therefore, must be relatively difficult and insulated from shifts in which political party has won the last election.
- Nurture regional identity for public support. Where the public identifies a region as distinct and special, it will demand that government protect the natural resources or community character that defines the region's unique identity. Regional identity needs to be fostered and constantly cultivated through education, visioning processes, news coverage, and events.

MANAGING CHANGE FOR SUSTAINABILITY

To meets its promise, regional planning must manage change without stultifying the creative dynamism of American society. Some defend fragmented government and condemn large-scale growth and land use management on the theory that regional governance and planning would suppress innovation, block market efficiencies, or lock in the particular built environment that today's governing elite happens to like (e.g., Garreau 1991). Indeed, we cannot and should note hope to stop change on a regional scale. Today's regional planning programs aim instead to shape change for the common good. It is also true, however, that many regional planning programs do try to preserve a part of the landscape as it is—that is, to stop change—on some geographic scale, in some parts of their region, in order to save characteristic landscapes, large contiguous forests, critical habitats and water resources, threatened or endangered plant and animal populations, or an agricultural countryside. Since we are not making more land, our regions must choose whether to sprawl until they literally run out of green fields, or instead draw permanent boundaries and build in and up, not out. For some regions, like my own in New Jersey, that choice is already very much upon us and cannot be deferred. For others, the discomforts of sprawl are growing acute long before they run out of buildable hinterlands. In either case, it is past time to use the intellectual, legal, and fiscal tools we have to anticipate the day when all acknowledge it is no longer possible to keep doing what we have been doing to the landscape over the past half century and more.

Is it even possible, given the dynamism of our economy and the unquenchable thirst for more and better that dominates our popular culture, to shape the landscape by intention and to protect some natural and cultural resources as they are today? Only time will tell. But I believe the programs my colleagues describe in this book provide strong evidence that permanent patterns of preserved land and growth zones can survive the forces of economic change, if they have the benefit of a committed public, competent leaders, and rigorous application of sustainable growth principles to shaping the built environment.

Let us summarize the critical benefits of managing change through regional planning—benefits embodied in the programs my colleagues and I have described in this book. Our twenty-first century society faces key challenges from inefficient and unsustainable use of land and other natural resources, due to sprawl and poor community and construction design habits; industrial decline due to the globalization of competition, information, and finance, exacerbating the vulnerability of many regions and populations to economic shifts beyond their control; the fiscal weakness of poorer urban areas coupled with the concentration of poverty and its evils within the metropolitan matrix; the high cost of decent housing in our most economically vibrant regions; and inadequate transportation infrastructure to serve regionalized labor markets, particularly for those needing affordable public transit.

These challenges are only becoming more complex with current economic and demographic trends. The great recession that began in 2008 has thrown into sharp relief the dangers of regional economies that depend on ever-rising housing prices and a highly creative financial sector. It has also shown for all who care to see that municipal-based governance and taxation is inefficient and fiscally unsustainable, in addition to its legacy of sprawl. While the arrival of poor immigrants slowed during this recession, it is sure to continue its long-term growth trend, presenting many regions with the need to provide greater fiscal relief and investments to communities laboring to give their residents decent education, housing, and job opportunities. And over all our endeavors now hangs the sword of global warming, necessitating new approaches to achieve efficiency and adapt to long-term environmental changes.

Recent events only clarify the need for diverse regional economies, fiscal equity and efficiency among the communities within the region, landscape-scale protection of natural resources, and the concentration of investment and growth in existing cities and town centers. Regional planning and governance structures provide the best, most adaptable means to promote these outcomes, because only regional strategies can accomplish the following:

- Slow or stop sprawl, focusing energy and money on existing cities and communities while protecting natural resources of water, forests, and airsheds
- Direct policies and funds, both public and private sector, to diversify regional economies and improve the economic "bones," such as educational institutions, appealing urban centers, and transportation networks that will sustain those efforts
- Provide for the equitable sharing of resources among diverse communities, to solve fiscal disparities, and fight the concentration of poverty that creates a harmful cycle of decline, subsidies, and social resentments
- Make infrastructure investments that will benefit an entire region over the long term, rather than today's most powerful player within the region
- Bring greater efficiency to public spending and break the stranglehold of inefficient, parochial, often corrupt local governments over tax collection, provision of services, and shaping of land use change
- Impose better community design and construction practices that have proven their value but struggle against parochial governance and business interests— such as low-impact design, and mixed use, denser, center-based, and transit-oriented development
- Resolve conflicts between environmental, business, and social justice goals by enabling the creation of common regional visions and plans instead of the mutually assured destruction of case-by-case struggles over investments and environmental permitting practices
- Move advocates and experts from diverse but connected fields, such as housing and environment, to work together toward common agendas rather than at cross-purposes

REFERENCES

Abbott, C. 2002. Planning a Sustainable City: The Process and Performance of Portland's Urban Growth Boundary. In *Urban Sprawl: Causes, Consequences and Policy Responses,* ed. G. D. Squires, 207–235. Washington, DC: Urban Institute Press.

Abbott, C., S. Adler, and M. P. Abbott. 1997. *Planning a New West: The Columbia River Gorge National Scenic Area.* Corvallis: Oregon State University Press.

Abelsohn, A., R. Bray, C. Vakil, and D. Elliot. 2005. *Report on Public Health and Urban Sprawl in Ontario: A Review of the Pertinent Literature.* Ontario: Ontario College of Family Physicians.

Albert, Richard C. 2005. *Damming the Delaware.* 2nd ed. University Park: Penn State University Press.

Allen, J. 1984. *The Magnificent Gateway: A Layman's Guide to the Geology of the Columbia River Gorge.* Portland, OR: Timber Press.

Altshuler, A., W. Morrill, H. Wolman, and F. Mitchell, eds. 1999. *Governance and Opportunity in Metropolitan America.* Washington, DC: National Academy Press.

Ameregis. 2006. Bluegrass Metropatterns: An Agenda for Economic and Community Progress in Central Kentucky. *Ameregis.* http://www.bluegrasstomorrow.org/pdf files/ Official First Draft Sept 26.pdf.

America 2050. Regional Plan Association. http://www.america2050.org.

Anderson, M. G. 1999. Viability and Spatial Assessment of Ecological Communities in the Northern Appalachian Ecoregion. Ph.D. diss., University of New Hampshire.

Anderson, M. G., F. Biasi, and S. Buttrick. 1998. *Conservation Site Selection: Ecoregional Planning for Biodiversity.* Boston: Nature Conservancy, Eastern Regional Office.

Aoki, K. 2005. All the King's Horses and All the King's Men: Hurdles to Putting the Fragmented Metropolis Back Together Again? Statewide Land Use Planning, Portland Metro and Oregon's Measure 37. *Journal of Law and Policy* 21:397–450.

Aytur, S. A., D. A. Rodriguez, K. R. Evenson, and D. J. Catellier. 2008. Urban Containment Policy and Physical Activity: A Time-Series Analysis of Metropolitan Areas 1990–2002. *American Journal of Preventative Medicine* 34 (4): 320–332.

Babbitt, B. 2005. *Cities in the Wilderness: A New Vision of Land Use in America.* Washington, DC: Island Press.

Barnett, J., ed. 2001. *Planning for a New Century: The Regional Agenda.* Washington, DC: Island Press.

Blair, B. Jr. 1987. The Columbia River Gorge National Scenic Area: The Act, Its Genesis and Legislative History. *Environmental Law* 17:863–969.

Blankenship, K. 2008. Bay Leaders Say They'll Not Meet 2010 Cleanup Goal. *Chesapeake Bay Journal* (January 2008). http://www.bayjournal.com/article.cfm?article=3232.

Blumm, M., and J. Smith. 2006. Protecting the Columbia River Gorge: A Twenty-Year Experiment in Land-Use Federalism. *Journal of Land Use and Environmental Law* 21 (Spring 2006): 201–232.

Bosselman, F., and D. Callies. 1971. *The Quiet Revolution in Land Use Control.* Washington, DC: U.S. Council on Environmental Quality.

Briffault, R. 2000. Localism and Regionalism. *Buffalo Law Review* 48 (1): 1–30.

Brookings Metropolitan Policy Program. 2008. *MetroPolicy: Shaping a New Federal Partnership for a Metropolitan Nation.* Washington, DC: Brooking Institution. http://www.brookings.edu/reports/2008/06_metropolicy.aspx.

Brueckner, J. 2000. Urban Sprawl: A Diagnosis and Remedies. *International Regional Science Review* 23:160–171.

Burby, R. J., and P. J. May. 1998. Intergovernmental Environmental Planning: Addressing the Commitment Conundrum. *Journal of Environmental Planning and Management* 41 (1): 95–110.

Burchell, R. 1992. *Impact Assessment of the New Jersey Interim State Development and Redevelopment Plan, Report II: Research Findings.* Trenton, NJ: New Jersey Office of State Planning.

Burchell, R. W., A. Downs, and S. Seskin. 1998. *The Costs of Sprawl Revisited.* Transit Cooperative Research Program, Transportation Research Board, National Research Council. TCRP Report 39.

Bush, P. M. 2004. Transboundary Water Allocation in the Delaware River Basin—A History of Conflict Management and Growing Challenges. Eastern Water Resources: Law, Policy and Technology Conference. Hollywood, FL, May 6–7, 2007.

Byers, E., and K. M. Ponte. 2005. *The Conservation Easement Handbook.* 2d ed. Washington, DC: Land Trust Alliance and Trust for Public Land. http://www.tpl.org/content_documents/CEH_TOC_Ch1_forWEB.pdf.

Byrum, O. E. 1992. *Old Problems in New Times: Urban Strategies for the 1990s.* Chicago: APA Planners Press.

Calthorpe, P., and W. Fulton. 2001. *The Regional City: Planning for the End of Sprawl.* Washington, DC: Island Press.

Carbonell, A., and R. Yaro. 2005. American Spatial Development and the New Megalopolis. *Land Lines* (April). http://www.lincolninst.edu/pubs/1009_American-Spatial-Development-and-the-New-Megalopolis.

Carruthers, J. I. 2002a. The Impacts of State Growth Management Programmes: A Comparative Analysis. *Urban Studies* 39 (11): 1959–1982.

———. 2002b. Evaluating the Effectiveness of Regulatory Growth Management Programs: An Analytical Framework. *Journal of Planning Education and Research* 21 (4): 391–405.

Cartright, S. D., and V. R. Wilbur. 2005. Translating a Regional Vision into Action. *Urban Land Institute, Community Catalyst Report No. 2.* http://www.uli.org.

Cashin, S. D. 2000. Localism, Self-Interest and the Tyranny of the Favored Quarter: Addressing the Barriers to the New Regionalism. *Georgetown Law Journal* 88:1985–2048.

Central Pine Barrens Joint Planning and Policy Commission. 1995. *The Central Pine Barrens Comprehensive Plan* (amended through 2004). http://pb.state.ny.us.

Chambers, S. 2004. Highlands Plan Spurs Call for a Water Tax. *Star Ledger.* June 7, 2004.

Chapin, T. S. 2007. Local Governments as Entrepreneurs: Evaluating Florida's "Concurrency Experiment." *Urban Affairs Review* 42 (4): 505–532.

Chapman, N., and H. Lund. 2004. Housing Density and Livability in Portland. In *Portland Edge: Challenges and Successes in Growing Communities,* ed. C. Ozawa, 206–229. Washington, DC: Island Press.

Chen, D. 2008. Corzine Seeks to Cut N.J. Budget and Work Force. *New York Times.* February 27, 2008.

Chesapeake Bay Authority. 1933. Conference Proceedings from the Chesapeake Bay Authority Meeting, Baltimore, October 6.

Chesapeake Bay Commission. 2003. The Cost of a Clean Bay. http://www.chesbay.state.va.us/Publications/C2Kfunding.pdf.

Chesapeake Bay Program. 2009. Chesapeake Bay Executive Order. http://executiveorder.chesapeakebay.net.

———. 2006. Annual Assessment. http://www.chesapeakebay.net/indicators.htm.

Chichilnisky, G., and G. Heal. 1998. Economic Returns from the Biosphere. *Nature* 391 (February 1998): 629–630.

City of Portland Office of Transportation. 2007. Portland Bicycle Counts 2007. http://www.portlandonline.com/transportation/index.cfm?c=eefjh&a=bfgeja.

Clemons, J. 2003. Supreme Court Rules for Virginia in Potomac Conflict. *National Sea Grant Law Center.* http://www.olemiss.edu/orgs/SGLC/National/SandBar/2.4supreme.htm (accessed January 24, 2008).

Clifford, J. (n.d.). Digging a Ditch toward a New Form of Government. National Park Service. http://www.nps.gov/archive/thst/mtver.htm.

Coalition for Utah's Future. 2007. *The Coalition for Utah's Future: Its History and Impact.* Salt Lake City: Coalition for Utah's Future.

Collier, C. R. 2004. Sustainable Water Resources Management in the United States: Use of River Basin Commissions to Promote Economic Development, While Protecting the Environment and Improving Community Quality, in *Promoting Sustainable River Basin: Governance: Crafting Japan-U,* 47–59. Institute of Developing Economies IDE-JETRO, Japan.

Collingham, Y. C., and B. Huntley. 2000. Impacts of Habitat Fragmentation and Patch Size upon Migration Rates. *Ecological Applications* 10:131–144.

Collins, B. R., and E.W.B. Russell. 1988. *Protecting the New Jersey Pinelands: A New Direction in Land-Use Management.* New Brunswick, NJ: Rutgers University Press.

Cortright, J. 2007. Portland's Green Dividend, White Paper for CEOs for Cities. *CEOs for Cities.* http://www.ceosforcities.org/files/PGD%20FINAL.pdf.

Daniel, C. 2003. The Twin Cities Metropolitan Council: Novel Initiative, Futile Effort. *William Mitchell Law Review* 27:1941.

Danielson, M. N. 1976. *The Politics of Exclusion.* New York: Columbia University Press.

Davis, C., S. Diegel, and R. Boundy. 2009. *Transportation Energy Data Book: Edition 28.* U.S. Department of Energy. http://www-cta.ornl.gov/data/Index.shtml.

Degrove, J. 2005. *Planning Policy and Politics: Smart Growth and the States.* Cambridge, MA: Lincoln Institute of Land Policy.

Delaware River Basin Commission. 2006. Delaware River Basin Water Code. http://www.state.nj.us/drbc/regs/watercode031109.pdf.

———. 1961. Compact. *State of New Jersey Website.* http://www.state.nj.us/drbc/over.htm.

Dewar, M., and D. Epstein. 2007. Planning for "Megaregions" in the United States. *Journal of Planning Literature* 22 (2):108–124.

Downs, A. 2005. Smart Growth: Why We Discuss It More than We Do It. *Journal of the American Planning Association* 71 (4):367–380.

———. 1994. *New Visions for Metropolitan America.* Washington, DC: Brookings Institution Press.

Dreier, P., J. Mollenkopf, and T. Swanstrom. 2001. *Place Matters: Metropolitics for the 21st Century*. Lawrence: University Press of Kansas.

Echeverria, J. D., and T. Hansen-Young. 2008. *The Track Record on Takings Legislation: Lessons from Democracy's Laboratories*. Washington, DC: Georgetown Environmental Law and Policy Institute, Georgetown University Law Center. http://www.law.georgetown.edu/gelpi/TrackRecord.pdf.

Edwards, M., and A. Haines. 2007. Evaluating Smart Growth: Implications for Small Communities. *Journal of Planning Education and Research* 27:49–64.

Envision Utah. 2006. *Wasatch Choices 2040: A Four County Land-Use and Transportation Vision*. Salt Lake City: Envision Utah. http://www.wfrc.org/cms/publications/wasatchchoices 2040report.pdf.

———. 2003. *The History of Envision Utah*. Salt Lake City: Envision Utah. http://www .envisionutah.org/historyenvisonutahv5p1.pdf.

———. 2002. *Urban Planning Tools for Quality Growth*. Salt Lake City: Envision Utah. http://www.envisionutah.org/eu_resources_toolboxes.html.

Ernst, H. R. 2009. *Fight for the Bay: Why a Dark Green Awakening Is Needed to Save the Chesapeake Bay*. Lanham, MD: Rowman & Littlefield.

———. 2003. *Chesapeake Bay Blues: Science, Politics, and the Struggle to Save the Bay*. Lanham, MD: Rowman & Littlefield.

Euler, G. 1996. *Scenery as Policy: Public Involvement in Developing a Management Plan for the Scenic Resources of the Columbia River Gorge*. Ph.D. diss., Portland State University.

Ewing, R. 2000. Florida's Growth Management Learning Curve. *Virginia Environmental Law Review* 19:375.

Ewing, R., K. Bartholemew, S. Winkelman, J. Walters, and D. Chen. 2007. *Growing Cooler*. Washington, DC: Urban Land Institute.

Ewing, R., R. Pendall, and D. Chen. N.d. *Measuring Sprawl*. Washington, DC: Smart Growth America. http://www.smartgrowthamerica.org/sprawlindex/MeasuringSprawl.PDF.

Fahrenthold, D.A. 2007. Wide-Open, Um, Plastic Spaces in Md. *Washington Post*, November 23, 2007.

Faludi, A. 2002. *European Spatial Planning*. Cambridge: Lincoln Institute of Land Policy.

Farmer, J. D. 2007. *Methodology for Forest Guardians' Carbon Offset Program*. Santa Fe, NM: Santa Fe Institute. http://www.fguardians.org/support_docs/document_carbon-calculation-methodology_2–07.pdf.

Federal Highway Administration. N.d. Highway Performance Monitoring System (HPMS). http://www.metro-region.org/files/maps/02-portland-dmvt-us-avrg.pdf.

Federal Railroad Administration. 2010. High-Speed Intercity Passenger Rail Program Northeast Region Fact Sheet. http://www.fra.dot.gov/downloads/Research/northeast_region.pdf.

Federal Transit Administration. 2005. Annual Transit Ridership 2005. http://www.metro-region.org/files/maps/04–2005-annual-transit-ridership.pdf.

Fischel, W. A. 1992. Property Taxation and the Tiebout Model: Evidence for the Benefit View from Zoning and Voting. *Journal of Economic Literature* 30:171–177.

Flynn, E. 2005. *Thinking and Acting Regionally in the Greater Wasatch Area: Implications for Local Economic Development Practice*. Salt Lake City: Envision Utah.

Forman, R.T.T. 2002. Foreword to *Applying Landscape Ecology in Biological Conservation*. Ed. K. J. Gutzwiller. vii–x. New York: Springer-Verlag.

———. 1995. *Land Mosaics: The Ecology of Landscapes and Regions*. New York: Cambridge University Press.

Forman, R.T.T., and L. E. Alexander. 1998. Roads and Their Major Ecological Effects. *Annual Review of Ecology and Systematics* 29:207–231.

Franklin, H. M., D. Falk, and A. J. Levin. 1974. *In-Zoning: A Guide for Policy-Makers on Inclusionary Land Use Programs.* Arlington, VA: Potomac Institute.

Franklin, J. F. 1993. Preserving Biodiversity: Species, Ecosystems, or Landscapes? *Ecological Applications* 3:202–205.

Frece, J. W. 2004. Twenty Lessons from Maryland's Smart Growth Initiative. *Vermont Journal of Environmental Law* 6 (3): 106–132.

Frisken, R., and D. F. Norris. 2001. Regionalism Reconsidered. *Journal of Urban Affairs* 23 (5): 467–478.

Frug, G. E. 1999. *City Making: Building Communities without Building Walls.* Princeton, NJ: Princeton University Press.

Frumhoff, P. C., J. J. McCarthy, J. M. Melillo, and S. C. Moser. 2007. *Confronting Climate Change in the U.S. Northeast.* Cambridge, MA: Union of Concerned Scientists.

Fulton, W., J. Mazurek, R. Pruetz, and C. Williamson. 2004. TDRs and Other Market-Based Land Mechanisms: How They Work and Their Role in Shaping Metropolitan Growth. A discussion paper prepared for the Brookings Institution Center on Urban and Metropolitan Policy. http://www.brookings.edu/reports/2004/06metropolitanpolicy_fulton.aspx.

Gainsborough, J. F. 2001. *Fenced Off: The Suburbanization of American Politics.* Washington, DC: Georgetown University Press.

Garreau, J. 1991. *Edge Cities: Life on the New Frontier.* New York: Doubleday.

Gillham, O. 2002. *The Limitless City: A Primer on the Urban Sprawl Debate.* Washington, DC: Island Press.

Goertzman, W., M. Spiegel, and S. Wachter. 1998. Do Cities and Suburbs Cluster? *Citiscape: A Journal of Policy Development and Research* 3 (3): 193–202.

Good, R. E. 1982. *Ecological Solutions to Environmental Management Concerns in the Pinelands National Reserve.* New Brunswick, NJ: Center for Coastal and Environmental Studies, Rutgers State University.

Good, R. E., and N. F. Good. 1984. The Pinelands National Reserve: An Ecosystem Approach to Management. *BioScience* 34:169–173.

Gottlieb, P. D. 1999. Do Economists Have Anything to Contribute to the Debate on Urban Sprawl (and Would Anybody Listen to Them If They Did)? *Forum for Social Economics* 28 (2): 51–64.

Gottlieb, P. D., and J. Reilly. 1990. *Projecting Costs for Roads under Various Growth Scenarios: Technical Reference Document.* Trenton: New Jersey Office of State Planning.

Gottmann, J. 1961. *Megalopolis: The Urbanized Northeastern Seaboard of the United States.* New York: Twentieth Century Fund.

Government Accountability Office. 2006. *Improved Strategies Needed to Better Guide Restoration Efforts.* GAO-06–614T. http://www.gao.gov/new.items/d06614t.pdf.

Governor's Conference 1971. A Statement to Governor Reubin O'D. Askew. Governor's Conference on Water Management in South Florida. Miami Beach, FL. September 24.

Green, M. 2006. *Causes of Haze in the Gorge: Final Report Submitted to Southwest Clean Air Agency and Oregon Department of Environmental Quality.* Reno, NV: Desert Research Institute, University of Nevada. http://www.deq.state.or.us/aq/gorgeair/docs/causesofHazeGorge.pdf.

GreenGauge21. 2010. High Speed Rail in Britain: Consequences for Employment and Economic Growth. *GreenGauge21.* http://www.greengauge21.net/publications/consequences-for-employment-and-economic-growth/.

Griffith, J. 2005. Regional Governance Reconsidered. *Journal of Law and Policy* 21:505–559.

Groves, C. R., D. B. Jensen, L. I. Valutis, K. H. Redford, M. L. Shaffer, J. M. Scott, J. V. Baumgartner, J. V. Higgins, M. W. Beck, and M. G. Anderson. 2002. Planning for

Biodiversity Conservation: Putting Conservation Science into Practice. *BioScience* 52 (6): 499–512.

Harris Interactive. 2007. *Utah Values and Future Growth.* New York, NY: Harris Interactive.

Hershberg, T. 2001. Regional Imperatives of Global Competition. In *Planning for a New Century,* ed. J. Barnett, 11–29. Washington, DC: Island Press.

Hills, R. M. 2000. Romancing the Town: Why We (Still) Need a Democratic Defense of City Power. *Harvard Law Review* 113 (8): 2009.

Hinze, S., and K. Baker. 2005. Minnesota's Fiscal Disparities Programs. *Minnesota House of Representatives Research* (January). http://www.leg.state.mn.us/docs/2005/other/050169.pdf.

Hooper, B. P. 2006a. Integrating River Basin Governance and Key Performance Indicators. *IWA Yearbook 2006.* London: IWA Publishing.

———. 2006b. Key Performance Indicators of River Basin Organizations. Submitted for publication as a Technical Note to the Institute of Water Resources, U.S. Army Corps of Engineers, Virginia.

Hooper, B., and J. Parzen. 2006. Livability and Smart Growth: Lessons from a Surdna Foundation Initiative. New Haven, CT: Yale School of Forestry and Environmental Studies. http://environment.yale.edu/publication-series/land_use_and_environmental_planning/938.

Horton, T. 2003. *Turning the Tide: Saving the Bay.* Rev. ed. Washington, DC: Island Press.

Howe, D. 2004. The Reality of Portland's Housing Market. In *Portland Edge: Challenges and Successes in Growing Communities,* ed. C. Ozawa, 184–205. Washington, DC: Island Press.

Hughes, J., and J. Seneca. 2006. New Jersey's New Economy Growth Challenges. Edward J. Boustein School of Planning and Public Policy. http://www.heartland.org/policybot/results/19571/New_Jerseys_New_Economy_Growth_Challenges.html.

ICLEI—Local Governments for Sustainability. N.d. List of Members. http://www.iclei.org/index.php?id=global-members.

Ingram, G. K., A. Carbonell, Y. Hong, and A. Flint. 2009. *Smart Growth Policies: An Evaluation of Programs and Outcomes.* Cambridge, MA: Lincoln Institute of Land Policy.

Intergovernmental Panel on Climate Change (IPCC). 2007. Mitigation of Climate Change. http://www.mnp.nl/ipcc.

Karr, J., and D. R. Dudley. 1981. Ecological Perspective on Water Quality Goals. *Environmental Management* 5:55–68.

Katz, B., ed. 2000. *Reflections on Regionalism.* Washington, DC: Brookings Institution Press.

Katz, B., and R. Puentes. 2006. *Prosperity at Risk: Toward a Competitive New Jersey.* Washington, DC: Brookings Institution, Metropolitan Policy Program. http://www.brookings.edu/~/media/Files/rc/speeches/2006/0501metropolitanpolicy_katz/20060501_Trenton.pdf.

Kennish, M. J., S. B. Bricker, W. C. Dennison, P. M. Gilbert, R. J. Livingston, K. A. Moore, R. T. Noble, H. W. Paerl, J. M. Ramstack, S. Seitzinger, D. A. Tomasko, and I. Valiela. 2007. Barnegat Bay-Little Egg Harbor Estuary: Case Study of a Highly Eutrophic Coastal Bay System. *Ecological Applications* 17 (5): S3–S16.

King, A. W. 1993. Considerations of Scale and Hierarchy. In *Ecological Integrity and the Management of Ecosystems,* ed. S. Woodley, J. Kay, and G. Francis, 19–42. Boca Raton, FL: St. Lucie Press.

Knaap, G., and E. Lewis. 2007. State Agency Spending under Maryland's Smart Growth Areas Act. College Park: National Center for Smart Growth Research and Education, University of Maryland.

Knaap, G., and E. Talen. 2005. New Urbanism and Smart Growth: A Few Words from the Academy. *International Regional Science Review* 28 (2): 107–118.

Lahr, M. 2003. Is New York City Still Propelling Growth in Its Suburbs? A Study of Economic Spillover Effects through Spatial Contiguity. Unpublished paper delivered at the 42nd Annual Meeting of the Southern Regional Science Association International, Louisville, KY, April. http://ideas.repec.org/p/wpa/wuwpur/0403007.html.

Lancaster County. 2006. Growing Together. Lancaster County Planning Commission. http://www.co.lancaster.pa.us/planning/cwp/view.asp?a=776&q=534082.

Lang, R., and A. C. Nelson. 2007. The Rise of the Megapolitans. *Planning: The Magazine of the American Planning Association,* January 2007.

Layzer, J. A. 2008. *Natural Experiments: Ecosystem-Based Management and the Environment.* Cambridge, MA: MIT Press.

Leinberger, C. B. N.d. Footloose and Fancy Free: A Field Survey of Walkable Urban Places in the Top 30 U.S. Metropolitan Areas. Washington, DC: Brookings Institution. http://www.brookings.edu/~/media/Files/rc/papers/2007/1128_walkableurbanism_leinberg/1128_walkableurbanism_leinberger.pdf.

Leopold, A. 1949. *A Sand County Almanac and Sketches Here and There.* New York: Oxford University Press.

Levine, J. 2006. *Zoned Out: Regulation, Markets, and Choices in Transportation and Metropolitan Land-use.* Washington, DC: Resources for the Future.

Lewis, L., G. Knapp, and J. Sohn. 2009. Managing Growth with Priority Funding Areas: A Good Idea Whose Time Has Yet to Come. *Journal of the American Planning Association* 75 (4): 457–478.

Listokin, D. 1976. *Fair Share Housing Allocation.* New Brunswick, NJ: Rutgers University Center for Urban Policy Research.

Luce, T. F. 1998a. Applying the Twin Cities Model of Tax-Base Sharing in Other Metropolitan Areas: Simulations for Chicago, Philadelphia, Portland, and Seattle. In *National Tax Association 1997* Annual Conference Proceedings. Washington, DC: National Tax Association.

———. 1998b. Regional Tax Base Sharing: The Twin Cities Experience. In *Local Government Tax and Land Use Policies in the United States: Understanding the Links,* ed. H. Ladd, 234–254. Cambridge, MA: Lincoln Institute of Land Policy.

Martin Prosperity Insight. 2010. *High Costs, High Speeds, Hidden Benefits: A Broader Perspective on High-Speed Rail.* Toronto: Rothman School of Management, University of Toronto.

Mason, R. J. 2008. *Collaborative Land Use Management: The Quieter Revolution in Place-Based Planning.* Lanham, MD: Rowman & Littlefield.

———. 1992. *Contested Lands: Conflict and Compromise in New Jersey's Pine Barrens.* Philadelphia: Temple University Press.

Maybury, K. P., ed. 1999. *Seeing the Forest and the Trees: Ecological Classification for Conservation.* Arlington, VA: The Nature Conservancy.

McConnell, V., M. Walls, and E. Kopits. 2006. Zoning, TDRs and the Density of Development. *Journal of Urban Economics* 59:440–457.

McKinney, M. J., and S. Johnson. 2009. *Working Across Boundaries: People, Nature, and Regions.* Cambridge, MA: Lincoln Institute of Land Policy.

Meck, S., R. Retzlaff, and J. Schwab. 2003. *Regional Approaches to Affordable Housing.* Washington, DC: American Planning Association.

Messer, K. D. 2007. Transferable Development Rights Programs: An Economic Framework for Success. *Journal of Conservation Planning* 3:47–53.

Ministry of Public Infrastructure Renewal. 2006. *Growth Plan for the Greater Golden Horseshoe, 2006.* Ontario: Queen's Printer for Ontario. http://www.placestogrow.ca.

Montgomery County. 2001. *Montgomery County (Ohio) Economic Development/ Government Equity (Ed/Ge) Handbook: 2001–2010.* Dayton, OH: Montgomery County.

Mountford, K. 2003. No Matter What Shells Are Fired in Oyster Wars, the Resource Always Loses. *Bay Journal* (March). http://www.bayjournal.com/article.cfm?article=835.

Muro, M., and R. Puentes. 2004. *Investing in a Better Future: A Review of the Fiscal and Competitive Advantages of Smarter Growth Development Patterns.* Washington, DC: Brookings Institution Center on Urban and Metropolitan Policy. http://www.brookings .edu/reports/2004/03metropolitanpolicy_muro.aspx.

Myers, P. 1974. *Slow Start in Paradise: An Account of the Development, Passage, and Implementation of State Land-Use Legislation in Florida.* Washington, DC: Conservation Foundation.

National Fish and Wildlife Foundation. 2010. Grant Programs. http://www.nfwf.org/ Content/NavigationMenu/ChesapeakeBayStewardshipFund/ApplyforaGrant/default.htm.

National Oceanic and Atmospheric Administration. 2007. *2007 Chesapeake Bay Blue Crab Advisory Report.* http://www.mdsg.umd.edu/images/uploads/siteimages/Living_ Chesapeake/bluecrabs/cbsac/pdfs/2007BCAR.pdf.

Nelson, A. C. 2006. Leadership in a New Era. *Journal of the American Planning Association.* 72 (4): 393–407.

———. 1999. Comparing States with and without Growth Management: Analysis Based on Indicators with Policy Implications. *Land Use Policy* 16:121–127.

Nelson, A. C., and C. J. Dawkins. 2004. *Urban Containment in the United States: History, Models and Techniques for Regional and Metropolitan Growth Management.* American Planning Association PAS Report 520. Chicago: American Planning Association.

Nelson, E. 2008. Bay Area Anchors Megaregion. *Contra Costa Times,* January 13.

Neptis Foundation. 2002. Toronto-Related Futures Study. Summary available at http://www.neptis.org/library/show.cfm?id=61&cat_id=23.

Norton, R. 2005. More and Better Local Planning: State-Mandated Local Planning in Coastal North Carolina. *Journal of the American Planning Association* 71 (1): 55–71.

Noss, R. F. 1990. Can We Maintain Biological and Ecological Integrity? *Conservation Biology* 4:241–243.

Okun, A. 1975. *Equality and Efficiency: The Big Trade-off.* Washington, DC: Brookings Institution Press.

Ontario Government. 2005a. Places to Grow Act, 2005. http://www.e-laws.gov.on.ca/html/ statutes/english/elaws_statutes_05p13_e.htm.

———. 2005b. Greenbelt Act, 2005. http://www.e-laws.gov.on.ca/html/statutes/english/ elaws_statutes_05g01_e.htm.

Ontario Government. 2006. Planning Act (as amended 2006). http://www.e-laws.gov.on .ca/html/statutes/english/elaws_statutes_90p13_e.htm.

Ontario Ministry of Municipal Affairs and Housing. 2005. *Greenbelt Plan.* Ontario: Queen's Printer for Ontario.

Ontario Ministry of Public Infrastructure Renewal. 2006. *Growth Plan for the Greater Golden Horseshoe, 2006.* Ontario: Queen's Printer for Ontario.

Oregon Department of Agriculture. Oregon Agricultural Facts. http://www.oregon.gov/ ODA/about_ag.shtml.

Orfield, M. 2002. *American Metropolitics: The New Suburban Reality.* Washington, DC: Brookings Institution Press.

———. 1997. *Metropolitics: A Regional Agenda for Community and Stability.* Washington, DC: Brookings Institution Press and the Lincoln Institute of Land Policy.

Orfield, M., and N. Wallace. 2007. The Minnesota Fiscal Disparities Act of 1971: The Twin Cities' Struggle and Blueprint for Regional Cooperation. *William Mitchell Law Review* 33 (2): 591–612.

Ozawa, C., ed. 2004. *The Portland Edge: Challenges and Successes in Growing Communities.* Washington, DC: Island Press.

Pearson, R. G., and T. P. Dawson. 2005. Long-Distance Plant Dispersal and Habitat Fragmentation: Identifying Conservation Targets for Spatial Landscape Planning under Climate Change. *Biological Conservation* 123:389–401.

Pendall, R. 2000. Local Land Use Regulation and the Chain of Exclusion. *Journal of the American Planning Association* 66 (2): 125–142.

Pendell, R., J. Martin, and W. Fulton. 2002. Holding the Line: Urban Containment in the United States. A discussion paper prepared for the Brookings Institution Center on Urban and Metropolitan Policy. http://www.brookings.edu/reports/2002/08metropolitanpolicy_pendall.aspx.

Perschel, R. T., A. M. Evans, and M. J. Summers. 2007. Climate Change, Carbon, and the Forests of the Northeast. *Forest Guild.* http://www.forestguild.org/publications/research/2007/ForestGuild_climate_carbon_forests.pdf.

Pew Center on Global Climate Change. 2008. A Look at Emissions Targets. http://www.pewclimate.org/what_s_being_done/targets#state.

———. 2006. Greenhouse Gas Emissions By Sector. http://www.pewclimate.org/global-warming-basics/facts_and_figures/us_emissions/usghgemsector.cfm.

Pierce, N. 1993. *Citistates: How Urban America Can Prosper in a Competitive World.* Washington, DC: Seven Locks Press.

Pindell, N. 2005. Planning for Housing Requirements. In *The Legal Guide to Affordable Housing Development*, ed. T. Iglesias and R. E. Lento, 3–38. Chicago: ABA Publishing.

Pinelands Commission. 1980. *New Jersey Pinelands Comprehensive Management Plan for the Pinelands National Reserve (National Parks and Recreation Act, 1978) and Pinelands Area (New Jersey Pinelands Protection Act, 1979).* New Lisbon: New Jersey Pinelands Commission.

Pinelands Development Credit Bank. 2008. Annual Report Fiscal Year 2007. *State of New Jersey Department of Banking and Insurance.* http://www.state.nj.us/dobi/pinelands/pinelandsbank.htm.

Poiani, K. A., B. D. Richter, M. G. Anderson, and H. Richter. 2000. Biodiversity Conservation at Multiple Scales: Functional Sites, Landscapes, and Networks. *BioScience* 50 (2): 133–146.

Porter, D. 1999. Reinventing Growth Management for the 21st Century. *William and Mary Environmental Law and Policy Review* 23:705.

Portland Metro. 2008. Portland Metro 2035 Regional Transportation Plan. http://www.oregonmetro.gov/index.cfm/go/by.web/id=25036.

———. 2005. Portland Regional Framework Plan. http://www.oregonmetro.gov/index.cfm/go/by.web/id=432.

———. 2004. *2004 Annual Compliance Report of the Urban Growth Management Functional Plan, Titled 7 (Affordable Housing) Component.* http://www.metro-region.org/index.cfm/go/by.web/id=7498.

———. 2000. Portland Metro Charter. http://www.oregonmetro.gov/index.cfm/go/by.web/id=629.

powell, j. a. 2000. Addressing Regional Dilemmas for Minority Communities. In *Reflections on Regionalism*, ed. B. Katz, 218–246. Washington, DC: Brookings Institution Press.

Prime Minister's Caucus Task Force on Urban Issues. 2002. *Canada's Urban Strategy: A Vision for the 21st Century, Interim Report.* April.

Prime Minister's Task Force on Urban Issues. 2002. *Canada's Urban Strategy: A Blueprint for Action, Final Report.* November.

Randolph, J. 2004. *Environmental Land Use Planning and Management.* Washington, DC: Island Press.

Regional Plan Association. 2007. *Northeast Megaregion 2050: A Common Future.* New York: Regional Plan Association.

———. 2006. *America 2050: A Prospectus.* New York: Regional Plan Association.

———. 1967. *The Region's Growth.* New York: Regional Plan Association.

Reilly, J. 1990. Projecting Wastewater Treatment Costs under Various Growth Scenarios, Technical Reference Document. Trenton: New Jersey Office of State Planning.

Reynolds, L. 2007. Local Governments and Regional Governance. *Urban Lawyer* 39 (3): 483.

Richmond, H. 2000. Metropolitan Land-Use Reform: The Promise and Challenge of Majority Consensus. In *Reflections on Regionalism,* ed. B. Katz, 9–39. Washington, DC: Brookings Institution Press.

Ring, R. 2006. Taking Liberties. *High Country News.* July 24. http://www.hcn.org/issues/326/16409.

Robert Charles Lesser & Co. 2007. Wasatch Front Development Trends. *Envision Utah.* http://www.envisionutah.org/plans.phtml?type=research.

Robichaud-Collins, B., and E.W.B. Russell. 1988. *Protecting the New Jersey Pinelands: A New Direction in Land-Use Management.* New Brunswick, NJ: Rutgers University Press.

Rusk, D. 2003. *Cities without Suburbs.* Washington, DC: Woodrow Wilson Center Press.

Sagoff, M. 2002. On the Value of Natural Ecosystems: The Catskills Parable. *Politics and the Life Sciences* 21 (1): 16–21.

Salt Lake City Chamber. 2007. *Downtown Rising: A New Vision for Salt Lake City.* Salt Lake City: Salt Lake City Chamber.

Seltzer, E. 2004. It's Not an Experiment: Regional Planning at Metro 1990 to the Present. In *The Portland Edge: Challenges and Successes in Growing Communities,* ed. C. P. Ozawa, 35–60. Washington, DC: Island Press.

Sierra Club. *Cool Cities.* http://coolcities.us.

Song, Y., and G. Knaap. 2004. Measuring Urban Form: Is Portland Winning the War on Sprawl. *Journal of the American Planning Association* 70 (2): 210–225.

Squires, G. D., ed. 2002. *Urban Sprawl: Causes, Consequences and Policy Responses.* Washington, DC: Urban Institute Press.

Staley, S. R., J. G. Edgens, and G. Mildner. 1999. A Line in the Land: Urban-Growth Boundaries, Smart Growth, and Housing Affordability. *Policy Study 263.* Los Angeles: Reason Foundation.

Statistics Canada. 2006. Census 2006. http://www12.statcan.gc.ca/census-recensement/2006/dp-pd/index-eng.cfm.

Stern, Sir N. 2007. Stern Review on the Economics of Climate Change. HM Treasury. http://www.hm-treasury.gov.uk/sternreview_index.htm.

Surface Transportation Policy Project. 2005. *Driven To Spend: Pumping Dollars Out of Our Households and Communities.* http://www.transact.org/library/reports_pdfs/driven_to_spend/Driven_to_Spend_Report.pdf.

Swanstrom, T. 2001. What We Argue About When We Argue About Regionalism. *Journal of Urban Affairs* 23 (5): 479–496.

Talen, E. 2008. Beyond the Front Porch: Regionalist Ideals in the New Urbanist Movement. *Journal of Planning History* 7 (1): 20–47.

Texas Transportation Institute. 2007. *2007 Annual Urban Mobility Report.* http://mobility.tamu.edu/ums/.

Urban Strategies Inc. 2005. *Application of a Land-Use Intensification Target for the Greater Golden Horseshoe.* Paper prepared for the Ontario Growth Secretariat Ministry of Public Infrastructure Renewal. http://www.mei.gov.on.ca/en/pdf/infrastructure/IntensificationTargetForGGH.pdf.

U.S. Census Bureau. 2007. American Community Survey. http://www.portlandonline.com/transportation/index.cfm?c=eefjh&a=bfgeja.

U.S. Climate Action Partnership. N.d. *Our Report: A Call for Action.* http://www.us-cap.org/about-us/our-report-a-call-for-action/.

U.S. Conference of Mayors. 2007. 2007 Mayors Climate Protection Summit in Seattle. *Mayors Climate Protection Center.* http://www.usmayors.org/climateprotection/2007summit.htm.

U.S. Corps of Engineers. 1977. *Chesapeake Bay Future Conditions Report.* Baltimore: Army Corps of Engineers.

———. 1973. *Chesapeake Bay Existing Conditions Report.* Baltimore: Army Corps of Engineers.

U.S. Department of Energy. 2009. Energy Efficiency and Renewable Energy. http://www.eere.energy.gov/states/maps/renewable_portfolio_states.cfm.

U.S. Energy Information Administration. Emissions of Greenhouse Gases Report. http://www.eia.doe.gov/oiaf/1605/ggrpt/index.html.

U.S. Environmental Protection Agency. 2007. Representative Carbon Sequestration Rates and Saturation Periods for Key Agricultural and Forestry Practices. http://www.epa.gov/sequestration/rates.html.

Walls, M. 2008. *Smart Growth @ 10: A Critical Examination of Maryland's Landmark Land Use Program, Conference Report.* College Park: National Center for Smart Growth Research and Education, University of Maryland.

Walls, M., and V. McConnell. 2007. *Transfer of Development Rights in U.S. Communities: Evaluating Program Design, Implementation and Outcomes.* Resources for the Future. Washington, DC: RFF Press.

Wannop, U. A. 1995. *The Regional Imperative: Regional Planning and Governance in Britain, Europe and the United States.* London: Jessica Kingsley Publishers.

Weitz, J. 1999. *Sprawl Busting: State Programs to Guide Growth.* Chicago: Planners Press, American Planning Association.

Weitz, J., and E. Seltzer. 1998. Regional Planning and Regional Governance in the United States 1979–1996. *Journal of Planning Literature* 12 (3): 361–392.

Wennersten, J. R. 1981. *The Oyster Wars of Chesapeake Bay.* Centreville, MD: Tidewater Publishers.

Wheeler, S. 2002. The New Regionalism: Key Characteristics of an Emerging Movement. *Journal of the American Planning Association* 68 (3): 267–278.

———. 2000. Planning for Metropolitan Sustainability. *Journal of Planning Education and Research* 20:133–145.

Whittaker, R. H. 1979. Vegetational Relationships of the Pine Barrens. In *Pine Barrens: Ecosystem and Landscape,* ed. R.T.T. Forman, 315–331. New York: Academic Press.

Williams, C. 1980. *Bridge of the Gods Mountains of Fire: A Return to the Columbia Gorge.* New York: Friends of the Earth.

Wiser, S. K., R. K. Peet, and P. W. White. 1998. Prediction of Rare-Plant Occurrence: A Southern Appalachian Example. *Ecological Applications* 8:909–920.

Zampella, R. A., N. A. Procopio, M. U. Du Brul, and J. F. Bunnell. 2008. *An Ecological-Integrity Assessment of the New Jersey Pinelands: A Comprehensive Assessment of the Landscape and Aquatic and Wetland Systems of the Region.* New Lisbon, NJ: New Jersey Pinelands Commission.

ONLINE RESOURCES

Adirondack Council, http://www.adirondackcouncil.org
Adirondack Park Agency, http://www.apa.state.ny.us
Ameregis, http://www.ameregis.com
America 2050, http://www.america2050.org
Association to Preserve Cape Cod, http://www.apcc.org
Atlanta Regional Commission, http://www.atlantaregional.com
Brookings Metropolitan Policy Program, http://www.brookings.edu/METRO
    .ASPX
California Coastal Commission, http://www.coastal.ca.gov
Cape Cod Commission, http://www.capecodcommission.org
Chesapeake Bay Commission, http://www.chesbay.state.va.us
Chesapeake Bay Foundation, http://www.cbf.org
Chesapeake Bay Program, http://www.chesapeakebay.net
Chicago Metropolitan Agency for Planning, http://www.cmap.illinois.gov
Clarke, Caton, Hintz, http://www.clarkecatonhintz.com
Coalition for Utah's Future, http://www.envisionutah.org
Columbia River Gorge Commission, http://www.gorgecommission.org
Conservation Resources, http://www.conservationresourcesinc.org
Delaware River Basin Commission, http://www.state.nj.us/drbc
Delaware Valley Regional Planning Commission, http://www.dvrpc.org
Eastern Shore Land Conservancy, http://www.eslc.org
Environmental Defense Fund, http://www.edf.org
Envision Utah, http://www.envisionutah.org
Evergreen Capital Advisors, http://evergreenca.com
Friends of the Columbia Gorge, http://www.gorgefriends.org
Highlands Coalition, http://www.highlandscoalition.org
Interstate Commission on the Potomac River Basin,
    http://www.potomacriver.org
Keystone Conservation Trust, http://www.keystoneconservation.org

Lancaster County Planning Commission, http://www.co.lancaster.pa.us/planning

Lincoln Institute of Land Policy, http://www.lincolninst.edu

Maine Office of State Planning, http://maine.gov/spo

Maryland Department of Planning, http://www.mdp.state.md.us

Metrolinx, http://www.metrolinx.com

National Center for Smart Growth Research and Education, http://www
.smartgrowth.umd.edu

Nature Serve, http://www.natureserve.org

New Jersey Future, http://www.njfuture.org

New Jersey Highlands Coalition, http://www.njhighlandscoalition.org

New Jersey Highlands Council, http://www.highlands.state.nj.us

New Jersey Meadowlands Commission, http://www.njmeadowlands.gov

New Jersey Office of Smart Growth, http://www.nj.gov/dca/divisions/osg

New Jersey Pinelands Commission, http://www.state.nj.us/pinelands

New York Central Pine Barrens Commission, http://www.pb.state.ny.us

Ontario—Places to Grow, http://www.placestogrow.ca

Oregon Department of Land Conservation and Development, http://www.lcd
.state.or.us/LCD/goals.shtml

Pacific Forest Trust, http://www.pacificforest.org

Piedmont Environmental Council, http://www.pecva.org

Pinelands Preservation Alliance, http://www.pinelandsalliance.org

PlanSmart NJ, http://www.plansmartnj.org

Portland Metro, http://www.oregonmetro.gov

Puget Sound Regional Council, http://www.psrc.org

Regional Plan Association, http://www.rpa.org

Regional Planning for a Sustainable America, http://www.regionalplans.com

Sacramento Area Council of Governments, http://www.sacog.org

San Diego Association of Governments, http://www.sandag.org

Siemon and Larsen, http://www.siemonlarsen.com

Smart Growth America, http://www.smartgrowthamerica.org

Tahoe Regional Planning Agency, http://www.trpa.org

INDEX

ABOUT THE AUTHORS

CARL ABBOTT is professor of urban studies and planning at Portland State University.

MARGERY POST ABBOTT is an independent scholar in Portland, Oregon.

SY ADLER is professor of urban studies and planning at Portland State University.

BOB ALLEN is director of science of the New Jersey chapter of the Nature Conservancy.

MARK G. ANDERSON is Eastern Region conservation science director of the Nature Conservancy.

GORDON BARRETT leads the Shorezone/Watercraft program of the Tahoe Regional Planning Agency.

RICHARD BENNER is senior Metro attorney of Portland Metro.

JOHN BERNSTEIN is president of the Northern Sierra Partnership.

ROBERT CEBERIO is a former executive director of the Meadowlands Commission.

CAROL R. COLLIER is executive director of the Delaware River Basin Commission.

RAYMOND P. CORWIN was the executive director of the New York Central Pine Barrens Commission.

ANDREW COTUGNO is director of planning of Portland Metro.

RAY D'AGOSTINO is township manager of West Lampeter Township, Pennsylvania.

ROBERT DREWEL is executive director of the Puget Sound Regional Council.

HOWARD R. ERNST is associate professor of political science at the United States Naval Academy.

ROB ETGEN is executive director of the Eastern Shore Land Conservancy.

MARY L. FREY is principal planner of the Lancaster County Planning Commission.

MAGGIE GEIST is executive director of the Association to Preserve Cape Cod.